MW01119815

Disability in the Global Sport Arena

Sport is often at the centre of battles for rights to inclusion linked to class, race and gender, and this book explores struggles centred on disability in different cultural settings in Europe, North America, Africa, Asia and Oceania. It challenges oversights and assumptions about the 'normal' body, and describes how individual and organizational transformations can occur through sport. The abilities of a person are recognised and placed centre stage - instead of the individual being forgotten, excluded, or placed at the margins simply because they have a disability.

National, regional and global change is part of the shift to the rights based approach reflected in the 2006 UN Convention on the Rights of Persons with Disabilities. Making sport inclusive affects the accessibility of facilities, funding, the media, policies, programs, organisations, sponsors and spectators, and at the same time changes the cultural values of the wider society. It also raises issues about competition access and eligibility for 'different' and technologically enhanced 'cyborg' bodies, and for those most socially disadvantaged. Addressing these questions which ultimately touch on the real meaning of sport can lead to profound changes in people's attitudes, and how sport is organized locally and globally.

Growth in the influential global organisations of the Paralympic Games, Special Olympics and Deaflympics is examined, as is the approach to disability in sport in both advantaged and resource poor countries. The embodied lives of persons with disabilities are explored utilizing new theoretical models, perspectives and approaches.

This book was previously published as a special issue of *Sport in Society*.

Jill M. Le Clair is a Professor of Anthropology, in the School of Liberal Arts & Sciences at Humber College Institute, Toronto, Canada, and the Founding Chair of the Global Disability Research in Sport and Health Network.

Disability in the Global Sport Arena
A Sporting Chance

Edited by
Jill M. Le Clair

Routledge
Taylor & Francis Group

LONDON AND NEW YORK

First published 2012
by Routledge
2 Park Square, Milton Park, Abingdon, Oxon, OX14 4RN

Simultaneously published in the USA and Canada
by Routledge
711 Third Avenue, New York, NY 10017

Routledge is an imprint of the Taylor & Francis Group, an informa business

British Library Cataloguing in Publication Data
A catalogue record for this book is available from the British Library

ISBN13: 978-0-415-48851-8

Typeset in Times New Roman
by Taylor & Francis Books

Publisher's Note
The publisher would like to make readers aware that the chapters in this book may be referred to as articles as they are identical to the articles published in the special issue. The publisher accepts responsibility for any inconsistencies that may have arisen in the course of preparing this volume for print.

Printed and bound in the United States of America by Publishers Graphics, LLC on sustainably sourced paper.

Contents

CONTENTS

SPORT IN THE GLOBAL SOCIETY –
CONTEMPORARY PERSPECTIVES

Series Editor: Boria Majumdar

DISABILITY IN THE GLOBAL SPORT ARENA
A Sporting Chance

Sport in the Global Society – Contemporary Perspectives
Series Editor: Boria Majumdar

The social, cultural (including media) and political study of sport is an expanding area of scholarship and related research. While this area has been well served by the *Sport in the Global Society* series, the surge in quality scholarship over the last few years has necessitated the creation of *Sport in the Global Society: Contemporary Perspectives*. The series will publish the work of leading scholars in fields as diverse as sociology, cultural studies, media studies, gender studies, cultural geography and history, political science and political economy. If the social and cultural study of sport is to receive the scholarly attention and readership it warrants, a cross-disciplinary series dedicated to taking sport beyond the narrow confines of physical education and sport science academic domains is necessary. *Sport in the Global Society: Contemporary Perspectives* will answer this need.

Titles in the Series

Australian Sport
Antipodean Waves of Change
Edited by Kristine Toohey and Tracy Taylor

Australia's Asian Sporting Context
1920s and 1930s
Edited by Sean Brawley and Nick Guoth

'Critical Support' for Sport
Bruce Kidd

Disability in the Global Sport Arena
A Sporting Chance
Edited by Jill M. Le Clair

Diversity and Division – Race, Ethnicity and Sport in Australia
Christopher J. Hallinan

Documenting the Beijing Olympics
Edited by D. P. Martinez and Kevin Latham

Football in Brazil
Edited by Martin Curi

Football Supporters and the Commercialisation of Football
Comparative Responses across Europe
Edited by Peter Kennedy and David Kennedy

Football's Relationship with Art: The Beautiful Game?
John E. Hughson

Preface

Bruce Kidd

Faculty of Physical Education and Health, University of Toronto, Toronto, Canada

This Special Issue is the second to be drawn from the papers presented to a conference at the University of Toronto in 2008 on sport and social change during the four decades between 1968 and 2008. The conference was held under the banner of 'To remember is to resist', the rallying cry of historian, poet and anti-racist campaigner Lennox Farrell.[1] The premise was that historical understanding is essential to both scholarship and the struggle for human rights and equality, more urgent than ever during the shrinking historical horizons of globalizing neo-liberalism in the electronic age. The idea was expressed even more poignantly by Richard Poplack in a review of South African writers on the eve of the 2010 World Cup. In such a racially charged atmosphere, he observed, 'to forget was itself an act of evil.'[2]

The struggle for access to and the enjoyment of sport is almost as old as modern sport itself, but much of this important history has been lost from view. In its origins in the industrializing countries, sport can best be understood as male, upper-class, able-bodied culture, providing both socialization for and the physical and social rewards of privilege, a far cry from the universal practice claimed in popular ideology. But such was the appeal of sport that subordinate groups very quickly took it up, and sought to conduct and play it for themselves. In some cases, they managed to climb over the fences and other barriers excluding them and compete successfully with the elites on their own terms, but in many other cases, they had to form their own associations and conduct their own competitions in isolation and exclusion, as women, the working classes, the indigenous peoples, blacks, ethnic and immigrant minorities, and persons with disabilities did in most countries until well after World War II.[3] It is instructive that both women and the organized working classes held their own versions of Olympic Games up until the late 1930s, black athletes in the USA had their own professional leagues, and minority ethnic communities in many countries had their own sports and associations.

The struggles for full inclusion in sport and physical activity were accelerated during the four decades covered by this volume, buoyed by the decolonization of Africa, Asia and the Caribbean, the youth radicalization of the 1960s, and the creative, uncompromising ambition of so many social movements and campaigns, especially those for civil and human rights, a peaceful, non-nuclear world, women's liberation, sexual diversity and universal accessibility. Activists fought against discrimination and for opportunities with a wide variety of strategies and tactics, from international, national and local human rights legislation to court challenges, media embarrassment, collective bargaining and in the case of the anti-war and anti-apartheid movement, internationally coordinated boycotts and mass protests. In their efforts to win opportunities for themselves, subordinate groups were often aided by the growing international support for human rights, and two deeply rooted currents of establishment sport, the liberal ideology of 'fair play' and the belief in 'sport for good', that playing or watching a sport could serve as education for citizenship. Subordinate groups could evoke the protections and opportunities of the Universal Declaration of Human Rights and other statements of human entitlement, such as the International Conventions on the Elimination of All Forms of Racial Discrimination (1969), All Forms of Discrimination Against Women (1979) and On the Rights of the Child (1989). They could argue that the logic of 'fair play' and a 'level playing field' required that class, racial, gender and ablest prohibitions be eliminated; they often found allies among those who sought to promote sport as a form of education, an antidote to delinquency and a strategy of social cohesion. But even with such favourable circumstances, the removal of barriers to full participation in sport, and the actual realization of opportunities for all peoples have been difficult and incomplete struggles. Moreover, the victories of one generation can be turned back in another. In Canada, the remarkable achievements of first-wave feminists in the 1920s and 1930s, including extensive participation, their own influential national organization, widespread media coverage of their best athletes, and a healthy spectatorship were so dramatically reversed in the 1940s and 1950s that the leaders of second-wave feminist sport had to start from scratch. As I write, the successful test cases of the 1980s, which gave young women the opportunity to compete on men's teams where comparable opportunities did not exist for them, are being revisited, and the International Olympic Committee has reinstituted the sexist gender-verification test. Widening class and region inequality belie the promise of opportunity. Children and youth from the upper classes are three times more likely to participate in sport than those from impoverished backgrounds.[4] Of course, these reversals and retreats have been conditioned by the sweeping economic, social, demographic and political transformations of the places and times in which they occur. The current ebb and flow of equity initiatives and the decline of public opportunities in sport and physical activities in many countries are a direct consequence of triumphal neo-liberalism and the assault on the idea of the enabling state.

These reflections underscore the importance of this special issue on the struggles of persons with disabilities (PWD) for full access to sport and physical activity. In a cultural practice that has idolized the able male body and citius, altius, fortius, PWD have long been marginalized in sport, if not excluded altogether through the systemic barriers of inaccessible and/or hard-to-reach facilities, unprepared instructors, patronizing and other forms of inappropriate language and of course, poverty and disease. Most opportunities are limited to periods of rehabilitation from accident or injury. Given the cultural place of twenty-first century sport as a marker of citizenship, and the seeming increase in disability, through wars, environmental catastrophes and diseases that plague so many parts of the world, ongoing, mainstreamed opportunities for PWD are more urgently needed than ever before.

It took longer than any other human rights struggle, more than five decades of concerted effort, to achieve the International Convention on the Rights of Persons with Disabilities in 2006. PWD are simultaneously women, persons of colour, gays, lesbians, bisexual, transgender and queer (LGBTQ), children and youth, and from low- and middle-income countries as well as the economically advanced societies, i.e. they have many other forms of identity,[5] and for the most part, their campaigns for opportunities in sport and physical activity have been astutely linked to those of other disadvantaged groups. The sorry exception was the 1976 Paralympic Games in Toronto, Canada, when they ran afoul of the international campaign against apartheid sport by inviting athletes from pro-apartheid South Africa. PWD and their allies have been remarkably successful in winning opportunities and recognition for themselves at every level of sporting practice and competition, overcoming bitter prejudice and seemingly implacable resistance, through the creation of new organizations and events, breathtaking athletic accomplishments, astute politics, affirming research and the generous support of some governments and donors. It's a remarkable story, as great an achievement as any of the equity victories in the period under review. Yet much remains to be done. What is particularly helpful about this Special Issue is the way it draws upon the victories and experiences of activists from so many countries. I congratulate the editor and organizer, Jill Le Clair, for her insight, commitment and persistence. The collection offers many valuable lessons for the next round of struggles.

Notes

[1] 'Black Rhythms in White Rituals'.
[2] 'Writing Johannesburg', 65.
[3] As in Canada, Kidd, *The Struggle for Canadian Sport*.
[4] Active Healthy Kids Canada.
[5] Parnes and Hashemi, 'Sport as a Means to Foster Inclusion'.

References

Active Healthy Kids Canada. *2010 Report Card*. http://www.activehealthykids.ca/ReportCard/PhysicalActivityandInactivity.aspx
Farrell, Lennox. 'Black Rhythms in White Rituals'. http://www.timbooktu.com/lennox/rituals.htm
Kidd, Bruce. *The Struggle for Canadian Sport*. Toronto: University of Toronto Press, 1996.
Parnes, Penny, and Goli Hashemi. 'Sport as a Means to Foster Inclusion, Health and Well-being of Persons with Disabilities'. In *Literature Reviews on Sport for Development and Peace*, edited by Bruce Kidd and Peter Donnelly, 124–57. Toronto: International Working Group on Sport for Development and Peace, 2007. http://www.righttoplay.com/International/news-and-media/Documents/Policy%20Reports%20docs/Literature%20Reviews%20SDP.pdf
Poplack, Richard. 'Writing Johannesburg'. *Walrus*, July/August (2010): 65.

Introduction

Global organizational change in sport and the shifting meaning of disability

Jill M. Le Clair

Humber College ITAL, Toronto, Canada; Global Disability Research in Sport and Health Network

There are 650 million people with disabilities worldwide and 450 million of them are in the global south. They are the largest minority, the poorest and the most marginalized. Sport has underlined the contradictions of prejudice and discrimination and the gap between low expectations and ability. The passage of the 2006 UN Convention on the Rights of Persons with Disabilities included Article 30, which defined rights in sport, physical activity and recreation, and shifted the meaning of disability globally. The historical framing of disability as a social welfare issue, charity-based and medically defined, was replaced by a rights-based approach to support inclusion. This Introduction outlines the issues related to disability in sport and physical activity in different cultural settings intersected by gender, race and ethnicity, class and age, and situates the articles that follow.

This collection of articles came out of the international conference 'To Remember is to Resist: 40 Years of Sport and Social Change, 1968–2008' hosted by the University of Toronto and Humber College ITAL. This conference upheld the importance of mainstreaming disability within sport. The articles in this Special Issue focus on the reorganization of and rethinking about disability in sport and the impact on persons with disabilities globally. The themes reflect inequities in power and discrepancies in economic development and resources, as well as in access and support for sport and physical activities. They are rooted in changes tied to global disability rights, and challenges to segregation, ableism and the hegemony of normalcy linked to shifting definitions of sport. The articles examine disability in global, regional, national and local sport, reflecting pioneering policies and they have suggestions about important issues for research in this new field. The articles describe political struggles in sport, sometimes with constraints because there is an absence of free speech.[1] The framework reflects the need to recognize the embodied nature of disability within sport, and assumes that all citizens have the right to fully participate in all aspects of social life, including sport and physical activity. In any collection of articles there are omissions and this is the case here.

There are 650 million people with disabilities around the world and 450 million of them are in the global south or resource-poor countries. The disability sport literature does not reflect this reality and these articles hope to help address this imbalance. Disability touches all families because approximately 10% of people of working age in each country have a disability. Only 15% of people are born with their impairment and typically by age 65 more than 40% of the population have a disability.[2] It could be said that we are all temporarily able-bodied. One of the challenges for disability research is that many countries do not have accurate national statistics, and the Poverty Assessments of the World Bank have not extensively addressed disability.[3] It is known that the disabled constitute the largest minority in the world and are often overlooked. They face stigma, prejudice, discrimination, poverty, inaccessible school systems and are chronically underemployed and unemployed. Social, financial and medical resources vary enormously from community to community which directly impacts on both health and sport opportunities.[4] Although the UN Millennium Development Goals (MDGs) of 2005 do not specifically mention the disabled, these goals directly impact many disabled as their focus is on extreme poverty.[5] Discrimination is global and includes being routinely subjected to physical abuse and social ostracism.[6] Documented in a 2007 Kenyan disability rights report, a former student described his daily treatment at school:

> As I was at … Thika Joy School, the teachers would beat me up when I got late, yet I could not push my wheelchair fast enough. Once I got late for lunch, I never used to go to eat because I would not be allowed to eat … Even in the dining hall I used to be beaten … [7]

A Canadian Paralympian interviewed in 2003, described her experience while training in the local community pool when she was younger. Two children asked her why she moved the way she did. 'When I told them I was disabled they ran away', in effect erasing her from their normative experience.[8] Effective mechanisms to challenge these kinds of responses towards the disabled have yet to be fully developed.

These behaviours are not simply isolated incidents, but are linked to inherently discriminatory legal, social and political policies. This is why disabled individuals find it necessary to assert their rights and challenge perceptions in the public arena. This was the aim of what have become global initiatives of disabled Canadians Terry Fox (Marathon of Hope) and Rick Hansen (Man in Motion World Tour), who both used physical activity (daily marathons and wheelchair travel) to change attitudes, to support inclusion and to raise research money. The physical achievements of these athletes, and others in sport around the world, contest negative assumptions about disability and limitations. Issues of 'voice' and representation are very important in this context. James Charlton's *Nothing About Us Without Us* is an ongoing demand in response to the history of paternalism and exclusion. The editor of the volume is permanently disabled from a spinal cord injury after a car crash and this reality informs the work. The lack of rights for persons with disabilities in the workplace means that there still is a serious under-representation of the disabled within academic discourse.

Disability rights, UN Convention Article 30 and globalization

Battles for individual civil and human rights have a long history in Western democracies and include the English Magna Carta Libertatum of 1215, the American Declaration of Independence in 1776, the French Constitution of 1791 and the UN Universal Declaration of Human Rights in 1948, but disability was not included in any of these documents. There has been ongoing tension between Western democracies supporting universal human rights and the often community/collective focused perspective of non-Western countries who argue that there is a colonial hegemonic and ethnocentric character to these values.[9] These arguments were set aside and, after literally years of delay and disagreement (and for the first time negotiations included the disabled), the passage of the 2006 UN Convention on the

Rights of Persons with Disabilities was possible with the support of countries from both the north and the south; this meant a profound shift in the meaning of disability in the global arena. Mashall McLuhan predicted a 'global village' through communication in *Understanding Media,* decades before the profound impact of technology globally was understood. Gupta and Ferguson argue that there are now transnational identities that reframe traditional nationalism and global sport is part of these shifting experiences and values.

The Convention has global impact and Article 30 of the Convention states that its aims are 'to encourage and promote the participation, to the fullest extent possible, of persons with disabilities in mainstream sporting activities at all levels, disability-specific activities, recreational activities, inclusion in physical education and school activities and recreation and tourism'.[10] Support for these activities is also to be provided; this includes coaches, trainers, management, the built environment, facilities and accessible equipment. Programmes and policies for both adults and children are addressed with a framework to benchmark change. Brock, J. Donnelly, Gupta, Gupta and Ferguson, and Pothier and Devlin discuss current rights issues in a cultural and globalized context, and Kidd and P. Donnelly within sport (Kidd, 2008; Kidd & Donnelly, 2008).[11] In the first article 'Disability Rights and Change in a Global Perspective', Marcia Rioux explains the key aspects of Article 30 in the UN Convention and the importance of monitoring.

Many of the articles address policy and programmes in disability sport. Jarvis, the former President of the Canadian Paralympic Committee explains that good policy is good for governments, politicians, bureaucrats and stakeholders:

> Policy is the language of governments … In the culture of government, policy is typically a necessary prerequisite for meaningful and sustained action. For sport generally, there can be successful outcomes in programming, providing support and athlete development from intentional intervention, but the absence of formal policy leaves initiatives in a precarious state.[12]

Disability rights policy and legislation are important, but so is the implementation of them within sport. The whole question of the gaps between legislation and policy that outline rights and the reality for those who want to exercise them, is a key concern in this next stage of disability sport. Monitoring frameworks of the UN Convention organizations such as Disability Rights Promotion International (DRPI) and national guidelines such as proposed by Spraklen and others[13] will play an important role as more individuals and organizations invoke these national and international rights in disability.

Sport has proven to be an arena in which to challenge oppression and discrimination faced by people with disabilities, just as it has been a site of contestation for women as Jennifer Hargreaves has described in her work and ethnic minorities in many countries.[14] Disabled athletes globally have challenged limitation and fought for access to public space. Also, innovators within governments have provided funding and supported both inclusive sport policies and disabled athletes, as has Sport Canada, beginning in the early 1990s and solidified in 2006 with the *Policy on Sport for Persons with a Disability.*[15] In addition, non-governmental organizations provide programmes, such as the inclusive sport and recreation centre of Variety Village in Toronto. Innovative pioneers, such as Dr Hehama Baum, who founded the MukiBaum Treatment Centres (also in Toronto, Canada), and HH Sheikha Mozah Bint Nasser Al-Missned, who founded the Shafallah Centre in Doha, Qatar to provide medical services, but also programmes in the arts and sport in addition to hosting international conferences. This all undertaken, to support the reframing of disability both in their own countries and internationally.[16] However, discrimination and hostility continue and centres such as these are few in number.

The growth of the disability rights movements around the world, and the UN Convention of the Rights of Persons with Disabilities, provide the framework for the greater inclusion of the disabled in all aspects of society in many countries, with new technologies to support shared information and globalization. Connected to disability rights is the reality that there has been a shift in the positioning and meaning of international disability sport. In 1996, the Paralympic Games were a second-tier games with much good will, but without adequate support and funding. By 2010, the Paralympic Games were genuinely partnered and funded with the Winter Olympic Games, and the logos for each of the Games were used jointly for promotion. The medal count for the Paralympic Games in Vancouver was eagerly watched, as was the debate over the government-funded 'Own the Podium 2010' programme,[17] but the controversy faded away with medal successes. Paralympians were seen as national heroes.

The articles in this Special Issue examine organizational change in the global sport organizations of the Paralympic Games, IPC Swimming, Special Olympics and Deaflympics, change to support mainstreaming, and the different strategies of the earlier incarnation of the Paralympic Games towards the sport boycott of apartheid South Africa. Regional organizational change is outlined in China, Oceania and East Africa, with a focus on Kenya. There are diverse articles on the individual and these include community sport in Ghana, transgressive 'cyborg' bodies and the role of sport in a tension-filled community in a resource-poor school in South Africa. Other articles argue for the need for research in disability sport in a number of areas and these include physical education, countries like Malaysia, female athletes in the media, the rates of participation in disability sport, the increase in risk-taking in sport and the concomitant increase in catastrophic injuries, and Islamic women in sport. The articles are organized around the theme of global disability rights, recognizing the inequities between the north and south in the context of the role of ableism and the hegemony of normalcy in the changing meaning of disability and the importance of language, and the impact of technology and disability linked to the shifting definition of sport. The Special Issue also includes discussion about the important issues to be addressed in this new field and directions for ongoing research. In any collection of articles there are omissions and this is the case here.[18]

Sport definitions: disability definitions – shifting meanings

What is sport?

The 2007 *Literature Reviews on Sport for Development and Peace* by Parnes and Hashemi clearly supports the importance of sport and physical activity to foster inclusion, health and well-being, and the articles in this Special Issue build on this work.[19] Sport is a cultural construct and is usually defined as including five elements: it is competitive, involves vigorous and complex physical skills, has rules with officials, has a tradition in a cultural context, and has rewards either public or personal.[20] The articles discuss both high-performance sport and recreational activities. They include disabilities of different kinds – physical and intellectual – and also raise the issue that a disability defined as an impairment by the medical community is not necessarily seen by others to be a disability, as is the case with some members of the Deaf community. What is defined 'officially' as sport is contested. In the Olympic Games, golf has been included and excluded, tug-of war has vanished; extreme sports have battled to be included as they grow in popularity and have attracted ever larger audiences. The media plays a role in this as the pressure to hand audiences to sponsors increases. So what is sport? Hunting foxes was part of rural cultural life in Great Britain and bull-fighting has a long history in Spain, but both face hostile opposition from those who want the 'sports' banned as unsporting, and although Ultimate Fighting Championships are seen as unsafe or even barbaric, ticket sales are phenomenal. Wushu was unheard of in the West and is not included in the Olympic or Paralympic Games, but is enormously popular in Asia and has a growing global audience. Modern international sport is Western in origin, but has come to include Asian forms like judo and tae kwando. Sport now includes the disabled, some participating in 'traditional' sports and some in new forms of sport such as goal ball, sit-ski and wheelchair basketball in which specialized equipment is used or new forms are created, as with wheelchair skateboarding.

Disability sport has evolved from being almost non-existent to extensive formal organizations that are local, national and international. The Glasgow Deaf and Dumb Football Club was founded in 1871 and the first international match took place between England and Scotland in 1891. The International Silent Games (Les Jeux Internationaux Silencieux) are the second oldest multisport international games after the Olympic Games and were held for the first time in Paris, France in 1924 with athletes from nine countries. However, the foundations for modern disability sport began at Stoke Mandeville Hospital in 1948 where neurosurgeon Dr Ludwig Guttman held a small sport event, with fewer than 20 athletes, parallel to the London Olympic Games. Spinal-cord-injured young veterans from World War II were depressed and isolated, and Guttman saw sport as not merely providing medical physiotherapy, but as a path to social inclusion.[21] From these small beginnings developed the current global Paralympic Games with its focus on sport performance. The Paralympic Games have also evolved and grown over time to include athletes with different disabilities, more sports and more events within the sports (as with skiing in the Winter Games).

What is disability?

In *Discipline and Punish*, Foucault describes power and control in the context of visibility, one 'organized entirely around a dominating, overseeing gaze'.[22] It is a perception, but also an active mode of seeing as the gaze is both disciplined and disciplining.[23] The active view or 'the disciplining gaze' is the panoptican of the able-bodied world, so powerful that disabled children were and still are labelled crippled, often hidden from view because of shame and in the hope of sheltering them from dehumanizing discrimination or abandonment. Gavin Smith describes the important interconnectedness between fear, memory and the law, and that historically, oppressive policies create a real fear of discriminatory government policies.[24] Although not unpacked in this Special Issue, these global restructurings of policy and practices try to address the fear so closely embedded in disability.

The necessity for a strong and healthy body in a world of limited technology frames disability as a liability for both survival and success. In highly industrialized and wealthy societies, technology supports the ideology of individual rights and impacts on all bodies. Technology is more available to support the physical challenges of a different body; however, we do find wide discrepancies in access and use. The shaping and limiting of the disabled means that their bodies are disciplined as they are inevitably subject to control, segregation and isolation. Assumptions about the normalcy of the able human body and the Christian blessedness of the healthy body are part of the heritage of the Western world.[25] Historical and religious values about morality and a 'polluted' or tainted status, as well as taboos,[26] have led to isolation and marginalization. Attitudes toward disability are recorded in the myths of the Ancient World through to present-day writing. Edwards outlines how the idealized body was the powerful body and the flawed body was seen to be dangerous or to be destroyed. The Greek gods fell from the skies if they had bodily deformities.[27]

Sport for the disabled has also been part of this struggle to challenge ancient views and achieve social inclusion.

Ableism and normalcy

Those who hold power define and frame knowledge.[28] A Western legacy is that essentialist assumptions are made about the human body. The body is seen to be biologically framed, unchanged and 'neutral'. This identity is usually described as able-bodied and the term used to describe this oversight or perspective of assuming the same physical ability for all is labelled 'ableism'. There is a hegemony of the normal that is at the heart of cultural production.[29] This critique is not political correctness, but an attempt to eliminate bias by correctly analysing a physical movement hegemony that is ideologized and oppressive because of its oversights. Criticisms of the literature are attempts to have better research analysis and understanding. This is also linked to the attempt to challenge the power relationship of the 'able-bodied gaze', which defined the world and the disabled as 'the other'. Labels and definitions are social constructs and are important in the debate about disability.

In the nineteenth century, the concepts of the 'norm', 'normality' and 'normalcy'[30] were developed as part of the wholesale attempt to classify the world. From the medical world to the 'natural', labelling, classifying and naming the 'normal' took place. Who and what are considered normal are always ideologically and politically based. Rosemarie Garland-Thomson created the term 'normate' to describe the centrality of the 'normal'[31] and the insidious power of that concept. Normal is meant to describe the centre, so the other is abnormal and the two concepts are in a binary relationship.[32] Sport has played a central role in this discussion because it has glorified the 'able' body and emphasized its normalcy and superiority both physically and, in some contexts, morally.[33]

Political identity and 'coming out'

Pushing back is part of any struggle against exclusion and discrimination, so tied to the gaze of abelism is the assertion of rights and the politicized aspects of 'coming out'. The wheelchair, whether as a symbol on bathroom doors or used by an athlete is universally understood, but being defined as disabled involves social transformation.

> Coming out, then, for disabled people, is a process of redefinition of one's personal identity through rejecting the tyranny of the *normate*, positive recognition of impairment and embracing disability as a valid social identity. Having come out, the disabled person no longer regards disability as a reason for self-disgust, or as something to be denied or hidden, but rather as an imposed oppressive social category to be challenged and broken down. ... Coming out, in our analysis, involves a political commitment.[34]

There is disagreement about 'coming out'. Swain and Cameron argue that identity status is tied to coming out to others, similar to the change in sexual-orientation status for gays and lesbians. Others argue that disability status is complicated by the 'visible' and the 'nonvisible' and 'invisible' nature of disability, and the changing dynamic of some disabilities.[35] Negotiating disability in social interaction is part of everyday life and is informed by the nature of the individual disability.[36] In sport, all athletes have had to negotiate their disability identity, as each disabled athlete has no choice because being part of the competitive sport system necessitates coming out through the classification process, which is public.[37]

However, disability has many different identities and meanings. Disability is often equated with inferiority and deficiency rather than a neutral difference that may require some adaptation; there is an implicit cultural moral judgement. The meaning of disability is culturally framed and what is defined as a disability in one context is not in another. Therefore, disability has been described as 'slippery' and fluid because there are many kinds. What is defined as a disability by some is not by others. There is tension over the issue of surgical interventions to address disability in children (and adults) which is heightened in discussion over the use of cochlear implants to mediate deafness. Some argue that they want their children to experience the hearing world, and others not. This is one of the most important debates in the Deaf community, as many see deafness as part of Deaf Culture and *not* a disability. Sparrow has used the term ethnocide in reference to implants.[38] This disagreement is part of the battle to maintain an independent Deaflympics separate from the Paralympic Games, managed by the Deaf. Donalda Ammons and Jordan Eickman argue this position in their article 'Deaflympics and the Paralympics: Eradicating Misconceptions'.

Disability is an inevitable, but often not recognized, consequence of violence, war and environmental disaster (such as the 2010 earthquake in Haiti and floods in Pakistan). Disability is framed differently in times of war, linked to sacrifice and nationalism. Events for soldiers such as the first Warrior Games held May 2010 in the USA, and programmes like the UK Battle Back, only exist because of the military injuries in Iraq and Afghanistan. Increasingly, disabled soldiers are participating in the Paralympic Games, and some in Special Olympics.

Intellectual disability

Almost totally overlooked in the past, there is now increasing support for the rights, personal independence and participation in sport of persons with intellectual disabilities, but often data are limited and support varies greatly by country.[39] In the past, persons with intellectual disabilities were often subject to cruel harassment and demeaning language. The activists of the Community Living movement have reframed the previously segregated and often institutionalized lives of the disabled. In the West, it has become expected that children are integrated into the school and community in ways that were unimaginable 40 years ago. The Special Olympics started by Eunice Kennedy Shriver in the USA in 1968, with separate sport events, has become a worldwide phenomenon in 180 countries with over 600,000 participants in China alone.[40] Previously criticized by some for their separate programmes, Unified Sports and Camp Shriver reflect initiatives for inclusion to bring non-disabled and disabled individuals and communities together. 'Promoting Social Inclusion for People with Intellectual Disabilities through Sport: Special Olympics International, Global Sport Initiatives and Strategies' by Coreen M. Harada, Gary N. Siperstein, Robin C. Parker and David Lenox provides insights into the current changes taking place globally in this area.

Theories of disability

Disability models

Historically, disability has been associated with religious or spiritual punishment and images of evil, so irrational fears led to active policies of discrimination, abuse and even extermination. Persons with visible and invisible disabilities have to negotiate disability on a daily basis. Those with different bodies have to face negative attitudes and those with invisible disabilities, such as deafness, often face irritation and a lack of comprehension. This reality means that persons with disabilities often use a great deal of energy in what Erving Goffman describes as 'passing' as non-disabled, to avoid the stigma of disability[41] because accommodations are not available to them. Disability in a non-technologized world of work and an absence of 'corrective' medical attention leads to poverty and begging for survival.

In the twentieth century, science became the ideological framework for prejudice. Scientists and doctors championed genetic management through eugenics, using sterilization and institutionalization; the idealized, nationalist, sporting, sometimes racialized body was incorporated into state policy. In Nazi Germany of the 1930s, the government generated propaganda and then programmes of discrimination, abuse and finally the disabled were the first group targeted for extermination.[42] After World War II, in response to these horrors rooted in eugenics, governments in the West framed disability within a *medical model* in which the focus was on the individual, impairment and rehabilitation. Social and welfare legislation was introduced to support and 'care for' the so-called weak and vulnerable, including the disabled.

By the 1970s, there was a rejection of the social welfare model with its paternalist approach and its implicit dependency, which saw the individual as having a medical health 'problem'. In response, the social construction model, which included a number of social–contextual approaches, argued that society itself creates disability because of barriers to participation that result in social oppression. Academics and activists such as Barnes, Davis, Oliver, Tom Shakespeare and Snyder, rejected the medical model and argued that social conditions were the source of oppression – the built environment in particular excludes, and lifts (elevators), curb cuts, ramps and computer-assisted technology minimized impairments and disabling conditions, and supported inclusion in all aspects of society. The 1990 Americans with Disabilities Act (ADA) helped pave the way globally for disability rights activists to invoke a new rights-based approach for inclusion. With this model, the term disability was transformed into a political rallying cry for rights and self-determination with the focus on *abilities*. The very concept of disability became challenged and issues of 'voice', representation and power became central. Swartz, who is South African, argues that this is particularly important in a post-colonial context in which capacity development in low-income countries needs to be directed by the disabled themselves.[43] Limited resources in non-Western, low- or middle-income countries means there are even greater battles to have disability recognized as an issue at all, in order to gain access to education, health services, transportation and all other aspects of social and political life. Currently, there is increasing recognition of the need for inclusion in all aspects of societies globally and for the first time the UN Economic and Social Council approved the policy of 'Mainstreaming Disability in the Development Agenda' in December 2009.[44]

Over time, criticisms of the social construction model developed because of its focus on society and the built environment. In his 2006 *Disability Rights and Wrongs*, Tom Shakespeare argues that the reality of the lived body was minimized, and increasingly researchers and activists have called for the recognition of the embodied nature of the disabled body by including the notion of *embodiment and the role of impairment*.[45] In spite of the sophistication of analysis of disability, Rioux and Valentine point out that the theoretical approaches to disability can be divided into four major groups; the individual–pathology approach includes a biomedical model and a functional model, and the social–pathology approach includes an environmental model and a human rights model. Rioux and Valentine argue that even if there are legal, human rights in place, there is no agreement on the theoretical approaches that are used in policy on the meaning of disablement, so patterns of inequality remain.[46]

Sport models: disability based to sport based

The medical model was used for classification at the beginnings of disability sport, at Stoke Mandeville Hospital, to ensure the much-problematized 'fair play'.[47] Parallel to the political and social changes in models of disability, disability-based sport evolved and changed over time. Disability-based competition using a medical assessment was replaced by sport-based competition with an evaluation of how the athlete functioned in the sport itself.[48] 'The Paralympic Games and 60 Years of Change (1948-2008): Unification and Restructuring from a Disability and Medical Model to Sport-Based Competition by David Legg, President of the Canadian Paralympic Committee and Robert Steadward, who write as academic researchers and key members of the organization, provides a history of this shift. Although there is disagreement over the significance, meaning and direction of the Games, Brittain in *The Paralympic Games Explained,* Howe in *The Cultural Politics of the Paralympic Games*, Hums and MacLean in *Governance and Policy*, Gilbert and Schantz in *The Paralympic Games*, Steadward and Petersen in *Paralympics*, Thomas and Smith in *Disabiity Sport and Society* and Wolff in 'Inclusion of the Sport for Athletes with Disabilities into Non-Disabled Sport Organizations' each describe how the Games have evolved and grown over time to include athletes with different disabilities, and more sports and more events within the sports (as with skiing in the Winter Games).[49] 'Transformed Identity: From Disabled Person to Global Paralympian' by Jill Le Clair illustrates these changes in IPC Swimming, through athlete narratives; identity at the personal level transformed at the same time as the international sport organization itself. By 1996, in Atlanta, swimmers were no longer organized into four separate disability-based swim teams (amputee, blind, cerebral palsy and wheelchair sport–spinal cord injury), competition was sport-based and there was only one national swim team consisting of athletes with different disabilities.

The importance of language

Part of the struggle for disability rights has been over language. *Claiming Disability: Knowledge and Identity* by Simi Linton[50] outlines the history of disability language with the destructiveness of negative and demeaning language. It explores the significant efforts made by disability activists, government agencies and educators to use 'neutral' or respectful language and abandon the labels of 'cripples' and 'freaks'. There is still tension over the basic terms of 'disabled' and 'persons with disabilities'. Generally in North America, the goal has been to emphasize the person, so within sport this means using the terms 'athlete with a disability' or 'athlete who is hearing impaired' rather than blind athlete or deaf athlete. Although there have been challenges to this individual-focus approach as in Titchkosky's critique 'Disability - A Rose by any Other Name: People First Language in Canadian Society' written over ten years ago. However, people in the UK and South Africa argue that disability is a political social status, and using disabled as the descriptor for the discriminated group and disabled person is more accurate. The South African Aids Council explains their position in these words:

> 'Disabled people' is the preferred term. We believe that disability should be accorded a similar status to sexuality, gender or race and just as we would not talk about a 'person with a

black skin' or 'a person with homosexual desires', we prefer not to talk about 'people with disabilities'. Where necessary, the latter term will be used in recognition of external environmental barriers experienced by disabled people.[51]

In many countries, persons with disabilities are fighting to get disability rights recognized and to also gain access to and participate in, the workplace, education, health services, transportation and all other aspects of social and political life. Sport has become a visible site for these struggles and language reflects differing perspectives. In her article 'Contested Perspectives of "Marvel" and "Mockery" in Disability Sport: Accra, Ghana', Anne-Marie Bourgeois analyses the structural position of disabled women and men in Accra. Through fieldwork and interviews, her research outlines the contested perspectives of the basketball players who are alternatively admired for their role and skills as athletes, and dismissed because of negative stereotypes that stem from the reality that many of the 'disableds' in the city beg to survive.

Inequities

Economic development

Where you are born, north or south, in a rich or poor neighbourhood, has a huge impact on the meaning of disability. There are enormous disparities within nations and regions, as well as between countries. Many countries have limited economic development and sport infrastructure and may be able to send only one or two athletes to international games, but there is limited published comparative data available. 'Participation Rates of Developing Countries in International Disability Sport: A Summary and the Importance of Statistics for Understanding and Planning' summaries Jackie Lauff's research goals.[52] She has made a detailed analysis of the Deaflympic, Paralympic and Special Olympics World Games from 1991 to 2006. She provides a valuable statistical resource for understanding the participation rates of developing countries in disability sport by gender, region and economic development. The article also provides a platform for further research to guide development assistance and improve international participation in disability sport.

Inequities tied to racism are usually linked to economic and political inequities. The historic worldwide sport boycott of South Africa with its discriminatory policy of apartheid is well known, unlike the different path taken in disability sport, which struggled to keep disabled athletes included in international competition. Ian Brittain provides a detailed analysis of this history in his article 'South Africa, "Apartheid" and the Paralympic Games'. The intersections of race, ethnicity and disability have been under-theorized and under-researched in disability sport, although discrimination in non-disabled sport has received considerable attention in terms of monitoring. Richard R. Lapchick the Director of the Institute for Diversity and Ethics in Sport puts out a Racial and Gender Report each year.[53] Hopefully, in the future scholars, will contribute to this important area.

We rarely read about some regions from the perspective of those who live there. China has initiated new national policies to support disabled people and disability in sport and recreation. China has undergone enormous social change from its status as a low-income country, and has become the second most important economy in the world. Brownell outlines the importance of the Olympic Games for repositioning the country internationally in her book *Beijing's Games: What the Olympics Means for China*. Having no international standing in 1983, China came first in the medal rankings at the 2008 Paralympic Games.[54] Hosting the Paralympic Games was an additional impetus for changes in sport and social policy. Sun Shuhan, Yan Rui, Mao Ailin, Chao Liu and Jing

Tang of Renmin University of China in Beijing provide a history of these changes in their article 'China and the Development of Sport for Persons with a Disability, 1978–2008: A Review'.

Large countries have divergent environmental conditions and their populations have different sport interests. There are dense, urbanized populations where global sports like soccer are popular, and widely scattered small populations, where citizens have limited resources of any kind. Some want, or are forced, to live a 'traditional' lifestyle off the resources of the land and some have very vibrant traditional sport games such as the Indigenous or Aboriginal Games in Canada, but they do not usually include disability games. Oceania is a region made up of many small countries and is rarely discussed in the sport literature; its population is widely dispersed, scattered across the Pacific Ocean, with the additional challenge that travel has to be by boat or expensive flights. Dr Jagdish Maharaj, a rehabilitation doctor and one of the founders of the Fiji Paralympic Committee, outlines some of the challenges for athletes and organizations in his article 'Living Disability and Restructuring IPC Sport in Oceania: The Challenge of Perceptions, Spatial Dispersal and Limited Resources'.

Malaysia has had a leading role in the Asia Pacific region, previously through the FESPIC Games and ASEAN Para Games, and its innovative policies. In many countries, disability sport is little documented. Selina Khoo has played a pioneering role in recording the history of disabled athletes and the short history of disability sport organizations in Malaysia. The national governing body of sport is the Malaysian Paralympic Council and in her article 'New Direction: Disability Sport in Malaysia', Khoo explains the challenges to increasing the growth in programmes and support and access that face countries with diverse populations.

Technology and prosthesis

Disability and impairment as they relate to participation in physical activity are also viewed differently at different ages. Priestley found that 'voluntary organizations in the UK did not perceive the older people they worked with as "disabled" unless they were unable "to carry out what a normal elderly person could do"'.[55] Motor limitations in children and seniors are expected, and often not labelled as disabilities. Impairment also changes in cultural contexts and 'attempts to alter the effects of impairment are historically bound'.[56] Technology is reframing the meaning of disability in many ways and for all age groups, sometimes making the impairment disappear. New technologies such as smart phones help support and evaluate people who are engaging in recreational activities, but need support or medical monitoring.[57] Cyborg bodies and Internet atavars are changing perceptions of the 'natural' body and the sport body.[58] All around the world, children with disabilities engage in social networking and experience sport events through the computer. YouTube generates sport celebrities like Aaron Fotheringham, the first person to do wheelchair skateboarding, what he calls 'hardcore sitting', and do backflips in a wheelchair in skateboard parks, creating a new sport.[59]

The world of prosthetics has been revolutionized through microtechnology. Prostheses can be visible or invisible – as in the use of hip replacements, increasingly for younger people who have sport injuries – and so people who in the past were severely disabled can now return to be active in sports.[60] 'Bladerunner or Boundary Runner? Oscar Pistorius, Cyborg Transgressions and Strategies of Containment' by Moss E. Norman and Nicola Moola discusses the significance of the South African runner Oscar Pistorius, who has artificial feet, his goal of competing in the Olympic Games, and the meaning of the modified cyborg bodies in the context of normalcy, humanness and technology. The question of disabled athletes leaving disabled sport to compete in the 'glamour' events of the Olympic Games has been debated because some think this could 'weaken' the Paralympic Games.[61] In any discussion of prostheses, individual and societal financial issues and availability vary. Devices are simply not accessible in many countries because high-tech prostheses can cost thousands of dollars. Cultural design issues also apply to prostheses – the Jaipur Foot Prosthesis was designed in India specifically for use by those who sit cross-legged on the floor and walk barefooted and 'it is cheap, enduring, and efficient'.[62]

Risk, health and schools

There are risks in sport and physical activity, and varying risks in the communities in which they take place. Disabling injuries differ by gender, and there are often misconceptions about risks.[63] Who would have imagined that fishing is one of the most dangerous recreational activities? 'Risk of Catastrophic Injury in Sports and Recreation' by the renowned neurosurgeon Dr Charles H. Tator summarizes the results of an extensive Canadian study that lays out the increasing disabling injuries resulting from increased risk taking in sport and recreation activities. It is the only study of this kind, and Tator argues the need for additional research because there is no cure for spinal cord injuries. Clearly, the preventative work of sport organizations and health and disability foundations like Think First Canada and the Rick Hanson Foundation also play an important role in disability prevention, but more needs to be done.

Risk-taking in sport can cause disability when the emphasis is on performance,[64] but recreational activities and exercise can improve or sustain health, and reduce the risk of disability. Some communities have much higher rates of disability because of greater risks to health. The Health Promoting Schools programmes see health as encompassing all aspects of children's lives.[65] With a broader definition of health in a social context, as distinct from a medical definition, choice and risk play important roles. Unfortunately, violence is the second major cause of death for youth (after traffic accidents), and drugs are often at the root of disabling violence in many sections of cities in both the south and the north. In an environment created out of the legacy of poverty and unemployment from South Africa's apartheid policies, Patricia Struthers paints a vivid picture of a community in which violence and drug dealing are part of everyday life. In this setting, efforts are made to create a healthy environment by including school netball that creates a temporary, conflict-free zone reminiscent of the Olympic peace of Ancient Greece; how this unfolds is outlined in the article 'The Use of Sport by a Health Promoting School to Address Community Conflict'.

One of the key elements in the UN Convention is the right of access by children to sport and games activities in schools, however, access to education is a privilege in many countries because even elementary schools have fees. It is the ethnocentrism of Western countries which assumes that schools can automatically be the site of delivery of sport opportunities as many schools are still inaccessible to disabled children, and educators do not receive training in inclusive programmes. In the past, schools for children with disabilities were often totally separate. Today, more and more physical education curricula across the globe are including adaptive and inclusive training, and programmes and training in the use of adaptive equipment to better include children.[66] In East Africa, the disability rights movement began in Zimbabwe, and Kenya formed its first disability organization in the 1950s,[67] but the issue of sport and physical activities in schools has only recently received attention. Physiotherapists José Frantz, Julie S. Phillips Joseph M. Matheri and Joanne J. Kibet conducted the first research in Kenya in schools on this topic and they analyse new approaches for supporting inclusion and increased activity in 'Physical Activity and Sport as a Tool to Include Disabled Children in Kenyan Schools'.

Oscar Pistorius captured international attention as he ran what seemed impossibly fast and then, ironically, he was seen to be 'advantaged' because of technology.[68] For athletes like Pistorius, disability is not from choice, but now legal and legislative challenges are taking place over what some have called 'lifestyle' disabling conditions such as obesity, which are often tied to decisions to be inactive and overeat. While many in the world suffer from hunger and malnutrition, weight-related disability is becoming a problem in an increasing number of countries. More than one third of Americans are obese and the Centres for Disease Control have called the country 'obesogenic' ('environments that promote increase food intake, non-healthy foods and physical inactivity'). At the same time, there is a call for anti-discrimination legislation because fatness is seen to be a source of oppression and the American Obesity Association wants to include obesity as a disability, to be grounds for discrimination law suits, and BMI to become a vital sign for children. In response, the US and UK governments are now calling for initiatives to support nutrition education and a return to compulsory physical education and sport in schools as a solution to prevent children from disabling overweight.[69]

Gender

The 2010 G8–G20 World Summit made maternal and child care a central issue in its planning and budgeting because the second-class status of women is problematic globally.[70] Social inequity is reflected in sport, recreation and leisure inequities. This is exacerbated for many women by the triple discriminations of gender, disability and poverty. There is also a gap in disability theory as the approach is often 'gender-neutral' and the literature is sometimes essentialized. Sampson argues for the need to recognize the specificity of the diversity of female experience and the context of gendered disability, not just as an 'additive' analysis.[71] The inequities of females in sport and recreation have been well documented in non-disabled sport in the west, but only explored in a limited fashion in disability sport, although DePauw and Gavron published their pioneer book *Disability in Sport* in 1995 and Jennifer Hargreaves provided a thoughtful analysis in her book *Heroines of Sport: The Politics of Difference and Identity* in 2000.[72]

Media

The political and economic context impacts on the presence or absence of media coverage. In the past, lack of coverage was a problem as few knew about sporting events, or saw women in competition. In some countries, women's sport is not covered by the media because of social restrictions.[73] Female Iranian athletes (and those in other countries) do not get publicity and recognition because male cameramen do not have access, and the events are not shown on national television. Key to sport coverage is who will watch, in what numbers and will the sponsors pay? The IPC has had difficulty in finding sponsors because the Games do not have the regular daily audiences that other commercial sports do, which is also similar to the less-popular sports in the Olympic Games (such as the javelin and the shot put). The impact of live coverage through ParalympicSport.tv may change this as anyone with access to the internet can watch events streamed live, or delayed.[74]

Table 1. Male and female participants in the Winter Paralympic Games.[77]

Year	Location	Men	Women	Total
1988	Innsbruck, Austria	300	77	377
1992	Tignes-Albertville, France	288	77	365
1994	Lillehammer, Norway	381	90	471
1998	Nagano, Japan	440	121	561
2002	Salt Lake City, USA	329	87	416
2006	Torino, Italy	375	99	474
2010	Vancouver, Canada	381	121	502

Table 2. Male and female participants in the Summer Paralympic Games.

Year	Location	Men	Women	Total
1988	Seoul, Korea	2,503	710	3,213
1992	Barcelona, Spain	2,323	697	3,020
1996	Atlanta, USA	2,415	780	3,195
2000	Sydney, Australia	2,867	978	3,843
2004	Athens, Greece	2,646	1,160	3,806
2008	Beijing, China	2,584	1,367	3,951

Inequities in access to sport itself are reflected in the participation statistics for female athletes in the Paralympic Games. There are also inequities tied to economic resources because women and men from some regions have a much better chance of sport participation, as is clear from Lauff's statistical analysis of international disability sport.[75] In 1988, 300 men and 77 women participated in the Innsbruck, Austria Winter Paralympic Games. In 2010, these numbers grew to 381 and 121 (32% of the total). At the 1988 Summer Games in Seoul, Korea, 2503 men participated and 710 women, and the 2008 Beijing Games involved 2584 men and 1367 women (52%). The proportion of female athletes in relation to the numbers of male athletes has increased, although there are comparatively more participants in the Summer Games (Tables 1 and 2). Financial issues are a factor and Smith and Twomey found that more female disabled athletes are unemployed.[76] Also, some national teams have no women at all, and others very few.

In their wide-ranging four-country study, Athanasios (Sakis) Pappous, Eric de Léséleuc and Anne Marcellini compared press coverage in Germany, France, Spain and the UK, and found that disabled female athletes are framed somewhat differently from non-disabled athletes in terms of presentation, description and sexuality. Their initial findings are presented in the article 'Contested Issues in Research on the Media Coverage of Female Paralympic Athletes'.

Constructed modesty, cultural values: inclusion or separation

Inclusion and exclusion are limited by perceptions of not only disability, but also gender. Women are participating in increasing numbers and there have been a number of new directions in women's sport. Since 2000, Western female athletes have seen themselves as part of a post-feminist world and used their bodies as commodities to brand and market themselves.[78] Disabled women athletes have been used to showcase athletic skills. In 2008, the swimmer Stephanie Dixon, who has one leg, was used in dramatic advertisements set in the pool to illustrate the successes of Canadian Paralympians.

The politics of gender often means that women are discouraged, prevented or even excluded from many kinds of physical activity, and whenever we hear the term modesty it is in always associated with girls and women, never men. What are defined as appropriate modest behaviour and clothes are always culturally constructed and in an historical context.[78] As late as the 1920s, women in Chicago were arrested for wearing bathing suits that were too short and showed too much thigh.[80] The increasing briefness of sport uniforms in international competition has created new challenges. One fifth of the world's female population are members of the Islamic faith and the cultural expectation is that they are expected to compete in sport wearing Muslim dress, hijab. In some countries, the government defines appropriate women's dress (as in Iran and Saudi Arabia), whereas in others individuals make their own choices.[81] The headscarf has become an emotional and volatile political lighting rod, but some sports like table tennis and soccer have grown significantly because of allowing accommodations in uniforms.[82] Sima Limoochi, a member of the Iran Paralympic Committee and the IPC Women's Sport Committee, describes two very different approaches to the support and encouragement of women in sport in 'Reflections on the Participation of Muslim Women in Disability Sport: Hijab, Burkini, Modesty and Changing Strategies'. One is the training of women within Paralympic sport and the other is the separate and segregated female only, Islamic Women's Games held in Tehran, Iran.

Conclusion

It is difficult for a non-disabled person to imagine not being able to breathe, walk or move with ease. However, it is hoped that articles will help bring about some understanding of this reality and the complexity of the disability rights movement. In this context, sport performance and participation have played an important role in questioning the meaning of disability as spectators see competition in public spaces, and performances often challenge assumptions abilities.

Most of these articles were written by researchers who are members of the Global Disability Research in Sport and Health Network and are also active as managers, administrators, coaches, officials and classifiers in their sport communities. This group evolved from conferences held in a number of cities where disability in low-income countries was a concern.[83] These articles illustrate a profound shift in the perceptions and meanings of disability within countries and globally, as persons with disabilities have increasingly moved from the margins of society. The result of disability activism and organizations is increased inclusion in the mainstream. The focus is primarily on the organizational context of disability sport, mindful of the lived experiences and perspectives of athletes with disabilities. This follows what Charlton has summarized succinctly, and has become an important premise, 'nothing about us without us'. The authors reflect these political struggles, which are wide ranging. They also reflect the need to recognize the embodied nature of disability, which is different from seeing disability as primarily a social construct. The framework is one of disability rights and assumes that all citizens have the right to fully participate in all aspects of social life including sport and physical activity.

Frequently lacking attention in academia, and in the past lumped into the portfolios of health and welfare by governments, sport and recreation often play an important role in the lives of individual families and in the wider context of political policies and national identities. Sport is *always* political whether in the context of the Ancient Olympic Games or currently with debates about the organization and management of global sports like football and the Paralmpic Games. Issues that are part of sport itself such as the inclusion of women's events, classification, the meanings of sport and gender, the significance of race and ethnicity, the role of technology whether in terms of assistive devices or cyborg bodies, will continue to be contested. Hopefully these papers will make a contribution to encourage debate and new research.

Acknowledgements

The early part of this work was funded by the Canadian Social Science and Humanities Research Council (SSHRC). This collection of papers would not have been possible without the support of a large number of people and the contributing authors I want to thank some of them. Executive Editor, Boria Majumdar for his commitment to global discourse in sport; Review Editor Jessica Robinson for her support and advice; Bruce Kidd and Greg Malszecki for their support and ongoing commitment to inclusive sport, as well as John Davies, Robert Gordon, Marcia Rioux, Melanie Panitch, Rebeccah Bournemann HH Sheikha Mozah Bint Nasser Al-Missned and Chair Hassan Ali Bin Ali of the Shafallah Center, Doha, Qatar; and the reviewers. Those whose assistance was essential to make travel and fieldwork feasible: Tommy Lord (Atlanta), Daniele Laumann Hart (Mar del Plata), Lindy Allery (Athens), and Jing Li (Beijing). Student research assistants: Margaret Shalma, Linda Kalbun and Anne-Marie Bourgeois helped make this volume possible, and Raquel Deveza without whose kindness and help I could not live independently.

Notes

[1] Kidd, 'Human Rights and the Olympic Movement'.

[2] Statistics Canada, Census, 2001. 'Prevalence of Disability in Canada'. In 2001, 3.6 million Canadians were living in households reported having disability limitations, which represented disability rate of 12.4%. http://www.statcan.gc.ca/pub/89-577-x/4151361-eng.htm. Siebers, *Disability Theory*, 7; Priestley, *Disability*.

[3] In most countries, disability statistics are often unreliable because of the self-reporting nature of the data and the different definitions of disability between and within countries. These factors are considered a challenge to accurate figures in South Africa, but they apply to other countries as well. (1) There are different definitions of disability; (2) dfferent survey technologies are used to collect information; (3) there are negative traditional attitudes towards people with disabilities; (4) there is a poor service infrastructure for people with disabilities in underdeveloped areas; (5) violence levels (in particular areas at particular times) have impeded the collection of data, affecting the overall picture, http://www.independentliving.org/docs5/SANatlDisStrat1.html#anchor4; Braithwaite and Mont, *Disability and Poverty*, 8; they argue for the need for additional quantitative research, especially in developing countries.

[4] Often forgotten, but many disabling conditions are rooted in poverty and malnutrition, such as a lack of vitamin A and blindness, vitamin B and beri beri, pellagra and anaemia, vitamin D and rickets, and diabetes.

[5] United Nations Development Programme, 'Millennium Development Goals'. They include goals and targets on income poverty, hunger, maternal and child mortality, disease, inadequate shelter, gender inequality, environmental degradation and the Global Partnership for Development, http://www.undp.org/mdg/basics.shtml.

[6] In the summer of 2011 *Scope*, the British charity and disability rights organization for the disabled argued that the disabled are often targeted and crimes against the Deaf and disabled in the UK should be classified as hate crimes whereas commonly they are simply overlooked. http://www.scope.org.uk/campaigns/disability-discrimination/disability-hate-crime.

[7] African Union of the Blind, *State of Disabled Peoples Rights in Kenya 2007 Report*, 47–48, http://www.yorku.ca/drpi/files/KenyaReport07.pdf.

[8] Le Clair, 'Water, Senses and the Experiences of the Pool'.

[9] Kidd and Donnelly, 'Human Rights in Sport';, 'Disjuncture and Difference in the Global'; Brysk, *Globalization and Human Rights*.

[10] United Nations Enable, 'The Rights and Dignity of Persons with Disabilities. The 2006 UN Convention', http://www.un.org/disabilities

[11] Brock, *Global Justice*; Donnelly, *Universal Human Rights in Theory*; Gupta, 'The Song of the Nonaligned World'; Gupta and Ferguson, 'Beyond Culture'; Pothier and Devlin, *Critical Disability Theory*; Kidd, 'Human Rights and the Olympic Movement'; Kidd and Donnelly, 'Human Rights in Sport'.

[12] Jarvis, 'People, Policy and Sports', http://www.paralympicfoundation.ca/index.cfm/about-us/staff/.

[13] Spraklen, Hylton, and Long, 'Managing and Monitoring Equality'.

[14] Hargreaves, *Sporting Females*; *Heroines of Sport*.

[15] Sport Canada, 'The Policy on Sport for Persons with a Disability, 2006', Canadian Heritage, http://www.pch.gc.ca/pgm/sc/pol/spt/tdm-eng.cfm.

[16] Variety Village, http://varietyontario.ca/village/index.htm; MukiBaum Treatment Centres, http://www.mukibaum.com/home.php; Shafallah Center, http://www.shafallah.org.qa/cms/english/default.aspx#.

[17] Own the Podium 2010, http://www.ownthepodium2010.com/About/. Across the country the hope was for a 'three-peat' with a gold in men's sledge hockey added to the women's and men's gold in non-disabled hockey.

[18] There are no articles from the newly emerging powerhouse of India, South America or related to sport and the impact of environmental degradation, the importance of classification, visual impairment/blindness, sexual orientation (LGBTQ), blindness, asylums and the disabling impact on families, communities and nations of HIV/AIDS. Watermeyer et al in *Disability and Social Change* discuss the impact of HIV/AIDS on southern Africa. For the total absence of non-work physical activity sport in asylums, see Rheaume, *Remembrance of Patients Past*.

[19] Parnes and Hashemi, 'Sport as a Means to Foster Inclusion'.

[20] Coakley, *Sports in Society*.

[21] Guttman, 'Sport for the Disabled'.

[22] Foucault, *Discipline and Punish*, 159; *The Birth of the Clinic*.

[23] Armstrong, 'Foucault and the Sociology of Health', 20–21.

[24] Smith, 'Formal Culture'. Smith points out that the repressive regimes of Hitler, Stalin and Mao used fear as a tool of social regulation.

[25] Snyder and Mitchell, 'Re-engaging the Body'.

[26] Douglas, *Purity and Danger*.

[27] Edwards, 'Constructions of Disability in the Ancient Greek World', 28.

[28] Foucault, *Power/Knowledge*.

[29] L.J. Davis, 'Constructing Normalcy', 47; Titchkosky and Michalko, *Rethinking Normalcy* and *Reading and Writing Disability Differently*.

[30] L.J. Davis, 'Constructing Normalcy', 10.

[31] Linton, *Claiming Disability*, 24.

[32] Ibid., 22.

[33] Kidd, *The Struggle for Canadian Sport*.

[34] Swain and Cameron, 'Unless Otherwise Stated', in Samuels, 'My Body, My Closet', 237.

[35] Samuels, 'My Body, My Closet', 237–243.

[36] Goffmn, *Stigma*; Wendell, *The Rejected Body*.

[37] See Classification – Solutions for the Future; Le Clair, 'Diverse Experiences of the Swimming Classification Process'; Le Clair, 'Sport and Health'; Le Clair, 'High Performance Swimming'.

[38] Biderman, *Wired for Sound*; Sparrow, 'Implants and Ethnocide'.

[39] Herr, Koh, and Gostin, *Different But Equal*; Fujiura, Park, and Rutkowski-Kmitta, 'Disability Statistics in the Developing World'; Lynnes, Nicholas, and Temple, 'Fostering Independence in Health-Promoting Exercise'.

[40] Herr *et al.*, *Different but Equal*; Solish, Perry, and Minnes, 'Participation of Children'; Braddock 'Honouring Eunice Kennedy Shriver's Legacy'.

[41] Goffman, *Stigma*.

[42] Mangan, *Shaping the Superman*.

[43] Swartz, 'Building Disability Research Capacity'; *Able-Bodied*.

[44] UN Nations Social and Economic Council, Commission for Social Development. Secretary General Report. February 2010. http://www.un.org/disabilities/documents/reports/csocd48.pdf

[45] Brenkenridge and Volger, 'The Critical Limits of Embodiment'. Shakespeare, 'Disability, Identity and Difference', 94–113; Titchkosky, *Reading and Writing Disability Differently*.

[46] Rioux and Valentine, 'Does Theory Matter?', 49.

[47] Kennedy and Hills, *Sport, Media and Society*.

48 Swimming is a sport that now classifies on the basis of how an athlete functions in the water, regardless of a medical classification, see Le Clair, 'Diverse Experiences of the Swimming Classification Process', 2.
49 Brittain, *The Paralympic Games Explained*; Howe, *The Cultural Politics of the Paralympic Games*; Hums and Maclean, *Governance and Policy*; Gilbert and Schantz, *The Paralympic Games*; Legg et al., 'Historical Overview of the Paralympics'; Steadward and Petersen, *Paralymics*; Thomas and Smith, *Disability Sport and Society*; Wolff, 'Inclusion of the Sport for Athletes with Disabilities'.
50 Linton, *Claiming Disability*.
51 South African Aids Council, 'HIV/AIDS and Disability in South Africa'. May 2008, ii. http://www.icdr.utoronto.ca/Files/PDF/94a3663acf97d5f.pdf
52 Lauff, 'Developing Country Participation'.
53 See www.tidesport.org.
54 Xu, *Olympic Dreams*; Brownell, *Beijing's Games*; *Training the Body for China*; 2008 Beijing Paralympics Medal Tally, http://www.china.org.cn/paralympics/node_7052638.htm
55 Priestley, *Disability*, 152.
56 Ott, 'The Sum of its Parts', 5.
57 Diabetes. Posadzki, 'Prescribing Blackberries'.
58 Butryn, 'Posthuman Podiums'.
59 Wheelchair backflops, http://www.youtube.com/watch?v=z43PXkvVC5c
60 Faulkner, 'Casing the Joint'.
61 Thomas and Smith, *Disability Sport and Society*, 158.
62 Sriniasan, Technology Sits Cross-Legged, 328.
63 Sparkes and Smith, 'Disabled Bodies'; Tator, *Catastrophic Injuries*; www.thinkfirst.ca; Prowidenza and Tator, 'Sports Injury Prevention', 58-78'.
64 Theberge, 'It's Not About Health'. Young, *Sporting Bodies*.
65 Skinner, stresses the importance of health first and medicine second in 'The Big Idea; Denman et al., *The Health Promoting School*.
66 R.W. Davis, *Inclusion Through Sports*; Lieberman and Houston-Wilson, *Strategies for Inclusion*.
67 'State of Disabled People's Rights in Kenya, 2007', http://www.yorku.ca/drpi/Kenya07Ch3.html.
68 Swartz and Watermeyer, 'Cyborg Anxiety'.
69 Aphramor, 'Disability and the Anti-Obesity Offensive'; Overweight and Obesity website; http://www.cdc.gov/obesity/index.html; Centers for Disease Control, 'State Based Programs', http://www.cdc.gov/obesity/stateprograms/index.html; NHS Health and Social Care Information Centre, 'Statistics on Obesity, Physical Activity and Diet: England 2010', http://www.ic.nhs.uk/webfiles/publications/opad10/Statistics_on_Obesity_Physical_Activity_and_Diet_England_20
70 Editorial. 'Maternal Health Plan Something of a Start'. *Globe and Mail* June 25, 2010.
71 Sampson, 'Beyond Compassion', 267–270; Wendell, *The Rejected Body*.
72 Schantz and Gilbert, 'An Ideal Misconstrued'.
73 Pfister, 'Islam and Women's Sport'; Hargreaves, 'Sport Exercise and the Female Muslim Body'.
74 See http://brandstagetv.net/ParalympicSportTV/Newsletter/edition06_2010.html
75 Lauff, 'Developing Country Participation'.
76 Quoted in Brittain, *The Paralympic Games Explained*, 110.
77 Brittain, *The Paralympic Games Explained*, 107; 'Paralympic Games Vancouver 2010', IPC Official website, http://www.paralympic.org/Paralympic_Games/Past_Games/Vancouver_2010/index.html
78 Maloney, 'A New Image Exposed', A18; Lenskyj, 'More Fallen Heroes'.
79 Hansen, 'The World of Dress'.
80 Kennedy, *The Swimsuit*; Hargreaves, 'Sport, Exercise and the Female Muslim Body'.
81 Pfister, 'Islam and Women's Sport', 13.
82 Scott, *The Politics of the Veil*, especially Chapter 1 'The Headscarf Controversies' and Chapter 4 'Individualism'. Often Muslim women are essentialized but *hijab* has many different meanings, some of them reflecting different identities and sometimes in conflict.
83 Development, Sport and Youth, Cape Town, South Africa, 2006; the FESPIC Games Confernce, Kuala Lumpur, Malaysia, 2006; the Festival of International Conferences on Caregiving, Disability, Aging and Technology (FICCDAT), Toronto, Canada, 2007; and formalized at the 2008 International Conference on Sport and Disability held at the Shafallah Centre in Doha, Qatar.

References

Aphramor, Lucy. 'Disability and the Anti-Obesity Offensive'. *Disability & Society* 24, no. 7 (2009): 879–909.

Armstrong, David. 'Foucault and the Sociology of Health and Illness: A Prismatic Reading'. In *Foucault Health and Medicine*, edited by Alan Petersen and Robin Bunton, 15–30. New York: Routledge, 1997.

Barnes, Colin, Geoff Mercer, and Tom Shakespeare. *Exploring Disability: A Sociological Introduction*. Cambridge: Polity Press, 1999.

Biderman, Beverly. *Wired for Sound: A Journey into Hearing*. Toronto: Trifolium Books.

Braddock, David. 'Honouring Eunice Shriver's Legacy in Intellectual Disability'. *Intellectual and Developmental Disabilities* 48, no. 1 (2010): 63–72.

Braithwaite, Jeanine, and Daniel Mont. 'Disability and Poverty: A Survey of World Bank Poverty Assessments and Implications. Social Protection and Labour: The World Bank'. SP Discussion Paper no. 0805, February 2008.

Brenkenridge, Carol A., and Candace Volger ed. 'The Critical Limits of Embodiment: Reflections on Disability Criticism'. *Public Culture* 14, no. 3 (2001): Special Issue.

Brittain, Ian. *The Paralympic Games Explained*. London: Routledge, 2010.

Brock, Gillian. *Global Justice: A Cosmopolitan Account*. New York: Oxford University Press, 2009.

Brownell, Susan. *Beijing's Games: What the Olympics Means to China*. New York: Rowman & Littlefield, 2008.

Brysk, Alison, ed. *Globalization and Human Rights*. Los Angeles: University of California, 2002.

Butryn, Ted M. 'Posthuman Podiums: Cyborg Narratives of Elite Track and Field Athletes'. *Sociology of Sport Journal* 20, no. 1 (2003): 17–39.

Charlton, James L. *Nothing About Us Without Us: Disability Oppression and Empowerment*. Berkeley: University of California Press, 1998.

Classification – Solutions for the Future. Proceedings of the VISTA 2006 Conference Bonn, Germany: IPC, 2006.

Coakley, Jay. *Sports in Society: Issues and Controversies*. Columbus, OH: McGraw Hill, 2008.

Davis, Lennard J. 'Constructing Normalcy, the Bell Curve, the Novel, and the Invention of the Disabled Body in the Nineteenth Century'. In *The Disability Studies Reader*, edited by Lennard J. Davis, 9–28. New York: Routledge, 1997.

Davis, Ronald W. *Inclusion through Sports*. Champaign, IL: Human Kinetics, 2002.

De Pauw, Karen P., and Susan Gavron. *Disability and Sport*. 2nd edn. Champaign, IL: Human Kinetics.

Denman, Susan, Alysoun Moon, Carl Parsons, and David Stears. *The Health Promoting School: Policy, Research and Practice*. London: Routledge, 2002.

Doll-Tepper, Gudrun, Kroner, Michael, and Werner Sonnenschein, eds. *New Horizons in Sport for Athletes with a Disability,* Vols 1 & 2. *Proceedings of the International VISTA '99 Conference. Cologne, Germany*. Oxford: Meyer and Meyer Sport, 2001.

Donnelly, Jack. 'Human Rights, Globalizing Flows, and State Power'. In *Globalization and Human Rights*, edited by Alison Brysk, 226–41. Los Angeles: University of California Press, 2002.

Donnelly, Jack. *Universal Human Rights in Theory and Practice*. 2nd edn. Ithaca, NY: Cornell University Press, 2003.

Douglas, Mary. *Purity and Danger: An Analysis of the Concepts of Pollution and Taboo*. London: Routledge, 1994.

Edwards, Martha, L. 'Constructions of Physical Disability in the Ancient Greek World'. In *The Body and Physical Difference: Discourses of Disability*, edited by David T. Mitchell and Sharon L. Snyder, 35–50. Ann Arbor: University of Michigan Press, 1997.

Faulkner, Alex. 'Casing the Joint: The Material Development of Artificial Hips'. In *Artificial Parts, Practical Lives: Modern History of Prosthetics*, edited by Katherine Ott, David Serlin, and Stephen Mihm, 199–226. New York: New York University Press, 2002.

Foucault, Michel. *Power/Knowledge: Selected Interviews and Other Writings 1972–1977*. Toronto: Random House of Canada, 1980.

Foucault, Michel. *The Birth of the Clinic: An Archaeology of Medical Perception*. New York: Vintage, 1994.

Foucault, Michel. *Discipline and Punish: The Birth of the Prison*. New York: Vintage, 1995.

Fujiura, Glenn T., Hye J. Park, and Violet Rutkowski-Kmitta. 'Disability Statistics in the Developing World: A Reflection on the Meaning in our Numbers'. *Journal of Applied Research in Intellectual Disabilities* 18, no. 4 (2005): 295–304.

Gilbert, Keith, and Otto Schantz. 'Reconceptualizing the Paralympic Movement'. In *The Paralympic Games: Empowerment or Side Show?* edited by Keith Gilbert and Otto Schantz, 8–18. Maidenhead, UK: Meyer & Meyer, 2008.

Gilbert, Keith, and Otto Schantz. *The Paralympic Games: Empowerment or Side Show?* Maidenhead, UK: Meyer & Meyer, 2008.

Goffman, Erving. *Stigma: Notes on the Management of Spoiled Identity*. New York: Touchstone Books, 1986.

Gupta, Akhil. 'The Song of the Nonaligned World: Transnational Identities and the Reinscription of Space in Late Capitalism'. In *The Anthropology of Space and Place: Locating Culture*, edited by Setha M. Low and Denise Lawrence Zuniga, 321–36. Malden, ME: Blackwell, 2003.

Gupta, Akhil, and James Ferguson. 'Beyond Culture: Space, Identity, and the Politics of Difference'. In *The Anthropology of Globalization: A Reader*, edited by Jonathan Xavier Inda and Renata Rosalda, 65–80. Malden, ME: Blackwell, 2002.

Guttman, Sir Ludwig. 'Sport for the Disabled as a World Problem'. *Rehabilitation* (1969): 29–43.

Hansen, Karen Tranberg. 'The World of Dress: Anthropological Perspectives on Clothing, Fashion, and Culture'. *Annual Review of Anthropology* 33 (2004): 369–92.

Hargreaves, Jennifer. *Sporting Females: Critical Issues in the History and Sociology of Women's Sports*. London: Routledge, 1994.

Hargreaves, Jennifer. *Heroines of Sport: The Politics of Difference and Identity*. New York: Routledge, 2000.

Hargreaves, Jennifer. 'Sport Exercise and the Female Muslim Body: Negotiating Islam, Politics and Male Power'. In *Physical Culture, Power, and the Body*, edited by Jennifer Hargreaves and Patricia Vertinsky, 74–100. London: Routledge, 2007.

Hargreaves, Jennifer and Vertinsky, Patricia, eds. *Physical Culture, Power, and the Bod*. London: Routledge, 2007.

Herr, Stanley, Koh, Harold, and Lawrence Gostin, eds. *Different But Equal: The Rights of Persons with Intellectual Disabilities*. New York: Oxford University Press, 2003.

Howe, P. David. *The Cultural Politics of the Paralympic Movement: Through an Anthropological Lens*. New York: Routledge, 2008.

Hums, Mary, and Joanne C. MacLean. *Governance and Policy in Sport Organizations*. 2nd edn. Scottsdale, AZ: Holcomb-Hathaway, 2008.

Jarvis, Patrick. 'People, Policy and Sports: A Canadian Perspective'. Paper presented at the FESPIC-APC Sports Congress. Kuala Lumpur, Malaysia. November 23, 2006.

Kennedy, Eileen, and Laura Hills. *Sport, Media and Society*. New York: Berg, 2009.

Kennedy, Sarah. *The Swimsuit*. London: Carlton, 2007.

Kidd, Bruce. *The Struggle for Canadian Sport*. Toronto: University of Toronto Press, 1996.

Kidd, Bruce. 'Human Rights and the Olympic Movement after Beijing'. *Sport in Society* 13, no. 5 (2010): 901–10.

Kidd, Bruce, and Peter Donnelly. 'Human Rights in Sport'. *International Review for the Sociology of Sport* 35, no. 2 (2000): 131–48.

Lauff, Jackie. 'Developing Country Participation in International Disability Sport Competition: A Historical Perspective'. MA Thesis, Norwegian School of Sport Sciences, 2007. http://assets. sportanddev.org/downloads/70__developing_country_participation_in_international_disabili ty_sport_competition.pdf

Le Clair, Jill M. 'High Performance Swimming: Equity or Political Correctness'. In *New Horizons in Sport for Athletes with a Disability*. Vol. 1. *Proceedings of the International VISTA 99 Conference Cologne, Germany*, edited by Gudrun Doll-Tepper, Michael Kroner, and Werner Sonnenschein, 465–82. Quebec: Meyer & Meyer Sport, 2001.

Le Clair, Jill M. 'Diverse Experiences of the Swimming Classification Process in Canadian Paralympian Narratives'. In *Classification – Solutions for the Future. Proceedings of the VISTA 2006 Conference*. Bonn, Germany: IPC, 2006.

Le Clair, Jill. 'Sport and Health: Global Challenges to Biomedical Definitions of Disability'. *Vis-à-Vis: Explorations in Anthropology* 9, no. 2 (2009): 203–19.

Le Clair, Jill M. 'Water, Senses and the Experiences of the Pool: Paralympic Athletes and Swimming'. Come to Your Senses: Creating Supportive Environments to Nurture the Sensory Capital Within. Priceedings of the 3rd International Sensory Therapy Conference, October 21–25, 2009.Toronto, Canada.

Legg, David, Claudia Emes, David Stewart, and Robert Steadward. 'Historical Overview of the Paralympics, Special Olympics and Deaflympics'. *Palaestra* 20, no. 1 (2002): 30–5.

Lenskyj, H.J. 'More Fallen Heroes: The Nude Calendar Phenomenon'. In *Olympic Industry Resistance: Challenging Olympic Power and Propaganda*, edited by Helen Jefferson Lenskyj, 129–48. Albany: State University of New York Press, 2008.

Lieberman, Laura J., and Cathy Houston-Wilson. *Strategies for Inclusion*. Champaign, IL: Human Kinetics, 2002.

Linton, Simi. *Claiming Disability: Knowledge and Identity*. New York: New York University Press, 1998.

Lynnes, Michelle D., Doug Nicholas, and Vivienne A. Temple. 'Fostering Independence in Health Promoting Exercise'. *Journal of Intellectual Disabilities* 13, no. 2 (2009): 143–59.

Mangan, J.A., ed. *Shaping the Superman: Fascist Body as Political Icon – Aryan Fascism*. London: Frank Cass, 1999.

Maloney, Tom. 'A New Image Exposed. Are Female Athletes being Exploited by Showing off their Muscular Bodies in Photos?' *National Post*, August 29 (2000): A18.

McLuhan, Marshall. *Understanding Media: The Extensions of Man*. Cambridge, MA: MIT Press, 1994.

Ott, Katherine. 'The Sum of Its Parts: An Introduction to Modern Histories of Prosthetics'. In *Artificial Parts, Practical Lives: Modern History of Prosthetics*, edited by Katherine Ott, David Serlin, and Stephen Mihm, 1–44. New York: New York University Press, 2002.

Parnes, Penny, and Goli Hashemi. 'Sport as a Means to Foster Inclusion, Health and Well-being of Persons with Disabilities'. In *Literature Reviews on Sport for Development and Peace*, edited by Bruce Kidd and Peter Donnelly, 124–57. Toronto: International Working Group on Sport for Development and Peace, 2007. http://www.righttoplay.com/International/news-and-media/Documents/Policy%20Reports%20docs/Literature%20Reviews%20SDP.pdf

Pfister, Gertrud. 'Islam and Women's Sport: More and More Muslim Women are Taking up Sports, and Tehran is Setting an Example'. *SangSaeng* Summer (2006): 12–15.

Posadzki, Alexandra. 'Prescribing Blackberries to Battle Disease'. *The Toronto Star*, April 19, 2010.

Pothier, Dianne and Richard Devlin, eds. *Critical Disability Theory: Essays in Philosophy, Politics, Policy, and Law*. Toronto: UBC Press, 2006.

Priestley, Mark. *Disability: A Life Course Approach*. Malden, ME: Polity, 2003.

Provvidenza, Christine, and Charles H. Tator. 'Sports Injury Prevention: General Principles'. In *Catastrophic Injuries in Sport and Recreation: Causes and Prevention – A Canadian Study*, edited by Charles Tator, 58–78. Toronto: University of Toronto Press, 2008.

Rheaume, Geoffrey. *Remembrance of Patients Past: Patient Life at the Toronto Hospital for the Insane, 1870–1940*. Toronto: University of Toronto Press, 2009.

Rioux, Marcia H., and Fraser Valentine. 'Does Theory Matter? Exploring the Nexus between Disability, Human Rights, and Public Policy'. In *Critical Disability Theory: Essays in Philosophy, Politics, Policy, and Law*, edited by Dianne Pothier and Richard Devlin, 47–69. Toronto: UBC Press, 2006.

Sampson, Fiona. 'Beyond Compassion and Sympathy to Respect and Equality: Gendered Disability and Equality Rights Law'. In *Critical Disability Theory: Essays in Philosophy, Politics, Policy, and Law*, edited by Dianne Pothier and Richard Devlin, 267–84. Toronto: UBC Press, 2006.

Samuels, Ellen. 'My Body, My Closet: Invisible Disability and the Limits of Coming-Out Discourse'. *GLQ: A Journal of Lesbian and Gay Studies* 9, no. 2 (2003): 233–55.

Schantz, Otto, and Keith Gilbert. 'An Ideal Misconstrued: Newspaper Coverage of the Atlanta Paralympic Games in France and Germany'. *Sociology of Sport Journal* 18, no. 1 (2001): 69–94, Special Issue.

Scott, Joan Wallach. *The Politics of the Veil*. Princeton, NJ: Princeton University Press, 2007.

Shakespeare, Tom. 'Disability, Identity and Difference'. In *Exploring the Divide: Illness and Disability*, edited by Colin Barnes and Geof Mercer, 94–113. Leeds: Disability, 1996.

Siebers, Tobin. *Disability Theory*. Ann Arbor: Univesity of Michigan Press, 2008.

Skinner, Harvey. 'The Big Idea: First Health and then Medicine'. www.yorku.ca/health/about.html

Smith, Gavin. 'Formal Culture, Practical Sense and the Structure of Fear in Spain'. *Anthropologica* 51, no. 2 (2009): 279–88.

Snyder, Sharon L., and David T. Mitchell. 'Re-Engaging the Body: Disability Studies and the Resistance to Embodiment'. *Public Culture* 13, no. 3 (2001): 367–90.

Solish, Abbie, Adrienne Perry, and Patricia Minnes. 'Participation of Children with and without Disabilities in Social, Recreational and Leisure Activities'. *Journal of Applied Research on Intellectual Disabilities* 23, no. 3 (2010): 226–36.

Sparkes, Andrew C., and Brett Smith. 'Disabled Bodies and Narrative Time: Men, Sport, and Spinal Cord Injury'. In *Physical Culture, Power, and the Body*, edited by Jennifer Hargreaves and Patricia Vertinsky, 158–75. London: Routledge, 2007.

Spraklen, Kari, Kevin Hylton, and Jonathan Long. 'Managing and Monotoring Rquality and Diversity on UK Sport'. *Journal of Sport and Social Issues* 30, no. 3 (2006): 289–305.

Sparrow, Robert. 'Implants and Ethnocide: Learning from the Cochlear Implant Controversy'. *Disability & Society* 25, no. 4 (2010): 455–66.

Srinivasan, Raman. 'Technology Sits Cross-Legged: Developing the Jaipur Foot Prosthesis'. In *Artificial Parts, Practical Lives:Modern History of Prosthetics*, edited by Katherine Ott, David Serlin, and Stephen Mihm, 327–47. New York: New York University Press, 2002.

Steadward, Robert, and Cynthia Petersen. *Paralypmics: Where Heroes Come*. Edmonton: One Shot Publishing Division, 1997.

Sutherland, Alan. 'Black Hats and Twisted Bodies'. In *Framed: Interrogating Disability in the Media*, edited by Ann Pointon and Chris Davies, 16–20. London: British Film Institute, 1997.

Swartz, Leslie. 'Building Disability Research Capacity in Low-Income Contexts: Possibilities and Challenges'. In *Disability and International Development: Towards Inclusive Global Health*, edited by Malcolm MacLachlan and Leslie Swartz, 91–103. New York: Springer, 2009.

Swartz, Leslie. *Able Bodied: A Memoir*. Cape Town: Zebra Press, 2010.

Swartz, Leslie, and Brian Watermeyer. 'Cyborg Anxiety: Oscar Pistorius and the Boundaries of What It Means to Be Human'. *Disability and Society* 23, no. 2 (2008): 187–90.

Tator, Charles H., ed. *Catastrophic Injuries in Sport and Recreation: Causes and Prevention – A Canadian Study*. Toronto: University of Toronto Press, 2008.

Theberge, Nancy. '"It's Not About Health, It's About Performance": Sport Medicine, Health, and the Culture of Risk in Canadian Sport'. In *Physical Culture, Power, and the Body*, edited by Jennifer Hargreaves and Patricia Vertinsky, 176–94. London: Routledge, 2007.

Titchkosky, Tanya. 'Disability – A Rose by Any Other Name. People First Language in Canadian Society'. *Canadian Review of Sociology and Anthropology* 18, no. 2 (2001): 125–40.

Titchkosky, Tanya. *Reading and Writing Disability Differently: The Textured Life of Embodiment*. Toronto: University of Toronto Press, 2007.

Titchkosky, Tanya and Michalko, Rod, eds. *Rethinking Normalcy: A Disability Studies Reader*. Canadian Scholars Press, 2009.

Thomas, Nigel, and Andy Smith. *Disability Sport and Society: An Introduction*. New York: Routledge, 2009.

Watermeyer, Brian, Leslie Swartz, Marguerite Schneider, and Mark Priestley. *Disability and Social Change: A South African Agenda*. Cape Town: HSRC Press, 2006.

Wendell, Susan. *The Rejected Body: Feminist Philosophical Reflections on Disability*. New York: Routledge, 1996.

Wolff, Eli. 'Inclusion of the Sport for Athletes with Disabilities into Non-Disabled Sport Organizations: Strategies and Recommendations'. Paper presented at VISTA '99: International Conference on Sport for Athletes with a Disability, Cologne, Germany, 1999.

Xu, Guoqi. *Olympic Dreams: China and Sports 1895–2008*. Cambridge, MA: Harvard University Press, 2008.

Disability rights and change in a global perspective

Marcia H. Rioux

Professor, Critical Disability Studies, School of Health Policy and Management; York Institute for Health Research; Disability Rights Promotion International (DRPI), York University, Toronto, Canada

The 2006 UN Convention on the Rights of Persons with Disabilities (CRPD) brought in a new era of disability rights, and as a human rights instrument Article 30 of the Convention addresses rights in sport and physical activity. Rights include those in disability-specific sport and mainstream sport, games, recreation, leisure, tourist sites and activities. The Convention also addresses other aspects of sport including coaching, training, management, barrier-free facilities and physical education. This article argues that the shift from a disability and charity-based approach to a rights-based approach fundamentally changes the playing field, the players, the spectators and the society. It also argues that the UN Convention provides a framework by which policies and programmes can be measured, and the public recognition of different bodies and abilities to support inclusive societies in the global context.

The 2006 UN Convention on the Rights of Persons with Disabilities (CDRP) was the beginning of a new era in disability rights, but it was the end of a 30 year struggle by advocates of human rights and by people in the disability rights movement to clearly assert the recognition that all persons, no matter what their disability, must enjoy all human rights and fundamental freedoms. It changed the playing field for people everywhere as it was the formal recognition that disability is a rights issue. The Convention is a human rights instrument, but it also has a social development aspect. At the same time, it identifies areas where adaptations have to be made for disabled people to effectively exercise their rights and have their rights protected and reinforced.

Article 30 of the UN Convention addresses rights related to sport and physical activity and is entitled 'Participation in Cultural Life, Recreation and Sport' and clearly states the following:

5. With a view to enabling persons with disabilities to participate on an equal basis with others in recreational, leisure and sporting activities, States Parties shall take appropriate measures:

    (a) To encourage and promote the participation, to the fullest extent possible, of *persons with disabilities in mainstream sporting activities at all levels*;

    (b) To ensure that persons with disabilities have an opportunity to organize, develop and participate in disability-specific sporting and recreational activities and, to this end, encourage the provision, on an equal basis with others, of appropriate instruction, training and resources;

    (c) To ensure that persons with disabilities have access to sporting, recreational and tourism venues;

    (d) To ensure that children with disabilities have equal access with other children to participation in play, recreation and leisure and sporting activities, including those activities in the school system;

    (e) To ensure that persons with disabilities have access to services from those involved in the organization of recreational, tourism, leisure and sporting activities.[1]

Article 30 recognizes that barrier-free design in the built environment must take place so that people can actually swim, play games, etc. in the sport, recreational and tourism facilities available. Appropriate training must be provided in coaching and physical education programmes, and in the services in all areas so that everyone can be included, as often in the past 'experts' often ignored or felt uncomfortable addressing the needs of persons with disabilities. Inclusion has to be incorporated so that children with disabilities can be included in play, recreation, leisure and sport activities, both inside and outside school systems, as often these children are sidelined or excluded entirely. It is also recognized that individuals may prefer to participate in mainstream sport or, in some cases, because they are not accommodated or because they prefer, may decide to engage in disability-specific activities. Swimming is an example where there may be varied paths within the sport that can provide different choices including recreational programmes, mainstream swimming or the Paralympic Games. At some point, it may be that there is sufficient accommodation of persons with disabilities in sports and the rules of sports that everyone will be able to complete together.

The Convention is based on eight guiding principles that underlie the Convention and each one of its specific articles:

    (1) respect for inherent dignity, individual autonomy including the freedom to make one's own choices, and independence of persons;

    (2) non-discrimination;

    (3) full and effective participation and inclusion in society;

    (4) respect for difference and acceptance of persons with disabilities as part of human diversity and humanity;

    (5) equality of opportunity;

    (6) accessibility;

    (7) equality between men and women; and

    (8) respect for the evolving capacities of children with disabilities and respect for the right of children with disabilities to preserve their identities.

These are strong principles against which all policies, programmes and services have to be measured. This calls for a strong commitment from governments, from the private sector and from non-government voluntary organizations. This aspirational document then provides a road map for a cohesive and comprehensive plan for moving towards an inclusive society, one in which discrimination is addressed.

The new human rights era in the disability field provides a direction for the full participation of disabled people in practice, at the local level. Disability rights recognize the complex and diverse range of people who make up the population. As a rights issue, disability is changing the playing field, the players and the rules of the game. It is a new era and it provides a chance to redirect energies away from diagnosis and rehabilitation of people with disabilities to diagnosis and rehabilitation of a social and economic structure that has built barriers to participation and engagement.

The paramount presumption that disability was an individual pathology was the dominant guiding principle for policy, programmes and services for most of the twentieth century. This idea assumed that a charitable approach to the condition of the individual was the most appropriate framework, and that the rights of the individual could be traded in return for receiving handouts from the state, and services and opportunities from non-government organizations.[2] Consequently, the emphasis was on either treating the individual or creating separate opportunities for people who were diagnosed as disabled. A disability diagnosis opened the path to benefits that enabled participation in 'special' activities – activities designed for people who had impairments. Disability is then treated as a form of deviance which is often privatized as the responsibility of non-government or charitable organizations and of families.[3] It does not create any pressure to change the discriminatory structure that was built into the institutions of society.

Disability understood as 'social' pathology,[4] can create an impetus for social change at every level. Realizing that impairment is part of the human fabric, disability is seen as inherent to the social structure,[5] so there is an emphasis on interventions directed at political, social and physical environments rather than cures or therapies for individuals. Inclusion of persons is seen as a public responsibility, given that the characteristics associated with disability are interpreted as normal occurrences within the range of human diversity and difference, rather than as deviant abnormalities. A rights-outcome approach constructs an analysis which sees society marginalizing people, and how society can be adjusted to eliminate this marginalization. As Quinn and Degener argued in a report evaluating UN human rights instruments in a disability context:

> [T]he human rights perspective means viewing people with disabilities as subjects and not as objects. It entails moving away from viewing people with disabilities as problems toward viewing them as rights holders. Importantly, it means locating any problems outside the person and especially in the manner by which various economic and social processes accommodate the difference of disability or not as the case may be. The debate about disability rights is therefore connected to a larger debate about the place of difference in society.[6]

With the ratification of the Convention on the Rights of Persons with Disabilities and the adoption of the realization that disability is a rights issue, monitoring of those rights becomes of key importance. States are required to report on their progress in achieving the rights.[7] This will necessitate reporting on the current situation – that is, establishing the bench marks as a basis for implementation – and to do long-term tracking that shows if and when the situation changes. This is not the sole task of national governments, however. It needs to be the mission of local governments and organizations engaged in services and programmes that are specifically directed to people with disabilities and organizations that do not include people with disabilities. The goal of monitoring is to work in a systemic way that is transformative in building alliances with governments, with the private sector and with the disability movement.[8] It involves tracking services and programmes within the context of rights – do they meet the guiding principles of the CDRP including autonomy, self-determination, equality, participation and so on? These are much more significant criteria than asking if they serve people with disabilities. A key criterion of the CRPD is how engaged people with disabilities themselves are in the monitoring of the rights – not simply as consultants – or board members, but as part of the monitoring teams.

There is a fundamental change in expectations about rights related to the experience of sport and physical activities. Instead of having to constantly negotiate on an individual basis, the assumption is that *persons with disabilities are entitled to have access, and participate in mainstream sport and disability sport*; to have accessible sport facilities and recreational and tourist sites, and access to training and coaching. Also children must have equal access, with other children, to play and to recreation activities in schools and elsewhere.

In the words of the High Court Justice of Australia, the Honourable Mary Gaudron:

> An important issue is how to take difference and needs into account in arriving at equality while avoiding discrimination'.[9] It is a challenge that is fundamental to making us able to respond to the diversity of people with whom we live on a daily basis. Levelling the playing field means addressing the very nature of how we run the business of society. We are at the beginning of a new era – one that places the responsibility on everyone to be creative and to find new ways to ensure inclusion and participation of those we have traditionally been excluded. It is a huge challenge but it is one that if we do not respond, we fail ourselves in continuing to sanction discrimination, benevolent perhaps, but still discrimination. It is fair, it is just and it entrenches disability rights.

Notes

[1] UN Enable, Comprehensive and Integral International Convention to Protect the Rights and Dignity of Persons with Disabilities (A/RES/56/583/Add.2), http://www.un.org/disabilities/default.asp?id=70. The Convention on the Rights of Persons with Disabilities and its Optional Protocol were adopted on 13 December 2006 at the United Nations Headquarters in New York, and was opened for signature on 30 March 2007. There were 82 signatories to the Convention, 44 signatories to the Optional Protocol, and one ratification of the Convention. This is the highest number of signatories in history to a UN Convention on its opening day. It is the first comprehensive human rights treaty of the twenty-first century and is the first human rights convention to be open for signature by regional integration organizations. The Convention entered into force on 3 May 2008.

[2] Barnes, Mercer, and Shakespeare, *Exploring Disability*; Oliver, *The Politics of Disablement*.

[3] Rioux and Zubrow, 'Social Disability and the Public Good', 148.

[4] Rioux, 'Disability: The Place of Judgement in a World of Fact', 102; Rioux, 'On Second Thought: Constructing Knowledge, Law, Disability and Inequality'; Oliver, *The Politics of Disablement*; Michalko, *The Difference Disability Makes*.

[5] WHO, International Classification of Impairments, Disabilities and Handicaps, http://www.who.int/classifications/icf/wha-en.pdf. WHO defines disability as a process that includes biomedical aspects, functional limitations and restrictions within environments, resulting in disadvantage.

[6] Quinn *et al.*, *Human Rights and Disability*.

[7] The CRPD Reporting Guidelines can be found online at: http://www.ohchr.org/EN/HRBodies/CRPD/Pages/CRPDIndex.aspx.

[8] Disability Rights Promotion International (DRPI) has developed tools and methodology for holistic monitoring. See http://www.yorku.ca/drpi.

[9] Mary Gaudron (Hon Justice), 'In the Eye of the Law; the Jurisprudence of Equality' (August 24, 1990) for the Mitchell Oration 1990, http://www.eoc.sa.gov.au/site/eo_resources/media_and_events/events/mitchell_orations.jsp.

References

Barnes, Colin, Geof Mercer, and Tom Shakespeare. *Exploring Disability: A Sociological Introduction*. Cambridge: Polity Press, 1999.

Michalko, Rod. *The Difference Disability Makes*. Philadelphia: Temple University Press, 2002.

Oliver, Michael. *The Politics of Disablement: Critical Texts in Social Work and the Welfare State*. Basingstroke, UK: McMillan, 1990.

Quinn, Gerard, Theresia Degener, Anna Bruce, Christine Burke, Joshua Castellino, Padraic Kenna, Ursula Kilkelly, and Shivaun Quinlivan. *Human Rights and Disability: The Current Use and Future Potential of United Nations Human Rights Instruments in the Context of Disability*. Geneva: United Nations, 2002.

Rioux, Marcia. 'Disability: The Place of Judgement in a World of Fact'. *Journal of Intellectual Disability Research* 41, no. 2 (1997): 102.

Rioux, Marcia. 'On Second Thought: Constructing Knowledge, Law, Disability and Inequality'. In *Different but Equal: The Rights of Persons with Intellectual Disabilities*, edited by Stanley Herr, Harold Koh, and Lawrence Gostin. London: Oxford University Press, 2003.

Rioux, Marcia, and Ezra Zubrow. 'Social Disability and the Public Good'. In *The Market and the Public Domain: Global Governance and the Asymmetry of Power*, edited by Daniel Drache. London: Routledge, 2001.

United Nations Enable. *Comprehensive and Integral International Convention to Protect the Rights and Dignity of Persons with Disabilities (A/RES/56/583/Add.2)*. New York: United Nations Enable (19 December), 2001.

World Health Organization. *World Health. International Classification of Impairments, Disabilities, and Handicaps*. Resolution WHA 54.21 Ninth Plenary Meeting A54/VR/9. Geneva: World Health Organization (22 May), 2001.

The Paralympic Games and 60 years of change (1948–2008): unification and restructuring from a disability and medical model to sport-based competition

David Legg[a] and Robert Steadward[b]

[a]Department of Physical Education and Recreation, Mount Royal University, Calgary, Canada;
[b]The Robert Steadward Centre, University of Alberta, Canada

The Paralympic Games began officially in 1960 and have evolved to become the second largest multisport event in the world, and the pinnacle of sporting achievement for athletes with disability. The transformation from a medical model in which sport was used for the purposes of rehabilitation to one focusing on elite athlete performance has occurred due to a myriad of personalities and events that led to significant organizational and structural change. For the purposes of this article, determination of what events constituted major change was based on a synthesis of the authors' personal experiences and suggestions from a number of international experts. The examples are embedded throughout the article within three time frames; burgeoning awareness, rise to prominence and transcendence. The conclusion is that the Paralympic Games had an indelible impact on disability, sport and society and that in the future this will only continue.

There has been a great deal written about the Olympic Games, but there has been significantly less dedicated to the Paralympic Games. There are signs, however, that this is changing with the recent publications of Cashman and Darcy, Howe, Brittain, Bailey and Wolbring,[1] among others. In part, this can be understood by the relatively short history of the Paralympic Games with the first official Games being held in 1960 and the modern Games starting in 1988. Nonetheless, enough time has now elapsed to provide us with adequate distance and perspective to better appreciate the growth of the Paralympic Games, and to consider future directions that it may take.

Looking at the Games in an Olympic context it is important to examine the difference between the Paralympics as an expression of elite sport competition – the Games – and the Paralympics as the expression of a movement (which may be akin to 'Olympism', the philosophy underpinning the Olympic ideals of Pierre de Coubertin, the founder of the modern Olympic Games). This is especially significant as, to date, an in-depth understanding of the Paralympic 'movement' or 'Paralympism' has not been published, although it is used widely. This is despite the fact that those using it appear to be basing their understanding of the 'movement' on an undefined set of values and beliefs. This leads to people talking past each other, unsure of just what underpins this thing they call 'Paralympism'. According to the International Paralympic Committee (IPC) Style Guide, the Paralympic Movement is viewed more from an organizational perspective, in which the 'Movement' encompasses all athletes and officials belonging to the National

Paralympic Committees (NPCs), the International Organizations of Sport for the Disabled (IOSDs), the International Federations (IFs), the Regional Organizations (ROs), the IPC Regional Committees, the IOSD Sports, the IPC Sports Committees, IPC Councils, IPC Standing Committees, other IPC bodies and any other persons or organizations who agree to be guided by the IPC Constitution and Bylaws. The criteria for belonging to the Paralympic Movement then are formal membership or recognition by the IPC. The values that form the foundation for the movement are courage, determination, inspiration and equality, and are espoused under the IPC's motto of Sprit in Motion.[2] As this article is intended, in part, as a retrospective, we focus on the Paralympic Games and not on the broader aspects of disability rights movements and related artistic and cultural events. Before embarking on this journey, however, it is first important to clarify what is meant by the term 'disability sport'. This has been previously reviewed in greater detail by Legg, Fay, Hums and Wolff[3] who used the definition of DePauw and Gavron[4] in which athletes with disability compete in many cases in activities specifically for them, and this is done to ensure an even playing field based on an accepted functional classification system adjudicated by the IPC. Disability itself is often not specifically defined and as an example, for the Canadian Paralympic Committee (CPC), the term disability is not addressed in its lexicon of terms. Instead what tends to happen is each sport governing body defines eligibility either by stating that a person is precluded by competing in 'able-bodied' sport and uses, for instance, a wheelchair for daily living or is based on a medical definition that reflects an athlete's classification.

It is important to note that Paralympic sport is part of disability sport, but not all disability sport is Paralympic sport. More specifically, Paralympic sport is administered using a classification system that determines an athlete's eligibility, with whom they would compete, allowable equipment modifications and team composition.

There are of course many athletes with disability that have also competed in non-disabled bodied sports. An example is Jim Abbot who has a congenital disability of one hand. He pitched with a variety of professional Major League Baseball teams from 1988 to 1998.[5] There have also been a number of athletes with disability that have competed in both non-disabled sport competitions as well as disability sport, such as Natalie du Toit from South Africa, and Natalia Partyka from Poland. Both competed in the Beijing Olympic and Paralympic Games, du Toit in swimming and Partyka in table tennis. For athletes who meet the minimum disability requirement in order to be categorized as a Paralympic athlete, however, the disability usually makes it so that competition against non-disabled competitors would be unfair.[6]

Methodology

The key issues presented here as leading to social change during the Paralympic Games' history stem from a presentation made at the 'To Remember is to Resist: 40 Years of Sport and Social Change 1968–2008', conference at the University of Toronto, Canada in May, 2008. The authors of the presentation were asked to identify key elements from the Paralympic Games that impacted social change during the 1968–2008 time frame.

Prior to attending the conference, the two authors met to identify key changes they observed based on their own experiences as administrators and leaders within the Paralympic movement. To supplement and enrich their perspectives they approached 24 experts from eight countries and four continents and asked them to respond between January and March, 2008 with examples of events in Paralympic sport (with the assumption most would focus on the Paralympic Games) which led to social change. The time frame required a focus on events occurring post 1968, which closely coincided with the genesis of the Paralympic Games following World War II, with the first official Games being held in 1960. Events that fall outside this time frame, however, were included for the purposes of this article. Responses from the 24 experts were collated, synthesized and added to the opinions of the two authors (who between them have over 60 years of experience as researchers, administrators and leaders of sport internationally, although primarily in Canada, and Paralympic sport in particular).

Using the period 1968–2008, we argue there were three eras that captured all of the examples submitted.[7] We have defined these as: burgeoning awareness, rise to prominence and transcendence. These did not have specific start and end dates, but instead represent general eras used to better guide our historical review.

Burgeoning awareness: the growth of disability in sport

The first theme suggests a time when the Paralympic Games were in their nascent stage. Whereas the Olympic Games and Olympic Movement celebrate a modern history beginning in 1896 with original roots in 776 BC,[8] the initial seeds of the Paralympic Games began only shortly after World War II, resulting in part, from vastly improved medical knowledge and evacuation procedures regarding spinal cord and other previously fatal injuries. This translated into a longer life expectancy for persons with spinal cord injuries which created a need for increased emphasis on rehabilitation.[9]

The British government responded to these changes and in 1944 opened the Spinal Injuries Centre at Stoke Mandeville Hospital in Aylesbury, UK. Under the direction of Dr Ludwig Guttmann, sport was introduced to the war veterans as part of rehabilitation. This completely transformed attitudes towards rehabilitation, and in recognition of this work, Guttmann was knighted in 1966. Wheelchair recreational activities at the hospital grew to include ward-versus-ward competitions and on July 28, 1948 the Stoke Mandeville Games took place on the same day the Olympic Games began as the aim of the Stoke organizers was to hold the Games parallel to each other. The initial Stoke Games included archery, with 14 male and 2 female participants. The Stoke Games for those with spinal paralysis continued on a yearly basis and in 1952 become international in scope through the participation of several Dutch ex-servicemen. Over 130 athletes competed in snooker, darts, archery and table tennis.[10]

Following the slow and deliberate growth of the Stoke Mandeville Games in the 1950s, Sir Guttmann contacted the International Olympic Committee with the hopes of holding the Stoke Games in Rome to coincide with their hosting of the 1960 Summer Olympic Games. The IOC leadership agreed and wheelchair events were held for 400 athletes from 23 countries with these exhibition events now viewed as the founding Paralympic Games. At these Games, Pope John XXIII in expressing the event's effect on the public stated:

> You are the living demonstration of the marvels of the virtue of energy. You have given a great example, which we would like to emphasize: you have shown what an energetic soul can achieve, in spite of apparently insurmountable obstacles imposed by the body.[11]

Pope Paul XXIII, further declared Guttmann '... the Coubertin of the paralyzed'.[12]

The Paralympic Games have since been held every four years, parallel to the Winter and Summer Olympic Games. To better demonstrate the rapid growth of the Paralympic Games in a relatively short period, it is worthwhile noting that the Summer Paralympic Games grew from 400 athletes representing 23 countries in 1960 to 3951 athletes from 146 countries in 2008.[13] (Table 1)

Table 1.   Summer Paralympic Games overview[14]

Year	Location	Number of countries	Number of athletes
2012	London	150*	4200*
2008	Beijing	146	3951
2004	Athens	135	3808
2000	Sydney	122	3881
1996	Atlanta	104	3259
1992	Barcelona	83	3001
1988	Seoul	61	3057
1984	Stoke Mandeville & New York	41	1100
		45	1800
1980	Arnhem	42	1973
1976	Toronto	38	1657
1972	Heidelberg	43	984
1968	Tel Aviv	29	750
1964	Tokyo	21	375
1960	Rome	23	400
1952	Stoke Mandeville	2	130

*These numbers are projected.

In 1964, four years following the inaugural Paralympic Games in Rome, the Games were held in Tokyo, which also hosted the Olympic Games. In 1968, the Paralympic Games were moved to Tel Aviv, Israel, while the Olympic Games were hosted in Mexico City. Mexico did not host the Paralympic Games as officials were fearful that persons with spinal injuries would not survive in the high altitudes and there were no organizations providing services for athletes with disabilities in Mexico to provide the necessary expertise to assist with hosting. Israeli officials, meanwhile, had an interest in wheelchair sport, particularly in terms of rehabilitation due to armed conflicts in the Middle East.

Other disability sport events were also taking place at this time around the world at regional, national and local levels. In Canada, events included the first Pan American Games for athletes with disability in Winnipeg in 1967 and the first national wheelchair games in Canada at the University of Alberta in Edmonton in 1968.[15] Special Olympics, for persons with intellectual disability, meanwhile, held their first International Games in 1968 in Chicago.

Rise to prominence: the growth of national disability organizations and disability-based competition

In 1972, the Summer Paralympic Games were held in Heidelberg, Germany, while Munich was the site of the Summer Olympic Games. In 1976, a similar relationship existed where the Olympiad for the Physically Disabled or TORONTOLYMPIAD (as it was then called) was held in Toronto only a few hours from Montreal, host of the Summer Olympic Games. The Toronto Games were unique in that they included those with visual impairments and amputation for the first time. In 1980, when the Summer Paralympic Games were held in Arnhem, the Netherlands, athletes with cerebral palsy were included, and in 1996 athletes with intellectual disabilities competed in Atlanta. In 1992, a separate Paralympic Games for athletes with an intellectual disability were held in Madrid, whereas the other disability groups competed in Barcelona.[16]

From 1996, athletes with an intellectual disability were included in the Paralympic Games, but following the discovery, at the 2000 Summer Paralympic Games in Sydney, of athletes in competition who did not have an intellectual disability, they were excluded and this issue has been a point of ongoing serious debate. For some it is a philosophical and moral imperative to include all those who wish to compete. While for others, those with physical disabilities have too often mistakenly been seen as having intellectual disabilities, and thus are hesitant to invite their return. There are also additional challenges because of disagreements over the classification process, as there is debate over the cultural bias of IQ tests used in determining intellectual disability. This will likely be further debated as athletes with an intellectual disability may be re-included within the Paralympic schedule for the 2012 Summer Paralympic Games in London.

Returning to 1976, the addition of athletes with disabilities other than those that were spinal cord related had a significant and long-term impact on the Paralympic Games. Interestingly it was the addition of these athletes that forced local organizers to change the name of the event from Paralympics to the Olympiad for the Physically Disabled. Dr Robert Jackson, Chairperson of the Game's host organizing committee noted that the term Paralympics was studiously avoided because it had the connotation of paraplegic games and was therefore objected to by athletes with visual impairments and amputations.[17] Ironically, Paralympics, which was originally coined at the 1964 Paralympic Games in Tokyo, would eventually be chosen as the official term for the four-year event with Para denoting 'in parallel to the Olympics,' and not what some perceived to be a shortened version of paraplegic.[18]

Following the Games, to better administer the services in Canada for wheelchair athletes and the new categories of athletes with disability, including those with visual impairments, cerebral palsy and amputations, the Canadian federal government created one umbrella organization called the Coordinating Committee of Sports for the Physically Disabled (CC-SFD). In 1980, it was renamed the Canadian Federation of Sport Organizations for the Disabled (CFSOD) and later encouraged by the IPC in 1989, it changed its name again to the Canadian Paralympic Committee (CPC). This, or similar steps, also occurred in many other countries. It would appear that the change was due in part to an evolution of language used to describe athletes, and also the profound shift from a focus on disability, to a focus on sport.

Interestingly, the CC-SFD might not have been created except for political turmoil during the Toronto Games. The Canadian federal government's financial commitment for hosting the Games was withdrawn due to South Africa's participation. At that time the IOC, IPC and other international sports organizations excluded South Africa because of its apartheid policies of discrimination towards non-white South Africans. The South African wheelchair sports team, however, was racially mixed and for this reason, the international governing body responsible for the Games accepted their participation. The Canadian government eventually relented to public pressure and while still not granting funding to the host organizing committee re-allocated its original financial commitment to create and support the CC-SFD.[19]

The year 1976 was also significant in that Winter Paralympic Games were held for the first time in Örnsköldsvik, Sweden (then called the Winter Olympic Games for the Disabled). In 1980, the Games were held in Geilo, Norway and in 1984 and 1988, the Games were hosted in Innsbruck, Austria. In 1992 and 1994, the Paralympic Games were held in the same cities as the Olympics: Albertville, France in 1992 and Lillehammer, Norway in 1994. This then began the practice of Paralympic Winter Games being held in the same cities as the Olympic Games,[20] which was the case for 2010 in Vancouver, and will be in 2014 in Sochi (Table 2).

Table 2. Winter Paralympic Games overview[21]

Year	Location	Number of countries	Number of athletes
2010	Vancouver	45*	600*
2006	Torino	39	477
2002	Salt Lake City	36	416
1998	Nagano	32	571
1994	Lillehammer	31	492
1992	Tignes-Albertville	24	475
1988	Innsbruck	22	397
1984	Innsbruck	21	457
1980	Geilo	18	350
1976	Örnsköldsvik	17	250 +

*These numbers are projected.

Rise to prominence (II): the shift from medical, patient and disability-based competition to sport and athlete-based competition

In the early 1980s, in addition to the many significant structural and organizational changes taking place specific to the Paralympic Games, key individuals were also helping to create a profound shift in the perception of disability and physical achievement. One example from a Canadian context includes Terry Fox who in 1980 during his Marathon of Hope attempted to run across Canada after having a leg amputated because of cancer. This run initially received little attention, but eventually attracted huge media attention. Fox's journey was cut short close to the halfway mark, due to his cancer spreading and he passed away soon thereafter, but as a tribute to his courage and vision, the Terry Fox run is hosted internationally and almost 30 years later it is the largest fundraiser worldwide for cancer research.

Five years after Fox's quest, wheelchair athlete Rick Hansen, who had sustained a spinal cord injury as a teenager, embarked on a similar type of odyssey with the goal of wheeling the equivalent of the earth's circumference in two years. The resultant Foundation created from donations received from the 1985–1987 tour, as well as the Rick Hansen Wheels in Motion fundraisers that occur across Canada, are now responsible for funding a multitude of sport, recreation and research endeavours related to spinal cord injury. Disability sport was beginning to be seen as more than simply a medical tool to help with rehabilitation. These were elite athletes. While both odysseys were independent of the Paralympic Games, both individuals were Paralympic athletes and wheelchair basketball teammates. As well, both likely had a significant impact on the perception of athletes with disabilities, although this may be perceived as being both positive and negative as some believe that persons with disability are seen in one of two bipolar lights; either to be pitied or as super human.

The Paralympic Games themselves, continued to evolve during the early 1980s, but were still being held in different cities from the Olympic competitions. In 1980, the Paralympic Games were held in Arnhem, the Netherlands because Soviet government officials who were hosting the Olympic Games in Moscow did not have organizations providing sport opportunities for citizens with disability and thus felt it was inappropriate to host the Paralympic contests. Interestingly, at the 2008 Summer Paralympic Games, Russia finished eight in the medal tally with 63 medals (and the Ukraine a former member of the Soviet Union finished fourth with 74 medals). Had the Ukraine and Russia combined their teams they would have theoretically won 137 medals thus finishing second only to China – a significant achievement considering only 28 years earlier Soviet officials did not host the Paralympic Games. Similarly, Mexico, which did not host the Games in 1968, finished in 14th place in 2008 with 20 medals (including 10 gold).[22]

In 1984, the Summer Olympic Games were held in Los Angeles and the Winter Games in Sarajevo, and these were milestones for Paralympic sport in that athletes with disabilities where invited to compete in demonstration events in the Olympic Games; alpine for winter and wheelchair athletics for summer. The inclusion of wheelchair athletic events in the Olympic Games lasted 20 years and is discussed in greater detail later in this article.

However, 1984 also proved a setback; the Paralympic Games were set to be hosted in two separate locations because the University of Illinois organizing committee was only prepared to host the wheelchair section of the summer Paralympic Games. Faculty from the University had originally agreed to host the Paralympic Games, which had been multi-disability in nature since 1976, but soon thereafter, they circulated a memo stating they were only prepared to host wheelchair events. As a result, disability sport leaders Ben Lipton and Jack Weinstein agreed to host the events for athletes with cerebral palsy, amputations and visual impairments in New York. Then, because of organizational challenges and financial problems, the Games were cancelled by the original hosts at the University of Illinois. In January 1984, Dr Robert Jackson, President of the International Stoke Mandeville Games Federation, approached Dr Robert Steadward, a professor at the University of Alberta and volunteer leader in Paralympic sport, to consider hosting the wheelchair events at the University of Alberta in Edmonton, Canada. Unfortunately, there was not enough time to raise the necessary funding and also Dr Steadward believed that the Games should be fully integrated and multi-disability. As a result, he respectfully declined. With little time to prepare the wheelchair competitions were moved to the Stoke Mandeville hospital in Aylesbury, UK.

Amalgamation: the formation of the IPC

As had happened in Canada following the Games in 1976 with the creation of several new disability sport organizations, a number of other sport organizations specific to various disabilities (i.e. visual impairment, cerebral palsy) emerged at the international level. Four of the international sport organizations, including those that represented athletes with spinal injuries, cerebral palsy, amputations and visual impairments, had determined that there was a need to coordinate Games and thus in 1982 created an International Coordinating Committee Sports for the Disabled (ICC). This came about, in part, because of the IOC's request to correspond and collaborate with one umbrella organization. Two years following, in the autumn of 1984, Dr Robert Steadward, on behalf of the Canadian Federation, circulated a proposal to every member nation in the ICC recommending a new organizational structure for disability sport, with democratically elected governance. He also requested that other nations and disability sport organizations consider submitting alternative proposals from their national perspective. The ICC Secretariat, which was situated in Arnhem as a result of funds remaining from the 1980 Summer Paralympic Games, helped to organize a seminar in March 1987 at which representatives could debate and discuss these various proposals. Disability sport leaders spent the first day or two presenting their proposals, with the following two days dedicated to sifting through the various ideas from which 23 resolutions emerged.

The most essential of these were as follows:

- to change the structure of the existing organization;
- to include national representation, as well as regional and athlete representation;

- to reduce the number of classifications;
- to implement a functional classification system;
- to develop a structure by sport and not by disability;
- work towards integration with the International Olympic Committee and other International Sport Federations.[23]

At the end of the meetings in Arnhem, the Netherlands, an ad hoc committee was elected with the mandate to take the 23 resolutions and develop a constitution and bylaws for a new worldwide organization for disability sport. Specific to the last resolution, Dr Steadward, as President of CFSOD met with IOC President Juan Antonio Samaranch in Calgary, Canada during IOC meetings leading up to the 1988 Olympic Winter Games. Steadward presented to Samaranch the results of the Arnhem Seminar and impressed upon him the importance of leaders from Paralympic sport continuing to meet with the IOC leadership in the hopes of developing a formal working relationship with the creation of a Memorandum of Understanding, and to move forward on our integration policy.

Returning to the Arnhem Seminars, Carl Wang, President of the Norway Handicapped Sport Association, was asked to chair the task force developing the governing structure and to present the committee's report in Seoul at a meeting held in conjunction with the Summer Paralympic Games in 1988. In a hotly debated forum, the proposal was not accepted, but it was decided, however, to have members reconvene in one year's time with the same task force addressing the concerns presented by the nations present in Seoul. The task force presented their recommendations to the member nations in Dusseldorf, Germany where some of the ideas were accepted in principle and on September 22 1989, at the end of the meetings, Dr Robert Steadward of Canada was elected as the IPC's founding president. Steadward and the Executive Committee then spent the following year preparing a formal constitution and bylaws which were presented and ratified at the General Assembly in 1990.

For the next several years the IPC then operated without a formal headquarters but in 1997, selected Bonn, Germany as the host city, which officially opened in 1999. The IPC sent out a tender to all member nations to submit bids to host the IPC headquarters. These bids were reviewed by the IPC Executive Committee which made a recommendation to the IPC General Assembly held in Sydney, Australia in the fall of 1997. The General Assembly voted to select Bonn, Germany as the new IPC headquarters.

When viewed by today's standards and expectations, it is truly remarkable to think that in the earliest days, the IPC was run and operated by a president and board of directors on a totally voluntary basis, with a global cadre of supporters. Today, Sir Phillip Craven continues to provide outstanding leadership to the IPC, which has grown to have over 30 staff, 162 NPCs and several issue specific standing committees.

The modern Paralympic Games – 1988 Paralympic Games, Seoul, Korea

Enabling, in part, the new found direction and enthusiasm for the IPC in 1989 was the 1988 Summer Paralympic Games held in Seoul. These Games are now perceived by many as the start of the modern Paralympic Games, in part, because they were held in the same venues as those used for the Summer Olympic Games. Also, the Games were different in their focus on sporting excellence, with Tony Sainsbury a long-time volunteer and professional leader in Paralympic sport, referring to them as the line in the sand that marked the end of disabled sport and rehabilitation and the commencement of the modern Paralympics and elite sport.

Although this shift was welcomed in retrospect, it is important to note that whereas the medical model was problematic, the elite sport-based one was no less so. The shift resulted in more full-time coaches, increased bureaucratization, a need for athletes to train full time, and increased media and sponsor scrutiny. One unintended consequence of this may have been a further prioritization shown towards those who were the least disabled and thus perceived to be most athletic. Those with more severe disabilities, therefore, may have been forgotten or at least marginalized. Other unintended consequences may have included an increase in cheating and particularly the use of performance-enhancing drugs.

Impact on Korea: legacy

While the 1988 Games were significant internationally, they were also important nationally and are an example of how hosting Paralympic Games can leave a legacy for the host country. Dr Youn-Dai Whang, Vice President of the Korea Association for the Disabled and Korean NPC and founder of the IPC Whang Youn Dai Overcome Prize noted that, within Korea, the Games accomplished in one year what would have taken 20 to 30 years to accomplish in the promotion of people with disability.[24]

Korea first participated in international disability sport in 1965 at the Stoke Mandeville Games. Like many other countries, Korea initially supported disability sport through a military-based organization with the Korean Veterans Association, sending three athletes in the sports of table tennis and power lifting. In 1967, Korea hosted their first Annual Korean War Veterans Games and in 1968 participated for the first time in an official Paralympic Games in Tel Aviv. Seven years later, the Jung-Lip Polio Centre was opened in Korea which included a gymnasium, indoor pool, shooting range and archery field. Here, from 1976 until 1990, they hosted a National Youth Games for Disabled that at its largest included close to 2000 athletes. In 1981, and due in part to it being the International Year of the Disabled, the Korean National Games for the Disabled were held with over 1000 participants in five sport disciplines and six disability categories. Starting in 1985, the Seoul Paralympic Games Organizing Committee took over management of the national Games so as to best prepare a team to compete at the 1988 Games. More recently, these national Games have grown exponentially and in 2007 the summer version hosted 3500 athletes in 20 sports and the winter Games had 224 athletes competing in five sports. This phenomenal growth would likely not have taken place were it not for the Paralympic Games being held in Seoul in 1988.[25]

Reflecting on the impact in Korea from hosting the Games, Tony Sainsbury remembered that, prior to the Games, he suspected that having a disability in Korea was regarded as 'some ordained travesty visited on a person or family for some long-past misdeed. Koreans were ashamed to have a disabled person in their family and did all in their power to hide the person and the issue'. Gatherings of persons with disability seldom happened and the few that did occurred in secrecy, or in the safe confines of a hospital. Attitudes were paternalistic and based on pity. This changed for Sainsbury during the Olympic Games, when he found himself in the shopping centre of Itchewon. All the decoration and bunting erected for the Olympic Games was being dismantled and Sainsbury asked his guide if this was premature with the Paralympics Games starting a few weeks later. The guide responded that shopkeepers had no interest in attracting customers from those Games as they likely had no buying power and would be more of a nuisance. One suit maker noted 'Paralympics! Bah! Not interested'. Two weeks later Sainsbury returned to the same street that was buzzing with activity:

> The same tailor had now employed four men to carry wheelchair athletes up the four flights of stairs to measure them for new suits. He was doing a roaring trade with those he had

previously thought of only as beggars. He was amazed that these clients had jobs, university degrees, owned their own businesses and homes, were married and had children – that they lived 'normal' lives.[26]

This recognition still occurs today, with one example being a recent partnership between Flight Centre and the CPC. Flight Centre has recognized the benefits of 'handicapitalism' and the buying power of those with a disability, whether as individuals, families or groups, and is recognizing the partnership not as a 'feel good' donation, but as a marketing investment.

A second example of how the Games impacted on Korean society is that following the 1988 Games it was reported that from a base of approximately 90,000 people in Korea registered in 1987 as having a disability this number rose to over 500,000 six months following the Games, 'a statistic so indicative of a nation who in a few short weeks had the blindfold of prejudice so irrecoverably removed'.[27] Hong-Jae Lee, Director of the Korean Paralympic Committee recognized this impact, noting that these changes were the result of newfound pride by persons with disability, 'they belonged and were valued and integral members of their community'.[28] In Korea, this legacy continues to evolve and 20 years later the media is continuing to do its part, having correspondents from all four major television stations and over 50 members of the media attend the 2008 Summer Paralympic Games in Beijing.[29]

Organizational integration with the IOC

Internationally, the 1988 Paralympic Games were also significant in that this was the first time that the Olympic Games Organizing Committee had a Paralympic Games Department; not unlike the 2010 Vancouver Organizing Committee for the Winter Olympic Games. Seoul's organizing committee also committed, for the first time, to using the same venues for both Games. Finally, there was a decision to host 'Olympic style' opening and closing ceremonies for the Paralympic Games, with the first day being declared open by Mr Ro Tae-Woo, the President of the Republic of Korea. It is important to remember that prior to 1988, the Paralympic Games had not been held in the same city as the Olympic Games, other than those in 1960 and 1964. Following the Games in Seoul, however, every Olympic and Paralympic Games, including those in the winter, have been held in the same city, and since 2000 both Games have been included in the same bid.[30] Tony Sainsbury recounted that

> as many of the early leadership have now passed on from the early 1980s it is difficult to separate out truth from myth or legend. But the story goes that when asked 'What are the Paralympics?' by the Seoul Organizing Committee for the Olympic Games, the Government and the city of Seoul, the answer given to them was 'it's just like a smaller version of the Olympic Games'. The Korean delegation appeared to take this literally'.[31]

The Seoul Paralympic Organizing Committee (SPOC), as a sister organizing committee within the Seoul Olympic Games Organizing Committee, worked hard to ensure appropriate infrastructure, including new facilities, but also focused on those areas they knew would enable the Paralympic Games to benefit the most. These included spectators and full venues, television and media interest, and presidential support for the project.[32] In Games that followed, this model was often mirrored, but not always to the same degree, and it was not until following the Sydney Paralympic Games in 2000 that organizing committees of future Games were required to bid jointly for both Paralympic and Olympic Games.

As noted earlier, for many, the changes with the 1988 Games were seen as a positive evolution, but it has likely not been without its challenges. What has not been fully understood, is whether the changes increased opportunities, or discouraged some from pursuing sport. The increased focus on performance, for example, may have resulted in a narrowing of opportunities for those from Third World countries. As an example, prosthetics used by amputee sprinters often cost anywhere between $US10 and $US20,000 and certainly wheelchair sporting events tend to be dominated by athletes and teams from countries that are financially better off.

The 1992 Summer Paralympic Games were held in Barcelona and these mirrored many of the initiatives begun in Seoul and are widely recognized as being hugely successful. Four years later in Atlanta, however, the 1996 Summer Games are perhaps the one example that best demonstrates the challenges of a non-unified approach to hosting the Games. Lois Appleby, CEO of the 2000 Paralympic Games in Sydney remembered being in Atlanta three days after the 1996 Olympic Games closing ceremonies and walking around the village and venues with colleagues from the Sydney Olympic Organizing Committee where she observed in her opinion total chaos.

> Television cables to scoreboards required for the Paralympics had been cut; the garbage in the main stadium and other venues had been left for the Paralympic organizing committee to clean, the village needed to be refigured because the Georgia Tech University did not have an agreement for the Paralympic athletes, and keys from most of the rooms in the Athletes' Village had been thrown into a box unlabeled thus requiring all of the locks to be changed.[33]

To Appleby, the Olympic organizers had simply walked away. They did not have any responsibility for the Paralympic Games, nor did they care.[34] Four years later, when Appleby helped host the 2000 Summer Paralympic Games they returned to the precedents set in Seoul and in some people's minds took the Games to another level of professionalism.

Symbols, logos and legacies

A third reason why the Seoul Games have special significance is the IPC logo. Prior to 1988, a variety of logos mirroring the Olympic rings were used, but in 1988 the Seoul organizing committee replaced the five rings with Tae Geuks which are a traditional Korean symbol.

> At the end of the Seoul 1988 Paralympics, the symbol was adopted by the International Coordinating Committee of World Sports Organizations for the Disabled (ICC) and used as a symbol for the co-ordination of the Paralympic Games of the various international organizations of sport for the disabled. When the International Paralympic Committee (IPC) was created in 1989, the five Tae Geuks were incorporated as the symbol of the IPC.[35]

In 1991, the British Olympic Committee protested the use of this logo, suggesting that it was too close to the Olympic logo and thus was adversely affecting their ability to attract sponsors and raise funds. Gerhard Heiberg, Chairman and President of the Olympic and Paralympic Organizing Committee in Lillehammer, had already begun using the logo for the promotion of the 1994 Games. It was thus decided that the IPC's logo should be changed to reflect the motto 'mind, body and spirit' after the 1994 Games, and the resultant logo included only three Tae Geuks in red, blue and green. In 2003 the logo was further altered using the same colours but replacing the Tae Geuks with Agitos (from the Latin word *agito*, meaning 'I move') encircling a centre point.[36]

The Seoul Games were also the second time that athletes with disability competed in the Olympic Games in the category of a demonstration status, which as noted earlier was a practice that had begun in Los Angeles and Sarajevo in 1984. At the time, this was seen as an appropriate avenue from which attention could be drawn to Paralympic athletes, but for many the ultimate goal was to have the events changed from demonstration to full medal status.[37] This was never achieved and in 2008 the demonstration events were cancelled outright.[38] What is important to note here is that many within the Paralympic community saw the ending of this practice as a positive decision. Unless the athletes were to be included as full medal status, and perhaps even if they were, there were to some too many negative consequences for their continuance to be justified. These included perceptions of tokenism, a focus only on athletics and wheelchair athletes, and more specifically paraplegics or those perceived to be the 'least disabled'. Others, however, saw the events as tremendous marketing opportunities for athletes with disability when television audiences were at their highest.

Transcendence

Who is eligible to compete?

Displaying the transcendence of the Paralympic Games was how the ending of the demonstration events in 2008 was overshadowed by the inclusion of two athletes with disability in the Olympic Games; Natalie du Toit, from South Africa and table tennis player Natalia Partyka from Poland.[39] What is interesting is that the examples of du Toit and Partyka were not the first times that athletes with disability had competed in Olympic Games. George Eyser (gymnastics, 1904), Oliver Halassy (water polo, 1928, 1932, 1936), Karoly Takács (pistol shooting, 1948) Liz Hartel (dressage, 1952, 1956), Naroli Fairhall (archery, 1984), Paola Fantato (archery, 1996) and Marla Runyan (athletics, 2000, 2004) had all previously achieved this status, with Fantato competing in the two Games during the same year.[40] Additionally, there have been athletes with disability competing in the Olympic Games since 1904, but their exploits have seldom received attention.[41]

Also, and possibly more noteworthy, to the media anyway, was the absence in the Olympic Games of another athlete with disability, Oscar Pistorius.[42] The notoriety was likely the result of his challenge to the International Association of Athletics Federation (IAAF) on their ruling regarding his eligibility to compete against non-disabled runners; which he won through an appeal to the IOC Court of Arbitration for Sport.[43]

The controversy about Pistorius also seemed to spur on media interest in disability sport in general and several questions related to the future of the Paralympic Games. These included where athletes with disability should compete, and whether they should be forced to choose or encouraged to compete in one or both. The underlying question then was whether one Games was 'better' than the other? The Pistorius story also brought to the forefront the question of at what point should athletes with disabilities no longer be allowed or encouraged to compete under the Paralympic umbrella.[44] It could be argued that athletes with more severe disabilities are being limited due to finite resources spread too thinly servicing those who are more 'able-bodied'? Thus, it could be further argued that a gradual transference of opportunities for athletes with disability who can compete equitably against able-bodied athletes could unlock these financial and human resources and provide better services for those who cannot.

A third question emerging from Pistorius's pursuit of Olympic competition is where does this discussion lead, especially considering technological advancements?[45] Will athletes with disability be readily referred to as bionic,[46] or super-abled?[47] The attempt to minimize the impact of technology is already occurring, with some nations banning the use of Speedo drag-reduction full-body LRZ swimsuits by non-disabled athletes, yet other forms of technological enhancement or technological doping such as pre-emptive Lasik eye surgery, and carbon sole shoe implants remain acceptable.[48] As further evidence of this shift it has been suggested that people rethink the use of legal drugs and accept the benefits of enhancement for daily activities.[49] The authors of this premise make it clear that they do not include sport, as participation does not lead to an improved 'world', but it is not difficult to see where an acceptance of one leads to the other.

A second metric demonstrating the transcendence of the Paralympic Games was the increased number of athletes and spectators. The 2000 Summer Paralympic Games in Sydney broke all previous ticket sales records with 1.1 million tickets sold and the Games attracted 360,000 organized school and community groups.[50] Beyond ticketing, Appleby further recognized that the 2000 Paralympic Games transcended all previous events for Games excellence. Before the Games she noted that, while garnering greater recognition than any time previous, the Paralympic Games were still an event with no brand, little to no international sponsor interest, little public understanding and a high resistance by the public to watch 'handicapped people' or 'supercrips in sexy chairs' and, it was up against the biggest sport brand in the world, the Olympic Games.[51] The Sydney host organizing committee, however, took on this mammoth task and agreed that they must plan for a 60-day event, and with this, increased the international profile and marketing potential.

What is less well known is whether this increased profile translated into long-term improved public perception, greater funding or other opportunities. For instance, a few select athletes in Australia and abroad may now be recognized as elite performers, but it is debatable whether this has transcended to all levels and whether the bias and prejudice of athletes with disability not being considered, at least publically, as true 'athletes' has changed.

Nonetheless, the Games continued to grow and the 2002 Salt Lake City Winter Paralympic Games were the first to take place under the IOC–IPC cooperation agreement. These Games were also unique in that there was a decrease in the number of competitors from prior Games due to new and higher qualification standards, designed to ensure a more elite level of competition. Since 2002, the Paralympic Games have been held in Athens (2004), Torino (2006) and Beijing (2008), each witnessing phenomenal growth and development of athlete performances, organizational sophistication and awareness. The 2010 Olympic and Paralympic Winter Games logos were presented together in many Canadian media and the 2012 Summer Games organizers will take this one step further using essentially the same logo with only a very slight variation between them. Perhaps one day there might just be one.

A final area where Paralympic sport has transcended its development, although not necessarily related to the Games, is in academia. In 1993, Dr Steadward hosted the inaugural VISTA conference in Jasper, Canada; the first international conference that brought together Paralympic coaches, athletes, administrators and scientists. The VISTA conference has now become part of the IPC's educational calendar and will next be hosted in 2011. Since the VISTA conference in 1993 many other sport-related conferences in areas such as sociology, history and management now have streams or sessions that incorporate athletes with disability. What remains reminiscent of long-standing segregation, however, is that these conferences often host separate streams which attract those who are already involved in the 'movement'. The first conference the authors are aware of that was truly integrated was the *To Remember is To Resist 1968–2008* in Toronto where the genesis for this paper occurred.

This brings us to 2010, when the Vancouver Games was proud to be the first to initiate a number of significant changes. 2010 was the first to include Paralympic Games in its official name, the first to have a joint marketing agreement with the host NPC, the first to include a Paralympian on one of its subcommittees, the first to unveil its Paralympic

Games emblem more than three years before the Games, the first to integrate design and marketing of Olympic and Paralympic mascots and the first to create a Paralympic School Days programme. These Games were also the first to have a separate Paralympic Games countdown clock, and the first to fly the Olympic and Paralympic flags side by side and the first to depict Paralympic sports on circulating coins.

The future

As with any industry, with growth come challenges and opportunities. Consequences, unintended or not, are that expectations for athlete services have risen, in some cases, without corresponding increases in sponsorship; questions continue regarding the legitimacy of athletes with disability such as Oscar Pistorius competing against the non-disabled; and strategies to ensure opportunities for those with severe disabilities and to provide equitable opportunities for female athletes with disability remain unanswered.

This article has attempted to provide a broad overview of the history of the Paralympic Games and to demonstrate that sport has and can continue to be a catalyst for social change, with the focus in this particular case on persons with disability. One could argue that this is already taking place with examples of public figures such as the former Mayor of Vancouver, Sam Sullivan who has a spinal cord injury accepting the Olympic and Paralympic Flags at the 2006 closing ceremonies in Torino. Another indication of how far understanding of athletes with disability has changed is that up until 1976, due to concerns about a person with disability's cardiovascular endurance, male paraplegic athletes were only allowed to compete in the track events up to 100 metres in length, women paraplegics 60 metres and quadriplegics 40 metres. Today, athletes with disability compete in most international sanctioned marathons. At the same time, there are still many examples of where Paralympic Sport has not moved far beyond the medical origins; and perhaps in some contexts this is not such a bad thing.

The Paralympic Games has come a long way in a short time. The Games in its entirety is only 60 years old and the modern Games is just over 20 years old. Over this period, passionate individuals have fought for the rights and recognition of athletes with disability and in order to do so they have had to adapt. By adapting, through sport, persons with disability have made the transition from patient to athlete and from athlete to citizen and this will likely continue to evolve and change.

Notes

[1] Cashman and Darcy, *Benchmark Games*; Howe, *The Cultural Politics*; Brittain, *The Paralympic Games Explained*; Bailey, *Athlete First*; Wolbring, 'Oscar Pistorius'.

[2] International Paralympic Committee, *About the IPC*; Official Jim Abbott Website, *Famed Major League Baseball Player*.

[3] Legg *et al.*, *Examining the Inclusion*.

[4] DePauw and Gavron, *Disability and Sport*.

[5] Official Jim Abbott Website, *Famed Major League Baseball Player*.

[6] Legg *et al.*, *Examining the Inclusion*.

[7] The authors are grateful to Dr Wheeler for suggesting this framework. Dr Wheeler is the former Research Coordinator at the Rick Hansen Centre (now called the Steadward Centre) which is a fitness and research centre for persons with a disability at the University of Alberta in Canada.

[8] Canadian Olympic Committee, *How the Olympic Games Began*.

[9] Legg *et al.*, *Historical Overview of Paralympics*; Steadward and Foster, 'History of Disability Sport'; Stewart, and Ammons, 'Future Directions of Deaflympics'. It is also important to note that there were other examples of disability sport taking place even prior to World War II such as the Deaflympics, which were held for the first time in 1924.

[10] Legg et al., *Historical Overview of Paralympics*; Steadward and Foster, 'History of Disability Sport'.
[11] Guttmann, *Textbook of Sport*.
[12] Illinois Parks and Recreation, *A Brief History of Paralympic Games*.
[13] International Paralympic Committee, *Past Games – Summer Games*. It is also important to note that the although the Paralympic Games in 1960 were the first 'Olympic style' Games for the Paralympians, some people see the Modern Paralympic Games as really only beginning at Seoul in 1988 after the IPC was given full status by the IOC.
[14] International Paralympic Committee, *Past Games – Summer Games*.
[15] Legg, 'Strategy Formation in Amateur Sport'; Legg et al., Historical Overview of the Paralympics'.
[16] Legg, 'Strategy Formation in Amateur Sport'; Legg et al., Historical Overview of the Paralympics'; Steadward and Foster, 'History of Disability Sport'.
[17] Legg, 'Strategy Formation in Amateur Sport'.
[18] Legg et al., 'Historical Overview of the Paralympics'.
[19] Legg, 'Strategy Formation in Amateur Sport'. See Brittain, 'South Africa, Apartheid and the Paralympic Games' in this issue for a more in-depth discussion on this.
[20] Steadward and Foster, 'History of Disability Sport'.
[21] International Paralympic Committee, *Past Games – Summer Games*.
[22] International Paralympic Committee, Medal Standings Beijing 2008.
[23] Steadward and Foster, 'History of Disability Sport'.
[24] Y.D. Whang, in discussion with the author. Seoul, Korea. August 14, 2008.
[25] Kyu, Lee, and Jeon, 'Paralympic Sport in Korea'.
[26] Tony Sainsbury, personal correspondence to author. February 12, 2008.
[27] Ibid.
[28] Hong-Jae Lee in discussion with the author. Seoul, Korea. Agust 14, 2008.
[29] Kyu, Lee, and Jeon, 'Paralympic Sport in Korea'.
[30] Ibid.
[31] Tony Sainsbury, personal correspondence to author. February 12, 2008.
[32] Ibid.
[33] Appleby, 'Legacy of the 2000 Sydney Paralympic Games'.
[34] Ibid.
[35] International Paralympic Committee, *About the IPC*.
[36] Ibid.
[37] DePauw and Gavron, *Disability and Sport*.
[38] Legg et al., *Examining the Inclusion*.
[39] Carter, *Games without Frontiers*; du Toit, *Road to Beijing*; Longman, 'South Africa's du Toit'.
[40] Legg et al., 'The Athletic Ability Debate'; International Olympic Committee, *Neroli Fairhall*; Mascagni, *Paola Fantato*; Runyan, *Marla's Story*.
[41] International Olympic Committee, *St. Louis 1904*.
[42] Legg et al., 'The Athletic Ability Debate'.
[43] Ibid.
[44] Ibid.
[45] Ibid.
[46] Miah, *Paralympics 2.0*.
[47] Adelson, 'Let'em Play'.
[48] Anderson, 'The War of the Swimsuits'.
[49] Greely et al., 'Towards Responsible Use'.
[50] Appleby, 'Legacy of the 2000 Sydney Paralympic Games'.
[51] Ibid.

References

Adelson, Eric. 'Let'em Play'. *ESPN Magazine* 11, no. 9 (2002): 53–6.
Anderson, Kelli. 'The War of the Swimsuits'. *Sports Illustrated Vault*, June 23, 2008. http://vault.sportsillustrated.cnn.com/vault/article/magazine/MAG1140911/index.htm
Appleby, Lois. 'Legacy of the 2000 Sydney Paralympic Games'. Paper presented at the Sport Event Hosting Conference, Taipei, Taiwan, 2007.

Bailey, Steve. *Athlete First: A History of the Paralympic Movement*. Chichester, UK: Wiley, 2007.

Brittain, Ian. *The Paralympic Games Explained*. London: Routledge, 2009.

Canadian Olympic Committee. *How the Olympic Games Began*. Ottawa: Canadian Olympic Committee, 2010. http://www.olympic.ca/EN/games/olympic/history.shtml

Carter, Paul, *Games Without Frontiers*. http://www.disabilitynow.org.uk/living/features/games-without-frontiers

Cashman, Richard, and Darcy Simon. *Benchmark Games: The Sydney 2000 Paralympic Games*. Sydney: Walla Walla, 2000.

DePauw, Karen, and Susan Gavron. *Disability and Sport*. 2nd edn. Champaign, IL: Human Kinetics, 2005.

du Toit, Natalie. *Road to Beijing*. Cape Town: Multi-Code Sport, 2010. http://www.nataliedutoit.com/

Greely, Henry, Barbara Sahakian, John Harris, Robert Kessler, Michael Gazzaniga, Philip Campbell, and Martha Farah. 'Towards Responsible Use of Cognitive-Enhancing Drugs by the Healthy'. *Nature* 456 (2008): 702–5.

Guttmann, Ludwig. *Textbook of Sport for the Disabled*. Aylesbury, UK: HM+M, 1986.

Howe, David. *The Cultural Politics of the Paralympic Movement: Through an Anthropological Lens*. New York: Routledge, 2008.

Illinois Parks and Recreation. *A Brief History of the Paralympic Games*, 2010. http://www.lib.niu.edu/ipo/1996/ip960722.html

International Olympic Committee. *Neroli Fairhall. Lausanne*. Switzerland: International Olympic Committee, 2010. http://www.olympic.org/uk/athletes/profiles/bio_uk.asp?par_i_id=33007

International Olympic Committee. *St. Louis 1904*. Lausanne, Switzerland: International Olympic Committee, 2010. http://www.olympic.org/uk/games/past/index_uk.asp?OLGT=1&OLGY=1904

International Paralympic Committee. *About the IPC – IPC Symbol and Motto*. Bonn, Germany: International Paralympic Committee, 2010. http://www.paralympic.org/release/Main_Sections_Menu/IPC/About_the_IPC/IPC_Symbol_and_Motto/

International Paralympic Committee. *Medal Standings Beijing 2008 Paralympic Games*. Bonn, Germany: International Paralympic Committee, 2010. http://www.paralympic.org/release/Main_Sections_Menu/Sports/Results/paralympics_reports.html?type=medalstandings&games=2008PG

International Paralympic Committee. *Past Games – Summer Games Overview*. Bonn, Germany: International Paralympic Committee, 2010. http://www.paralympic.org/release/Main_Sections_Menu/Paralympic_Games/Past_Games/Summer_Games_Overview.html

Jeon, J. & Legg, D. 'Seoul 1988 – The First Modern Paralympic Games'. In *Paralympic Legacies*, edited by D. Legg & K. Gilbert, 47–52. Illinois: Commonground Publishing, USA, 2011.

Kyu Han, Jae Lee, and Justin Jeon. 'Paralympic Sport in Korea'. Presentation made at the 2007 International Paralympic Committee General Assembly, Seoul, Korea 2007.

Legg, David. 'Strategy Formation in Amateur Sport Organization: A Case Study'. *International Journal of Sport Management* 4, no. 3 (2003): 205–23.

Legg, David, Allison Burchell, Patrick Jarvis, and Tony Sainsbury. 'The Athletic Ability Debate: Have We Reached a Tipping Point?' *Palaestra* (forthcoming).

Legg, David, Claudia Emes, David Stewart, and Robert Steadward. 'Historical Overview of the Paralympics, Special Olympics and Deaflympics'. *Palaestra* 20, no. 1 (2002): 30–5.

Legg, David, Ted Fay, Mary Hums, and Eli Wolff. 'Examining the Inclusion of Wheelchair Exhibition Events within the Olympic Games: 1984–2004'. *European Journal of Sport Management* 9, no. 13 (2009): 243–58.

Longman, Jere. 'South Africa's du Toit Fulfills a Dream Derailed'. *New York Times*, 2008. http://www.nytimes.com/2008/08/18/sports/olympics/18longman.html

Mascagni, K., *Paola Fantato: Sports as a Means of Social Integration*. http://www.la84foundation.org/OlympicInformationCenter/OlympicReview/1996/oreXXVI10/oreXXVI10zc.pdf

Miah, Andy. *Paralympics 2.0*. London: Author, 2010 http://www.bioethicsforum.org

Official Jim Abbott Website. *Famed Major League Baseball Player*, 2010. http://www.jimabbott.info/

Runyan, Marla, *Marla's Story*, 2010 http://www.marlarunyan.com/story.php

Steadward, Robert, and Susan Foster. 'History of Disability Sport: From Rehabilitation to Athletic Excellence'. In *Adapted Physical Activity*, edited by R. Steadward, G. Wheeler, and J. Watkinson, 471–96. Edmonton: University of Alberta, 2003.

Stewart, Donald A., and Donalda K. Ammons. 'Future Directions of the Deaflympics'. *Palaestra* 17, no. 3 (2003): 45–9.

Wolbring, Gregor. 'Oscar Pistorius and the Future nature of Olympic, Paralympic and Other Sports'. *SCRIPTed* 5, no. 1 (2008): 139. http://www.law.ed.ac.uk/ahrc/script-ed/vol5-1/wolbring.asp

Transformed identity: from disabled person to global Paralympian

Jill M. Le Clair

Humber College ITAL, Toronto, Canada

Transformations can take place at the organizational and personal level. This article is about both. It presents the narratives of the careers of Canadian swimmers with a disability who, through their training and hard work, went from being defined as persons with disabilities to become Paralympians, as the sport system of Paralympic Games swimming changed from being disability-based to sport-based. Their stories are similar to athletes in other countries who compete in the global Paralympic Games system, but with one difference, this sport events take place without the use of high tech wheelchair equipment and prostheses, as in athletics. Athletes compete with unadorned bodies in the water of the pool, and the pool is also transformative in its own way, allowing for mobility and movement that gravity on dry land does not sustain.

I think the word handicapped is probably a bad word. It's kind of like when you use the 'N' word for a black person. It's outdated. It has no place being in society, there are so many better words.

Veteran Paralympian, 2003

The global disability sport system

In 1948, a handful of veterans at Stoke Mandeville Hospital in England competed in the first ever disability sport event held parallel to the Olympic Games. At the time, neurosurgeon Ludwig Guttman was thought to be unrealistic because he envisaged these marginalized men with spinal cord injuries using sport as a route to social inclusion.[1] The naysayers were wrong and Guttman was right. It turns out that the impact of international disability sport movements has been very important because these organizations have helped reframe the meaning of disability, and provided new sport opportunities for elite competition and social inclusion.[2]

This paper presents the personal narratives of Canadian swimmers with a disability (SWAD) team members who were, or became Paralympians.[3] Their careers took place at a time of profound change in the Paralympic Games sport system as it evolved from a relatively little-known disability-based, disability-specific group of organizations to become a genuinely global, sport-based umbrella organization.[4] It is a story of organizationally transformation and of transformation in the lives of individuals with disabilities. It is also the story of individual hard work with a focus on achieving, and this experience is replicated by athletes in many other countries.

Two main stages or transformations in the careers of Canadian Paralympic swimmers are discussed. The first is the recognition of their socially defined disability identity, and the rejection of the limitations of this label. The second is the transformation to athlete and competitive swimmer, as each individual negotiated the differences between the perceived body and the lived body in relation to the presentation of the self as a person with a disabled body.[5] There is also a brief discussion of the classification process required to obtain the status of a Paralympic swimmer and of the macro-organizational change in International Paralympic Committee (IPC) swimming which switched from disability-based classification to sport-based classification and competition.

Background: historical moments

This research resulted from the author attending an Atlanta Sports Council meeting in 1995 that was held at Georgia Tech University, in order to showcase the new Olympic aquatics facility and to see the first international event being held in the pool, the Paralympic Games Swim Trials. This event was quite different from a conventional non-disabled swimming event in which the competitor bodies are very similar – tall, wide shoulders and long, muscular arms. There were athletes of varied sizes and shapes in swimsuits of different designs and colours. When competition began some swimmers stood with arms raised in the conventional start position, others were positioned for the same event in the water. The starts were varied – some held onto a rope in the water, some were steadied by an assistant while standing, and others sat on the starting block, but in the water, all swam unaided, with no fins or prostheses. It was obvious that these athletes had different disabilities, but they were competing in the same pool. The daily newssheet, the *ISPT News*, explained that the swimmers were competing in different classes, so we saw the 'same' event take place more than once as those with different degrees of disability were grouped together.[6] I had stumbled on part of the profound shift in disability swimming.

Once competition started, the swimmers raced through the water and the athletes in the lower classes, with more severe disabilities, we had seen moving carefully or with assistance on land moved surprisingly (to the author) speedily through the water. Perhaps part of the author's reaction was emotional as the author was jealous of their athletic vigour as she sat on a bench hardly able to sit and watch, or move up and down the stands because of a spinal cord injury from a car crash. Early in 1996 an introduction to the coach and team followed, and out of that serendipitous event in Atlanta came a decade of following the team and this research.

The author has lived in two worlds, as a non-disabled person who loved movement and physical activity. Her life was then suddenly transformed into the world of disability where every movement was restricted, painful and challenging. This research is part of a reflexive analysis of the world of international swimming while on her own odyssey she was also experiencing a range of issues including stigma and disability identity,[7] the knowledge/power axis, medical 'disciplining',[8] globalization,[9] odysseys[10] and disability rights[11] symbolized locally in the passage of the Accessibility for Ontarians with Disabilities Act (2005),[12] nationally with the Americans with Disabilities Act (ADA)[13] and globally in the UN Declaration of the Rights of Persons with Disabilities (2006).[14] The lived reality of disability allowed for research insights that were informed by experience.

The fieldwork context

The analysis in this article is drawn from participant observation and interviews conducted between 1996 and 2008, the bulk of the interviews being conducted between 2000 and

2003. To understand the lives of these athletes it was necessary to follow them as they travelled from one end of the country to the other, and around the world, as best I could, to attend provincial, national and international competitions, training camps and classification sessions and seminars. Similarly to other researchers in our globalized world, Frohlick describes this as researchers 'chasing' people around the world for interviews, and fieldwork as 'fleeing and transient'[15] because of the required mobility of globalization. Between 2002 and 2004, the swimmers on the team literally travelled around the world. They travelled across Canada, to South America and Europe to train and compete: in Canada the pools ranged from Victoria, British Columbia, Winnipeg, Manitoba, Edmonton, Alberta to Toronto, Ontario; overseas the World Championships took place in Mar del Plata, Argentina, and the Paralympic Games in Athens, Greece, in the autumn of 2004. The interviews were primarily conducted at training camps and also on the telephone, and consisted of open-ended questions that related to the five stages of their swimming careers, including retirement.[16]

Stage one: transformation to disability identity

Link and Phelan argue that the development of disability identity takes place in the context of three mechanisms of discrimination – individual, structural, and discrimination that operates through the stigmatized person's beliefs and behaviours.[17] The series of steps or changes in this process of transformation includes, first their awareness of their own self-conception of disability status and its emotional component; and second, what Goffman describes as the rejection of 'virtual' identity replaced with 'authentic social identity'[18] and true identity through friendship and acceptance. All of this takes place in the context of the dominating 'normate' and the social construction of the 'normal'.[19] The limiting disability or handicap label is rejected through sport, and there is a determination to overcome physical barriers using whatever strategies are necessary. In addition, there are changes specific to the acceptance of body shape and 'difference', especially related to the rejection of the concept of the 'missing' or different limb, or limbs, and there is change through the rejection of stereotypes about the 'feminine' body. The final part in transformation is that each and every one of these individuals has to be publicly recognized as a person with a disability and classified for swimming competition in the Paralympic Games. Sometimes impacting directly in one second, and at other times over a period, these myriad ways culminate in the individual reframing what disability means as a stigmatized public status under the hegemonic 'gaze' of the wider society.[20] Through a multiplicity of paths, there are different ways in which persons with a disability reject marginalization and seek empowerment through the physical activity of swimming, often very early in their lives.

Childhood teasing, ridicule and sport

The elements in this transition included sometimes being subject to bullying at school and an increasing awareness of disability. Non-disabled individuals often assume that those with a disability must automatically have a sense of self as a person with a disability from earliest childhood, but this is not necessarily the case. Sometimes the individual did not become aware of their disability until their teens or even early adulthood.[21] The child knows that they may be unable to do some of same physical activities as their schoolmates or their family, but they are 'normal' or 'average' in their own minds. This is at the same time that they are experiencing the reality of their physical challenges. One swimmer[22] describes the growing awareness of a different physical ability.

> I was in my teens. I never really thought about it … In grade seven is really when it started to come to my attention. Sort of in grades five, six and seven, but painfully so in grades seven and eight. But I always liked doing things. I loved my swimming lessons; we'd walk everywhere. My dad would say, run over to the tree, run back. He'd tell me to ride a bike – I know I fell a lot [laughter]. I had lots of skinned knees and skinned elbows, but I did all that stuff.

Some athletes described being at school as being a form of torture; they only began to make sense of it all as an adult.[23] They were made fun of at school, were the target of jokes, name calling or slurs, and their different motor movements were sometimes mimicked. Some, it must be said, had good friends and felt their disability had no impact. These seem to be those individuals who participated in physical activities and were integrated through team sport. Regardless, for some there was a sense of profound rejection. Some athletes had a miserable time at school because of the other children, teachers or sometimes both.

> My gait has definitely improved, but when I was growing up, they imitated the way I walked all the time in the hallways. They called me retard because the only thing that I knew and understood about my disability, I didn't know that I had cerebral palsy until I was just about twenty-one … … In grade six we had to write a story of our life. I wrote it, I wrote what it was like to have a disability – I didn't know I had CP – to be teased and to be made fun of, to be called names, and to be ridiculed and judged.

Awareness and self-naming

Each individual goes through the process of naming and self-naming,[24] and this is unique and occurs at different ages for each person. Each athlete was asked, 'When did you become aware of yourself with a disability?', and a number explained that they had been treated in the same way as other family members, with expectations to work hard and contribute like anyone else, so they had not really become aware of the differences until well into adolescence. Goffman might interpret the family focus on sport and opportunities as a form of 'deviance disavowal' – the ignoring of a dominant and determining factor,[25] but the athletes and their families said their focus was on doing whatever seemed possible and 'normalizing' the child's experience.

However, even though some athletes claimed that they had never experienced discrimination, the term disability or disabled nearly always engendered an emotional response. Goffman[26] states that the public recognition of a status, as for alcoholics at an Alcoholics Anonymous meeting, is an important part of identity making.[27] When each athlete was asked if they saw a parallel, this perspective was firmly rejected. The athletes did not see a parallel at all.

> I don't think it's important like that, because AA is, you know, a sociological problem you have. You have to admit it so you can get help. I don't need help. I'm a disabled person, I have a disability, and I'm swimming with a disability. I need help? No. It doesn't work like that.

The athletes felt there was a clear differentiation between a status that they saw as a choice, such as drinking alcohol or being overweight. These were regarded as lifestyle choices which individuals could change. The disabilities the swimmers had were unchangeable by lifestyle; a missing hand or limb, motor neurological limitations or visual limitations cannot be addressed by making different choices. Some seemed to imply that the use of the word disability indiscriminately diminished the reality of a 'genuine', severe and unchangeable disability. This attitude was also present in the magazines based on disability issues. There were debates at this time about the challenge to the gains made through the Americans with Disabilities Act by actions seen to weaken or demean serious concerns related to disability by conflating them with 'math challenges' or non-medical obesity issues in Americans with a Disability law suits.[28]

Stage two: the impact of sport on disability identity

Rejection disability and embracing ability

The swimmers with a disability rejected the concept of disability outright. In response to the question 'What do you think of the term disability?' these responses were typical.

> No, I never have and I never will (use the term) and if people use that kind of term, I don't know, it's like they're putting themselves down. It's just that word disgusts me so much that every time people use it, it makes me feel so irritated and so out of control because it just drives me crazy. It's like that word for me signifies low self-esteem. I don't like it. You were born that way? Well, go on with your life and do whatever it is that you have to do … and go on.

For those born with a disability it has been part of life from the first day, but what it signifies, represents and symbolizes changes with life experience and struggles. The individual becomes socially aware of their limitations or impairments in physical movement and bodily activity, and these necessitate a presentation of self as a person with a disability. But being physically active in the water and becoming involved in organized swimming challenges the 'victim' or limiting label of disability identity. There is a contradiction between the disability label and the abilities the athletes have in the water. The limitations implicit in the term disability are rejected absolutely, as the athletes see themselves as being able to do what they want and achieve the goals they want. The focus across the board was on what the athletes want to do and feel that they can do. The negative elements that disability identity represents are rejected outright.

> No. I don't see myself as disabled so I don't think there's any difference. I don't like that word. It's a very disgusting word. I will use it as somebody who is unable to jump, or go and run, and do something that you could do, I don't know, it's just I believe that word puts people down, makes their self-esteem low. I don't like using that word, find something else. It's a word in the dictionary, but, I don't like classifying people for who they are, what they do, what they are missing. They are who they are, no matter what. Everybody has a story to tell, everybody has something to learn from everybody, so just, respect everybody for the way they are, and live your life the fullest.

The discussion of the meaning of the term disability by athletes was nuanced. The athletes rejected the more common American term of the 1980s and 1990s 'physically challenged'. It was argued that there is physical challenge in many activities, and often there are physical challenges for those with disabilities, but it is not an accurate term because non-disabled individuals can take on physical challenges, but a person with a disability has no choice. However, it was recognized that each person had different strengths and weaknesses and the label disability was dependent on the context and the expected skills.

> Let's just use that stupid word, disability, everybody has one. (Not everyone) can sing; if you put me to sing people will start crying, I can't sing. I could dance, I'm a good dancer, but I can't sing. So that's it, I'm unable to sing, even if I try my best, I can't, so everybody has that in their life, not everybody knows how to do everything. Does that make them disabled? No. They might have the ability to do something, but they don't have the ability to do something else, so what?

Other athletes accepted their body shape from the start and said they never faced discrimination. They were certain that they had not faced discrimination or barriers.

Perhaps it needs to be remembered that most of the athletes were still relatively young, and most students, but they were clear in their answers, explaining: 'Well, I don't know, not really, nothing.' Another said:

> I've never seen (discrimination), I just view it as just being there (my disability), and I'm different than everybody else, it's just fun. I just always have been very aware of it and I don't really deny it, it's just it's there, right there, and face it and go with it. Go on with it, there's not much you could do.

It could be argued that athletes must adopt a specific frame of mind in order to compete; the athlete must think that it is possible to achieve the goals that they have in mind. So the individuals who participated in these interviews would not have chosen this path if they had not had a positive 'can-do' attitude. They must reject the negativity that discrimination presents in order to continue against the odds of achieving various goals.

Disabilities can be visible or invisible and create social margins. If visible, the athlete is forced to negotiate in each and every social situation. Expecting or feeling anxious about potential rejection can lead to social isolation. This expectation of stereotyping has been called 'stigma consciousnesses.'[29] Some persons with a disability become annoyed or irritated at having to constantly negotiate their disability identity, and others put down the endless questioning to 'lack of information' or 'lack of education'. Sometimes being at the receiving end of people staring was irritating, and some athletes, although comfortable and almost naked on the pool deck, felt different outside the pool. One man in his late twenties still felt uncomfortable about his different body and put it this way: 'I've got better, I mean before I wouldn't wear shorts that were short. I would cover up. I got a lot better'.

Older people will often use the term handicapped, meaning disability, and in training a coach referred to a male swimmer as handicapped. The swimmer found this usage inappropriate and explained why.

> 'I'm not handicapped', I said. I hate that word. I'm not handicapped. Sure I've got a disability (one leg) but am I any more handicapped than somebody who sits on the sofa, who eats a bag of chips and weighs 300 pounds? No. Am I any more handicapped than somebody who's on unemployment and won't go to find work because they feel sorry for themselves, no. And you know I train my ass off every day in the water and I swim 180,000 meters a week, a month, does that make me handicapped? No. So I think the word handicapped is probably a bad word. It's kind of like when you call the 'N' word for a black person. It's outdated you. It has no place being in society - there are so many better words.

Acceptance of 'true' identity through trust and acceptance

The process of swimming and sport activity often facilitated acceptance of disability status. At the swimming pool, it meant that there was an acceptance of difference, and of the person and the body, because of swimming.

> I don't think you can accept yourself right away. I'm still working on it. I think it's just a day-by-day thing. I think throughout your life you kind of deal with everything, one thing at a time. Something new will come up. They (others) might think that it's all going to be bad, but it's not, you know. For me I really met some true friends and the same thing will happen for them.

Transformation of IPC Swimming in the Paralympic Games

From disability-based to sport-based

Athletes train and compete within organizational structures that support or undermine opportunities and the framing of sport experiences. The first Stoke Mandeville Games focused on paralysed athletes with spinal cord injuries, but year by year sports were added (including volleyball, cycling, wheelchair marathon, tennis, wheelchair rugby and sailing). In addition, athletes with different disabilities began competing (cerebral palsy, amputee, *les autres*, visually impaired). Until the 1980s, international sport organizations had been disability based. Classification was based on a medical model and medical classification. The main sport organizations consisted of:

- Cerebral Palsy International Sport and Recreation (CP-ISRA);
- International Blind Sports Association (IBSA);
- International Association of Sport for Persons with a Mental Handicap (INAS-FMH; joined in 1992 and later became INAS-FID (suspended in 2000);
- International Stoke Mandeville Games Federation (ISMGF; later the ISMWSF);
- International Sports Organization for the Disabled (ISOD); and
- Comité International des Sports des Sourds (CISS; World Games for the Deaf) which withdrew without participating in the Paralympic Games and became the separate Deaflympics.[30]

In 1988, these previously independent disability sport organizations, under the leadership of Dr Robert Steadward, reorganized as one umbrella organization the International Paralympic Committee (IPC) that would oversee the Paralympic Games. Later the IPC reorganized to follow the global regions of the Olympic Games.[31] The IPC was to become structured in a way similar way to the Olympic Games organized by the International Olympic Committee (IOC) and became structurally and financially formally linked in the Olympic bid process and in the Olympic Games themselves. In 2010, the two events of the Olympic and Paralympic Games were planned together and the official title used was 'The Vancouver Organizing Committee for the 2010 Olympic and Paralympic Games' and in the media this was the official title of the Games, spoken of together.[32]

Globalization and unified national team

It is important to recognize that these changes took place in the context of an increasingly globalized world in which we see disability in what Appadurai calls 'postnational geography' and Gupta calls 'transnational identies' [33] where shared values and identities are not based on territoriality, but on shared values about human rights which play an increasingly important role in disability discourses.[34] The passage of the 2006 UN Convention on the Rights of Persons with Disabilities included a section directly addressing sport and physical activity which also strengthened a rights-based approach for inclusion.[35] As supporters in different countries lobbied (assisted by an exponential growth in communications' technology of the Internet, mobile phones and social networks like Facebook) as part of public discourse for national approval and passage by their own legislative assemblies, awareness of disability issues in sport increases.

Older swimmers had competed in a system in which the teams were disability-based and they had felt frustrated because they had wanted better competition and a greater sport focus. Swimming was divided by disability. In Canada, there had been four swim teams with different coaches, different training and different uniforms. Sports aim to create fair competition, and part of ensuring fairness is that athletes are placed in similar groupings as boxers classified by weight. IPC Swimming explains classification in this way:[36]

> Traditionally there are athletes who belong to six different disability groups in the Paralympic Movement: amputee, cerebral palsy, visual impairment, spinal cord injuries,

intellectual disability and a group which includes athletes who do not fit into the aforementioned groups (*les autres*).

Classes are determined by a variety of the 1989 international that may include a physical and technical assessment throughout the athlete's career. Sports certify individuals to conduct the process of classification and they are known as classifiers. Since the 1960s, the development of sport for athletes with a disability has produced and developed; and this continues to evolve to the present day.

By 1992, IPC Swimming had reorganized its classification system for competition to become sport-based. How fast did the athlete swim in the water? How effective was their propulsive force through the water? All athletes were grouped together *regardless of their disability* and were classified together. The focus became sport, not disability:

Swimming is governed by the IPC and co-ordinated by the IPC Swimming Technical Committee, which incorporates the rules of the International Swimming Federation (FINA). The FINA rules are followed with a few modifications, such as optional platform or in-water starts for some races and the use of signals or 'tappers' for swimmers with blindness/visual impairment; however, no prostheses or assistive devices are permitted.[37]

With a focus on sport in Canada, this meant that and there was only one Canadian swim team and this was the sport system athletes were part of in 1996. The team consisted of swimmers with a variety of disabilities who competed as one team. The 1989 international transformation laid the groundwork for Canadian technical classifier and coach James Hood to propose a Memorandum of Understanding for Swimming Canada to integrate the national Olympic swim team and the SWAD team. Therefore for the first time ever the non-disabled Junior National Team Trials and the SWAD Paralympic Trials were held together in Nepean near Ottawa, in 1996. By 2000, the Olympic and Paralympic Trials were held at the same Olympic pool and at the same time in Montreal. In 2004, at the Etobicoke Olympium, the Olympic and Paralympic Trials events alternated. There had been a sea change in attitude from 1996 as the media alternated in interviewing the athletes who were on the way to compete as either Olympians or Paralympians.[38] This was the kind of inclusion that Guttman had imagined over 60 years earlier.

'Coming out' – transformation from a person with a disability to classified swimmer

Public disability identity

These international and national organizational changes meant that the pool also provided an interesting contradiction in that everyone is present because of an official disability identity, but each person has a different disability. There is a shared normalcy and ease of social understanding with neither staring nor the need to explain. At the same time, there is a classification which creates a disability ranking. Each athlete is classified by their functioning in the water into a class for the stroke used in the specific event. It can be seen to be somewhat like the grouping in boxing to ensure fairness. The groupings are by number; an S1, SB1 is the most severely disabled and S10 or SB9 the least disabled, and athletes with visual impairments or blind S11 to S13; and the classification includes an on-land component and an in the water assessment. No swimmer can compete in the IPC system without being classified and hence a public statement 'coming out' as an athlete with a disability. There is no hiding of disability in this environment.

Many swimmers explained that although their identity is clearly labelled as a disability identity, they did not like the term as it categorized them and was seen to be restrictive. They saw themselves as capable and independent, not as disabled or limited. They rejected

Goffman's premise about the need for a public statement as 'swimmers with a disability' and rejected the disability label as negative.

One of the interesting differences between the literature in the past and the experience of those with disabilities in the last 20 years is that those very signs of disability (Goffman's stigma) have been transformed into symbols of excellence. In sport, the visible artificial Flex-foot is not hidden away because of stigma and shame; it is merely part of a post-modern cyborg elite body.[39] 'Passing' or 'covering' is the opposite to 'coming out'. Some theorists have argued that bodies today are by definition cyborg bodies, what Butryn calls 'post-humans'[40] because the 'so-called "natural" body has been impacted by technology whether minimally through a childhood inoculation or maximally through life support systems, heart transplants or prostheses'.[41]

Classification

In the case of competitive athletes 'coming out' is an institutionalized process, with assessments included in the process of classification. It is conceptualized collectively by society,[42] and specifically in this case by the swimming community. The individual recognizes either from birth or through trauma 'I am a person with a disability' (even if this identity is rejected), and in order to compete in disabled swimming, disability identity must be formally and publicly recognized. Those who participate in any sport must first state that they have a disability identity by presenting themselves as a swimmer with a disability who must be placed in the appropriate competition/skill group by being classified. Linton argues that a great deal of energy is put into 'passing' and that hiding is a response to prejudicial attitudes and it is important for individuals to claim and recognize their disability.[43] One female swimmer wrestled with the meaning of identifying with a disability identity.

> Prior to that time, I had never defined myself as having a disability, so it was an element that I struggled with because in order to participate in Paralympic sport you have to first say I have a disability. It's part of the whole eligibility process and then it's moving from that point. It has certainly coloured the kinds of choices that I've made in my own professional career of moving into a situation of saying you know what? I'm an athlete first and I happen to have a disability, and that's one of the really powerful things about the Paralympic sport movement in our society. It gives you the opportunity to take that societal notion of disability and turn it into something else that is constructive. It allows you to not only get on with your life but also to explore those ideas and those goals of excellence.

Athlete identity and team membership

Another athlete described the stressful experience of formally joining a team. The swimmer was nervous and the other non-disabled team members were anxious at having their first swimmer with a disability on the university team.

> For fear of being ignorant, or offending me, and I think too, part of it is me, because when I first started swimming with able-bodied clubs, I was scared out of my wits. I was terrified, terrified, and now, and part of it is that I've established myself, so I feel much more comfortable, I can go into the coach and say, Hi, I'm – – –, this is what I've done. I hold these Canadian records, I've swum at these international meets; I have a right to be here, whereas, before, it was very scary. And you're much more worried about what people will think about you, and I think where I did my undergrad, from the perspective of swimming with their able-bodied team and so on, and that was a real boost for me, but also being in an environment where we were encouraged not to judge people on the way that they looked but more on their abilities ...

It could be argued that we all present and think of ourselves by shaping and stressing those things that are most important, but others could define us as being in denial or unrealistic. For swimmers, regardless of disability, the water is always a source of a framing disability identity differently. The athlete feels and moves in different ways in the water, often 'in a liberating sense,' often leading to a different framing of the meaning of disability. 'My disability is different. It still does affect me in the water; it's simply that there are more things that I can do'.

Social marginalization can be a consequence of disability. Historically, the disabled were marginalized in all aspects of society – hidden from view, thought to be unmarriageable and usually unemployed.[44] Because of the global initiatives on the rights of athletes, the 2006 UN Convention on the Rights of Persons with Disabilities and the Sport for Development and Peace initiatives[45] we have seen a shift in attitudes and opportunities towards sport. So, for those who decide to compete and train in high-performance sport we have an interesting dichotomy. Training to perform well means reaching for an above-average sport performance while being marginalized as a person with a disability. Yet performances of higher classed swimmers are beyond the ability of all except for a small percentage of able-bodied swimmers.

Titchkosky uses the term 'between-ness'[46] to describe the marginality of a person with a disability. My findings are that the overriding aspect for swimmers is their love for the water and the freedom of movement in swimming. Most became exposed to swimming from their earliest memories and enjoyed the water from the start. Water was a medium that had a positive impact on their marginalization in various ways. In addition, because of their success with the physical achievements in sport, the marginality that Titchkosky describes as central is minimized. The swimmers see themselves as independent and empowered. One athlete felt the language of disability was inaccurate for athletes:

> I don't perceive myself as disabled. I feel like I'm able-bodied you know, but I just happen to have one leg, so maybe an able bodied swimmer with one leg; able-bodied swimmer with one arm, but that's not (a) universal (term).

Agency: high-performance athlete identity

Physicality is personal and experienced uniquely by each individual, although clearly there are shared experiences and values. 'The term rather than concept of physicality'[47] has been taken into use in describing people's experiences during physical activity. The body is a means through which each person experiences and learns about the world. It is also a means through which change can take place. Agency, in the context of learned bodily experiences at the personal level, has 'a transformative capacity that is socially and historically contextualized'.[48] In the recognition that there is human agency in movement (in all ways of moving), individuals present, interpret, choreograph and challenge bodily presentation in a constantly changing fashion; this includes 'the moving body',[49] a dynamic perspective on the body',[50] and what Harre calls 'causal powers theory'.[51] Here, the context is the competitive pool.

> Stigma is entirely dependent on social, economic, and political power – it takes power to stigmatize. In some instances the role of power is obvious. However, the role of power in stigma is frequently overlooked because in many instances power differences are so taken for granted as to seem unproblematic. When people think of mental illness, obesity, deafness, and having one leg instead of two, there is a tendency to focus on the attributes associated with these conditions rather than on power differences between people who have them and people who do not. But power, even in these circumstances, is essential to the social production of stigma.[52]

Link and Phelan argue that stigma is totally dependent on power differentials and we have seen that change in swimming as swimmers moved from competing in a disability-based system to one that increasingly viewed swimmers as world champions competing in the same venues in conjunction with the Olympic Games.

According to Hevey,[53] empowerment is part of the transforming aspect of the rejection of the aspects of stigmatization and the celebration of 'enfreakment' and the concept of 'Super Crips'. This transformation of the diminishing terms cripple/crips into something that transcends its demeaning framework has power. It means the symbol of inequity is turned on its head. It is also part of the *transformative process* of self-identifying and the structural redefinition from being a person with a disability to that of a high-performance swimmer with a disability.

There are three other main aspects to the transformation into national team member that are briefly outlined here that are inherent and required to be part of high-erformance swimming regardless of the athlete being disabled or not, and these automatically become part of the new elite swimmer identity. First, the individual swimmer's body is 'disciplined' in the ways of swimming. Here the terms of Mauss (the *technique du corp*) and Bourdieu (*habitus*)[54] are used to describe the results from the rigours of daily training at the pool, with the essential self-discipline necessary to master the technical aspects of the various strokes and the skills required for competition. This process is accompanied by a new high-performance team identity guided, or some might say dominated, by coaches. The individual team body is also part of the marketing of the team image while it changes shape and may be inscribed to reflect a changed identity.

The second aspect is the experience of the team, which includes the marketing and commodification of team bodies in the team uniform under the authority of the coach and with the support of the 'service specialists'. The team disciplining of the body is epitomized by the athlete's contract, legally specifying the financial, social and political demands of team membership.

Third is the experience of the events in the environment of the competition sites themselves, the competitive settings. This is the globalized part of the athletes' world as competition is international in nature and the Canadians once they are classified become part of this global system. They have potential competitors from 80 countries and changing sites for the swim meets, World Championships and the Olympic Games.

The speed at which the transformation takes place, the swim club membership, and the attitude of the coaches varies, but there are some shared elements for all athletes regardless of disability and gender. The swimmers and their bodies are now subject to the discipline of the team, and these embodied activities are socially constructed.[55] This discipline is more intense and different from what Mauss calls 'the circumstances of life in common'.[56] There is an increased intensity and seriousness:

> But whatever the level of participation, the formal disciplining of bodies that occurs within sport and dance involves not only the transmission of knowledge about, and the shaping of competence with, given techniques of the body, but also the proselytizing of particular schemes of preference, valuation, and meaning.[57]

Conclusion

Assumptions about disability identity are changing. The lives of persons with disabilities changed profoundly because of swimming as the sport reframed their childhood experiences of disability. Although each athlete had unique experiences and different disabilities, the term disability held negative connotations for these athletes, who although officially classified as disabled athletes, rejected the disability label as negative and restricting. Their transforming lives took place as the international disability sport system, the international Paralympic Games also shifted its focus from disability-based to sport-based competition.

Acknowledgements

The author would like to acknowledge the support of the Social Science and Humanities Research Council (SSHRC) of Canada for their two year graduate fellowship and the University of Toronto for their one year graduate fellowship that supported this research. I'd also like to thank Swimming Canada for its ongoing support and co-operations. The following provided personal assistance and without whose help the fieldwork research could not have been undertaken: Lilian Le Clair, 1996 Youth Nationals and Paralympic Trials, Ottawa, Canada; Tommy Lord, 1996 Paralympic Games, Atlanta, USA; Daniele Laumann Hart, 2002 Swimming World Championships, Mar del Plata, Argentina; Lindy Allery, 2004 Paralympic Games, Athens, Greece and Li Jing (Patricia) of Renmin University of China, 2008 Paralympic Games, Beijing, China. Most important I am very appreciative of the time that the athletes, coaches, officials, sport administrators, classifiers and others so generously spent with me, on what I am sure seemed to be a laboriously slow process, as I tried to document their experiences in their own words.

Notes

1. Guttman, 'Sport for the Disabled'.
2. This article only addresses issues related to athletes with physical disabilities as the International Sports Federation for Persons with Intellectual Diasabilities (INAS-FID) that provides opportunities for persons with intellectual disabilities to compete in sport was suspended from the Palympic Games in 2000 and its activities are under review.
3. The term 'Swimmers with a Disability' was initiated by the team itself, although there is some discussion about who first came up with the term. This article will use the term swimmers throughout to refer to the team. Conventional usage now is to use the term Paralympians in referring to swimmers with disabilities who compete in the Paralympic Games.
4. Steadward and Peterson, *Paralympics*; Duncan, 'The Sociology of Ability and Disability'.
5. Goffman, *Presentation of Self*.
6. ISPT News, 2.
7. Goffman, *Presentation of Self; Stigma*.
8. Foucault, *Discipline and Punish; The Birth of the Clinic*.
9. Brysk, *Globalization and Human Rights*.
10. Homer, *The Odyssey*.
11. Raphael, Bryant and Rioux, *Staying Alive*.
12. Accessibility for Ontarians with Disabilities Act (AODA), http://www.aoda.ca
13. Although the Americans with Disability Act (ADA) was only national legislation, it had a worldwide impact as other countries invoked its premise, See Americans with a Disability Act. The US Equal Opportunity Commission. http://www.ada.gov/
14. UN Convention of the Rights of Persons with Disabilities, http://www.un.org/disabilities
15. Frohlick, 'Negotiating the "Global"', 529.
16. Many of the interviews were conducted at different times for two reasons: (1) the limited time swimmers had available. In training camp, swimmers and coaches have virtually no 'free' time as almost every minute is scheduled. (2) The physical challenges of the author who had limitations due to her own disability.
17. Link and Phelan, 'Conceptualizing Stigma', 379.
18. Goffman, *Stigma*, 2.
19. Garland-Thompson, *Extraordinary Bodies*.
20. 'In the twentieth and twenty-first centuries, we are so used to hierarchical rankings based on race and colour it is sometimes forgotten that these rankings are grounded in differences in power. It becomes almost surprising to see that English colonists in the eighteenth century and old-order Americans in the nineteenth century were able to stigmatize the Dutch and the Irish because of their positions of power vis-à-vis these groups'. Link and Phelan, 'Conceptualizing Stigma', 375.

[21] This is perhaps is not dissimilar to the studies of children of colour who did not become aware of their own colour until their teens. They assumed they were like the white characters they saw on television.

[22] The confidentiality and anonymity of the swimmers was part of the research guidelines, as many were actively competing. This was to allow those interviewed to speak more freely and not feel that any criticisms they made might have a negative impact on their swimming careers or funding.

[23] Nussbaum, 'Feminotopias', 166. There is a long historical tradition of curiosity about differentess and the displaying of deviant or 'freak' bodies. 'Dwarfs, giants, Siamese twins, hermaphrodites and unusual being with various physical deformities were regularly exhibited for profit in London in the early decades of the (eighteenth) century' and this continued in Canada until the 1950s. Today television and the Internet have replaced travelling fairs.

[24] Singer, 'Why Can't You Be Normal'.

[25] Goffman, *Stigma.*

[26] Goffman, *Presentation of Self.*

[27] In the *New York Times* in 2000 Jennifer Egan writes about the then 'new' phenomenon of multiple identities on the Internet. 'While the Internet provides a safe haven for countless gay teenagers who wouldn't dare confide their sexual orientation to the people around them, it is also a very easy place to get burned'. December 10, 2000, 110–117, 128–133. Many people use aliases or fake identities, and there is a real concern that the Internet is dangerous, no one knows for sure who is responding, and there is the possibility that procurers and 'gay bashers' are using the Internet for these purposes. The SWAD team members told the author that they used the Internet as a source of information on swim events and used email as a means of keeping in touch with their friends and family, but they do not use the disability websites or chat rooms. Probably this experience is different today in that disability agencies now deliberately target youngsters with a disability and put advertisements in public places to reach their audience.

[28] At the same time the Disability Rights Education & Defence Fund (DREDF) (www.dredf.org) challenges legal definitions of disability eg. a lower leg amputee defined by the courts as 'not disabled'.

[29] Pinel, 'Social Consciousness'. However, this was not the experience of these informants in Canada in the 1970s to the 1990s.

[30] Depauw and Gavron, *Disability and Sport.*

[31] The last Far East and South Pacific Games for the Disabled (FESPIC) were held in 2006, after which the regions matched those of the Olympic Games.

[32] The official site of the Vancouver Olympic Games, http://www.vancouver2010.com

[33] Appadurai, 'Sovereignty Without Territoriality', 381; Gupta, 'The Song', 322.

[34] Brysk, *Globalization and Human Rights.*

[35] Wolff, Hums, and Roy, *Sport in the UN Convention.*

[36] The IPC provided its rules and regulations online, http://www.swimmingcoach.org/pdf/ipcrulebook.pdf

[37] Paralympic swimming is framed by the rules of the international non-disabled swimming organization FINA with few accommodations, http://www.ipc-swimming.org/About_the_Sport. Rules also include regulations about approved competition suits over which there has been much controversy.

[38] Le Clair, 'High Performance Swimming'. It was clear this integration was not based on some form of political correctness, but competition for the best high performance swimmers in the country.

[39] Haraway, 'A Cyborg Manifesto'.

[40] Butryn, 'Posthuman Podiums'

[41] Figueroa-Sarriera, 'Children of the Mind'.

[42] Goffman, *Stigma,* 124.

[43] Linton, *Claiming Disability.* Linton's choice of title for her book reflects her insistence that individuals claim or own disability and her emphasis on the power of language.

[44] O'Sullivan, 'Messy Business'. Disabling illness became front page news and the target of 24-hour media coverage in March 2005 when an American woman, Terri Schiavo, in a 'persistent vegetative state', became subject to adversarial legal suits within her family about whether to invoke state intervention to terminate artificial feeding that would lead to death. Heated moral and religious debate took place about 'quality' of life versus humane release, which were reminiscent to the practices of Grafeneck (Castle) Hospital in Germany during the 1940s when the families of

mentally disabled individuals received form letters after their relatives had been euthanized; 'In view of the nature of his serious, incurable aliment, his death, which saved him from a lifelong institutional sojourn is to be regarded merely as a release'.

[45] Sport rights; Peter Donnelly, 'Child Labour, Sport Labour'; Jack Donnelley, *Universal Human Rights*; Kidd, 'A New Social Movement'.

[46] Titchkosky, *Disability, Self and Society*, 217.

[47] McDermott, 'Toward a Feminist Understanding of Physicality', 12.

[48] Ibid., 20

[49] Langlan, 'Mobility, Disability'.

[50] Aronson, Harre, and Cornell Way, *Realism Rescued*.

[51] Harre in Farnell, 'Moving Bodies, Acting Selves', 342.

[52] Link and Phelan, 'Conceptualizing Stigma'.

[53] Language can also be challenged by inverting the meaning of demeaning words. One of the earliest websites that was a source of information for persons with a disability on the Internet was *Cripworld*, which saw itself as a resource site for information and advocacy, and a site of empowerment through the use of this term.

[54] Mauss, Techniques du Corps'; Bourdieu, *Distinction*.

[55] Dyck and Archetti, *Sport*, 11.

[56] Ibid., 9.

[57] Ibid.

References

Appadurai, Arjun. 'Sovereignty Without Territoriality: Notes for a Postnational Geography'. In *The Anthropology of Space and Place: Locating Culture*, edited by Setha M. Low and Denise Lawrence-Zuniga, 337–50. Malden, MA: Blackwell, 2003.

Bourdieu, Pierre. *Distinction: A Social Critique of the Judgement of Taste*. Cambridge, MA: Harvard University Press, 1990.

Brysk, Alison, ed. *Globalization and Human Rights*. Los Angeles: University of California Press, 2002.

Butryn, Ted. 'Posthuman Podiums: Cyborg Narratives of Elite Track and Field Athletes'. *Sociology of Sport Journal* 20, no. 1 (2003): 17–39.

Depauw, Karen, and Susan J. Gavron, eds. *Disability and Sport*. Champaign, IL: Human Kinetics, 2005.

Doll-Tepper, Gudrun, Michael Kroner, and Wenner Sonnenschein, ed. *New Horizons in Sport for Athletes with a Disability. Proceedings of the International VISTA '99 Conference, Cologne, Germany*. Vols 1 and 2. Oxford: Meyer and Meyer Sport, 2001.

Donnelly, Jack. *Universal Human Rights in Theory and Practice*. 2nd edn. Ithaca, NY: Cornell University Press, 2003.

Donnelly, Peter. 'Child Labour, Sport Labour: Applying Child Labour Laws to Sport'. *International Review for the Sociology of Sport* 32, no. 4 (1997): 389–406.

Duncan, Margaret Carlisle. 'The Sociology of Ability and Disability in Physical Activity'. *Sociology of Sport Journal* 18, no. 1 (2001): 51–68.

Dyck, Noel, and Eduardo P. Archetti. *Sport, Dance and Embodied Identities*. New York: Berg, 2003.

Dyck, Noel, and Eduardo P. Archetti. 'Getting into the Game: Anthropological Perspectives on Sport – Introduction'. *Anthropologica* 46, no. 1 (2004): 3–8.

Farnell, Brenda. 'Moving Bodies, Acting Selves'. *Annual Review of Anthropology* 28 (1999): 341–73.

Figueroa-Sarriera, Heidi J. 'Children of the Mind with Disposable Bodies'. In *The Cyborg Handbook*, edited by Chris Hables Gray. New York: Routledge, 1995.

Foucault, Michel. *The Birth of the Clinic: An Archaeology of Medical Perception*. New York: Vintage, 1994.

Foucault, Michel. *Discipline and Punish: The Birth of the Prison*. New York: Vintage, 1995.

Frohlick, Susan E. 'Negotiating the "Global" Within the Global Playscapes of Mount Everest'. *The Canadian Review of Sociology and Anthropology* 40, no. 5 (2003): 525–42.

Garland-Thomson, Rosemarie. *Extraordinary Bodies: Figuring Physical Disability in American Culture and Literature*. New York: Columbia University Press, 1997.

Goffman, Erving. *Stigma: Notes on the Management of Spoiled Identity*. New York: Touchstone Press, 1986.

Goffman, Erving. *The Presentation of Self in Everyday Life*. New York: Anchor Books, 1963.

Gupta, Akhil. 'The Song of the Non-Aligned World: Transnational Identities and the Reinscription of Space in Late Capitalism'. In *The Anthropology of Space and Place: Locating Culture*, edited by Setha M. Low and Denise Lawrence-Zuniga, 321–36. Malden, MA: Blackwell, 2003.

Guttman, Ludwig. 'Sport for the Disabled as a World Problem'. *Rehabilitation* 68 (1969): 29–43.

Haraway, Donna. 'Cyborg Manifesto'. In *The Cultural Studies Reader*, edited by Simon During, 271–91, 2nd edn New York: Routledge, 2000.

Homer. *The Odyssey*. London: Penguin Books, 2003.

ISPT News. *IPST Facts and Figures*. International Paralympic Swim Trials. Thursday, August 17, 1995. Evening session. No 2: 1–2.

Kidd, Bruce. 'A New Social Movement: Sport for Development and Peace'. *Sport in Society* 11, no. 4 (2008): 370–80.

Langlan, Celeste. 'Mobility, Disability'. *Public Culture* 13, no. 3 (2001): 459–484.

Linton, Simi. *Claiming Disability: Knowledge and Identity*. New York: New York University Press, 1998.

Le Clair, Jill. 'High Performance Swimming or Political Correctness'. In *New Horizons in Sport for Athletes with a Disability. Proceedings of the International VISTA '99 Conference, Cologne, Germany*, Vol. 2. edited by Gudrun Doll-Tepper, Michael Kroner, and Wenner Sonnenschein, 465–92. Oxford: Meyer and Meyer Sport, 2001.

Link, Buce G., and Jo C. Phelan. 'Conceptualizing Stigma'. *Annual Review of Sociology* 27 (2001): 363–85.

Low, Setha M., and Denise Lawrence-Zuniga. *The Anthropology of Space and Place: Locating Culture*, 321–36. Malden, MA: Blackwell, 2003.

Mauss, Marcel. 'Techniques du Corps'. *Economy and Society* 2, no. 1 (1974): 70–88.

McDermott, Lisa. 'Toward a Feminist Understanding of Physicality Within the Context of Women's Physically Active and Sporting Lives'. *Sociology of Sport Journal* 1 (1996): 12–31.

Nussbaum, Felicity. 'Feminotopias: The Pleasures of Deformity in Mid-Eighteenth Century England'. In *The Body and Physical Difference: Discourses of Disability*, edited by David T. Mitchell and Sharon L. Snyder, 161–73. Ann Arbor: University of Michigan Press, 1997.

O'Sullivan, John. 'Messy Business'. *National Post*, March 23, 2005, A22.

Pinel, Elizabeth C. 'Stigma Consciousness: The Psychological Legacy of Social Stereotypes'. *Journal of Personality and Social Psychology* 76 (1999): 114–28.

Raphael, Dennis, Toba Bryant, and Marcia Rioux, eds. *Staying Alive: Critical Perspectives on Health, Illness, and Health Care*. Toronto: Canadian Scholars' Press, 2006.

Singer, Judy. '"Why Can't You Be Normal for Once Once in Your Life": From a Problem With No Name to the Emergence of a New Category with a Difference'. In *Disability Discourse*, edited by Mariaan Corker and Sally French, 59–67. Philadelphia: Open University Press, 1999.

Steadward, Robert, and Cynthia Peterson. *Paralympics: Where Heroes Come*. Edmonton, AB: One Shot Publishing, 1997.

Titchkosky, Tanya. *Disability, Self and Society*. Toronto: University of Toronto Press, 2003.

Warner, Rick. 'Stylish, Swift Swimsuits Help Promote Brands'. *National Post*, August 21, 2004, A10.

Wolff, Eli, Mary Hums, Elise Roy. *Sport in the UN Convention on the Rights of Persons with Disabilities*. New York: United Nations Office of Sport for Development & Peace, 2007.

Promoting social inclusion for people with intellectual disabilities through sport: Special Olympics International, global sport initiatives and strategies

Coreen M. Harada[a], Gary N. Siperstein[b], Robin C. Parker[b] and David Lenox[c]

[a]Comprehensive Soldier Fitness – Performance and Resilience Enhancement Program, Arlington, USA; [b]Centre for Social Development and Education, University of Massachusetts, Boston, USA; [c]Special Olympics International, Washington, USA

Little is known of sport in the lives of people with intellectual disabilities, but emerging evidence suggests that it provides the same benefits as for people without disabilities. Historically, people with intellectual disabilities have been on the periphery of society, including learning in separate classrooms, and sport has served as a portal into the mainstream. Since its inception in 1968, Special Olympics has been at the forefront in providing opportunities for sport participation and has grown to serve nearly three million people with intellectual disabilities in over 180 countries. Special Olympics has been an engine of change to provide opportunities for individuals with intellectual disabilities to be visible in society and has actively promoted their inclusion through Unified Sports and Camp Shriver programming. The value of these inclusive programmes is explored in terms of the connection they provide among and between individuals with intellectual disabilities, their families and the surrounding community.

In many ways, sport can be considered the cultural and social link between people of all ages, ethnic and racial backgrounds, and ability levels. Since the time of Ancient Greece, sport has been both a unifying and divisive social experience for both spectators and athletes.[1] In modern times, sport has maintained, if not increased, its important role in society. Through sport, participants can socialize with others, contribute to common team goals, gain mastery in a variety of sport skills, and improve health and well-being.[2]

One of the most exceptional, but less recognized contributions to society by the sport world has been the integration of groups that historically have been marginalized, in particular ethnic minorities and women.[3] The acceptance and inclusion of individuals from these groups as athletes was an arduous process and although the first formal sport opportunities were through separate sport leagues, the fact remains that the sport world has been a leading force for inclusion. Moreover, sport has allowed people of colour and women to take part in a common life experience and compete as equals alongside all other athletes. In keeping with this 'tradition' of sport as a vehicle for inclusion, in recent years there has been a surge in sport opportunities for another group on the margin of society, people with disabilities.[4]

Understanding disability sport

Historically, there have been relatively few programmes providing opportunities for sport participation for athletes with disabilities of any nature. The three most prominent are the International Paralympic Committee (IPC), the International Committee of Sports for the Deaf, and the Special Olympics, all of which are recognized by the International Olympic Committee (IOC). The best known of these disability sport organizations is the IPC, whose Paralympic Games are held in conjunction with the Olympic Games. Started in 1948 at Stoke Mandeville Hospital, this organization evolved into the IPC by 1960. The IPC provides access to sport for people with disabilities such as spinal cord injuries, cerebral palsy, blindness and other physical disabilities, to participate in 12 winter and summer sports at all levels, however, the organization has been most focused on providing athletes with physical disabilities the opportunity to compete at elite levels.

The Paralympic movement received an immense amount of media attention in the USA after the 2005 release of the documentary *Murderball*.[5] This documentary followed the 2004 US Paralympic men's rugby team and won acclaim for its depiction of athletes with physical disabilities as 'real athletes'. The film portrayed the athletes' capabilities as well as their struggles to reach elite levels of competition. Perhaps most importantly, this film signalled a turning point in public awareness of athletes with physical disabilities – seeing them as capable sportsmen and women and just like any other athletes without disabilities.[6]

Sport for people with intellectual disabilities: the Special Olympics Movement

The beginnings of Special Olympics

While there have been opportunities for individuals with intellectual disabilities to participate in elite sport through the IPC,[7] the primary provider of sport programming for these atheletes is Special Olympics. What sets Special Olympics apart is that, whereas the IPC is focused on providing athletes with disabilities the opportunity to compete at elite levels, Special Olympics promotes sport participation for athletes with intellectual disabilities at all levels, regardless of ability. The specific mission of Special Olympics is to

> Provide year-round sports training and athletic competition … for children and adults with intellectual disabilities, giving them continuing opportunities to develop physical fitness, demonstrate courage, experience joy and participate in a sharing of gifts, skills and friendship with their families, other Special Olympics athletes and the community.[8]

Any individual with intellectual disabilities over eight years old is eligible to train and compete in Special Olympics in any of 30 summer and winter Olympic-type sports. Training and competition are focused on demonstrating competence rather than winning, a fact which is emphasized by the athlete oath: 'Let me win. But if I cannot win, let me be brave in the attempt'. A unique feature of Special Olympics is that all athletes, regardless of how they place in an event, are awarded for their efforts.

The idea that individuals with intellectual disabilities could participate and benefit from sport originated in 1968 when the Special Olympics movement was formally established as an international non-profit organization, with the First International Summer Games at Soldier Field in Chicago, Illinois. One thousand athletes with intellectual disabilities from 26 US states and Canada participated in these Games in four sports. Special Olympics was borne out of the desire of Eunice Kennedy Shriver, a well-known advocate for people with intellectual disabilities, to provide such individuals the opportunities to demonstrate their abilities rather than their disabilities, and to be given the opportunity to participate in the normative life experience of sport as enjoyed by individuals without disabilities.

It is important to remember that Special Olympics was founded in the USA amid a climate of segregation. During the 1960s, people with intellectual disabilities were routinely isolated from society; many lived in institutions, there was limited access to education among their peers without disabilities, and few employment opportunities in the community. While the work of early disability advocates yielded government policies and the creation of special education programming, during this time, individuals with intellectual disabilities and their families were likely to be socially isolated in their own neighbourhoods and communities.[9]

For example, during this time, new federal educational policies were put in place that supported teacher training and resources for public schools to implement special education programmes. However, students with intellectual disabilities were routinely educated in segregated classrooms and rarely interacted with their peers without disabilities. Therefore, it is perhaps not surprising that the idea of people with intellectual disabilities participating in sports was completely unheard of during this time, and by default was also unsupported by community sport and recreation programmes. Special Olympics provided for many individuals with intellectual disabilities, their first opportunity to participate in sports.

Just as the educational opportunities for people with intellectual disabilities have progressed, clinical as well as colloquial understanding of intellectual disability has also evolved. Over the last century, there have been 10 revisions to the clinical definition of intellectual disability alone. In addition, the terminology used to describe this population has also changed dramatically over time to reflect this greater understanding. For example, the terminology used to describe the spectrum of impairment within this population has included 'feeble-minded', 'idiot', 'imbecile' and 'moron', although starting in the 1940s advocates pushed for the more neutral term, 'mental retardation'.[10] In 2002, the field began to shift again from 'mental retardation' to the more person-centred term, 'intellectual disability'.[11,12]

The global reach of the Special Olympics movement

Today, Special Olympics serves nearly three million individuals with intellectual disabilities from over 180 countries across the globe. These individuals participate in community- and school-based Special Olympics programmes, organized primarily by volunteers,[13] across seven regions: North America, Latin America, Asia Pacific, East Asia, Middle East/North Africa, Africa and Europe Eurasia (Table 1).

Together, these programmes offer approximately 30,000 competitions annually, ranging from school or community tournaments to regional and worldwide competitions. While this may seem to be an extraordinary number of participants, it is only a fraction of the total number of individuals with intellectual disabilities worldwide which is estimated at 200 million people. However, it is important to consider that there are few statistics that accurately represent the number of people with intellectual disabilities around the world; frequently, any available statistics do not differentiate type of disability.

In countries like the USA, where Special Olympics has been a part of the landscape of programmes available to people with intellectual disabilities for four decades, it is common to find athletes who have been involved for a significant portion of their lives, with many having participated throughout their school years and into adulthood. Conversely, in regions where the development of programmes and policies supporting people with intellectual disabilities has been more recent, such as Asia and Eastern Europe, athletes' participation is more frequently concentrated in the school years. In fact,

Table 1. Special Olympics programmes, organized by region.

Region						
North America	52 US states	Belize	Guam	Cayman Islands	Jamaica	St. Vincent & The Grenadines
	American Samoa	Suriname	Guyana	Trinidad & Tobago	Martinique	US Virgin Islands
	Aruba	Bermuda	Turks & Caicos	Curacao	St. Lucia	St. Kitts & Nevis
	Bahamas	Antigua & Barbuda	Canada	Grenada	Barbados	Guadeloupe
		Bonaire	Caribbean	Dominica	Mexico	Dominican Republic
Latin America	Argentina	El Salvador	Honduras	Ecuador	Paraguay	Venezuela
	Brazil	Bolivia	Panama	Guatemala	Puerto Rico	Cuba
	Costa Rica	Chile	Peru	Uruguay		
Asia Pacific	Afghanistan	Nepal	India	Indonesia	Singapore	New Zealand
	Bangladesh	Pakistan	Timor Leste	Laos	Thailand	Brunei Darusalaam
	Bhutan	Samoa	Australia	Vietnam	Philippines	
	Cambodia	Sri Lanka		Myanmar	Malaysia	
East Asia	China	Hong Kong	Japan	Chinese Taipei	Korea	
			Macao			
Middle East/North Africa	Algeria	Palestine	Jordan	Kuwait	United Arab Emirates	Oman
	Egypt	Saudi Arabia	Lebanon	Libya	Lebanon	Qatar
	Iraq	Syria	Mauritania	Monaco		Sudan
	Bahrain	Iran	Tunisia			
Africa	Benin	Democratic Republic of Congo	Niger	Congo	Lesotho	The Gambia
	Burkina Faso	Kenya	Nigeria	Rwanda	Malawi	Togo
	Botswana	Cote d'Ivoire	Reunion	Senegal	Mali	Uganda
	Cameroon	Namibia	Seychelles	South Africa	Mauritius	Zimbabwe
	Chad		Swaziland	Tanzania		
Europe Eurasia	Albania	Croatia	Gibraltar	Kosovo	Moldova	Slovakia
	Andorra	Cyprus	Great Britain	Kyrgyz Republic	Montenegro	Slovenia
	Armenia	Czech Republic	Greece	Latvia	Netherlands	Spain
	Austria	Denmark	Hungary	Liechtenstein	Norway	Sweden
	Azerbaijan	Estonia	Iceland	Lithuania	Poland	Switzerland
	Belarus	Faroe Islands	Ireland	Luxembourg	Portugal	Tajikistan
	Belgium	Finland	Isle of Man	FYR Macedonia	Romania	Turkey
	Bulgaria	France	Israel	Malta	Russia	Turkmenistan
	Monaco	Georgia	Italy	Bosnia & Herzegovina	San Marino	Ukraine
	Germany	Kazakhstan	Serbia		Uzbekistan	

in countries where children with intellectual disabilities are educated in separate schools, many athletes begin participating in Special Olympics at a young age through programmes in their elementary or middle school.[14]

Criticisms of Special Olympics

Despite its worldwide appeal, criticism of Special Olympics has emerged over the years, particularly among those in the disability field.[15] There are many who believe that Special Olympics is not a 'serious' sport programme and solely exists to provide opportunities for athletes to feel good about themselves by receiving medals and making friends. This is an image that is often perpetuated by the media through stories about volunteer 'huggers' who congratulate athletes at the end of a race. Many also question the segregated nature of traditional Special Olympics events in light of the push for inclusion both in the USA and more recently, around the globe. For example, with regard to the USA in particular, critics believe that Special Olympics operates in contrast to educational initiatives aimed at promoting inclusion by supporting the participation of children with intellectual disabilities in segregated sport programmes.[16] A related criticism of Special Olympics is its virtual monopoly as a provider of sport programming for people with intellectual disabilities. Opponents suggest that the depth and breadth of Special Olympics have allowed, if not encouraged, community sport and recreation providers to avoid serving people with intellectual disabilities without reproach. In fact, there is a dearth of opportunities for recreation and physical activity for people with intellectual disabilities beyond Special Olympics.[17] As a result, much of the knowledge about sport participation for people with intellectual disabilities is anchored in the Special Olympics experience, one that has a great impact on not only the individual with intellectual disabilities, but their families as well.

Understanding the impact of Special Olympics

Impact on the athlete

Numerous studies conducted over the past several decades have revealed that participation in Special Olympics impacts the lives of athletes in many ways. Individuals participating in Special Olympics not only experience improvements in their sport skills, but also in their feelings about themselves (including self-esteem, self-efficacy and self-confidence), and in their social and physical competence.[18] In addition, Special Olympics provides people with intellectual disabilities of all ages with opportunities to develop social relationships with their teammates which often carry over into their lives off the playing field.[19] It is interesting to note that athletes themselves recognize the positive personal benefits of participation in sports as they report similar improvements in their own development.[20]

More recent research has also begun to demonstrate that athletes with intellectual disabilities around the globe are more like athletes without disabilities than might be expected. In fact, a recent series of cross-cultural studies conducted involving large random samples of Special Olympics athletes from across the world have shown that Special Olympics athletes come to sport for the same types of reasons as other athletes, because they enjoy playing sports and want to learn new skills, in addition to their desire to make friends.[21] Many of these athletes are also interested in and capable of participating in rigorous sport training to develop their skills for competition. Moreover, their interests are diverse in that many participate in individual as well as team sports during their time with

Special Olympics. Overall, athletes across the globe often participate in several sports over the course of their involvement in Special Olympics with most athletes participating in at least two sports per year.[22]

Interestingly, most Special Olympics athletes are also involved in leisure-time physical activities (LTPA). Much of the literature on physical activity and health suggests that people with intellectual disabilities are generally sedentary due to a lack of opportunities and support for these activities, and as a result they are physically unfit, much more so than the general population of adults.[23] In the USA, however, Special Olympics athletes are more physically active than the general population, not to mention their peers with intellectual disabilities who do not participate in Special Olympics. While Special Olympics athletes around the world report similar levels of physical activity outside of their participation in Special Olympics, these findings unfortunately cannot be compared to physical activity statistics in their respective countries, as few countries collect this type of data.

Many family members of athletes with intellectual disabilities frequently emphasize the role of Special Olympics in providing their child with an opportunity to develop socially, emotionally and physically through sport, similar to the benefits afforded to athletes without disabilities.[24] Most view Special Olympics as providing the normative life experience of sport participation and camaraderie that are more readily available to individuals without disabilities. It is also important to note that family members from around the world recognize that without Special Olympics, their children would most likely be alone at home,[25] as the types of experiences offered through Special Olympics are not widely available in the community or even through the school.[26] In those countries where individuals with intellectual disabilities and their families are still generally segregated from society, Special Olympics has the opportunity to fill an exceptionally large void in the life of the person with an intellectual disability by providing access to the community through sport.

Impact on the family

The benefits of participation in Special Olympics are not limited to the athlete however, as there are also direct impacts on the family, as parents and siblings are provided the opportunity to see their family member with an intellectual disability in a new way. Studies including families of Special Olympics athletes around the world have demonstrated that family members' perceptions of their children and expectations for their future were significantly more positive after observing their participation in Special Olympics.[27] Specifically, family members report that participation in Special Olympics has improved their understanding of their child's abilities and raised expectations as to what their child with intellectual disabilities can achieve. For example, one family member in Argentina commented that after witnessing her child participate in Special Olympics she '... now believe[s] that everything in life is difficult but not impossible'. Similar sentiments were reported by family members in China, one of whom stated,

> We felt helpless before, because we did not know what his future would be. Since participating in Special Olympics, he [has changed] significantly, and we see the hope. They [people with intellectual disabilities] can merge into society.

Many family members, particularly in countries with newly developed policies supporting individuals with intellectual disabilities, believe that through participation in Special Olympics, their children will become more confident, more competent and come to be accepted by society. Family members also frequently report the positive impact of their child's participation in Special Olympics on their interactions within the family, including sibling relationships, and on their participation in daily life tasks in the home.

It is clear that individuals with intellectual disabilities gain valuable personal benefits as a result of their participation in Special Olympics as do the family members who support them. Moreover, these findings are consistent for athletes around the world, providing evidence to support the notion that the impact of sport participation for people with intellectual disabilities is universal, regardless of where it occurs, and that the value of Special Olympics to the athletes and their families transcends local cultural values about intellectual disability. Just like the women and people of colour who came before them, Special Olympics has provided athletes with intellectual disabilities the opportunity to participate in the common life experience of sport and allowed them the opportunity to demonstrate their abilities and similarities to all athletes; remarkably, however, these similarities are rarely emphasized or even widely known outside the Special Olympics community.

Public attitudes toward people with intellectual disabilities

Unfortunately, the general public in many countries, including the USA, perceive individuals with intellectual disabilities as moderately impaired and able to perform only the simplest of tasks.[28] This image is often perpetuated by the media and other popular culture outlets that depict individuals with intellectual disabilities as objects of pity and as vulnerable.[29] Moreover, in many countries there are varying levels of 'visibility' of people with intellectual disabilities in general, as well as the support and treatment of people with intellectual disabilities within a particular culture. In fact, research suggests that a large percentage of people around the world have had either no contact or only superficial contact with someone with intellectual disabilities. As a result, it is perhaps not surprising public attitudes and perceptions are often negative.[30]

It is these negative perceptions that contribute to the continued exclusion of people with intellectual disabilities from their communities. Although Special Olympics was established to provide opportunities for people with intellectual disabilities to play sports, they are continually working to change attitudes by providing opportunities for the global public to see the similarities between themselves and people with intellectual disabilities through sport. Special Olympics is also striving to provide more opportunities for athletes with intellectual disabilities to demonstrate their abilities to society by promoting their inclusion in their own neighbourhoods and schools.

Innovative approaches to promoting inclusion through Special Olympics

Over the course of the last 40 years, Special Olympics has developed a variety of initiatives and programming for people with intellectual disabilities that are responsive to the critical societal needs for advocacy and inclusion, because it is clear that communities universally have generally struggled to meet the needs of people with intellectual disabilities.[31] For example, Special Olympics has capitalized on opportunities to educate world and community leaders and effect policy change, particularly in developing countries, through innovative programme demonstration projects and public awareness campaigns. The efforts of two regions, China and Latin America, are highlighted here. In addition, three programmes offered through Special Olympics aimed at promoting the inclusion of individuals with intellectual disabilities are also described: the Athlete Leadership Program, Unified Sports, and Camp Shriver.

China

Special Olympics China, in particular, organized by a government agency which supervises educational, vocational and recreational programmes for all people with disabilities (the Chinese Disabled Persons Federation [CDPF], founded in 1988), and currently the largest programme in the world with over 600,000 participants, has played an important role in the development of *Sunshine Homes*, which are supported by the national government. These homes meet the critical needs of adults with intellectual disabilities living in China by providing opportunities to learn job skills, stay physically active and maintain social relationships with others outside their families. While sport through Special Olympics is still important in the daily life of these individuals with intellectual disabilities, it is only one in a spectrum of components designed to improve the life of the person with an intellectual disability.

Latin America

Special Olympics Latin America has developed a relationship with CONMEBOL (South American Football Confederation), which is the governing body and one of the six regional confederations of the International Federation of Association Football (FIFA), to promote the inclusion of athletes with intellectual disabilities at major FIFA-sponsored events, including televising games played by athletes with intellectual disabilities nationally.[32] By capitalizing on the global social value of football, athletes with intellectual disabilities gain opportunities to demonstrate their competence on the playing field to the general public and also to be seen and accepted as members of their communities who share similar interests to those without disabilities.

Athlete Leadership Program

Special Olympics has also developed programming to promote the self-advocacy of individuals with intellectual disabilities through their Athlete Leadership Program. This programme provides athletes around the world with training in public speaking and opportunities to participate in governance in their local Special Olympics programmes, non-profit organizations and communities. For instance, athletes serve as members of their state or national Special Olympics Board of Directors or in community service organizations as advocates for themselves and other people with intellectual disabilities. In addition, many athletes who have participated in the Athlete Leadership Program have chosen to become Special Olympics coaches, allowing them to impart the lessons learned from leadership training to other athletes with intellectual disabilities in their communities. Athletes can also become certified sport officials, providing them with the opportunity to become more involved in their communities through mainstream sports.

Unified Sports

Unified Sports, initially called the Integrated Sports programme, was developed in the early 1980s in the USA to provide youth with and without intellectual disabilities opportunities to interact in meaningful ways, both on and off the playing field. Specifically, Unified Sports provides opportunities for individuals with and without intellectual disabilities of similar age and ability to come together to compete as equals on the playing field. The advent of this programme signalled a shift in the approach to sport for people with intellectual disabilities offered through Special Olympics because it eliminated the hierarchical arrangement that exists in the traditional model of Special Olympics, in which individuals without intellectual disabilities act as coaches, teachers and facilitators for athletes with intellectual disabilities. Unified Sports became an official part of the Special Olympics movement in 1989 although until recently, it was largely limited to US programmes. At present, Unified Sports has expanded in all seven of its regions to include over 150,000 athletes and partners around the world, including countries such as Serbia, Russia and South Africa.

Unified Sports seeks to promote the development of sport skills, teamwork and sportsmanship for all players, in addition to the social acceptance of people with intellectual disabilities among their peers without disabilities by allowing them to witness first-hand their similarities on and off the playing field. Creating opportunities for players with and without intellectual disabilities (called athletes and partners, respectively) with similar sport skills to train regularly, compete alongside one another, and contribute to shared team goals, is seen as a way to break down the barriers that have historically kept individuals with intellectual disabilities isolated from their peers without disabilities. Moreover, all players benefit in a model of equal status, as players see one another as skilled peers and capable contributors to the team, which supports the development of social relationships. This is of particular importance in countries that lack policies supporting the inclusion of students with intellectual disabilities in mainstream schools. In fact, there is considerable variation in inclusive practices worldwide, ranging from full inclusion in the regular classroom, separate classrooms in mainstream schools, completely separate school environments, to in some cases no education at all, despite UNESCO global mandates like *Education For All*.[33] This mandate,[34] along with the UNESCO *Salamanca Statement and Framework for Action on Special Education*,[35] emphasizes not only the importance of providing an education to all children with disabilities, but also the importance of creating inclusive schools.[36]

Despite these efforts, youth with intellectual disabilities remain isolated from their peers without disabilities, perhaps not always physically, but socially. For example even in the USA, where policies and laws have ensured that individuals with intellectual disabilities are included in mainstream schools and classrooms, a recent study showed that youth without disabilities have very little contact with their peers with intellectual disabilities in school and are unwilling to interact with their peers with intellectual disabilities in any type of activity that they would normally do with a friend.[37] A replication of this study with youth in China, although lacking the history of inclusive policy employed in the USA, revealed similar findings.[38] Further and perhaps most noteworthy, fewer than 10% of youth in either country reported having a friend with an intellectual disability.

Special Olympics has sought to promote the social inclusion of children and youth with intellectual disabilities among their peers without disabilities through Unified Sports programming both in the USA and across the globe. Early on, much of what was known about the impact of Unified Sports on participants came from programmes in the USA and many of the benefits to athletes mirror those of traditional Special Olympics programming, including improved sport skills and feelings about themselves. Interestingly, partners also experienced similar personal benefits as well as gaining a better understanding of their peers with intellectual disabilities.[39] More recently, an evaluation was conducted of a school-based Unified Sports football programme in Europe and results suggest that athletes and partners participating in Unified Sports developed themselves as sportsmen/women and formed positive social relationships with one another off the field.[40]

In addition, many partners noted that the social relationships they formed with their peers with intellectual disabilities did not exist before the Unified Sports experience because most attended separate schools. For example, although the participating athletes and partners in Romania attended schools that were in close proximity and sometimes even shared sport facilities, there are virtually no opportunities for the students to interact in ways that allow them to share experiences and learn from one another. Partners also spoke about how their perceptions of their peers with intellectual disabilities had improved, an improvement also noted by coaches and parents, as they now view their peers with intellectual disabilities as skilled athletes, friends and equals on and off the field. Coaches cited several examples of partners who had taken the initiative to ask their peers from the mainstream school to be mindful of the way they treated the students from the special school, as they had become their friends and teammates. It is important to note that, similar to adults, many youth worldwide hold misperceptions as to the capabilities of their peers with intellectual disabilities and quite often hold low expectations for what they can do.[41] However, it is clear that with opportunities to interact on the sport field and work together toward shared goals, youths' understanding and expectations of their peers with intellectual disabilities can be changed for the better.

Taken together, these findings suggest that Unified Sports is a successful venue for providing opportunities for individuals with intellectual disabilities to learn about sport as well as to interact with their peers without intellectual disabilities in meaningful ways. This is especially important in those countries where many of the participating athletes and partners are separated by their educational settings; in many ways, the Unified Sports experience provides the first opportunity for physical inclusion. Special Olympics Europe Eurasia, in particular, has used the Unified Sports programme to demonstrate the possibilities for inclusion among school-aged youth, which has been particularly important for countries that more recently became members of the European Union, like Romania and Poland.[42] The continued expansion of Unified Sports throughout the region using this school-based model has been most recently funded by the Vodafone Foundation, which 'recognizes that sport . . . [is a] vital tool for development for some of the most marginalised and disadvantaged groups in communities around the globe'.[43]

By tying inclusive sport to the educational setting, students can be encouraged to carry over the lessons they learn on the field into their interactions in the classroom. However, the model of Unified Sports is also being embedded into community sport clubs, which provides players with opportunities to apply the lessons learned into their lives as members of the community. These clubs attract players of all ages and abilities to competitive sports, where players are selected for teams based on their skill levels. Teams engage in rigorous training and compete regularly, and the club frequently plays an important role in the community social network. Through opportunities to participate on these club teams, people with intellectual disabilities are recognized for their skills on the field and treated as valued members of their communities off the field. In addition, these Unified Sports club opportunities are available to individuals with and without intellectual disabilities throughout the lifespan, which further supports healthy lifestyles through sport and recreation.

Camp Shriver

In addition to competitive sports through traditional Special Olympics programming, as well as Unified Sports, Special Olympics has also identified opportunities to promote inclusion through the recreational Camp Shriver programme. Established in 1962, Camp Shriver was conceived as a way to provide children with intellectual disabilities the normative life experience of summer camp enjoyed by children without disabilities.

This early camp model served as a catalyst for societal recognition of the interests and needs of people with intellectual disabilities in sport and recreation.[44] It is interesting to note that Camp Shriver's initial success spurred the development of hundreds of camps over the past 40 years for children and youth with not only intellectual disabilities, but other disabilities as well, including Prader–Willi syndrome, Tourette syndrome and autism.

More recently, however, Special Olympics re-examined the Camp Shriver model as an alternative approach to promoting the inclusion and social acceptance of people with intellectual disabilities alongside their peers without intellectual disabilities through recreation. This effort is currently focused within the USA, where summer camp is a well-established normative life experience for children and youth of all ages.[45]

It is important to note that each Camp Shriver site currently approaches inclusion in a way that addresses the diverse needs of their respective communities. A common element, however, is that each Camp Shriver site is recreational in nature and focuses on having fun and teaching sport skills for leisure and physical activity, as opposed to preparing for competition. One site in particular, Camp Shriver at the University of Massachusetts Boston, not only approaches recreational sport using a fully inclusive model, but also strives to promote the inclusion of the children with intellectual disabilities once they return to the classroom through their experiences and interactions in the summer camp environment.

At Camp Shriver Boston, an equal number of young school-aged children with and without intellectual disabilities from the same communities and schools attend summer camp together. Unique to Camp Shriver Boston is this opportunity for children with and without intellectual disabilities to interact outside the classroom setting in a number of recreational non-competitive sport and traditional camp activities as equal status participants. Too often, children with intellectual disabilities are singled out among their peers at school due to the specialized support they receive. In addition, classrooms are often fraught with negative perceptions about the abilities of students with intellectual disabilities due to their cognitive limitations. In fact, research has consistently demonstrated that while students with intellectual disabilities might be physically included in their schools and classrooms, they are not part of the social fabric of these settings.[46] The Camp Shriver Boston model stresses the importance of recognizing similarities among all children regardless of ability, to promote the social inclusion of children with intellectual disabilities. Most importantly, for all children the focus of the camp experience is having fun.

A recent study of children attending Camp Shriver Boston revealed that all children, regardless of disability status, derive a number of benefits as a result of their participation. Not only do most children improve their sport skills while attending camp, but they also develop positive social relationships with their peers; almost all children with and without intellectual disabilities made new friends while at camp.[47] It should be noted that similar to the Unified Sports programme cited above, most children with and without intellectual disabilities came to camp with similar sport skills. As a result, all campers were able to benefit from and participate equally in the same activities. Although this is just one of many Camp Shriver sites, Camp Shriver Boston serves as an example of what is possible when children with and without intellectual disabilities come together in a totally inclusive recreational setting.

Special Olympics plays an important role in the lives of individuals with intellectual disabilities and their families through its work with policymakers across the globe, the opportunities it provides athletes to distinguish themselves in the community and through its inclusive programming. Unified Sports, and more recently Camp Shriver in particular, have demonstrated what is possible when individuals with and without intellectual disabilities are brought together through sport. These programmes have found success in providing a platform for the development of social relationships and recognition of similarities and abilities between individuals with and without intellectual disabilities, thus promoting greater acceptance of individuals with intellectual disabilities among their peers. Moreover, when these opportunities are provided to children and youth the great potential for impacting school communities, inclusive or not, is immeasurable.

It is important to note that Special Olympics is not the only organization that has supported inclusive sport programming (e.g. Little League's Challenger Baseball programme), but rather that the efforts of Special Olympics have been far reaching, particularly on a global and large-scale level. The lessons learned by Special Olympics throughout the development, implementation and expansion of these initiatives can be valuable to schools, community sport and recreation providers, and other disability sport organizations. For example, while it is of vital importance for people with intellectual disabilities to have access to sport and recreation for their physical, social and personal development, it is critical that youth are afforded the opportunity to learn about intellectual disabilities and to engage with their peers with intellectual disabilities such that their similarities are highlighted. These opportunities are particularly meaningful when youth have opportunities to carry the lessons learned on the playing field into their interactions with their peers in the community, the school and the classroom, which is important given that research suggests that children and youth lack opportunities to interact with their peers with intellectual disabilities both in and outside of school. Inclusive sport can fill a void for those with and without intellectual disabilities by providing a venue to learn about one another that is structured as well as meaningful.

Societal implications of Special Olympics

Overall, sport in the life of people with intellectual disabilities can be conceptualized in much the same way as sport for women 35 years ago and for ethnic minorities 60 years ago; it is a common, empowering life experience. As the primary provider of sport opportunities for people with intellectual disabilities across the globe, Special Olympics has afforded athletes with intellectual disabilities in thousands of communities the normative life experience that is afforded to individuals without disabilities. The sport experience offered through Special Olympics is universal and fills a critical need in the lives of people with intellectual disabilities by providing opportunities for physical activity, social interaction, and demonstrating competence to themselves, their families and the community. Aside from the personal benefits that people with intellectual disabilities gain from the experience, seeing their family member with an intellectual disability excel through sport has a notable and positive impact on the family. The importance of Special Olympics is perhaps most salient in those communities where there may be few other services or opportunities for people with intellectual disabilities.

It is critical in the future, however, that individuals with intellectual disabilities have even greater opportunities to experience sport alongside their peers without disabilities as it is clear that sport is a powerful vehicle to promote their inclusion. People with intellectual disabilities are continually seeking opportunities to be included and accepted into the social fabric of their communities. If the opportunity is there, these athletes will seize it. What they are seizing is more than just a chance to play sport, but rather a chance to be a part of society.

Notes

[1] Public Broadcasting System, *The Real Olympics*.

[2] Carron and Hausenblas, *Group Dynamics in Sport*; Donaldson and Ronan, 'The Effects of Sport', 369–389; Hedstrom and Gould, *Research in Youth Sports*; Smith and Smoll, 'Youth Sports', 341–372; Ståhl *et al.*, 'The Importance of Social Environment', 1–10.

[3] Cockcroft, *Latinos in Béisbol*; Elling and Knoppers, 'Sport, Gender and Ethnicity', 257–268; Lumpkin, Stoll, and Beller, *Sport Ethics*; Rampersad, *Jackie Robinson*; Rappoport, *Ladies First*; Roberts, *A Necessary Spectacle*; Toohey and Veal, *The Olympic Games*.

[4] International Paralympic Committee, *History of Sport* (http://www.paralympic.org/release/Main_Sections_Menu/IPC/About_the_IPC/History_of_Sport_for_Persons_with_a_Disability/); International Sport Federation for Persons with Intellectual Disability, *About INAS-FID* (http://www.inas-fid.org/aboutinas.html); Special Olympics, *Who We Are* (http://www.specialolympics.org/Who_We_Are.aspx).

[5] Rubin and Shapiro, *Murderball*.

[6] McGrath, 'A Film's Stars'. http://www.nytimes.com/2005/03/26/movies/26murd.html?ex=1174881600&en=938d33f830ebb797&ei=5070.

[7] These opportunities through the INAS-FID/IPC have been suspended since the Sydney Paralympic Games in 2000 and are currently under review.

[8] Special Olympics, *Mission Statement* http://www.specialolympics.org/content.aspx?id=6186&terms=mission.

[9] Bentley, 'Lessons from the 1%', 543–561; Matthews, 'Teaching the "Invisible"', 229–239; Roulstone, 'Disability, Dependency', 427–443.

[10] Goode, 'Mental Retardation is Dead', 57–59; Switzky and Greenspan, *What is Mental Retardation*.

[11] Danforth, 'New Words', 51–55; Goode, 'Mental Retardation is Dead', 57–59; Schalock, 'What's in a Name?' 59–61; Turnbull *et al.*, 'Shakespeare Redux', 65–70; Walsh, 'Changing Mental Retardation', 70–75.

[12] AAIDD, *Definition of Intellectual Disability*, http://www.aaidd.org/intellectualdisabilitybook/content_2348.cfm?navID=267. The current definition of intellectual disability, according to the American Association on Intellectual and Developmental Disabilities, is 'characterized by significant limitations both in intellectual functioning and in adaptive behavior [and] originates before the age of 18'. One criterion is IQ; another equally important criterion is adaptive behaviour, which includes conceptual, social and practical skills. This definition is accepted as a standard among the international community. As a result of the continual changes within the intellectual disability community there is a range of terminology used throughout scholarly publications.

[13] Special Olympics, *Reach Report 2007*.

[14] Harada, Parker, and Siperstein, *Comprehensive National Study of Special Olympics Programs in China; Comprehensive National Study of Special Olympics Programs in Latin America*; Norins Bardon, Harada, and Parker, 'Evaluation of the Special Olympics Europe/Eurasia Unified Football'.

[15] Storey, 'The More Things Change'.

[16] Hourcade, 'Special Olympics,' 58–65; Orelove, Wehman, and Wood, 'An Evaluative Review of Special Olympics', 325–329; Porretta, Gillespie, and Jansma, 'Perceptions about Special Olympics', 44–54; Storey, 'Case Against Special Olympics', 35–42; Wolfensberger, 'Normalization, Lifestyles, Special Olympics', 128–131.

[17] Buttimer and Tierney, 'Patterns of Leisure Participation', 25–42; Dattilo and Schlein, 'Understanding Leisure Services', 53–59.

[18] Frith, Mitchell, and Roswal, 'Recreation for Mildly Retarded', 199–203; Krebs and Block, 'Transition of Students with Disabilities', 305–315; Orelove, Wehman, and Wood, 'An Evaluative Review of Special Olympics', 325–329; Sallis *et al.*, 'Determinants of Physical Activity', 248–257; Sherrill and Williams, 'Disability and Sport', 42–64.

[19] Farrell *et al.*, 'The Driving Force', 153–166; Shapiro, 'Participation Motives', 150–165.

[20] Gibbons and Bushakra, 'Effects of Special Olympics', 40–51.

[21] Feltz and Ewing, 'Psychological Characteristics', 98–105; Gill, Gross, and Huddleston, 'Participation Motivation', 1–14; Gould, Feltz, and Weiss, 'Motives for Participating in Competitive Youth Swimming', 126–140; Harada, Parker, and Siperstein, *Comprehensive National Study of Special Olympics Programs in China; Comprehensive National Study of Special Olympics Programs in Latin America*; Harada and Siperstein, 'The Sport Experience',

68–85; Siperstein, *et al.*, *Comprehensive National Study of Special Olympics Programs in the United States. A Special Report.*

22 Athletes begin their participation in SO through a programme in their school or through a community organization supporting individuals with ID.

23 Draheim, Williams, and McCubbin, 'Prevalence of Physical Inactivity', 436–444; Rimmer, Braddock, and Marks, 'Health Characteristics and Behaviors', 489–499; U.S. Center for Disease Control and Prevention (CDC), *Physical Activity for Everyone*; U.S. Department of Health and Human Services (USDHHS), *Physical Activity and Health.*

24 Dykens and Cohen, 'Effects of Special Olympics', 223–239; Weiss *et al.*, 'Involvement in Special Olympics', 281–305.

25 Kersh and Siperstein, *Positive of Special Olympics.*

26 Buttimer and Tierney, 'Patterns of Leisure Participation', 25–42; Dattilo and Schlein, 'Understanding Leisure Services', 53–59; Sparrow, Shinkfield, and Karnilowicz, 'Constraints on Participation in Mainstream Recreation', 403–11; Stanish, Temple, and Frey, 'Health-Promoting Physical Activity', 13–21; Temple and Walkley, 'Physical Activity of Adults with Intellectual Disability', 342–52.

27 Harada, Parker, and Siperstein, *Comprehensive National Study of Special Olympics Programs in China; Comprehensive National Study of Special Olympics Programs in Latin America*; Kersh and Siperstein, *Positive Contributions of Special Olympics*; Siperstein, Parker, and Norins Bardon, *Attitudes of Special Olympics Family Members.*

28 Siperstein *et al.*, *Multinational Study of Attitudes.*

29 Pardun, Corbin, and Engstrom, 'Media's Portrayal of People with Intellectual Disabilities'.

30 Norins Bardon, Siperstein, and Xiong, 'National Study of Chinese Youth Attitudes'; Siperstein Norins *et al.*, *Multinational Study of Attitudes*; Siperstein, Parker *et al.*, 'National Study of Youth Attitudes Toward Inclusion', 435–455.

31 McLean, 'Special Olympics'.

32 Olimpiadas Especiales América Latina, 'Fútbol de Olimpiadas Especiales', http://info.specialolympics. org/Special+Olympics+Public+Website/Spanish/Noticias/Noticias_de_Olimpiadas_Especiales/ Sudamericano+de+Futbol.htm.

33 UNESCO, *World Declaration on Education for All*, http://www.unesco.org/education/efa/ ed_for_a;;/background?jomtien_declaration.shtml.

34 The UNESCO *Education for All* mandate emphasizes the importance of providing an education to all children with disabilities.

35 UNESCO, *Salamanca Statement on Principles, Policy and Practice in Special Needs Education* emphasizes creating inclusive schools which '...celebrate differences, support learning, and respond to individual needs'.

36 UNESCO, *Salamanca Statement*, http://www.unesco.org/education/pdf/SALAMA_E.PDF.

37 Siperstein, Parker *et al.*, 'National Study of Youth Attitudes Toward the Inclusion', 435–455.

38 Norins Bardon, Siperstein, and Xiong, 'Chinese Youth Attitudes'; Siperstein, Parker *et al.*, 'National Study of Chinese Youth Attitudes'.

39 Siperstein, Hardman, Wappett, and Clary, 'National Evaluation of Unified Sports'.

40 Norins Bardon, Harada, and Parker, 'Evaluation of the Special Olympics Europe/Eurasia Unified Football'.

41 Norins Bardon, Siperstein, and Xiong, 'Chinese Youth Attitudes'; Siperstein, Parker *et al.*, 'National Study of Youth Attitudes Toward Inclusion', 435–55.

42 Poland's joined the EU in 2004 and Romania became a member in 2007, the year after the evaluation of the pilot project was completed. However, in both of these locations the Unified Football programme was important in demonstrating each country's efforts to promote inclusion among youth.

43 Vodafone Foundation, 'Sport and Music', http://www.vodafone.com/start/foundation/news/ the_vodafone_group1.html.

44 Special Olympics, History, http://www.specialolympics.org/history.aspx.

45 In addition, Camp Shriver has recently been expanded to include camps in Kazakhstan and India.

46 Heiman, 'Friendship Quality Among Children', 1–12; Siperstein, Leffert, and Widaman, 'Social Behavior and the Social Acceptance and Rejection', 271–281; Siperstein and Parker, 'Toward an Understanding of Social Integration', 119–124.

47 Siperstein, Glick, and Parker, 'The Social Inclusion of Children'.

References

American Association on Intellectual and Developmental Disabilities (AAIDD). *Definition of Intellectual Disability*. Washington, DC: AAIDD, 2010.

Australian Institute of Sport. *National Talent Search Program*. Bruce: Australian Institute of Sport.

Bentley, Judy K. 'Lessons from the 1%: Children with Labels of Severe Disabilities and Their Peers as Architects of Inclusive Education'. *International Journal of Inclusive Education* 12 (2008): 543–61.

Buttimer, John, and Edel Tierney. 'Patterns of Leisure Participation Among Adolescents with a Mild Intellectual Disability'. *Journal of Intellectual Disabilities* 9 (2005): 25–42.

Carron, Albert V., and Heather A. Hausenblas. *Group Dynamics in Sport*. 2nd edn. Morgantown, WV: Fitness Information Technology, 1998.

Cockcroft, James D. *Latinos in Béisbol*. New York: Franklin Watts, 1996.

Danforth, Scot. 'New Words for New Purposes: A Challenge for the AAMR'. *Mental Retardation* 40 (2002): 51–5.

Dattilo, John, and Stuart J. Schlein. 'Understanding Leisure Services for Individuals with Mental Retardation'. *Mental Retardation* 32 (1994): 53–9.

Donaldson, S.J., and K.R. Ronan. 'The Effects of Sport Participation on Young Adolescents' Emotional Well-Being'. *Adolescence* 41 (2006): 369–89.

Draheim, Christopher C., Daniel P. Williams, and Jeffrey A. McCubbin. 'Prevalence of Physical Inactivity and Recommended Physical Activity in Community-Based Adults with Mental Retardation'. *Mental Retardation* 40 (2002): 436–44.

Dykens, Elizabeth M., and Donald J. Cohen. 'Effects of Special Olympics International on Social Competence in Persons with Mental Retardation'. *Journal of the American Academy of Child and Adolescent Psychiatry* 35 (1996): 223–9.

Elling, Agnes, and Annelise Knoppers. 'Sport, Gender and Ethnicity: Practices of Symbolic Inclusion/Exclusion'. *Journal of Youth and Adolescence* 34 (2005): 257–68.

Farrell, Robin J., Peter R.E. Crocker, Meghan H. McDonough, and Whitney A. Sedgwick. 'The Driving Force: Motivation in Special Olympians'. *Adapted Physical Activity Quarterly* 21 (2004): 153–66.

Feltz, Deborah, and Martha Ewing. 'Psychological Characteristics of Elite Young Athletes'. *Medicine and Science in Sport and Exercise* 19 (1987): 98–105.

Frith, G.H., J.W. Mitchell, and Glenn Roswal. 'Recreation for Mildly Retarded Students: An Important Component of Individualized Education Plans'. *Education and Training of the Mentally Retarded* 13 (1980): 199–203.

Gibbons, Sandra L., and Frank B. Bushakra. 'Effects of Special Olympics Participation on the Perceived Competence and Social Acceptance of Mentally Retarded Children'. *Adapted Physical Activity Quarterly* 6 (1989): 40–51.

Gill, Diane L., John B. Gross, and Sharon Huddleston. 'Participation Motivation in Youth Sports'. *International Journal of Sport Psychology* 14 (1983): 1–14.

Goode, David. 'Mental Retardation is Dead: Long Live Mental Retardation!'. *Mental Retardation* 40 (2002): 57–9.

Gould, Daniel, Deborah Feltz, and Maureen Weiss. 'Motives for Participating in Competitive Youth Swimming'. *International Journal of Sport Psychology* 16 (1985): 126–40.

Harada, Coreen M., Robin C. Parker, and Gary N. Siperstein. *Comprehensive National Study of Special Olympics Programs in China*. Boston: University of Massachusetts, Centre for Social Development and Education, 2008.

Harada, Coreen M., and Gary N. Siperstein. 'The Sport Experience of Athletes with Intellectual Disabilities: A National Survey of Special Olympics Athletes and Their Families'. *Adapted Physical Activity Quarterly* 26 (2009): 68–85.

Harada, Coreen M., Robin C. Parker, and Gary N. Siperstein. *A Comprehensive Study of Special Olympics Programs in Latin America: Findings from Argentina, Brazil, and Peru*. Boston: University of Massachusetts, Centre for Social Development and Education, 2008.

Hedstrom, Ryan, and Daniel Gould. *Research in Youth Sports: Critical Issues Status: White Paper Summaries of the Existing Literature*. East Lansing: Michigan State University, Institute for the Study of Youth Sports, 2004.

Heiman, Tali. 'Friendship Quality Among Children in Three Educational Settings'. *Journal of Intellectual and Developmental Disabilities* 25 (2000): 1–12.

Hourcade, Jack Joseph. 'Special Olympics: A Review and Critical Analysis'. *Therapeutic Recreation Journal* 23 (1989): 58–65.

International Paralympic Committee. *History of Sport for Persons with a Disability*. Bonn, Germany: International Paralympic Committee, 2010.

International Sport Federation for Persons with Intellectual Disability (INAS-FID). *About INAS-FID*. Wakefield, UK: Mencap, 2010.

Kersh, Joanne, and Gary.N. Siperstein. *The Positive Contributions of Special Olympics to the Family*. Boston: University of Massachusetts, Centre for Social Development and Education, 2008.

Krebs, P.L., and Martin E. Block. 'Transition of Students with Disabilities into Community Recreation: The Role of the Adapted Physical Educator'. *Adapted Physical Activity Quarterly* 9 (1992): 305–15.

Lumpkin, Angela, Sharon Stoll, and Jennifer Beller. *Sport Ethics: Applications for Fair Play*. 3rd edn. Boston: McGraw Hill, 2003.

Matthews, Nicole. 'Teaching the "Invisible" Disabled Students in the Classroom: Disclosure, Inclusion and the Social Model of Disability'. *Teaching in Higher Education* 14 (2009): 229–39.

McGrath, Charles. 'A Film's Stars are Tough Athletes. They are also Paraplegics'. *New York Times*, March 26, 2005.

McLean, William. 'Special Olympics: The Rest of the Story'. *Research and Practice for Persons with Severe Disabilities* (forthcoming).

Norins Bardon, Jennifer, Coreen M. Harada, and Robin C. Parker. *Evaluation of the Special Olympics Europe/Eurasia Unified Football Pilot-Project: Findings from Austria, Poland, Romania, Serbia and Slovakia. Final Report for Special Olympics, Inc.* Boston: University of Massachusetts, Centre for Social Development and Education, 2008.

Norins Bardon, Jennifer, Gary N. Siperstein, and Yang Xiong. *National Study of Chinese Youth Attitudes toward Students with Intellectual Disabilities. Final Report for Special Olympics, Inc.* Boston: University of Massachusetts, Centre for Social Development and Education, 2008.

Olimpiadas Especiales América Latina. 'Sudamericano de Fútbol de Olimpiadas Especiales en Venezuela'. Washington: Special Olympics Inc.

Orelove, F.P., Paul Wehman, and J. Wood. 'An Evaluative Review of Special Olympics: Implications for Community Integration'. *Education and Training of the Mentally Retarded* 17 (1982): 325–9.

Pardun, Carol, Stephen Corbin, and Karen Engstrom. *Media's Portrayal of People with Intellectual Disabilities. Final Report for Special Olympics, Inc.* Columbia, SC: University of South Carolina, 2005.

Porretta, David L., Michael Gillespie, and Paul Jansma. 'Perceptions about Special Olympics from Service Delivery Groups in the United States: A Preliminary Investigation'. *Education and Training in Mental Retardation and Developmental Disabilities* 31 (1996): 44–54.

Public Broadcasting System. *The Real Olympics: A History of the Ancient and Modern Olympic Games*, DVD. Produced by Public Broadcasting System. Arlington, VA: Public Broadcasting System, 2004.

Rampersad, Arnold. *Jackie Robinson: A Biography*. New York: Ballantine, 1997.

Rappoport, Ken. *Ladies First: Women Athletes Who Made a Difference*. Atlanta: Peachtree, 2005.

Rimmer, James H., David Braddock, and Beth Marks. 'Health Characteristics and Behaviors of Adults with Mental Retardation Residing in Three Living Arrangements'. *Research in Developmental Disabilities* 16 (1995): 489–499.

Roberts, Selena. *A Necessary Spectacle: Billie Jean King, Bobby Riggs, and the Tennis Match that Levelled the Game*. New York: Crown Publishing, 2005.

Roulstone, Alan. 'Disability, Dependency, and the New Deal for Disabled People'. *Disability and Society* 15 (2000): 427–43.

Rubin, Henry.A., and Dana A. Shapiro. *Murderball*. DVD. Directed by Henry A. Rubin and Dana A. Shapiro. New York: A&E Indie Films, 2005.

Sallis, James F., Bruce G. Simons-Morton, Elaine J. Stone, Charles B. Corbin, Leonard H. Epstein, Nell Faucette, Ronald J. Iannotti, Joel D. Killen, Robert C. Klesges, Clayre K. Petray, Thomas W. Rowland, and Wendell C. Taylor. 'Determinants of Physical Activity and Interventions in Youth'. *Medicine and Science in Sports and Exercise* 24 (1992): 248–57.

Schalock, Robert L. 'What's in a Name?'. *Mental Retardation* 40 (2002): 59–61.

Shapiro, Deborah R. 'Participation Motives of Special Olympics Athletes'. *Adapted Physical Activity Quarterly* 20 (2003): 150–65.

Sherrill, Claudine, and Tennessee Williams. 'Disability and Sport: Psychosocial Perspectives on Inclusion, Integration, and Participation'. *Sport Science Review* 5 (1996): 42–64.

Siperstein, Gary N., and Robin C. Parker. 'Toward an Understanding of Social Integration: A Special Issue'. *Exceptionality* 16 (2008): 119–24.

Siperstein, Gary N., Gary C. Glick, and Robin C. Parker. 'The Social Inclusion of Children with Intellectual Disabilities in a Recreational Setting'. *Intellectual and Developmental Disabilities* 47, no. 2 (2009): 97–107.

Siperstein, Gary N., Coreen M. Harada, Robin C. Parker, Michael L. Hardman, and Jayne McGuire. *Comprehensive National Study of Special Olympics Programs in the United States. A Special Report.* Boston: University of Massachusetts Boston, 2005.

Siperstein, Gary N., Michael Hardman, Matthew Wappett, and Laura Clary. *National Evaluation of the Special Olympics Unified Sports Program: A Special Report.* Boston: University of Massachusetts Boston, 2001.

Siperstein, Gary N., James S. Leffert, and Keith F. Widaman. 'Social Behavior and the Social Acceptance and Rejection of Children with Mental Retardation'. *Education and Training in Mental Retardation and Developmental Disabilities* 31 (1996): 271–81.

Siperstein, Gary, Jennifer Norins, Stephen Corbin, and Timothy Shriver. *Multinational Study of Attitudes Toward Individuals with Intellectual Disabilities.* Washington, DC: Special Olympics Inc, 2003.

Siperstein, Gary N., Robin C. Parker, and Jennifer Norins Bardon. *Attitudes of Special Olympics Family Members in the United States, Japan, and China.* Boston: University of Massachusetts Boston, 2005.

Siperstein, Gary N., Robin C. Parker, Jennifer Norins Bardon, and Keith F. Widaman. 'A National Study of Youth Attitudes toward the Inclusion of Students with Intellectual Disabilities'. *Exceptional Children* 73 (2007): 435–55.

Siperstein, Gary N., Robin C. Parker, Jennifer Norins, and Keith F. Widaman. 'A National Study of Chinese Youth Attitudes toward Students with Intellectual Disabilities'. Unpublished, University of Massachusetts Boston.

Smith, Ronald E., and Frank L. Smoll. 'Youth Sports as a Behaviour Setting for Psychosocial Interventions'. In *Exploring Sport and Exercise Psychology*, edited by Judy L. Van Raalte and Britton W. Brewer, 341–72. Washington, DC: American Psychological Association, 2002.

Sparrow, William A., Anthony J. Shinkfield, and W. Karnilowicz. 'Constraints on the Participation of Individuals with Mental Retardation in Mainstream Recreation'. *Mental Retardation* 31 (1993): 403–11.

Special Olympics. *Reach Report 2007.* Washington, DC: Special Olympics Inc., 2007.

Special Olympics. *History of Special Olympics.* Washington, DC: Special Olympics Inc., 2010.

Special Olympics. *Mission Statement.* Washington, DC: Special Olympics Inc., 2010.

Special Olympics. *Who We Are.* Washington, DC: Special Olympics Inc., 2010.

Ståhl, Timo, Alfred Rütten, Don Nutbeam, Adrian Bauman, Lasse Kannas, Thomas Abel, Gunther Luschen, Diaz J.A. Rodriguez, Jan Vink, and Jouke van der Zee. 'The Importance of the Social Environment for Physically Active Lifestyle: Results from an International Study'. *Social Science & Medicine* 52 (2001): 1–10.

Stanish, Heidi I., Viviene A. Temple, and Georgia C. Frey. 'Health-Promoting Physical Activity of Adults with Mental Retardation'. *Mental Retardation and Developmental Disabilities Research Reviews* 12 (2006): 13–21.

Storey, Keith. 'The Case Against Special Olympics'. *Journal of Disability Policy Studies* 15 (2004): 35–42.

Storey, Keith. 'The More Things Change, The More They are the Same: Continuing Concerns with the Special Olympics'. *Research and Practice for Persons with Severe Disabilities*, (forthcoming).

Switzky, Harvey N. and Greenspan, Stephen, eds. *What is Mental Retardation: Ideas for an Evolving Disability in the 21st Century.* Washington, DC: American Association of Mental Retardation, 2006.

Temple, Viviene A., and Jeff W. Walkley. 'Physical Activity of Adults with Intellectual Disability'. *Journal of Intellectual & Developmental Disability* 28 (2003): 342–52.

Toohey, Kristine, and A.J. Veal. *The Olympic Games: A Social Science Perspective*. New York: CABI, 2000.

Turnbull, Rud, Ann Turnbull, Steve Warren, Steve Eidelman, and Paul Marchand. 'Shakespeare Redux, or Romeo and Juliet Revisited: Embedding a Terminology and Name Change in a New Agenda for the Field of Mental Retardation'. *Mental Retardation* 40 (2002): 65–70.

United Nations Educational, Scientific and Cultural Organization (UNESCO). *The World Declaration on Education for All 1990*. Paris: UNESCO, 1990.

United Nations Educational, Scientific and Cultural Organization (UNESCO). *The Salamanca Statement on Principles, Policy and Practice in Special Needs Education*. Paris: UNESCO, 1994.

U.S. Centre for Disease Control and Prevention (CDC). *Physical Activity for Everyone: Recommendations*. Atlanta, GA: CDC, 2005.

U.S. Department of Health and Human Services (USDHHS). *Physical Activity and Health: A Report of the Surgeon General*. Atlanta, GA: USDHHS, 1996.

Vodafone Foundation. *The Vodafone Group Foundation Makes Commitment to Support Special Olympics Unified Sports® Projects*. Berkshire: Vodafone Group Foundation, 2008.

Walsh, Kevin K. 'Thoughts on Changing the Term Mental Retardation'. *Mental Retardation* 40 (2002): 70–5.

Weiss, Jonathan, Terry Diamond, Jenny Demark, and Benedicte Lovald. 'Involvement in Special Olympics and its Relations to Self-Concept and Actual Competency in Participants with Developmental Disabilities'. *Research in Developmental Disabilities* 24 (2003): 281–305.

Wolfensberger, Wolf. 'Of Normalization, Lifestyles, the Special Olympics, Deinstitutionalization, Mainstreaming, Integration, and Cabbages and Kings'. *Mental Retardation* 33 (1995): 128–31.

Deaflympics and the Paralympics: eradicating misconceptions

Donalda Ammons[a] and Jordan Eickman[b]

[a]International Committee of Sports for the Deaf (former President) and Gallaudet University (Professor Emerita), Washington D.C, USA; [b]California State University, Northridge, California, USA

This article adds to the limited literature about the world of Deaf sport. It argues that deafness is not viewed within the Deaf community as a disability, and highlights the importance of Deaf culture and the shared meaning of being Deaf. The article then goes on to look at the debates around the Deaflympics, and the important role that this independent competition can play for Deaf athletes. The article addresses the problems that arise when it is argued that Deaf athletes, and thus the Deaflympics and national Deaf sport organizations, should be assimilated into the Paralympic Games under the umbrella of disability sport. This position has severely affected many national Deaf sports organizations and their ability to develop and fund their Deaflympics athletes. The history of the relationships between the Deaflympics and the Paralympics, and the International Committee of Sports for the Deaf and the International Paralympic Committee are also discussed.

Being Deaf, Deaf culture and the Deaflympics

The words Deaf and deaf have important and different meanings for the Deaf community, but the subtle distinction between the two is often not understood by society at large. 'Deaf' with a capital D is used to signify to signify deaf people who are primarily sign language users, members of the Deaf community, and share Deaf culture and common experiences. By the same token, the authors and others use 'deaf' to indicate the general population of deaf people (people who have hearing loss).[1] This distinction between a sociocultural understanding of Deaf people and a medicalized understanding of the condition of deafness is crucial for any analysis of what it means to be Deaf.

Deaf people see themselves as part of a linguistic and oppressed, cultural minority with its own culture, who often face prejudice, stigma and discrimination like other minority groups, even though deafness often appears to be invisible. Sport functions as an important social and psychological institution for identity and valorizations and that is why the independence of the Deaflympics is important for Deaf people in many different countries. Unlike in the so-called disability sports, the very specific cultural, community and identity issues at play here are a key component that motivates Deaf athletes' desire to maintain their own international sport events where their needs and aspirations can be met.

This article addresses the widely held position that Deaf athletes (and thus the Deaflympics and national Deaf sport organizations) should be assimilated into the Paralympic Games under the umbrella of disability sport. We argue that this demonstrates a profound misunderstanding as to what it means to be Deaf.[2] This misconception has severely affected many national Deaf sports organizations and their ability to develop and fund their Deaflympics athletes. In order to understand how this situation arose, the history of the relationships between the Deaflympics and the Paralympic Games, and the International Committee of Sports for the Deaf (ICSD) and the International Paralympic Committee (IPC) must also be examined.[3]

Being deaf is not a disability: Deaf culture, sport and communication in signed languages

Deaf people have always found a way to find each other and share their commonality and, in particular, their need for visual communication through sign language. The first free school for deaf children was established in Paris in the 1760s.[4] Deaf people began congregating in more formal situations, primarily for social and cultural reasons. Most Deaf people were (and still are) born into hearing families. They have experienced difficulties with communication and especially the misunderstanding of how deafness affects the ability to participate in society. This, in turn, has led to negative stereotypical attitudes towards Deaf people. When the first Deaflympics occurred, 'society viewed deaf people as intellectually inferior and linguistically impoverished beings'.[5] In recent years, there has been an increased interest in the global battle for Deaf human rights, as it has become clear that Deaf people have reduced access to education, government services and what equates to equal citizenship, based on their deafness alone. A significant reason for this, it has been found, is the lack of recognition of sign language and the associated translation services that are needed to allow Deaf people access to large sections of society.[6] These problems can also be seen in the context of Deaf sport.

Jerald Jordan, CISS President [CISS was renamed as the International Committee of Sports for the Deaf (ICSD)] from 1971 to 1995, argues that the central aspect for Deaf athletes is not sport, but that they are Deaf, and that being Deaf is the most important aspect of their identity: 'Deaf people do not consider themselves disabled, particularly in physical ability. Rather, we consider ourselves to be part of a cultural and linguistic minority'.[7]

He goes on to explain the importance of communication to Deaf people in the context of sports. The fact that Deaf people use sign language to communicate is a central aspect to their identity and Deaf culture. Mixing hearing and deaf people at sports events changes the event's very nature:

> The Deaf athlete views the disabled athlete as being a hearing person first and disabled second (italics added). When athletes congregate at the Paralympics, or when hearing and Deaf people congregate at any event, the hearing people, regardless of physical limitations, are able to communicate freely with each other as long as they have a common language. The Deaf athlete, however, is always excluded from the group. On the other hand, at the Deaf Games, or any other event at which Deaf people meet, Deaf athletes can usually communicate other Deaf athletes, regardless of which country they may be representing. In the Deaf Games, athletes are able to compete and interact with others freely and without sign language interpreters, except where hearing officials are involved. If Deaf athletes were to compete in the Paralympic Games, then numerous sign language interpreters would be necessary to bridge this communication barrier, otherwise the Deaf athletes would be completely separated from all disabled athletes. The very purpose of the Games – *to bring athletes together* – would be lost.

> ... As a group, Deaf people do not fit into either the able-bodied or disabled categories. It has been the oft-repeated experience of the Deaf community that our unique needs are lost when we are lumped into either category. Our limits are not physical; rather, they are outside of us, in the social realm of communication. Among hearing people, whether able-bodied or disabled, we are almost always excluded, invisible and unserved. Among ourselves however, we have no limits.[8]

In other words, a Deaf person in a setting full of non-signing hearing people would not have the same access to communication, conversations and information, and the same opportunity to socialize, make friends and have cultural exchanges through direct communication (in the Deaf person's case, via a signed language) as a hearing person in the same setting would. Likewise, a non-signing hearing person in a setting full of signing Deaf people would lack the same opportunities.

For Deaf people, information must be presented visually and communication must take place using a visual language, in contrast to hearing people for whom information and communication usually take place through a spoken language modality. For many in the Deaf community this has become a human rights issue, arguing that Deaf people have the equal right to information and communication opportunities as hearing people do.

In the past, many deaf children were placed in residential schools for deaf children, which impacted on their sport experience as well, and the deaf school experience was particularly important for them. Lane, Hoffmeister, and Bahan explain:

> Sports are one of the powerful bonding forces in the DEAF-WORLD. The love of individual and team sports is nurtured in the residential schools and whetted by rivalry among schools. Sports rapidly become a vehicle of acculturation for the Deaf child, a shared experience, a source of Deaf pride, and an avenue for understanding customs and values in the DEAF-WORLD ... However, sports frequently play a particularly important role in the lives of minorities, for they open a path to achievement and distinction where many others are closed by prejudice. In the DEAF-WORLD, moreover, athletics provide a level playing field when it comes to language ... Some Deaf people attend athletic tournaments to play, of course, but they and many more are there for another reason: to be with other members of the DEAF-WORLD (frequently impossible during the work day) and to see old friends who have become separated after graduation or marriage or a move to a new job.[9]

American Sign Language (ASL) for Americans is a national language so Deaf people are able to meet and communicate as a language minority group at sport events. Lane et al. elaborate further:

> Athletics in Deaf culture also serve linguistic and political functions. ASL is a *truly national language*, in part because of the co-mingling of Deaf people in the residential schools, in the clubs and in regional and national athletics. And athletic programs provide an opportunity for Deaf managers, so often disempowered in the larger society, to further their leadership abilities, to show what they can do, and to broker a certain amount of power in the DEAF-WORLD ... The DEAF-WORLD sees itself as a language minority, not a disability group ... With athletics organized formally in Deaf schools and clubs and at local, regional, national and international levels, and given the role of athletics in social life, leadership training, and cultural bonding, Deaf sports are clearly a major institution in the DEAF-WORLD.[10]

It is important to understand that signed languages are different from spoken languages. For example, ASL is different from English, and not just 'English conveyed through signs' or 'a manual code for English'. Signed languages are not based on sounds. For example, 'ASL signs have five [parameters, or components] — handshape, movement, location, orientation and non-manual signals (facial expression)'.[11]

Sign language is not universal. Signed languages differ from each other and furthermore have dialects, 'complex rules of grammar', large vocabularies, and can be used for 'everyday conversation, intellectual discourse, rhetoric, wit and poetry'.[12] Also, it is possible that in different countries where the spoken and written language, for the layman's purposes, are virtually identical (i.e. English in the UK and the USA), the signed languages in each country are very different from each other (British Sign Language and ASL). Lane *et al.* explain when Deaf people from different countries congregate, 'a contact language known as *International Sign*' is used, 'allowing speakers of mutually unintelligible signed languages to communicate'.[13]

Deaf sports history

Organized Deaf sport began in the late nineteenth century. Through the emergence of Deaf societies, church groups, reading clubs and so forth, Deaf sport clubs sprouted. The Ohio School for the Deaf had baseball and rugby teams circa 1870. The earliest known and established adult Deaf sport club is the Glasgow Deaf and Dumb Football Club (Scotland), set up by 1872. The six earliest adult Deaf sport clubs were found in Britain. Thus they developed pretty much in parallel to sports clubs for the hearing. By 1915, other clubs had appeared, mostly in Western Europe and Australia. In Europe, due to geographical proximity, local sporting clubs began to play 'friendlies' across national borders. A Scotland–England football match at Glasgow on March 28, 1891 is the earliest known full Deaf international match in any sport between two nations, a mere 19 years after the first Scotland–England match among the hearing teams. Germany's Deutscher Gehörlosen-Sportverband, dating from 1910, is the oldest national Deaf sport association.[14]

The Deaflympics, launched in 1924, are the second oldest international multisport event in the world, after the Olympic Games (1896), and are under the patronage of the International Olympic Committee (IOC). Eugène Rubens Alcais, the deaf French Deaf Sports Federation secretary-general visualized the idea 'of staging an international Deaf sporting event that would promote the growth of deaf sport federations all over Europe' and was ably assisted by Antoine Dresse, a young deaf Belgian, in making this a reality.[15]

The first Deaflympics were in Paris in 1924 (148 athletes from nine countries) and the first ever sports event for any group of people with disabilities. At the conclusion of the initial Paris Games, Deaf sporting leaders met at a nearby café and established an international governing body for Deaf sports named Comité International des Sports Silencieux (CISS or International Committee of Silent Sports).[16]

Subsequent summer Games were held every four years with a suspension during World War II. The first winter Deaflympics were held in Austria in 1949 with 33 athletes from five countries. The 2005 summer Deaflympics held in Melbourne experienced then-record participation with 3488 athletes/team officials from 74 countries, 21 international media groups, over five million hits to the Deaflympics website, and an over AU$19 million estimated economic benefit to the City of Melbourne.[17]

The IOC granted official recognition for the 'Deaflympics' appellation in 2001. Japan and the USA became the first non-European countries to affiliate with ICSD, and the USA was the first non-European country to confirm participation in the Deaflympics for the 1935 Games. Among relative newcomers (since 1977) enjoying the benefits of this worldwide network of sports and social inclusion are such geographically disparate countries as Mongolia, Bangladesh, Cyprus, Estonia, Uruguay, Iceland and Swaziland. As of May 2010, ICSD has 104 member nations geographically distributed amongst four regional confederations as follows: Africa (20 members), Asia Pacific (30), Europe (42), Pan America (8).[18]

Organization of the Deaflympics

The Deaflympics are distinguished from other IOC-sanctioned Games by the fact that they are organized and managed exclusively by the ICSD Executive Committee who are all Deaf. Oftentimes the local organizing committee includes hearing people in various managerial positions and they work collaboratively with deaf people. Only Deaf people are eligible to serve on the ICSD Executive Committee. ICSD currently limits Deaflympics eligibility to athletes who are both 'Deaf, defined as a hearing loss of at least 55 dB per tone average in the better ear (three-tone frequency average at 500, 1000 and 2000 Hertz, ISO 1969 Standard)' and 'members of an affiliated National Deaf Sports Federation and citizens of that country'.[19] This limitation was established in 1979 by the 25th ICSD Congress.[20] Eickman describes the history behind how ICSD developed eligibility rules based on hearing limits and notes how simulating being deaf and doping were analogous in the eyes of the then-ICSD Executive Committee, as 'an example of how Deaf people protect Deaf culture and Deaf identity.'[21]

The Deaflympics are typically organized by a national deaf sports federation, through an organizing committee, that also seeks financial support, to ensure the Deaflympics are held at an elite level. Sometimes, governments partner with the national deaf sports federation, playing a significant part in the Deaflympics' operation. International, national and local sport organizations are enlisted to assist with sport event operations, thus creating the need for a high level of sign/spoken language interpreting to facilitate communication between deaf athletes/officials and hearing sport/government officials. Also visual presentation of information, through using video screens, captioning and information boards, during the Deaflympics is crucial for both athletes and spectators.[22]

ICSD objectives and structure

ICSD's objectives include serving as Deaf sports' international representative organization, developing and promoting sports training and competition in the Deaf international sporting community, developing new training programmes and expanding existing opportunities for Deaf sport participation at international standards, promoting Deaf sport's organization and development in developing countries, liaising with the IOC and General Association of International Sport Federations (GAISF), in pursuance of ICSD objectives, and with the various international sports federations, in providing continued guidance and resources for Deaf athletes and Deaf sports programmes.

The ICSD Executive Committee is unique because it is run only by Deaf members. Members come from all parts of the world and communicate in different sign languages. Therefore, meetings are conducted in international signs. ICSD Congresses of all Full Members, each represented by three delegates, convene every two years, within the week preceding the Deaflympics. Voting delegates at ICSD Congresses must be able to understand and use international signs.[23] However, due to funding and support constraints, some full members are not able to send Congress delegates and rely on attending regional meetings.

Olympism in the Deaflympics

ICSD shares the same goals and beliefs as the IOC, such as a need for athletes to compete with each other and a need for a group of people with a commonality, in this case Deaf people, to come together and share their experiences. The Deaflympics actively promote the old ideal of the Olympics – brotherhood through sports and upholding to the ideals of Olympism. 'And it was also Coubertin who originated the idea that while the Olympics can instil national pride, the cooperation the world's nations may promote peace and prevent conflict'.[24]

> Olympism is a philosophy of life, exalting and combining in a balanced whole the qualities of body, will and mind. Blending sport with culture and education, Olympism seeks to create a way of life based on the joy found in effort, the educational value of good example and respect for universal fundamental ethical principles.[25]

Juan Antonio Samaranch, former IOC president, describes his first-hand observation of how the Deaflympics reflect Olympism:

> My first dealings with the CISS came when I attended the 1981 Deaf World Games in Cologne, Germany. I was inspired by the special sense of camaraderie amongst the athletes, officials and spectators, united together in a sea of moving hands. It did not matter that those people were deaf; I could easily see that these Games held a special meaning and purpose for all those involved, just like the Olympic Games. Unity through sport, differences put aside, the final push of a runner towards the finish line and a gold medal – it was all there in Cologne.[26]

Sport continues to be a bonding force in the local and global Deaf community. The value of coming together for a celebration of Deaf sport, where culture and language are not barriers, was clearly demonstrated at the 2009 Deaflympics where the biggest ever contingency of countries and athletes/team officials attended. The Deaflympics *do* play a large part in Deaf culture and the Deaf community, but this does not detract from the Deaflympics as an elite Olympic-level sports event. It is perhaps for this reason that some have pushed for inclusion in the Paralympic games. However, Baker and Cokely describe how ASL, in a signed modality, draws Deaf people in the USA together and its powerful impact on maintaining Deaf culture and community, which is something that would be lost if pulled under the Paralympic umbrella.[27] It is not hard to imagine or witness that other sign languages do the same thing for Deaf people all over the world.[28] Also, Stewart's *Deaf Sport: The Impact of Sports within the Deaf Community* describes the connection between Deaf sport and ASL, and it is obvious from elsewhere in this work that the Deaflympics fall under this scope of Deaf sport. His profiles of various Deaf sport leaders further affirm these points.[29] Deaf sport, however, is not the only context under which Deaf people gather, others occur under political, academic, and other special interest group banners such as the WFD, Deaf Academics and Deaf History International.[30] And so one must ask why it is that sport is so important.

Breivik, Haualand, and Solvang[31] describe the significance of Terence Parkin's (Deaf South African Olympic silver medallist) comments about his participation in the Deaflympics in their discussion of 'The Olympic Ideal and the deaf community', which appears to reflect their connection of Olympism with Parkin's Deaflympics experience:

> Terrence Parkin, made a statement, when coming from him, elegantly united the Olympic ideal of *citius – fortius – altius* and the outspoken joy of meeting and making friends with deaf people from all over the world ... Terrence Parkin made a metaphoric relation between the athletic achievements and the sense of being at home among ones' equals that many overtly expressed. Parkin officially announced that he had chosen to attend the Deaf World Games rather than a world cup swimming contest elsewhere, because being in Rome was like *being with his family*. Being a world-class swimmer, he broke several DWG-records during the Rome DWG, and his statement of being with here with his 'family' was visibly acclaimed and appreciated. Being both an outstanding athlete and a 'true' deaf person (by announcing his membership in the Deaf family in fluent international signs), he personalized not only the vibrant sense of *communitas* (Turner 1974) of the Deaf community that could be sensed through the games. In addition, he also used a symbolic language with parallels to the Olympic Truce, which underlines *the spirit of brotherhood* that shall be prevailing among groups and individuals all over the world during the period of the Olympic Games[32]. By using the family metaphor, both Parkin and the IOC make a moral statement ... Parkin did thus not only say that he felt like he was a part of the worldwide deaf family, he also stated that he was *like* them. So when he at the same time made outstanding Olympic achievements, the entire deaf world (his *family* or *equals*) was metaphorically lifted to higher levels, too.[33]

Gerhard Sperling's (a German/East Germany race walking athlete) comparative comments about competing at the Olympic Games and the Deaflympics, make it apparent that communication at the Deaflympics is also significant:

At the Olympics I experienced the beauty of color of many nation's flags, TV cameras, flashing lights, huge street and stadium turnouts, spectators' screams and their hand and facial expressions while I competed as a lone deaf walker, and at the World Games I was always the happiest man because I could freely converse and socialize with any foreign deaf athlete.[34]

Mike Cavanaugh, a former US Deaf men's team handball coach, has directly participated in four Deaflympics, eight Olympic Games and two Paralympic Games. His insights, as a hearing person able to communicate in ASL, in comparing the 1988 Olympic Games and the 1989 Deaflympics, are especially informative offering the perspective of an outsider–insider:

I experienced the exact same thrill in participating in the Opening Ceremonies of the 1988 Olympic Games in Seoul as I did in the Opening Ceremonies of the 1989 World Games for the Deaf (WGD) in Christchurch. I also observed that there was a remarkable level of genuine friendship displayed amongst the athletes at the WGD and I attributed that to the universality of sign language and the athletes from different nations being able to readily communicate with one another. The common bond of brotherhood and sisterhood through sport was pure and uplifting. This experience had a powerful and lasting impact on me and I am left with the impression that the deaf share a special experience through their deafness.[35]

We believe Cavanaugh's reference 'to the universality of sign language' includes his observation of the shared features of signed languages that allow Deaf athletes to communicate across language barriers by using International Sign, as we ourselves have experienced the same thing at the Deaflympics. Cavanuagh also appears to state that this ability of Deaf athletes to communicate with each other leads to building the bond he describes and sharing the experience of being Deaf.

It was obvious to me that before, during and after competition there was a greater enjoyment of just being in one another's company for the athletes in the WGD. Everyone wanted to win but there was seemingly greater respect for one another amongst the athletes which for me only enriched the level of competition. All athletes make sacrifices to compete in the Olympic Games and the WGD. I think however WGD athletes make greater sacrifices, personally and professionally to compete and perhaps that is why they enjoy the moment and the competitive experience perhaps to a greater degree.[36]

The testimonies of Parkin, Sperling and Cavanaugh, two Deaf and one hearing participant in the Deaflympics, offer more support of how the Deaflympics reflect Olympism, specifically in how the direct communication, sign language-using environment provides a platform for the aforementioned IOC-described 'joy found in effort, the educational value of good example and respect for universal fundamental ethical principles' that Deaflympics athletes and fans can impart to each other.[37]

ICSD–Paralympic Games relationship: self-governance and opportunities for athletes

Although the ICSD and the IPC have collaborated over the years, ICSD questioned the merit of a move towards the incorporation of the Deaflympics into the Paralympic Games. In the 1990s, some national Deaf sport governing bodies felt that hosting the Deaflympics were becoming increasingly more expensive, as was the cost of participating in them. Government and public money was not easy to obtain and the idea of joining with the IPC might not only reduce these costs, but take advantage of the high public profile the Paralympic Games enjoyed.[38] Some also felt that this might increase opportunities for athletes who were currently struggling with the increased expenses. The IOC was also keen for this partnership. In 1991, Jordan wrote:

As president of the CISS, I am constantly asked why deaf people have a separate international sports program. I am also asked why deaf people do not simply participate in games for the disabled. My first response is to say that *Deaf athletes are not disabled in any way when playing various sports*; in fact, fair competition can be achieved only with other deaf people, with whom communication comes easily. But being deaf in a hearing world means much more than simply having separate sports, teams, games and other social activities . . . Deaf athletes are neither fish nor fowl. On the one hand, they are medically disabled, which leads to the tendency of the hearing population to classify them with other disabled athletes. On the other hand, as far as sports are concerned, they are able-bodied. No adaptations to the rules of sports need be made. No new sport needs to be conceived to make participation of deaf persons possible. What deaf athletes do need is an environment that will meet their physical needs as well as their social needs. Where competition with able-bodied, hearing athletes provides ample opportunities to hone athletic skills, it often fails to satisfy basic social needs, like communication and getting to know fellow players on intimate terms.[39]

In recognition of the unique communication requirements of Deaf athletes, the prohibitive costs to the IPC of providing sign language interpreters, and the inability for the Paralympic Games to accommodate the growing numbers of Deaf competitors, the ICSD felt that they had no other recourse but to withdraw its membership with the IPC. Members of the ICSD Congress could not support eliminating the number of sporting events that would be offered for Deaf athletes if they were to compete at each Paralympic Games. The IPC made it clear that they could not afford to be the umbrella organization for the existing Deaf Games without a serious reduction in the number of events and given the number of sign language interpreters that would be required. Each of these factors merits discussion in further detail here.[40]

Currently, 19 summer and 5 winter disciplines are currently contested at the Deaflympics.[41] Similarly, there are 22 summer and 5 winter Paralympic Games sports.[42] Jordan explains that: 'in Deaf sport there is only one classification – deaf. No modification to any sport occurs, other than minor technical adjustments to make auditory cues visible'.[43] Jordan goes on to explain that, 'By comparison, in the Paralympic Games many events are adapted. Because of the great range of physical qualities, athletes competing in the Paralympic Games have had to be classified according to ability. This classification system is complex and intended to create a level playing field for the athletes' and he gives a few examples of the various numbers of classifications for the different types of Paralympic athletes.[44]

Thus, if Deaf athletes were incorporated into the Paralympic Games, instead of 19 summer disciplines, only three to five sports for Deaf athletes would be part of the Paralympic Games programme, and Jordan makes a similar point in his analysis of the Deaflympics and the Paralympics. For many this is a sacrifice not worth making. Table 1 provides a comparative listing of the sports/disciplines offered in each summer competition.[45]

Also, to ensure equal communication access between Deaf athletes and hearing Paralympic Games officials and athletes, qualified signed/spoken language interpreters fluent in the appropriate languages are required. For example, an interpreter fluent in Swedish Sign Language and spoken Swedish would be needed to facilitate communication between a Deaf Swedish athlete and hearing Swedish Paralympic Games officials and athletes. Approximately 3000 such interpreters, at a total cost of approximately US$3,000,000, would be needed to cover the demand. The IPC is not able or willing to fund this interpreting service.

Additionally, the ICSD organization had been (and continues to be) a role model for the national and local Deaf sporting organizations around the world. Since 1924, the ICSD has been organized and administered *by* Deaf people, experiencing self-governance and self-regulation. Without an equitable merger of the ICSD and the IPC, the outcome of any agreement with the IPC would result in ICSD and their Games being organized and

Table 1. Sport events in the Deaflympics and the 2008 Paralympic Games

Deaflympics	Paralympic Games
Athletics	Archery
Badminton	Athletics
Basketball	Boccia
Beach Volleyball	Cycling
Bowling	Equestrian
Cycling Road	Football 5-a-side
Football	Football 7-a-side
Judo	Goalball
Karate	Judo
Mountain Bike	Power lifting
Orienteering	Rowing
Shooting	Sailing
Swimming	Shooting
Table Tennis	Swimming
Taekwondo	Table Tennis
Tennis	Volleyball (Sitting)
Volleyball	Wheelchair Basketball
Wrestling Freestyle	Wheelchair Fencing
Wrestling Greco-Roman	Wheelchair Rugby
	Wheelchair Tennis

administered *for* Deaf people. This is an important concept for any organization which is self-governed – the organization *by* its constituents as opposed to being managed *by* an outside group on their behalf. Because of the ICSD's philosophy of leadership *by* Deaf people, this also became the model for local and national Deaf sports organizations, enabling Deaf people from all over the world to enjoy empowerment and self-governance in the arena of Deaf sports. The IOC has respected this decision and has continued to provide recognition and support. This is a model that could, and perhaps should, be expanded within the IPC, rather than pushed aside. Currently the IPC is neither self-governed nor self-regulated by those it represents. For many in the Deaf community this is an insurmountable problem that looks like a step back from the long-fought battle for self-determination by those who are socially marginalized.

A compromise of sorts has been reached, but its viability remains to be seen. In November 2004, officials from the ICSD and the IPC signed a memorandum of understanding (MOU) in the hope of creating a collaborative landscape in international competition and a clear understanding of the roles and responsibilities as separate organizations. There was further understanding that Deaf athletes with additional disabilities would be able to participate in various IPC events, and conversely, multidisabled Paralympic athletes with at least 55 dB hearing loss in the better ear could compete in the Deaflympics and Deaf World Championships. The agreement was developed with the intention that it would provide the National Olympic Committees (NOCs) and the National Paralympic Committees (NPCs) with better awareness and understanding of the ICSD and the IPC as two separate organizations that manage their own quadrennial event, the Deaflympics and Paralympic Games, respectively. Other stipulations of the MOU include to: mutually recognize and respect the autonomy of their organizations, as well as cooperate 'in informing ... sports authorities of the international structures of both organizations and addressing the conflicts that may arise at national level between the affiliated organizations'.[46]

Confusion and misconceptions at the NOC/NPC level: a struggle for retaining autonomy

The aforementioned factors have made it very difficult for NOCs and NPCs to understand the unique situation of and provide equal financial, logistical and other support to the Deaflympics and Deaf athletes. There are also several additional important factors adding to the confusion; first, the accord between the IPC and the IOC to make the Paralympic Games part of the Olympic bidding package.[47] Second, the recent IOC restructuring (the splitting of the IOC Sports department into two separate departments—Sports and Games) which transferred responsibility of the Olympics and Paralympic Games to the Games department, while leaving the Deaflympics (classed as a Recognized Federation) behind within the Sports department has led to a marginalization of this competition. Third, the regular turnover of NPC officials means that there needs to be an ongoing education of NPC officials about Deaf sport, Deaf people, signed languages and Deaflympics-related issues. The learning curve that these officials must undergo means that there are constantly periods of miscommunication between the NPC and the ICSD.

These factors have combined to make a 'perfect storm' of disability organizations stating that they speak for and represent Deaf sport and national governments taking actions that negatively impact national Deaf sport organizations. Given this comprehensive history and the positive interactions with IOC and IPC, there continue to be serious problems in educating disabled sports leaders and organizations throughout the world to the unique situation of the Deaf athlete.

Ammons illustrates five actions taken by disability sport organizations or national governments undermining Deaf sport autonomy. This includes disability sport organizations declaring control over Deaf sports on the continental level in Africa, in Botswana and the United Arab Emirates, the French government restructuring its sports program which ultimately led to the dissolution of the Federation Sportive des Sourds de France, an ICSD charter member, and mandated that the deaf sports operate under the Federation Francaise Handisport, and the British government took funding away from the 2009 British Deaflympics team due to the British government's desire to focus instead on British athletes for the 2008 and 2012 Olympic and Paralympic Games.[48] In a further development, French athletes could not participate in ICSD competition for some months, while negotiations were underway to re-establish a Deaf-led French Deaf sports representative entity. During the first attempt at negotiating a resolution, ICSD met stiff resistance from Federation Francaise Handisport.[49] This conflict encompasses the whole point of this section in a nutshell – hearing sport leaders failing to respect and support Deaf self-autonomy in running Deaf sports affairs. This is serious disenfranchisement and disempowering, and even more appalling in light of the key role Eugène Rubens Alcais, a deaf Frenchman, had in the Deaflympics' formation. In the most recent development, the French athletes have now resumed participation given the fact ICSD yielded to external pressure to re-admit France as a member in good standing.

These decisions illustrate the seriousness of the consequences of this lack of Deaflympics and Deaf sport awareness, and the need for continual, clear, strong messages from the IOC regarding the Deaflympics' autonomy and their sanction by the IOC. The actions taken by disability sport organizations and national governments suggest a tremendous lack of respect and support for Deaf sport and the Deaflympics, and the absence of a true understanding of the Deaflympics and their benefit to and meaning for Deaf athletes and the Deaf community, and thus the tremendous positive benefits of supporting the Deaflympic movement and their Deaf athletes.

National governments and National Olympic Committees: funding challenges and the potential end of the Deafympics?

In order to redress the balance of power in favour of the Deaf sports organizations work needs to be done at the national level. Ammons gives a succinct explanation of the roots of the problems and further examples.[50] The problems outlined above, along with many other problems we face, arise because there is no clear distinction in many governments and NOCs regarding disabled sports. To take it one step further, these problems exist because *there is no clear recognition of ICSD/Deaflympics as a separate, equal and independent body within the IOC family.*[51]

In other words, Ammons explains that as ICSD's scope encompasses all Deaf sports worldwide rather than solely the Deaflympics, there is no current 'International Deaflympic Committee' (IDC) existing that solely focuses on Deaflympics organization. This creates great difficulty and work for national Deaf sport federations in educating their national governments and/or NOCs about ICSD and the Deaflympics and that these national Deaf sport federations are actually responsible for their nation's Deaflympics participation.

This leads to either of two outcomes usually occurring. The first is the non-recognition of ICSD plus an assertion for Deaf sport to be under IPC governance. If more countries go down this road, Deaf sport will most likely disappear. The second is much more favourable for the Deaf community – establishment of a national Deaflympic committee that also supports and promotes Deaf athletics within that nation. When the IOC restricts the use of the name Deaflympics, it has been found that governments do not give equal recognition or funding for their Deaf sports federations. Other impacts include a decline in the number of Deaf athletes participating in the Deaflympics, primarily because of limited funds from their national governments which has led to the cancellation of some events due to insufficient number of athletes and/or teams.

Also, for both the 2005 Summer Deaflympics (Melbourne, Australia) and the 2011 Winter Deaflympics (High Tatras, Slovakia), the national government was anticipating working with a national Deaflympic committee. When this was not the case, a serious crisis appeared regarding either government or NOC support for the Deaflympics in question. For Australia, a resolution was found only after an IOC member stepped in, resulting in 'the use of the name of Deaflympics in Australia'. For Slovakia, the 'government was appalled to learn that there was no national Deaflympic committee in Slovakia and that IOC would not allow it'. A Slovak governmental ultimatum and deliberations resulted in a Slovak Deaflympic Committee being formed, which averted the Slovak Paralympic Committee's running of the 2011 Deaflympics.[52]

An interesting development took place in May 2010 when ICSD's Executive Board cancelled the 2011 Winter Deaflympics, with the apparent reasons being both funding and organization falling short of expectations.[53] Subsequently around September 2010, ICSD had a change of heart with a decision to reinstate the Winter Deaflympics in Slovakia after receiving strong and re-newed commitment from Jan Mokos, the Mayor of High Tatras. With much regret and sadness, the Games never materialized due to lack of necessary funds to fulfill the obligations.

Ammons reminds that:

> The CISS/ICSD has no control of the use of the term Deaflympics by national governments or NOCs. In adhering to the IOC'S basic universal principles for good governance, and adhering to the advice of President Rogge, given in August 2006, who told us that we could not interfere in each country's affairs, it would be inappropriate to do so.[54]

However, ICSD has seen a huge difference in support and funding for Deaflympic athletes between countries where a national Deaflympic committee has been established and countries where no national Deaflympic committee exists and a Deaf sport federation exists under a different name or where the national Paralympic organization runs Deaf sports. For ICSD and national Deaf sport federations, having ownership of the word 'Deaflympics' can and does make all the difference.

Conclusion

n recognition of the unique communication requirements of Deaf athletes, it is clearly evident that the Paralympic Games could not afford to include Deaf athletes, given the number of sign language interpreters that will be required, or offer a competition programme for Deaf athletes that is identical in scope and breadth to what the Deaflympics already offer.

It is not only the enjoyment of playing sport, but the importance of the social connection, central to how Deaf communities thrive and survive in today's world that makes the Deaflympics so important. In Stewart, Ammons is quoted:

> An important part of all international competition is the opportunity to meet and develop friendships with people all over the world. Deaf athletes are not so much rivals fiercely competing for a prize, as they are friends competing alongside and against one another ... no matter what sign language we use or what country we are from, the urge to socialize with one another will always be there because we are Deaf first and athletes second.[55]

This quote again highlights the importance for Deaf people of communicating in a signed language modality with other Deaf people and how Deaf sport is a platform for this environment.

There is work being done to correct some of the mis-steps that have been made. The ICSD has introduced policies and programmes to eradicate misconceptions about the Deaflympics and Paralympic Games by initiating Deaf Sports Reform (creating an IDC, re-focusing the ICSD on non-Deaflympics competitions, and forming a ICSD Youth committee) in 2008 which will lead to clearer distinctions between different aspects of elite Deaf sport.[56] In recent years, the ICSD administration under immediate past president Ammons spent much time and energy advocating ICSD, the Deaflympics, and Deaf sport to the IOC and IPC, and educating and dealing with various NOCs and NPCs regarding national Deaf sport organizations.

The IOC and IPC have responded positively to these efforts. In January 2009, IOC President Jacques Rogge gave his support to the Deaf Sport Reform changes.[57] Since November 2004, the ICSD and IPC have agreed to allow eligible athletes to participate in each other's Games.

Now it is time for the NOCs and NPCs to step up and fully support their Deaf athletes by recognizing the Deaflympics as an Olympic and Paralympic Games-level event, as the IOC and IPC already do, fully funding their Deaflympic teams and Deaf sport programmes (including elite, developmental, and grassroots programmes), respecting IDC/ICSD's authority over Deaf sports, working with IDC/ICSD/ICSD Youth to allow each Deaf athlete the opportunity to reach his fullest potential, both as a Deaf person and Deaf athlete, and raising awareness of Deaf athletes, signed languages, Deaf sport, and opportunities that Deaf sport offers through mainstream media channels, at training centres, and within the Deaf community throughout their geographic domain.

With a clear understanding of the unique issues involved with the Deaflympics and Paralympic Games, all who enjoy and support sport can and will work together in a positive way to eradicate misconceptions about the Deaflympics and Deaf athletes.

Notes

1. These definitions of 'Deaf' are drawn from the various definitions of 'Deaf' as offered by Eickman, 'The Role of Deaf Sport', 1; Lane, *The Mask of Benevolence*, xi; Lane, Hoffmeister, and Bahan, *A Journey into the Deaf-World*, ix, x, 5–8; Stewart, *Deaf Sport*, x; Padden and Humphries, *Deaf in America*, 2–3. Padden and Humphries, *Deaf in America*, 2–3, 129, is drawn from the work of Woodward, 'Implications for Sociolinguistics Research'.

2. Given the limited literature regarding Deaf sport that takes the position of the authors, this article is largely based on Ammons' report, 'Deaf Sports and Deaflympics'. Thus, the substantial portions of Ammons' report that have been quoted or paraphrased in this article are, for the most part, reproduced without quotation marks or citations to simplify the citing process. Also, Jordan, *World Games for the Deaf* serves as a very significant and valuable resource from which this article draws heavily. Additionally, the authors wish to acknowledge Jordan's use of the term 'misconception' in addressing the Deaflympics and the Paralympics.

3. Jordan, *World Games for the Deaf*. Jordan raises and addresses the same seminal points surrounding this misconception as well as the histories of ICSD, IOC, IPC, the Deaflympics, the Paralympics, and ICSD and the Deaflympics' relationships with the other entities, including funding. Additionally, Jordan emphasizes the importance of signed language communication to Deaf athletes and the Deaf people's view of themselves as 'not … disabled' but 'part of a cultural and linguistic minority', as well as argues as to 'Why the Deaf Community Needs Separate Games'. The authors use these ideas of Jordan's in the preceding two paragraphs, particularly the latter paragraph, and wish to acknowledge Jordan's work here.

4. Ministère de la Santé, *Institut National de Jeunes Sourds de Paris*, 1; Lane, When the Mind Hears, 57, 423; Lane, Hoffmeister and Bahan, *A Journey into the Deaf-World*, 51, 53.

5. Stewart and Ammons, 'Future Directions of the Deaflympics', 46. In this source, Stewart and Ammons cite this quoted sentence as a paraphrase from Moores, *Educating the Deaf*.

6. Haualand and Allen, *Deaf People and Human Rights*, 6–7. http://www.wfdeaf.org/pdf/Deaf%20People%20and%20Human%20Rights%20Report%20-%2023%20Feb%2009%20Version.pdf.

7. Jordan, *World Games for the Deaf*.

8. Ibid.

9. Lane, Hoffmeister, and Bahan, *A Journey into the Deaf-World*, 131–132. The authors refer to the DEAF-WORLD in the U.S. as 'a group (an estimated million people) possessing a unique language and culture' and that their 'focus is on the DEAF-WORLD in the United States, for it has been the most thoroughly investigated', ix.

10. Ibid.

11. Smith, Lentz, and Mikos, *Signing Naturally*, 3; Valli, Lucas, and Mulrooney, *Linguistics of American Sign Language*, 17.

12. World Federation of the Deaf, *Fact Sheet: Sign Language*, 2, http://www.wfdeaf.org/pdf/fact_signlanguage.pdf. Note: Weblink no longer exists as of 9–23–11.

13. Lane, Hoffmeister, and Bahan, *A Journey into the Deaf-World*, 207–208.

14. Eickman, 'A Concise History of Deaf Sport'; Ohio School for the Deaf, *OSD's Journey Toward Destiny*, http://www.ohioschoolforthedeaf.org/history.aspx; Smith, *The History of Glasgow Deaf Athletic*, 2, 3, 4–6. These authors give support for 1872 as a correct date to use. CISS, *World's Oldest Deaf Sports Club*, 17; Gorham, *The International Football Match in Glasgow*, 138; Deutscher Gehörlosen-Sportverband, *History*. These authors give support for 1871.

15. Ammons, *Deaf Sports and Deaflympics*, 3; Jordan and Giansanti, 'Origins of CISS', 12.

16. Ammons, *Deaf Sports and Deaflympics*, 3–4; Jordan and Giansanti, 'Origins of CISS', 12–13.

17. ICSD, *Games*. http://www.deaflympics.com/games/; Jordan and Giansanti, 'Origins of CISS' 13; ICSD, *1949 Seefeld*, http://www.deaflympics.com/games/participant.asp?GamesID=6; Ammons, 'Deaf Sports and Deaflympics', 3–4.

18. Ammons, *Deaf Sports and Deaflympics*, 4; CISS, 'Annexe A', 3, 4 (It is possible and likely that the person putting together this report was Antoine Dresse on behalf of the then-ICSD executive committee and then-ICSD President Eugène Rubens Alcais); Ammons, *Deaf Sports and Deaflympics*, 5; Stewart and Ammons, 'Future Directions of the Deaflympics', 46; ICSD, *Full Members*, http://www.deaflympics.com/about/contact.asp?ID=FM; *Regional Confederation Representatives*, http://www.deaflympics.com/about/contact.asp?ID=RC; Eickman, 'A Concise History of Deaf Sport'. See also reference Juan Samaranch to John Lovett, 'Re: Change of Name', 17 May 2001. This was a letter from then President of the International Olympic

Committee, Juan Samaranch to John Lovett, then President of the International Committee of Sports of the Deaf, confirming that as per Lovett's suggestion, the Deaf World Games would indeed change their name to Deaflympics.

[19] ICSD, *Constitution,* sections 9.3.2 and 9.1.6. http://www.deaflympics.com/about/index.asp?DID=545; ICSD, *Eligibility.* http://www.deaflympics.com/athletes/?ID=239.

[20] Eickman, 'The Role of Deaf Sport', 102; Søndergaard, 'CISS 25', 1153, art. 10.17; also see CISS, *XXVth congress XXVemè congrès,* Appendix D, sec. 17.2, 18.

[21] Eickman, 'The Role of Deaf Sport', 101–111; 108; Søndergaard, 'CISS Executive Committee Meeting', 1092'.

[22] Ammons, *Deaf Sports and Deaflympics,* 5.

[23] ICSD, Constitution, sections 9.3.2, 13.1, 9.1.1, 9.1.4, 9.1.2 & 9.1.6. http://www.deaflympics.com/about/index.asp?DID=545.

[24] McNamara, *The Founder of the Modern Olympics.*

[25] IOC, *Olympic Charter,* 11.

[26] Samaranch, *Foreword,* 7.

[27] Baker and Cokely, *American Sign Language,* 58.

[28] Lane, Hoffmeister, and Bahan, *A Journey into the Deaf World,* 5–6, 209–210; Stewart, *Deaf Sport,* 33–34.

[29] Stewart, *Deaf Sport,* 15–16, 33, 66–67, 89–92, 182–183. Profiles of several Deaf sport leaders also make the connection to the Deaflympics apparent, as well as make connections to sign language. Stewart offers examples of international Deaf gatherings such as a Deaf recreational organization, as well as describes different types of media coverage of Deaf community activity and other aspects of Deaf people's lives.

[30] Lane, Hoffmeister, and Bahan, *A Journey into the Deaf World,* 207. Authors illustrate how there are other types of international Deaf gatherings and have updated their examples with some of the more recent gatherings.

[31] Breivik, Haualand, and Solvang, *Rome.*

[32] Terence's name is misspelled as Terrence here. Deaflympics records for the South African roster for the 2001 Deaflympics attest to the correct spelling – see ICSD, *South Africa.* ICSD, *Games: Rome 2001: 19th Summer Deaflympics,* http://www.deaflympics.com/games/participant.asp?GamesID=33&CountryID = 193;ICSD, *2001 Rome,* http://www.deaflympics.com/games/index.asp?GamesID=33.

[33] Pinchas, 'Deaf Participants at the Olympic Games', 8; 'Deaf Olympians and World Games', 4.

[34] Cavanaugh, personal communication, August 6, 2009. The authors' commentary on Cavanaugh's observation of the 'universality of sign language', are based on their experiences as well as drawn from Lane, Hoffmeister, and Bahan, *A Journey into the Deaf World,* 208–209.

[35] Ibid.

[36] IOC, *Olympic Charter,* 11.

[37] Ammons, *Deaf Sports and Deaflympics,* 9; Stewart and Ammons, 'Awakenings', 27, 29.

[38] Stewart, *Deaf Sport,* vii–viii. The authors wish to point out that the use of the term 'medically disabled' by Jordan is significant. Lane, *When the Mind Hears,* xiii–xvii introduces and discusses the negative impact of labelling deaf people as having something medically wrong with them. Lane, *The Mask of Benevolence,* xii–xiv, xvi–xvii, 5, 18–20, 22–28 provides further description of the disability labelling and its impact. Stewart, *Deaf Sport,* 93–99 describes the medical view of deaf people by hearing people and the influence of this on Deaf sport.

[39] Eickman, 'The Role of Deaf Sport', 322–337, 88–94. Eickman provides a detailed historical account, dates, and describes selected events, additional factors and some of the frustrations involved in ICSD's relationships with the IPC and its predecessors, disabled sport organizations.

[40] ICSD, *Sports,* http://www.deaflympics.com/sports/.

[41] IPC, *Sport,* http://www.paralympic.org/Sport/.

[42] Stewart, *Deaf Sport,* 7.

[43] Jordan, *World Games for the Deaf.*

[44] Jordan, *World Games for the Deaf* (for Jordan's point); ICSD, *Sports,* http://www.deaflympics.com/sports/ (for Deaflympics disciplines); IPC, *Beijing 2008 6–17 September 2008 Beijing, China,* http://www.paralympic.org/Paralympic_Games/Past_Games/Beijing_2008/index.html (for 2008 Summer Paralympic Games sports).

[45] IPC, *IPC and Deaflympics Sign Memorandum of Understanding,* http://www.paralympic.org/Media_Centre/News/General_News/2004_11_30_a.html.

46 IPC, *Paralympic Games*, http://www.paralympic.org/Paralympic_Games/.
47 Ammons, *Deaf Sports and Deaflympics*, 14–15.
48 ICSD, *Full Members*, http://www.deaflympics.com/about/contact.asp?ID=FM and *ICSD Remains Committed to Find Solution for French Deaf Athletes*, http://www.deaflympics.com/news/pressreleases.asp?ID=1482.
49 Ammons, *Deaf Sports and Deaflympics*, 14–17.
50 Ibid., 15.
51 Ibid., 15–16.
52 ICSD Executive Board, *Cancellation of the 17th Winter Deaflympics in Slovakia*, http://www.deaflympics.com/news/pressreleases.asp?ID=1487.
53 Ammons, *Deaf Sports and Deaflympics*, 17.
54 Stewart, *Deaf Sport*, 191.
55 ICSD, *Deaf Sports Reform: Final Draft: 41st ICSD Extraordinary Congress*, http://www.deaflympics.com/news/enews/pdf/DeafSportReform.pdf; *Deaf Sports Reform: Voting Results*, http://www.deaflympics.com/news/enews/pdf/DeafSportReform-VotingResults.pdf; Ammons, *President's Message*, November 2008, http://www.deaflympics.com/news/enews/backissues.asp?ID=1383.
56 Ammons, *President's Message*, February 2009, http://www.deaflympics.com/news/enews/index.asp?ID=1400.
57 IPC, *IPC and Deaflympics sign Memorandum*.

References

Ammons, Donalda. *Deaf Sports and Deaflympics. Presented to the International Olympic Committee*. Frederick, MD: ICSD, 2008.
Baker, Charlotte, and Dennis Cokely. *American Sign Language: A Teacher's Resource Text on Grammar and Culture*. Silver Spring, MD: TJ Publishers, 1980.
Breivik, Jan-Kåre, Hilde Haualand, and Per Solvang. *Rome – a Temporary Deaf City!: Deaflympics 2001*, 28–29. http://www.ub.uib.no/elpub/rokkan/N/N02-02.pdf
Comité International des Sports Silencieux. 'Annexe A: Rapport du Comite Executif au Congres de Londres 1935'. Liége, Belgium: Comité International des Sports Silencieux, 1935, 3–4.
Comité International des Sports Silencieux. 'Lausanne, March 23rd, 1968: The C.I.S.S. is Awarded the Olympic Cup'. *Bulletin du Comité International des Sports Silencieux* 53 (1968): 532–3.
Comité International des Sports des Sourds. XXVTH CONGRESS XXVEME CONGRÈS MÉRIBEL, FRANCE 20-21 / 1 / 1979. Comité International des Sports des Sourds, 1979.
Comité International des Sports des Sourds. 'World's Oldest Deaf Sports Club'. *Bulletin du Comité International des Sports Silencieux* 173 (1994): 17.
Deutscher Gehörlosen-Sportverband. *History: The German Deaf Sports Federation is the Eldest Sports Organisation for People with Disabilities*. http://www.dg-sv.de/wir.php?page=0&lang=1
Eickman, Jordan A. 'Concise History of Deaf Sport: From the 1870s to the Present'. Paper presented at the Deaf Way II International Conference on Deaf Culture at the Washington D.C. Convention Centre, July 12, 2002.
Eickman, Jordan. 'The Role of Deaf Sport in Developing Deaf Identity'. PhD diss., University of Bristol, 2004.
Gorham, Charles. 'The International Football Match in Glasgow'. *The Deaf and Dumb Times* II, 10 (1891): 138–40.
Haualand, Hilde, and Colin Allen. *Deaf People and Human Rights*. Helsinki, Finland: World Federation of the Deaf and the Swedish National Association of the Deaf, 2009, 6–7.
IOC. *Olympic Charter: In Force as From 7 July 2007*. http://multimedia.olympic.org/pdf/en_report_122.pdf.
Jordan, Jerald M. *The World Games for the Deaf and the Paralympic Games*. http://www.deaflympics.com/news/publishedarticles.asp?ID=1131
Jordan, Jerald M., and Terry Giansanti. 'Origins of CISS'. In *CISS 2001: A Review*, edited by John M. Lovett, Terry Giansanti, and Jordan Eickman, 12–15. Redditch, UK: Red Lizard, 2001.
Lane, Harlan. *When the Mind Hears: A History of the Deaf*. New York: Random House, 1989.
Lane, Harlan. *The Mask of Benevolence: Disabling the Deaf Community*. San Diego, CA: Dawn Sign Press, 1999.

Lane, Harlan, Robert Hoffmeister, and Ben Bahan. *A Journey into the Deaf-World*. San Diego, CA: Dawn Sign Press, 1996.

Lovett, John M. 'From the President'. *Bulletin du Comité International des Sports Silencieux* 188 (1997): 3.

McNamara, Robert. *The Founder of the Modern Olympics, Pierre de Coubertin*. http://history1800s.about.com/od/sports/a/Coubertin.htm

Ministère de la Santé, de la Famille et des Personnes Handicapées. *Institut National de Jeunes Sourds de Paris*. Institut National de Jeunes Sourds de Paris, no date.

Moores, Donald F. *Educating the Deaf.*, 4th edn. Boston: Houghton Mifflin, 1996.

Padden, Carol, and Tom Humphries. *Deaf in America: Voices from a Culture*. Cambridge, MA: Harvard University Press, 1988.

Pinchas, Rafael. 'Deaf Participants at the Olympic Games'. *Bulletin du Comité International des Sports Silencieux* 179 (1995): 8.

Pinchas, Rafael. 'Deaf Olympians and World Games'. *Bulletin du Comité International des Sports Silencieux* 183 (1996): 4–5.

Samaranch, Juan A. *Foreword to CISS 2001: A Review*, edited by John M. Lovett, Terry Giansanti, and Jordan Eickman, 7 Redditch, UK: Red Lizard, 2001.

Smith, Cheri, Ella Mae Lentz, and Ken Mikos. *Signing Naturally: Student Workbook Level 1*, edited by Lisa Cahn. San Diego, CA: Dawn Sign Press, 1988.

Smith, Robert J. *The History of Glasgow Deaf Athletic*. Glasgow: Deaf connections, 2003.

Søndergaard, Knud. 'CISS Executive Committee Meeting 26th–27th May 1978, Copenhagen'. *Bulletin du Comité International des Sports Silencieux* 94 (1978): 1090–103.

Stewart, David A. *Deaf Sport: The Impact of Sports within the Deaf Community*. Washington, DC: Gallaudet University Press, 1991.

Stewart, David, and Donalda Ammons. 'Awakenings: The 1993 World Games for the Deaf'. *Palaestra* X, no. 2 (1994): 26–31.

Stewart, David, and Donalda Ammons. 'Future Directions of the Deaflympics'. *Palaestra* 17, no. 3 (2001): 45–9.

Valli, Clayton, Ceil Lucas, and Kristin J. Mulrooney. *Linguistics of American Sign Language: An Introduction*. 4th edn. Washington, DC: Clerc Books/Gallaudet University Press, 2005.

Woodward, James. 'Implications for Sociolinguistics Research Among the Deaf'. *Sign Language Studies* 1 (1972): 1–7.

South Africa, apartheid and the Paralympic Games

Ian Brittain

Centre for Peace and Reconciliation Studies, Coventry University, Coventry, UK

South Africa was excluded from the 1964 Tokyo and 1968 Mexico City Olympic Games over their government's apartheid policies, before being finally expelled from the Olympic Movement in 1970. In contrast, South Africa first competed in the International Stoke Mandeville Games, which in an Olympic year became known as the Paralympic Games, in 1962. South Africa continued to compete until 1985 (although they had been excluded from both the 1980 and 1984 Paralympic Games) when they were finally expelled from the movement despite having competed with a racially integrated team since 1975. This article looks at some of the events and issues, particularly the influence of international politics, which led to their exclusion and eventual expulsion from the disability sports movement, despite the claims by both the South African team and the organizers of international disability sport that the fully racially integrated team was challenging apartheid by setting an example for others to follow.

The story of South African participation in international disability sport, long beyond the expulsion of its Olympic team from the Olympic Games, is extremely complex with numerous individuals, organizations and issues all playing a part. In writing this article, the author has attempted to highlight a variety of these issues although the list is far from complete. The article will begin by describing why apartheid was such a major issue and the impact reactions to it, in both South Africa and around the world, had on South Africa's involvement in international sport. It will briefly outline South Africa's participation in both the Olympic and the international disability sports movements. It will then highlight some of the key reasons for the differences between the two, and look at some of the possible reasons why South Africa was able to continue competing in international disability sport despite their expulsion from the Olympic movement.

Apartheid in South Africa

Apartheid is an Afrikaans word meaning 'apartness'. It came about at a time when imperial rule was receding and enforcement of segregation was being relaxed. However, South Africa went against this world trend by strengthening barriers between blacks and whites and attempting to rationalize this in terms of ideas about racial purity.[1] At a time when many nations were moving away from using race as a device for social division, South Africa continued its segregationist policies. These segregationist practices really started when the Afrikaner National Party came to power in 1948. On the one hand, according to Beinart and Dubow, explanations of the segregation practices of the National Party vary between the materialist and the ideological, the structuralist and the individualist.[2] On the other hand, academics such as Whalley-Hammell claim that the cultural imperialism of colonial racism in apartheid South Africa was informed by specific interpretations of the Bible and of biology to justify the withholding of civil rights from those deemed 'inferior'.[3] Tatz describes the underlying cultural ideology of the Afrikaner's as being based in fundamental Calvinism, their belief in a divine calling or mission in life to preserve white civilization, their Puritanism and fanatical nationalism. Frank Braun, head of the white South African National Olympic Committee (SANOC), once 'scientifically' explained why there were no qualified non-white swimmers in South Africa by stating that 'some sports the Africans are not suited for. In swimming, the water closes their pores so that they cannot get rid of carbon dioxide and so they tire quickly'.[4] Whalley-Hammell goes on to claim that the function of this ideology was to preserve, protect and perpetuate minority white power, and that ideology and power, in combination, served to maintain power and dominance with such effectiveness that the white minority group wielded the majority of power and the black population, who make up the statistical majority, was accorded minority status.[5] In addition, racial discrimination helped to facilitate capitalist growth and provide whites with material and political benefits.[6] Turok claims that the National Party maintained its power through the introduction and maintenance of various Acts, and they then used the legal system in order to enforce its discriminatory practices. One such Act was the Native Land Act, which prohibited Africans from gaining any legal rights to any lands outside their so called 'traditional' areas.[7] According to Seedat, the political pressure for the passing of these Acts came almost entirely from those who wished to ensure a steady and cheap supply of labour. The only way that those in power could force people to accept low wages in the white-owned mines, farms and factories of South Africa was to destroy their self-sufficiency and alternative forms of livelihood. These laws were often enforced through police brutality, thus using fear as a means of ensuring compliance. Where there was any form of attempt to protest or challenge the status quo it would often end up with the protesters being seriously injured or in some instances with large numbers of protesters losing their lives such as in Sharpeville (1960) and Soweto (1976).[8]

Apartheid, disability and discrimination

In apartheid South Africa the ways in which people were classified determined the 'rights' to which they were entitled. Thus the rights of citizenship were traditionally allocated according to physique, with physical differences used to divide the powerful from the powerless.[9] In terms of apartheid in South Africa this was done purely on racial heritage and skin colour. Worldwide the same kind of classification based in physical difference has been used to discriminate against people with a variety of impairments in order to define, and often control, their lives.[10] People with disabilities and the organizations that support them, therefore, have a strong understanding of the impact of discrimination on their lives and what it really means to be discriminated against and alienated from the rest of society. Non-whites with a disability would also have been subject to a double discrimination in terms of both their skin colour and their impairment. This is one possible reason why the organizers of international disability sport were so adamant that the South African team should be allowed to continue to compete. Being ostracised from the rest of society, participation in sport may have been one of the very few opportunities that South Africans with disabilities, and non-whites in particular, might have had to prove to themselves and the rest of society that they were capable of contributing to society and achieving great things.

Apartheid and sport in South Africa

According to Booth, the National Party did not introduce specific legislation to prohibit racially mixed sport. However, apartheid legislation was so all-encompassing that it mitigated against integrated sport at almost every turn by such methods as making travel extremely difficult for non-whites and having specific sports facilities for each of the races, with white facilities being vastly superior in quality and quantity to non-white facilities.[11] On March 29, 1961, South African Minister of the Interior Jan De Klerk announced that the government would not approve the participation of mixed teams in global sporting events; that mixed teams from other nations would not be welcome in South Africa; and that only separate white and non-white teams could compete abroad in international competition.[12] The white sporting federations in South Africa, which were the ones affiliated to the international federations and thus controlled access to international competition, did not allow for non-white membership. This made access to international sport, including the Olympic Games, almost impossible for non-white sportsmen and women. In addition, those non-whites who did manage to compete for South Africa at the international level were not awarded their 'Springbok Colours', (national recognition and proof an individual had represented South Africa in international sporting competition), which were reserved purely for white competitors. In 1971, the international boycott of sporting links with South Africa (described later) led to the introduction of a multinational sports programme which allowed whites, coloureds (mixed heritage), Africans (blacks) and Asians (Indian subcontinent) to compete against each other as 'nations', provided they affiliated to one of the governments 'national' federations. As international links receded further, the government eventually permitted domestic competitions between 'nations' and eventually club-level competitions between 'nations'.[13] It is likely that it was this legislation that allowed the South African Sports Association for the Disabled to hold mixed trials and to send its first racially mixed team to Stoke Mandeville in 1975. As the disabled were affiliated to a separate 'national' federation they were, in essence, a distinct 'nation' for whom colour was a secondary consideration.

South Africa and the Olympic Games

South Africa first competed in the Olympic Games in St Louis in 1904 and continued to compete at every summer Games up to and including Rome in 1960.[14] The issue of discrimination within South Africa was not, however, officially discussed at the IOC until the IOC session in Rome in 1959. At the IOC session in Baden Baden in 1963 the South African IOC member, Reginald Honey, proposed that apartheid was an internal matter which did not concern the IOC. This led the IOC to decide that if there was no change to the discrimination in sport policy, then South Africa would be excluded from the Tokyo Olympic Games.[15] These changes did not occur and so South Africa did not participate in the Tokyo Games in 1964. However, three years later at the IOC session in Tehran the IOC voted that South Africa could enter a multiracial team for the Mexico Games on the understanding that the South African NOC continued to fight against all forms of racial discrimination in amateur sport.[16] This led to the newly emerging African states threatening a boycott and this was followed by boycott threats from the Soviet Union and black American athletes. Under pressure from the Mexican organizing committee, the IOC finally withdrew the invitation to the South African team in May 1968.[17] South Africa was finally expelled from the Olympic Movement at the Amsterdam IOC session in 1970 and did not compete in the Olympic Games again until 1992.[18]

Anti-apartheid and non-racial sports organizations

In the late 1950s Dennis Brutus, a coloured school teacher from Port Elizabeth, called a conference of black sports federations at which they formed the South African Sports Association (SASA). This was the first non-racial sports organization in South Africa and lobbied international sports federations to withdraw recognition of the whites-only South African member organization, as well as lobbying the IOC to insist on SANOC integrating black sports people. In 1960 SASA was effectively closed down by the police and the government, who placed a banning order on Dennis Brutus that made it illegal for him to belong to any organization, teach, write or attend any meeting of more than two people. In 1963, the former SASA officials formed the South African Non-Racial Olympic Committee (SANROC) whose aim it was to replace SANOC as members of the IOC. However, when Dennis Brutus, Chairman of SANROC, wrote to members of the IOC in 1963 asking them to join the struggle against racist sport, Arthur Porritt, the IOC member for New Zealand dismissed him as 'a well known trouble maker'.[19] Eventually, SANROC was forced to wind up its activities in South Africa and go into exile in London, where it continued its activities, applying pressure to any national and international sporting organizations and teams that continued to have sporting links with South Africa. Jarvie and Reid claim the strength of SANROC was their refusal to separate sporting demands from the broader demands of social change.[20] According to Miller, SANROC had no serious connection to sport. They were in fact a political arm of the black African protest movement, funded by Czechoslovakia and other Communist sources, which must have added fuel to western nations' claims that the anti-apartheid movement was a communist plot.[21]

Another major player in the black African protest was the Supreme Council for Sport in Africa (SCSA) set up in the mid-1960s by the newly independent African states who began to try and convince the rest of the world's sporting organizations to expel South Africa.[22] The impact of this organization was most clearly seen in the black African boycott of the Montreal Olympic Games in 1976 in protest at a New Zealand All Blacks rugby tour of South Africa. However, often the white nations found ways to negate the demands of organizations such as SANROC and SCSA by the adoption of tactics such as the weighted voting system. At the International Association of Athletics Federations (IAAF) meeting in Budapest in 1966 they adopted a weighted voting system that gave 37 predominantly white nations 244 votes and 99 predominantly non-white nations only 195 votes, possibly in reaction to mounting pressure from African nations calling for the banning of the South African member organization from the IAAF. In 1970, representatives from non-white countries had only 33% of the IOC voting power.[23]

The worldwide political background

It is important to note some of the other major political issues outside sport that acted as a backdrop to the whole issue of the boycott campaign against South Africa and the differing views that arose as a result of it. The Cold War between western nations and the Soviet bloc was at its height during this period, with fear of communism and communists at the very top of the agenda for some western governments. In addition, the civil rights movement was gaining momentum in 1960s America as non-whites attempted to attain equal rights with their fellow white countrymen and women. Both were extremely emotive issues. According to Lapchick, a 1970 survey showed that 68% of white nations were not opposed to South African participation in sport, believing that apartheid was an internal South African issue. However, 98% of non-white nations were opposed to South African participation in sport without complete sports integration. All 32% of white nations opposed to South Africa's participation were from the socialist bloc.[24] Booth claims most whites regarded the sports boycott of South Africa and the anti-apartheid movement as a whole to be part of a coordinated communist campaign.[25] Ramsamy also claims that support for Harry Edwards and his Project for Human Rights helped play a vital role in the exclusion of South Africa from the Olympic movement. Edwards' project was primarily aimed at seeking justice for African-American athletes, possibly as part of the wider civil rights movement, and felt a common cause in the exclusion of 'racist South Africa'.[26] Ramsamy goes on to claim that it is possible that some of the pro-South African lobby actually voted to exclude South Africa in the hope of countering Edwards' campaign for a boycott of the Olympic Games by black US athletes.

South Africa and the sporting boycott

According to Tatz, the most powerful, pervasive and pertinent force in South Africa was the Broederbond, a secret brotherhood of 12,000 'Super Afrikaners' which harnessed all political, administrative, social and, where possible, economic forces to its cause, namely, the sovereignty of Afrikanerdom and its values.[27] Tatz claims that the government's official sports policy was based on the Broederbond's recommendations of 1971. Huddlestone claimed sport may have been South Africa's Achilles' heel, in the sense that its national teams were so obviously good in certain sports, particularly rugby union, and so to deny South Africa the opportunity to demonstrate its excellence would shake its self-assurance very severely.[28] This appears to be borne out in a statement by the Broederbond in which they admitted that sport is important in international affairs for the prestige of countries and the promotion of a cause.[29] The eventual and almost total international sporting boycott of South Africa by the rest of the world played a major part in the downfall of the apartheid regime.

Having outlined the impact of apartheid on sport in South Africa and its impact on the participation of non-disabled, non-white sportsmen and women there now follows a brief description of what it was like to be a disabled sportsman or woman in South Africa under Apartheid.

People with disabilities in South Africa

There is very little information currently available about what it was like to be disabled in South Africa prior to the mid-1980s. In terms of health care for the general population, Bernstein claims that the white population of South Africa enjoyed an extremely high standard of health care. There were no malnutritional diseases to be found among them, there was a more than adequate supply of doctors, and hospitals had an excellent reputation for their treatment of their white patients. In general, white patients had better access to better facilities – less crowded hospitals, speedier referrals, better equipped surgeries and so on. With few exceptions, all facilities were segregated, those for whites being amongst the best in the world and those for blacks being greatly inferior.[30] Seedat claims that in a country where health and social services for the physically 'normal' black citizens were distinctly inferior to the facilities provided for whites, it should come as no surprise to discover that facilities for the physically disabled were practically non-existent. In 1981 there were a total of 40 institutions for whites, as well as protective workshops. For handicapped coloured people there were only seven workshops subsidised by the Department of Internal Affairs.[31] According to Seedat the following amounts were allocated to Welfare Services for the disabled in the 1982/83 budget:

- White – R 5,769,000
- Indians – R 81,000
- Coloured – R 305,000
- African – R 527,000

As can be seen from the figures, Africans, comprising 72.7% of the population, were allocated less than 10% of the amount allocated to whites, who comprised 15.5% of the population. Seedat also reports a high mortality rate amongst African paraplegics in Soweto, claiming this to be a reflection of the poor and overcrowded living conditions for the average Sowetan. She goes on to describe how difficult it was to accommodate a person in a wheelchair in a tiny house which might be crammed with 10 or even 20 people. Paraplegics, 70% of whom were unemployed in Soweto, were a burden on families already struggling to feed their children. Most paraplegics in Soweto lost their rights to their homes at the same time as losing their jobs on becoming disabled. They had to become lodgers, usually at exorbitant rents, and houses with special facilities for wheelchairs were unheard of.[32]

The Gross National Product of South Africa in the 1970s was one of the highest in Africa and amongst the top 30 in the world, but the wealth was very unevenly distributed. The minority white population received 64% of the national income in 1977, whilst Africans received 26%. On average, a white worker earned more than four times the monthly wage of an African.[33] According to Thompson, unemployment, which was always high amongst black South Africans, increased during the 1970s. Thompson cites South African economist Charles Simkins who estimated that African unemployment almost doubled from 1.2 million to 2.3 million between 1960 and 1977, by which time perhaps 26% of Africans were unemployed. Consequently, Blacks experienced high levels of poverty, under nutrition and disease, especially tuberculosis. The impact of this poverty meant that many Africans turned to crime in order to survive.[34] Little reports that in the late 1950s and early 1960s at the orthopaedic unit at Baragwaneth, one of the largest hospitals in the country serving only blacks and Indians, most of the patients were paraplegics, with 65% of this paraplegia caused by the Totse gangs. Apparently, these outcasts from various tribes roamed Johannesburg robbing and committing crimes against other non-whites. One of their favourite methods of dealing with a victim was to bend the them over and insert a sharpened bicycle spoke, screwdriver or other object into the spinal cord, severing it. Baragwaneth apparently received about 15 cases of this kind of crime a week.[35]

South Africa and disability sport

At a meeting of the International Stoke Mandeville Games Committee (ISMGC) held at Stoke Mandeville in July 1962, the President, Professor Ludwig Guttmann, reported that developments were ongoing in South Africa to form a Paraplegic Sports Association and a Spinal Unit in Cape Town. As a result of this, South Africa had sent their first official team to the 1962 Stoke Mandeville Games. The inaugural meeting of the South African

Paraplegic Games Association was held on November 12 that year at the Old Edwardian Club, Johannesburg. Although it was a multiracial club from its inception, in line with government policy, national Games were held in alternate years for the different race groups.[36] For as Barrish, the Chairman of the organization later pointed out 'whilst the practice of the Association was one of non-discrimination, the environment within which it had to operate continued to be a discriminatory one. For this reason, the activities of the Association over a long period were a microcosm of the social battle that was going on in South Africa.'[37] According to several sources,[38] up until 1975 South Africa sent alternate teams of black participants and white participants to the Stoke Mandeville Games. Interestingly this does not seem to have been an issue for the Games organizers, although in a letter from Charles Dunham, Secretary General of the International Sports Organization for the Disabled (ISOD) in July 1971, the South African Paraplegic Sports Association (SAPSA) was temporarily refused membership because paragraph 2f of their constitution did not conform to the ISOD constitution.[39]

It stated:

> To render its services to all racial groups throughout the territories specified in Para 2(a) hereof with the understanding that, in order that they may in time become interested and self-reliant and be able themselves responsibly and sincerely to serve their people the effort in relation to racial groups other than White will be in the direction of establishing, encouraging, helping and advising separate counterparts for these groups.[40]

This constitution was written in January 1968. No mention can be found that this paragraph ever caused any concern for the ISMGC, although they were not accepted as full members until 1972, so it is possible that it may have at some point. It took until 1975 for them to be accepted as full members of ISOD. South African teams competed at the Paralympic Games in Tokyo, 1964, Tel Aviv, 1968 and Heidelberg, 1972, and at all of the Games held at Stoke Mandeville in the intervening years with the exception of 1969, although it appears to have been the all-white teams that competed in the 'Paralympic' Games. The next Paralympic Games were due to be held in Toronto, Canada in 1976. According to Greig, the first hint for the organizers that the participation of a South African team might cause problems came in May 1974 when the Canadian Minister for Health and Welfare released a statement informing all sports federations that it would not fund athletes travelling to South Africa because of its apartheid practices. As the Federal Government had promised funding of C$500K for the Games, the organizing committee sought clarification from the Minister who in November 1974 wrote urging that South Africa not be invited as their presence would have embarrassing repercussions. South Africa was duly notified that it would not be invited. However, both the ISMGC and ISOD, of whom the SAPSA was now a full member in good standing, were against the expulsion and as such following a meeting in May 1975 the organizing committee informed SAPSA that a team would be welcome provided they had integrated trials and sent an integrated team,[41] which may well have had some impact upon their decision to send their first ever integrated team to Stoke Mandeville in 1975. In the end, South Africa sent a team of around thirty,[42] including nine black athletes. The Games in Toronto lost their Federal funding, but still broke even. However, eight countries withdrew either before or during the Games on the order of their governments. These were Kenya, Sudan and Yugoslavia, who withdrew before the Games, and Cuba, Jamaica, Hungary, India and Poland who turned up in Toronto, but either withdrew prior to the start of the Games or like Poland competed for several days (winning enough medals to place seventh in the medal table). Poland finally withdrew after a failed appeal to the organizing committee to have the South African team thrown out.[43]

South Africa continued to compete at the Stoke Mandeville Games in the period 1977 to 1979 with a racially integrated team. However, a small number of nations boycotted these Games as a result, including Jamaica, Finland and Yugoslavia. In July 1977, the decision was taken to award the 1980 Paralympic Games to Arnhem in the Netherlands, following a lack of any response from the Olympic organizers in Moscow.[44] However, the Dutch parliament, following much debate, decided that if the organizers of the 1980 Games allowed South Africa to compete they would be forced to withdraw their offer of financial support for the Games.[45] Unlike, the Toronto organizers, the organizers in Arnhem took the decision to cancel the South African entry. South Africa did, however, continue to compete at Stoke Mandeville from 1981 to 1983. The Paralympics for 1984 were due to be held on two sites; the wheelchair athletes at the University of Illinois and all other athletes on Long Island, New York. In June 1982, F. Don Miller, Executive Director of the United States Olympic Committee wrote a letter stating that 'the presence of any South African sports team on the soil of the United States would be a grave embarrassment'.[46] In the end, the wheelchair Games in Illinois hit a financial crisis and in March 1984 had to be moved to Stoke Mandeville at very short notice. Despite this, South Africa did not compete in either New York or Stoke Mandeville that year, but they did compete at Stoke Mandeville again the following year for one final time, before finally being expelled from the international disability sports movement.

The presidents and charismatic authority

Both Cantelon and McDermott,[47] with respect to Avery Brundage (IOC President throughout South Africa's expulsion from the Olympic Movement), and Novak,[48] with respect to Sir Ludwig Guttmann (founder of the Paralympic Games and President of both ISMGF and ISOD), apply Weber's concept of charismatic authority to the way each man ran their respective organizations. This concept of the charismatic leader is defined by Weber as applying to certain qualities of an individual by virtue of which they are set apart from others and treated as if endowed with specifically exceptional qualities. However, charisma is inherently unstable and, therefore, usually gets either erased or transferred to a specific office or position such as that of the president or to an organization as a whole such as the IOC.[49]

Avery Brundage's charismatic authority stemmed from his position as president of the IOC, but also from his slavish adherence to what he perceived to be the philosophical principles of the founding charismatic authority of the IOC, namely Baron Pierre de Coubertin.[50] Indeed Miller, in the official history of the Olympic Games and the IOC, describes Brundage as despotic, a moralistic bulldozer, fanatical defender of Coubertin's legacy.[51] As such, he was dead set against countries using the Olympic Games for political purposes.

Guttmann's charismatic authority is somewhat more complex and equally intangible. It has its roots in the medical–humanitarian basis for disability sport, which had at its core the drive to rehabilitate, both physically and socially, soldiers and civilians spinally injured in World War II. However, on top of this, right from the beginning, Guttmann drew distinct parallels between the Olympic Movement and that for disability sport. He modelled his own Games on the Olympic model with opening and closing ceremonies, athletes' oath and so forth.[52] He too was staunchly against the involvement of politics in sport. It even reached the stage where, at a time in the late 1970s when the IOC was mired in political controversies, Guttmann claimed that the disability sport Games were now the 'true Olympics' as they more clearly portrayed the Olympic ideals of Coubertin.[53] On this basis, Guttmann was adamant that the racially integrated team of South Africa would continue to be allowed to compete at all costs.

Some examples of this include:

- Lobbying repeatedly the IOC, the United Nations and many governments with his reasons why the racially integrated team of South Africa should continue to compete.[54]
- Threatening after Toronto to expel any nation that withdrew from the Games on political grounds.[55]
- Threatening to take the Paralympic Games away from Arnhem in 1980 when told South Africa would not be allowed to compete.[56]

It is hard to determine exactly what was behind this zeal to keep South Africa in the Games, but it may have its basis, at least partially, in the fact that Guttmann was a German Jew who had escaped the Nazis just prior to the onset of war.[57] However, Guttmann passed away in March 1980 and the new presidents of ISOD and ISMGF, perhaps lacking some of the charismatic authority of Guttmann, accepted South Africa's expulsion from the Arnhem Games. They did, however, continue to allow them to compete at the Stoke Mandeville Games up to and including 1985, when factors to be outlined shortly finally overtook them. During the period leading up to the 1984 Games, which was originally to be on two sites in the USA, they did soften their stance somewhat in that motions were passed by both organizations stating that where a government refused visas to the South African team they would not penalize the host organizing committee for abiding by their government's wishes.[58]

'Keep politics out of sport' – a slogan of its time

Numerous individuals and sporting organizations have, over the years, tried to claim that sport is above or transcends politics and as such politics should be kept out of sport, but as Cashmore points out:

> This is the reason sport and politics mix so well – because people think they shouldn't. So when political factions, or even whole nations, consciously manipulate events to make their points decisively and dramatically, they often opt for sport, knowing that the rest of the world will be so outraged they'll take immediate notice.[59]

Sport then, practised and watched by billions of people around the world, forms a ready-made conduit for governments and individuals to both make political statements about their own beliefs and to challenge the political ideologies of others that they strongly disagree with. As such, it is impossible for sports people to extract themselves from politics, while at the same time it is impossible to keep politicians out of sport, especially if they can see some advantage in making use of it. Clearly, the bigger the event, the bigger the audience and the media coverage of it and so the greater the potential impact of any political action. Therefore, an event such as the Olympic Games, the largest and most media-saturated sporting event in the world, is a prime opportunity to make a political statement, either during the Games themselves such as the 'black power salute' at the men's 200-m medal ceremony in Mexico City, or by deliberately boycotting the Games in protest at the presence of another country whom the boycotters may disagree with in some way, such as the African nations boycott of the Montreal Games due to the New Zealand rugby tour of South Africa.

Nearly all the protagonists on both sides involved in the boycott campaign against South Africa and their apartheid practices used the argument that politics should be kept out of sport. Avery Brundage, president of the IOC, claimed in 1956 that 'sport is completely free of politics'.[60] Sir Ludwig Guttmann, founder and head of the international disability sports movement, was staunchly against the involvement of politics in sport and even the South African government were not averse to claiming that politics should be kept out of sport by way of decrying the sporting boycott against them. It should be noted, however, that much of this occurred at a time in history when an understanding of how the world (and the world of politics in particular) works and how the world of sport interacts with the wider world were not widely understood in the way they are today. Seen through a current understanding of the world such claims appear extremely naive.

The rise of disability politics

The social model of disability was first theorized by the Union of Physically Impaired Against Segregation (UPIAS) in the UK in 1976,[61] as a way of overcoming the negative perceptions entrenched in the medical model of disability and to highlight the ways in which disabled people were actually disabled more by the built environment and these negative perceptions than they were by their own impairments. It led some people with disabilities to want to have a much greater say in the way they lived their lives and to take a much more active and often politicized role within the society in which they lived. Part of this was the desire to take a much greater role in the running of organizations that were aimed at improving their lives. Up to that point, it would be hard to argue that the disability sport movement had not done a great deal to improve the lives of those disabled individuals who chose to take part, but it would also appear that the underlying ethos of those in charge was a paternalistic one, with the athletes with disabilities who participated gratefully accepting the new opportunities afforded to them without question. This is perhaps best demonstrated in an exchange between a blind delegate from Denmark attending the eighth general assembly of ISOD for the first time in 1979 and Sir Ludwig, the ISOD president.[62] The blind delegate asked Sir Ludwig if ISOD was an organization of disabled or an organization for disabled and why he had not received the huge amount of information in an accessible format. Sir Ludwig replied that his work for the disabled was history and that the delegate was here for the first time and should sit and listen and learn, and not make impertinent remarks. In December 1983, the UPIAS newsletter stated that 'the very atmosphere around Stoke Mandeville reeks with dominance and authority … you will smell this odour mixed up with paternalism'.[63] In 1979, at a European table tennis event at Stoke Mandeville, Maggie Jones, twice a Paralympic medal winner, was banned for life from all ISMG events for handing out leaflets highlighting the healthcare facilities for disabled blacks in South Africa.[64] This led to the first protest at the International Stoke Mandeville Games by a group calling themselves Disabled People Against Apartheid. These protests continued every year the Games were held at Stoke Mandeville until South Africa were finally expelled from the Games in 1985 and got increasing amounts of media coverage both locally and nationally.[65]

Worldwide politics

Government intervention in national disability sports organizations

As the anti-apartheid cause gathered momentum, many governments signed treaties and various other UN resolutions and declarations such as the Gleneagles Agreement, which stated that signatories would strive 'vigorously to combat the evil of apartheid by withholding any form of support for, and by taking every practical step to discourage contact or competition by their nationals, with sporting organizations, teams or sportsmen from South Africa'.[66] As such, they did not want organizations within their borders going against the proscribed political direction. This was especially true for organizations that were dependent upon government funding for their activities, as was the case with many disability sports organizations, and so more and more governments applied political pressure to prevent their teams competing at events where South African teams were present.

Geo-Politics

As Novak points out the collective voice and power of the African nations within the Olympic movement were much more powerful than in the disability sports movement.[67] As Table 1 depicts, the number of African nations competing at the Olympic Games compared with the Paralympics was far, far higher, giving them a much more powerful voice within the Olympic Movement, although this was often mediated by tactics such as the weighted voting system highlighted earlier. This was made stronger still by the success of African athletes in sports such as track and field and boxing, which helped to draw large audiences. Issues such as poverty, lack of technology (e.g. wheelchairs) and the far slower pace of development of services for people with disabilities in Africa meant that far fewer were able to compete in sport for the disabled. This meant that within the Paralympic Movement their collective power was far weaker in determining policy within the movement.

Table 1.   Number of African nations participating by year (excluding South Africa).

Year	Olympic Games	Paralympic Games
1964	20	1
1968	23	2
1972	27	4
1976	6* (2)	3

*Four nations competed for three days before withdrawing.[68]

ISMGF and SANROC

In July 1979, there was a meeting between the ISMGF Executive Committee, Sam Ramsamy and Mr Stein of SANROC and Menzo Barrish, Dr Potgeiter and Paul Moeti of the South African Sports Association for the Physically Disabled at Stoke Mandeville.[69] At the meeting, Ramsamy claims that Dr Guttmann explained that he had fled to the UK in 1933 as he became aware of Nazi intentions. He also stated that he had visited South Africa and had met Mr Vorster, the then president of South Africa. Ramsamy reminded Sir Ludwig that Mr Vorster was interned during World War II because of his support for Nazi Germany to which Dr Guttmann claimed that Mr Vorster was fine now as 'he is totally anti-communist'.[70] Ramsamy claims it was at this point that he realized that it was useless pursuing their conversation. He also met with Ms Joan Scruton, Secretary General of ISMGF and ISOD, and gathered immediately that both Scruton and Guttman were using the notion of 'separating sport and politics' as a ruse to accommodate apartheid South Africa. According to the minutes of that meeting, despite the claims by the ISMGF Executive that the racially integrated South African disabled sports team marking a breakthrough in the fight against apartheid, Ramsamy and SANROC rejected this claim because they belonged to an organization that believed that the only way to see effective change inside South Africa was to completely isolate them.[71] This was a view that gained greatly in momentum over time, eventually spreading into the world of disability sport and leading to the eventual expulsion of South Africa from the movement despite their racially integrated team.

Attitudes towards the disabled

Interestingly, there appears to be two camps when it comes to government reactions to the participation of South Africa in the Paralympic Games. The first is illustrated by a quote in Novak from a British Foreign and Commonwealth Office official regarding the participation of Rhodesia in the Heidelberg Games in 1972 who stated that 'it would be wrong to bring cripples into the political arena',[72] which gives an indication of the Paralympics being seen as insignificant and beneath politics. The second kind of reaction is those countries who appear to have used the Paralympic Games as an easy and cheap political tool such as Cuba, Poland, Jamaica, Hungary, India and Yugoslavia who all boycotted the Toronto Paralympic Games, but sent large delegations to the Montreal Olympics. However, it should be noted that some of these countries were, unlike Poland, at least consistent in their boycott of both the Paralympic and Stoke Mandeville Games whilst South Africa continued to compete.

Media visibility and the scale of games

Prior to 1976, the Paralympic Games were small, wheelchair only and relatively unknown and unheard of outside the disabled community. Therefore, they were almost untouched by the kind of nationalist agenda and economic politics that plagued the Olympic Games. The Paralympic Games were all but ignored by the outside world. However, in 1976 events such as the Soweto riots, the New Zealand rugby tour of South Africa, the African boycott of the Montreal Olympics combined with the fact that the Paralympics were to be a much larger multidisability event for the first time and were to be held in Canada, whose Federal Government had co-sponsored a UN resolution against apartheid in November 1975, suddenly focused the world media spotlight upon the movement in a way never before encountered. In fact, Bob Jackson, Chairman of the Games organizing committee in Toronto claimed the Games were a victim of worldwide media and had become a political pawn.[73] Unfortunately, once the issue of South Africa's participation in international disability sport became an issue of media attention it became impossible to go back to the way things had been prior to the Toronto Games. Slowly, but surely, the issue became enveloped as another part of the worldwide anti-apartheid campaign. Interestingly, however, what it also highlighted was the increasing importance of the four-yearly Paralympic Games as opposed to the Stoke Mandeville Games from which they had sprung. This is perhaps best illustrated by the fact that Poland, who withdrew from the Toronto Games in protest at South Africa's participation, happily competed alongside the South Africans at the next three Stoke Mandeville Games, but then threatened to boycott the next Paralympic Games in Arnhem if South Africa were to compete.[74]

South African manoeuvring

According to Reddy, in order to overcome the increasing stranglehold of boycotts on South African sport in the 1970s, the South African government began to send teams abroad with no advance publicity in order to prevent protests, spend millions of rand in order to entice individuals and teams to play in South Africa, and periodically announce 'concessions' that Reddy claims were meant to do nothing more than deceive the gullible.[75] Although there is no absolute proof that this occurred in disability sport there is some evidence that it may have. In an attempt to prove to the ISMGF committee that the disability sports movement in South Africa was non-racial, the whole committee was invited to visit South Africa to spend time at disabled sports clubs and witness first-hand that the selection trials for international teams were multiracial and based purely on results. Menzo Barrish, long-time head of the disability sports movement in South Africa stated at the AGM of the South African Sports Association for Paraplegics and People with other Disabilities in 1978 that Minister of Sport Koornhof had personally obtained R26,880 from the State Treasury to pay for the visit of the ISMGF committee members.[76] In addition, Dr Guttmann had a personal meeting with Dr Koornhof in which Dr Guttmann was apparently given repeated assurances 'that it was the genuine desire of the South African government to make sport free from political, racial and religious interference'.[77] Dr Guttmann appears to have been totally taken in by these assurances as he refers to them on several occasions in letters to bodies such as the United Nations and in the minutes of ISMGF and ISOD.[78] In addition, Maggie Jones (the athlete banned from Stoke Mandeville for distributing anti-apartheid leaflets) stated that one of the reasons that Dr Guttmann kept fighting for the inclusion of South Africa in the Games was that they made regular substantial financial contributions to the Paraplegic Sports Endowment Fund, which helped finance the Games.[79] Although annual accounts for this fund certainly show this to be true – South Africa made a contribution of £281 in 1978 and £1000 in 1979,[80] it is also true that several other nations made similar sized contributions. A final possible example of political manoeuvring came when, following the political uproar regarding their participation in Toronto in 1976, and the refusal of Russia to host the Games in 1980, South Africa offered to host the Paralympic Games.[81] Although no reason can be found to explicitly explain why they were not chosen, there were originally five other bids and eventually Arnhem was chosen as it was decided the Games should be in Europe.

Boycotts finally start to bite

Following on from the boycotts in Toronto in 1976 some nations such as Yugoslavia continued to boycott the Stoke Mandeville Games as well, whereas others such as Poland did not, and were content to compete alongside the South African team. However, gradually as political pressure mounted on the South African regime worldwide and events in South Africa such as the Soweto riots in 1976, the death of Steve Biko in detention in 1978 and the declaration of a state of emergency in 1985, gave the government power to deal with all resistance to apartheid, the number of countries boycotting the Games steadily rose. It reached a point whereby in 1985 the British Paraplegic Sports Society, as hosts of the Games at Stoke Mandeville were forced to write to the ISMGF committee regarding the impact boycotts were now having on the Games.[82] Countries that had boycotted the 1985 Stoke Mandeville Games included Kenya, Zimbabwe, Finland, USA, Canada, New Zealand, Jamaica, Trinidad and Tobago & Yugoslavia. Finally, on July 29, 1985 a vote to no longer accept South African entries for the Games was carried by a narrow majority of 7 for, 5 against and one abstention.[83]

Conclusion

According to Booth, in 1982 Robert Archer and Antoine Bouillon concluded that 'one looks in vain' to find a single white sporting organization that disregarded or challenged racial segregation within apartheid South Africa.[84] Either they did not bother to look outside the world of non-disabled sport or, like many people at that time, did not consider disability sport as 'real' sport. It appears from the evidence that the South African Sports Association for the Disabled did its best to provide all athletes with a disability, irrespective of colour, the opportunity to compete in international sport, albeit within the confines of the prevailing political structure within South Africa at the time. The ISMGF and ISOD, led by Ludwig Guttmann appear to have done their best to ensure the participation of the South African team within their Games. At first this does not appear to have been difficult as disability sport appears to have been able to operate under the political radar, possibly because of its perceived lack of importance. However, as the Games grew in size and the desire of Dr Guttmann to link the Games to the Olympic movement by seeking the same host city as the Olympic Games began to take effect, the Games themselves became more visible along with their South African connections. As the worldwide political pressure to cut links with South Africa grew incessantly, and possibly aided by the death of Dr Guttmann in 1980, the pressure on the disability sports movement to cut its ties with its South African member slowly grew to the point that the movement itself was in danger of collapsing. This is possibly a rather simplistic overview of how South Africa was able to compete in international disability sport for so long after their Olympic counterparts had been excluded, but hopefully the various issues that have been highlighted in this article, which are all interconnected to varying and complex degrees, have gone some way to highlight some of the reasons.

Notes

[1] Cashmore, *Making Sense of Sport.*
[2] Beinart and Dubow, ed., *Segregation and Apartheid.*
[3] Whalley-Hammell, *Perspectives on Disability.*
[4] Tatz, *Sport in South Africa.*
[5] Whalley- Hammell, *Perspectives on Disability.*
[6] Beinart and Dubow, ed., *Segregation and Apartheid.*
[7] Turok, *Inequality as State Policy.*
[8] Seedat, *Crippling a Nation.*
[9] Whalley- Hammell, *Perspectives on Disability.*
[10] Brittain, 'Elite Athletes with Disabilities'.
[11] Booth, *Sport and Politics.*
[12] Keech, 'The Ties That Bind'.
[13] Cashmore, *Making Sense of Sport.*
[14] IOC Website, 2010, 'Rome 1960: All Facts: Consequences of Apartheid'. http://www.olympic. org/en/content/Olympic-Games/All-Past-Olympic-Games/Summer/Rome-1960/Rome-1960/
[15] Honey, 'South Africa and the Olympic Movement'.
[16] Olympic Review, 'About the South African Team'. http://www.la84foundation.org/Olympi cInformationCenter/OlympicReview/1968/ore05/ore05l.pdf.
[17] Killanin, *My Olympic Years*, 46.
[18] Olympic Review, 'Olympism Against Apartheid'. http://www.la84foundation.org/Olympi cInformationCenter/OlympicReview/1988/ore249/ORE249f.pdf.
[19] Booth, *Sport and Politics.*
[20] Jarvie and Reid, 'Sport in South Africa'.
[21] Miller, *The Official History*, 167.
[22] Cashmore, *Making Sense of Sport.*
[23] Lapchick, *The Politics of Race.*
[24] Ibid.
[25] Booth, *Sport and Politics.*
[26] Ramsamy, 'Apartheid'.
[27] Tatz, *Sport in South Africa.*

28 Huddlestone in Cashmore, *Making Sense of Sport*.
29 Booth, *Sport and Politics*.
30 Bernstein, *For Their Triumphs*.
31 Seedat, Crippling a Nation
32 Ibid.
33 Ibid.
34 Thompson, *A History of South Africa*.
35 Little, *African Safari Tour Journal*.
36 South African Sports Association for Persons with a Disability Website, 'Brief History of Sport for Disabled in South Africa'. http://www.sasapd.org.za/data/Sport%20structures%20and%20SASAPD%20June%202005.htm
37 Letter from Menzo Barrish to Paul Luedtke dated April 29, 1992 [International Wheelchair and Amputee Sports Federation (IWAS) Archives].
38 Letter from Menzo Barrish to Paul Luedtke dated April 29, 1992 (IWAS Archives); Minutes of a meeting between the Executive Board of the International Stoke Mandeville Games Federation with the Dutch Olympic Committees, Mr Sam Ramsamy Chairman (and SACOS overseas representative) and Mr Stein of SAN-ROC dated July 23, 1979 (IWAS Archives).
39 Letter dated March 19, 1971 from Charles Dunham, Secretary General – International Sports Organization for the Disabled to Menzo Barrish, South African Tean Manager (IWAS Archives).
40 The South African Paraplegic Games Association Constitution, January 1968 (IWAS Archives).
41 Grieg, 'South African Apartheid', 57.
42 Coetzee and Van Der Merwe, 'South Africa's Participation', 83.
43 Guttmann. 'Reflection', 233.
44 Minutes of the Meeting of the Executive Board of the International Stoke Mandeville Games Federation held at Stoke Mandeville, UK, Saturday July 23, 1977, 2 (IWAS Archives).
45 Minutes of the Meeting of the Executive Board of the International Stoke Mandeville Games Federation held at Stoke Mandeville, UK, December 1, 1979, 7. (IWAS Archives).
46 Letter dated June 17, 1982 from F. Don Miller, Executive Director – United States Olympic Committee to B. Dale Wiley, Chairman National Wheelchair Athletic Association (IWAS Archives).
47 Cantelon and McDermott, 'Charisma and the Rational'.
48 Novak, 'Politics and the Paralympic Games'.
49 Ibid.
50 Cantelon and McDermott, 'Charisma and the Rational'.
51 Miller, *The Official History*, 167.
52 Brittain, 'The Evolution of the Paralympic Games'.
53 Letter dated November 6, 1975 from Sir Ludwig Guttmann to Madame Berlioux, Secretary General – International Olympic Committee (IOC Archives).
54 For example, letter dated February 27, 1978 from Sir Ludwig Guttmann to the Tri-Partite Council Special Committee Against Apartheid, United Nations (IWAS Archives).
55 Minutes of the Council Meeting of the International Stoke Mandeville Games Federation held on Wednesday August 11, 1976 at Toronto, Canada, 5. (IWAS Archives).
56 Minutes of the Council Meeting of the International Stoke Mandeville Games Federation held on July 28, 1979 at Stoke Mandeville, UK, 3. (IWAS Archives).
57 Goodman, *Spirit of Stoke Mandeville*.
58 Minutes of the Meeting of the Executive Committee of the International Stoke Mandeville Games Federation held at Stoke Mandeville, UK, Saturday July 31, 1982 (IWAS Archives).
59 Cashmore, *Making Sense of Sport*.
60 Ibid.
61 Union of Physically Impaired Against Segregation (UPIAS), *Fundamental Principles of Disability*.
62 Minutes of the eighth General Assembly of the International Sports Organization for the Disabled held at Stoke Mandeville, UK, September 1 and 2, 1979, 16 (IWAS Archives).
63 UPIAS, 'Disabled People Against Apartheid' (IWAS Archives).
64 Scruton, Stoke Mandeville, 188.
65 For example, 'Soaked Protesters Fail to Dampen Wheelchair Games', *The Daily Telegraph* July 25, 1983, 11.
66 Cashmore, *Making Sense of Sport*.

67 Novak, 'Politics and the Paralympic Games'.
68 Wallechinsky, *The Complete Book of the Olympics*, X.
69 Minutes of a meeting between the Executive Board of the International Stoke Mandeville Games Federation with the Dutch Olympic Committees, Mr Sam Ramsamy (Chairman (and SACOS overseas representative) and Mr Stein of SAN-ROC dated July 23, 1979 (IWAS Archives).
70 Ramsamy, S., personal communication, e-mail dated June 28, 2009.
71 Minutes of the eighth General Assembly of the International Sports Organization for the Disabled held at Stoke Mandeville, UK, September 1 and 2, 1979, 16 (IWAS Archives).
72 Novak, 'Politics and the Paralympic Games'.
73 *Torontolympiad Daily News*, 'Politics Interfere – Again', Saturday August 7, 1976, 1. (IWAS Archives).
74 Minutes of the eighth General Assembly of the International Sports Organization for the Disabled held at Stoke Mandeville, UK, September 1 and 2, 1979, 8 (IWAS Archives).
75 Reddy, *Sports and the Liberation*. http://www.anc.org.za/un/reddy/sam-ram.html
76 Review by the National Chairman (Menzo Barrish) of the activities of the South African Sports Association for Paraplegics and Other Physically Disabled: Annual General Meeting to be held on March 26, 1978 in Cape Town (IWAS Archives).
77 Letter dated November 18, 1977 from Sir Ludwig Guttman to Dr Kurt Waldheim, Secretary General, United Nations (IWAS Archives).
78 Letter dated February 27, 1978 from Sir Ludwig Guttmann to the Tri-Partite Council Special Committee Against Apartheid, United Nations, 1–2. (IWAS Archives).
79 Jones, personal communication, e-mail dated August 30, 2007.
80 British Paraplegic Sports Society Limited, 1979, Seventh Annual Report and Accounts for the Year Ended March 31, 1979, 16. British Paraplegic Sports Society Limited, 1980, Eighth Annual Report and Accounts for the Year Ended March 31, 1980, 15.
81 Bailey, *Athlete First*, 37.
82 Minutes of the Meeting of the Executive Committee of the International Stoke Mandeville Games Federation held at Stoke Mandeville, UK, Friday July 26, 1985 (IWAS Archives).
83 Minutes of the Meeting of the Executive Committee of the International Stoke Mandeville Games Federation held at Stoke Mandeville, UK, Monday July 29, 1985 (IWAS Archives).
84 Booth, *Sport and Politics*.

References

Bailey, Steve. *Athlete First: A History of the Paralympic Movement*. Chichester: Wiley, 2008.
Beinart, William, and Saul Dubow. 'Introduction: The Historiography of Segregation and Apartheid'. In *Segregation and Apartheid in Twentieth Century South Africa*, edited by William Beinart and Saul Dubow, 1–24. London: Routledge, 1995.
Bernstein, Hilda. *For Their Triumphs & For Their Tears: Women in Apartheid South Africa*. London: International Defence Aid Fun for South Africa, 1985.
Booth, Douglas. *Sport and Politics in South Africa*. London: Frank Cass, 1998.
Brittain, Ian. 'Elite Athletes with Disabilities: Problems and Possibilities'. PhD diss., Buckinghamshire Chilterns University College, 2002.
Brittain, Ian. 'The Evolution of the Paralympic Games'. In *Benchmark Games: The Sydney 2000 Paralympic Games*, edited by Richard Cashman and Simon Darcy, 19–34. Petersham, NSW: Walla Walla Press, 2008.
Cantelon, Hart, and Lisa McDermott. 'Charisma and the Rational-Legal Organization'. *Olympika* X (2001): 33–58.
Cashmore, Ellis. *Making Sense of Sport*. 2nd edn. London: Routledge, 1996.
Coetzee, G.J., and Floris J.G. Van Der Merwe. 'South Africa's Participation in the International Stoke Mandeville Games'. *South African Journal for Research in Sport, Physical Education and Recreation* 13, no. 1 (1990): 79–85.
Goodman, Susan. *Spirit of Stoke Mandeville: The Story of Sir Ludwig Guttmann*. London: Collins, 1986.
Greig, David.A. 'South African Apartheid and the 1976 Torontolympiad: A Historical Analysis of Influential Actions and Events Affecting the 5th Paralympic Games'. Masters thesis, University of Windsor, 2005.

Guttmann, Ludwig. 'Reflection on the 1976 Toronto Olympiad for the Physically Disabled'. *Paraplegia* 14 (1976): 225–40.

Honey, Andrew. 'South Africa and the Olympic Movement'. *Fifth International Symposium for Olympic Research* (2000): 177–84.

Jarvie, Grant, and Irene Reid. 'Sport in South Africa'. In *The International Politics of Sport in the 20th Century*, edited by James Riorden and Arnd Kruger. London: E & FN Spon, 1999.

Keech, Malcolm. 'The Ties That Bind: South Africa And Sports Diplomacy 1958 – 1963'. *The Sports Historian* 21, no. 1 (2001): 71–93.

Killanin, Lord. *My Olympic Years: President of the International Olympic Committee 1972–80*. London: Secker & Warburg, 1983.

Lapchick, Richard. *The Politics of Race and International Sport*. Westport, CT: Greenwood Press, 1975.

Little, Jan. 'African Safari Tour Journal: USA Paraplegic Athletes' Tour of the Republic of South Africa and the Federation of Rhodesia and Nyasaland''. University of Illinois Archives, June 11 to July 25, 1962.

Miller, David. *The Official History of the Olympic Games and the IOC*. Edinburgh: Mainstream Publishing, 2008.

Novak, Andrew. 'Politics and the Paralympic Games: Disability Sport in Rhodesia–Zimbabwe'. *Journal of Olympic History* 16, no. 1 (2008): 47–55.

Ramsamy, Sam. 'Apartheid, Boycotts and the Games'. In *Five Ring Circus: Money, Power and Politics at the Olympic Games*, edited by Alan Tomlinson and Garry Whannell, 44–52. London: Pluto Press, 1984.

Scruton, Joan. *Stoke Mandeville: Road to the Paralympics*. Aylesbury: Peterhouse Press, 1998.

Seedat, Aziza. *Crippling a Nation: Health in Apartheid South Africa*. London: International Defence and Aid Fund for South Africa, 1984.

Tatz, Colin. *Sport in South Africa*. NSW: Australian Anti-Apartheid Movement, 1985.

Thompson, Leonard. *A History of South Africa*. New Haven, CT: Yale University Press, 1990.

Turok, Ben. *Inequality as State Policy: The South African Case*. Milton Keynes: Open University, 1976.

Union of Physically Impaired Against Segregation (UPIAS). *Fundamental Principles of Disability*. London: UPIAS, 1976.

Union of Physically Impaired Against Segregation (UPIAS). 'Disabled People Against Apartheid'. *Disability Challenge Newsletter* 2 (December 1983).

Wallechinsky, David. *The Complete Book of the Olympics*. Harmondsworth, UK: Penguin Books, 1984.

Whalley-Hammell, Karen. *Perspectives on Disability and Rehabilitation: Contesting Assumptions; Challenging Practice*. London: Elsevier, 2006.

Contested issues in research on the media coverage of female Paralympic athletes

Athanasios (Sakis) Pappous[a,b], Anne Marcellini[b] and Eric de Léséleuc[b]

[a]Centre for Sports Studies, University of Kent, Canterbury, UK; [b]Interdisciplinary Research Group: Santé, Education et Situations de Handicap, UFR-STAPS, University of Montpellier 1, Montpellier, France

The Paralympic Games are considered to be the second biggest sporting event in the world, after the Summer Olympic Games, however, research on the media coverage of athletes with disabilities is in its infancy. More specifically, there is a lack of studies focusing on whether quantitative and qualitative differences exist in the manner in which the female and male Paralympic athletes are represented in the print media. In contrast, there is an extensive body of scholarly research on the differential media treatment of female and male Olympic athletes. This article includes three aspects: (1) a brief summary of the media coverage of non-disabled female athletes, with the aim of providing some research indicators that could be used in analogous studies of Paralympic sport; (2) the examination of the limited media literature on the portrayals of female and male Paralympic athletes; and (3) a discussion of possible future research in this relatively unexplored, area of media, gender and Paralympic sport.

Even though the Paralympic Games are considered to be the second biggest sporting event in the world sport arena after the Summer Olympic Games, research on the media coverage of athletes with disabilities is in its infancy. Indeed, research on the media depiction of sports for people with disabilities has not changed much since 2001, when Schantz and Gilbert[1] stated that studies about print coverage of sports activities were rare. In fact, our review of the relevant literature published during the last 10 years identified only four studies that examined the media treatment of Paralympic athletes; two focused on American television[2] and two on European newspapers.[3] However, none of these studies focused on whether quantitative and qualitative differences exist in the manner in which female and male Paralympic athletes are represented in the print media. Contrary to the limited literature on media, gender and Paralympic athletes, their Olympic counterparts have attracted an extensive body of scholarly work regarding the differential media treatment of female and male athletes. Hence, the first part of this article presents a, non-exhaustive summary of the media coverage of non-disabled female athletes. The aim of this article is to provide some indicators of the nature of research that could be used in order to inspire analogous studies on Paralympic sport. It then goes on to discuss the limited literature on media portrayals of female and male Paralympic athletes. It concludes with a discussion of the possibilities for future studies in this relatively unexplored area.

The role of the media in the cultural construction of disability

Disability is viewed differently in each cultural context and in each historical period.[4] Merely a decade ago, for example, a lower leg amputee was considered a severe disability in South Africa, however, nowadays the achievements of Oscar Pistorius (the most universally famous Paralympic athlete at the present time) have contributed to the 'normalization' of amputation, in part because his use of highly sophisticated artificial feet has attracted global media attention.

Today the representation of people with disabilities in the media is 'regarded as confirming what it means to be a disabled person in this society'.[5] Indeed, media institutions are the most powerful agents in creating the *mediated reality* that most people live in, at least in western societies (which have also been called 'media societies'). Deni Elliott states that only a small percentage of what we know about the world is based on first-person sense experience. The media provide the vicarious experience and shape our perception of it.[6] With this incredible influence, the media can be found to transmit cultural stereotyping or, on the contrary, have the potential of generating alternative meanings of identity. Sport is also viewed as playing a crucial role in the transmission of dominant cultural ideologies. Media and sports are key agents in reproducing, constructing or transforming gender and disability stereotypes.[7]

Female non-disabled athletes and the media

The role of media in maintaining or reinforcing stereotyped portrayals of female athletes has been a common and well-documented theme in sports sociology research over the past 30 years.[8] Among the stereotyped reporting on female athletes we find humorous feature stories on women's sports and a frequent sexual objectification of female athletes.[9] Other common patterns are infantilization (female athletes frequently called 'girls', 'young ladies') and trivialization, that is, by focusing on the non-sport-related aspects (such as their appearance, their professional occupation, their roles as mothers, wives and so on) instead of offering information about their qualifications as sports champions.[10] Unless involved in a scandal, it is the sports skills that are invariably a focus for articles on their male counterparts. It is also important to mention that stereotyped portrayals are 'culturally sensitive'. For example, women wearing the hijab are often thought to be non-athletic in the west, but we find active segregated sport in many Muslim countries. In quantitative terms, researchers seem to agree that the overall space allotted to female athletes is significantly lower than the one reserved for male athletes. In a review of 12 scientific articles published over a 16-year period, Crossman[11] calculated that the total space dedicated to the coverage of female athletes was 24.7% for articles and 34.7% for photos (compared with coverage allotted to males).

In one of the most cited and prominent articles, Duncan[12] referred to the culturally constructed differences between men and women. These differences are usually highlighted by presenting women in passive frames and as emotionally dependent beings; two characteristics that constitute signs of weakness in capitalist, individual-oriented societies.[13] There are several ways to display gender differences in media. Kane[14] observed that in relation to female sports coverage, journalists are more likely to offer mediatized attention to sports that emphasize aesthetics, such as gymnastics or synchronized swimming. In a study that examined sports magazines, it was found that only 2% of the published images depicted women in a leadership position (referees, federative officials, trainers, etc.).[15] In another study, Messner, Duncan, and Cooky[16] chose a very illustrative title 'Silence, Sports Bras and Wrestling Porns: Women in Televised Sports News and

Highlights Shows', reflecting that the sexuality of female athletes is accentuated more than their athletic abilities. As Hardin *et al.*[17] stated: 'images of heroic sporting women have historically been usurped by sports cuties in mainstream media'. A good example of the increased focus that is being placed on the physical attributes of female athletes was the enormous media interest in Anna Kournikova, an athlete who attracted media comments that focused predominantly on her sex appeal rather than on her athletic performance. The description of journalist Simon Hooper in the web version of CNN *Sports Illustrated* is quite expressive of the way Kournikova was perceived by the male-dominated media: 'The Russian 21-year-old is one of the most recognizable and photographed stars in tennis thanks to her blonde looks and figure-hugging outfits'.[18] Sports sociology researcher John Vincent and his collaborators,[19] in an analysis of British newspaper narratives about female tennis competitors gave the characterization '*Sporting Lolita*' to describe the media frame of this Russian athlete. This term nuances a certain media portrayal of female athletes, especially in the sport of gymnastics,[20] a frame referring to perverse sexualization of the allured figure of preadolescent and adolescent girls.

In fact, sports media often produce and reproduce an image of women as eternal children, as if they remain in a liminal childish stage failing to become mature sexual beings. A number of studies have demonstrated that the use of language is a recurrent medium in the infantilization of female athletes by the sports media. Fullerton, and R. Jones *et al.* observed that the employment of terms such as 'girls' or 'young girls' is very common when addressing female athletes.[21] Their male counterparts, however, are rarely 'boys'. Another linguistic pattern that infantilizes women in sport is that journalists have the tendency to refer to female athletes using their given name, while using the family name for male athletes.[22]

Disabled female athletes and the media

Contrary to the plethora of studies that focus on media depictions of non-disabled female athletes, literature on the media coverage of disabled female athletes remains scarce. When analysing the results of the literature we identified two main categories of results. On the one hand, there are studies which indicate that disabled athletes receive identical treatment as the non-disabled female athletes: this first category of findings is usually addressed by researchers who have undertaken quantitative content analysis. On the other hand, there are studies which highlight the particularities of the gendered images concerning disabled female athletes.

Under-representation in sport coverage

As we have seen above, the overall space allotted to female athletes is significantly lower than the space reserved for male athletes. The under-representation in the news is a very common pattern in the media coverage of female non-disabled athletes, but there are few studies that have examined whether there is a denial of women's place in the Paralympic arena too.

In an investigation into the coverage of Paralympic Games in Spain, Pappous *et al.*[23] examined the proportion of male/female photographs in eight Spanish sport and mainstream newspapers over a period of three Olympiads (Atlanta 1996, Sydney 2000, and Athens 2004). In this study, it was observed that of 335 images, 207 featured a male athlete and only 60 depicted a female athlete as the main character (the remaining percentage were mixed photos).

A similar pattern appeared in the study carried out in Great Britain by Thomas and Smith[24] who analysed the British media coverage of the 2000 Paralympic Games and observed that female athletes were featured less often than their male counterparts. The authors of this study argued that a possible reason for a greater photographic coverage of male athletes was probably due to the smaller number of female athletes participating in the Games. Indeed, future studies which examine the gendered Paralympic media coverage should take into account this often overlooked but important structural factor which strongly influences the amount and nature of media coverage: the asymmetrical female/male demographics of Paralympic delegations. In the 1996 Paralympic Games, 47% of countries sent no female athletes at all. More recent data coming from the Spanish Paralympic Committee speaks loudly to this issue; only 24% of the 133 athletes that were part of the Spanish delegation at the 2008 Beijing Paralympic Games were women.[25] While parity in the Spanish Olympic delegation has almost been achieved, in the Paralympic Games the inequality is significant and women are a minority.

It should also be noted that there are also cultural barriers that limit female participation in Paralympic sports. In the recent Paralympic Games of 2008 there were no female swimmers competing from Middle Eastern Islamic countries. This definitively affects the media coverage both in their home countries and globally. If there are no women in these events there are no images of female athletes to be quantified and analysed.

Such demographic data highlights the necessity of in-depth studies of the factors leading to limited female participation in Paralympic sport. By means of both qualitative and quantitative methodology, through the use of in-depth interviews and questionnaires, researchers should identify the personal, sociocultural and institutional factors which intervene and set up the barriers that render difficult access to participation in the Paralympic sport arena by disabled women.

Future studies should evaluate the relative importance of an eventual greater amount of media attention given to male athletes by weighing the data into independent variables that structure the internal logic of media coverage in sports. Several researchers[26] who have worked with data coming from non-disabled athletes, and who were interested in whether the proportion of media coverage was fairly and accurately distributed between male and female athletes, decided to test the amount of media coverage against some independent standards which are relevant to the internal logic of sport. Future work should follow the paradigm of these studies by including independent variables (such as the proportion of male/female athletes participating in the Games and the proportion of medals won by the female Paralympians) to assure a more accurate comparison of the amount of coverage.

In a recent article, D. Jones[27] included these two simple 'representation' indices (participation and medal rates) and obtained results that contradicted the 'under-reporting' thesis according to which female athletes receive less coverage. In her study, D. Jones showed that when these two parameters were analysed, Australia's Olympic female athletes 'received more coverage than their medal wins and team population would seem to warrant'.[28] Thus, it will be interesting to explore whether a similar pattern will occur, when analysing the Paralympic media coverage.

However, numbers are not always sufficient to translate significance. By echoing G. Rose's suggestion, 'something that is kept out of the picture may nonetheless be extremely significant to meaning',[29] researchers should develop qualitative analysis in order to examine whether the depiction of female Paralympians is similar to the stereotyped patterns (trivialization and infantilization) that have been reported in earlier studies concerning the coverage of female non-disabled athletes.

Particularities in the media coverage of female disabled athletes

Nowadays, it is well known that gender identities are complex and hold a high degree of interaction and association with other important factors such as disability, race and sexual orientation. That is why we believe that if we aim to have a wider view of the representation of female sport in the media, then we should consider the inclusion of the dimensions of gender, race, disability and sexuality 'as intersecting aspects of subjectivity and not as independent categories'.[30] Sherrill asserts that disability should be included 'along with race/ethnicity, class and age as concerns and issues' to be explored in the study of sport and gender.[31] Until these categories of difference are analysed together, generalizations concerning, for example, the overall 'sexualization of female athletes by the mass media', carry the risk of becoming superficial, since female athletes do not form a homogenous group.

Therefore, the hypothesis that disabled athletes might not be subject to the identical kinds of stigma as their non-disabled counterparts merits further attention. Particular characteristics of the conditions of disabled athletes should be explored, because women with disabilities are at a risk of experiencing a double disadvantage for being both a woman and disabled.[32] The findings of Schell and Rodriguez[33] confirm the assertion of Ferri and Gregg, that women with disabilities are 'under a double silence, treated as asexual first and then denied any images (even an oppressive one) of their sexuality'.[34] In exploring the televised portrayal of a female Paralympic tennis player, Schell and Rodriguez observed that the athlete was depicted as 'genderless and asexual' and that the 'averted gaze of sports media served to de-eroticize Lewellen and to elide her identity as a sexual and social being'.[35] This discrepancy between the sexualization of non-disabled athletes, on the one hand, and the non-sexualisation/de-eroticisation, on the other hand, could probably be due to the fact that women with disabilities do not fit into the established sex–gender system. According to Ferri and Grecc, women with disabilities occupy 'neither the position of subject or the object of the desire',[36] thus are less sexualized than non-disabled women. The aforementioned findings suggest that women with disabilities do not face the same stigma as non-disabled women, and that is why specific media analysis of female athletes with disabilities is required. Meekosha and Dowse[37] also underline a potential contradiction between feminist researchers who condemn the eroticized images of women, when at the same time disabled women are hardly ever portrayed as sexual beings.

Schell and Duncan,[38] in one of the first studies that focused on the media portrayals of disabled athletes, observed that female Paralympians did not receive any sexist remarks at all, this element was in contrast with the recurring sexist journalistic writing on female Olympians.[39] In discussing this positive finding, Schell and Duncan remark that the absence of typically sexist commentaries about women's appearance, facial or bodily beauty, sexiness and 'cuteness' is probably due to the fact that people with disabilities are often perceived as 'aesthetically unpleasant' and 'asexual'.[40]

However, French scholars[41] undertook a qualitative analysis of the European newspapers coverage of Sydney 2000 Paralympic Games and provided some questioning of 'traditional' assumptions concerning the gendered nature of disabling imagery. Interestingly, in this study,[42] Paralympic female athletes in their sample were depicted highlighting what Duncan and Messner characterized as 'body parts that signalled female sexual difference'.[43] The results of this study show that the media coverage of Paralympic sport can challenge cultural representations which contradict the myth that disability implies asexuality.

Moreover, the qualitative analysis of this study revealed another facet in the media treatment of male Paralympians, by offering evidence that male athletes were also presented as childlike, emotive or in passive poses, trivialized and infantilized in the media treatment of the Paralympic Games.[44] This was a distinctive element because the literature concerning sports media coverage of male Olympic athletes does not offer evidence of an analogous stigma. The overall nonspecific gendered identification of Paralympic athletes may be considered to have a double reading: either a positive–progressive one or a negative–traditional one. In the first interpretation, the nonspecific gendered identification could be seen as highlighting progress, a move from the traditional masculine and feminine roles. According to Morris, the traditional social definition of masculinity is impregnated with images associated with strength and powerful ideal bodies; simultaneously implying that to be masculine is not to be vulnerable.[45] However, Barnes argues that women are 'already seen as vulnerable, passive and dependent' and that is why 'there is less artistic interest in portraying disabled women, unless it is as tragic saintly figures'.[46] The media coverage of the Paralympic Games offers the opportunity of an alternative to this traditional stereotyped image by offering images of heroic athletic female Paralympians, when at the same time it is not uncommon to see an illustration of male Paralympic athletes in childlike, emotional and trivialized scenes.[47] However, the neutralization of the sexual differences in the case of the Paralympic athletes could also be seen as a perpetuation of traditional stereotyped notions in the process of obliterating the gender dimension within the disabled population. The latter interpretation implies that Paralympic media coverage continues to stigmatize people with disabilities, irrespective of their gender, by presenting them as eternal childlike beings lacking agency, even when they are Paralympic champions.

Suggested framework for future research

The literature on sports media coverage offers evidence of unfair treatment of female non-disabled athletes. The most salient feature of the gender differentiation in sports media is, first, female athletes receive less coverage. Second, media discourses concerning coverage of female athletes are shaped with sexualization, infantilization and trivialization frames. But what about the media coverage of female elite athletes with disabilities? Are they subject to the same stigma as their able-bodied counterparts? As we have seen briefly throughout this article, the scarce research available yields contradictory results. There is need for future research designed to examine whether the stigmatization that has already been shown to operate in the media treatment of non-disabled female athletes is also present in the media coverage of Paralympic female athletes, and if it can be interpreted as part of the same paradigm. The proposals found in this review can guide the formulation of several research questions that seek answers about media portrayals of female athletes with disabilities:

- Are there any differences in the media coverage of female athletes with disabilities and the coverage of non-disabled female athletes?
- Do female disabled athletes receive less textual and photographic coverage on the whole than their male counterparts?
- Does the level of coverage accurately correlate with the demographics of the Paralympic national teams? Does the level of coverage reflect the number of medals won by female and male athletes?
- Does the media coverage offer evidence of infantilization/trivialization or sexualization frames toward female or male disabled athletes?
- While gender parity on the Olympic Teams has almost been achieved what are the reasons that women are a minority on most national Paralympic teams? What are the

sociocultural and institutional factors which intervene and set up the barriers that render difficult access to participation in the Paralympic sport arena by disabled women?

Last, but no less important, we need research in different cultural contexts. Up to now, most of the studies on media coverage of sport for people with disabilities originate from North America, English-speaking countries and from European Union countries. As we have seen above, disability does not have a universal character, thus it will be fruitful to obtain data from countries which are active in Paralympic sport (such as Cambodia, China, South and Central America) but remain under-represented until now in the scientific literature on media coverage of *disability in the global sport arena.*

Acknowledgements

This research was supported by a Marie Curie Intra-European Fellowship within the 6th European Community framework Programme (Contract No 042104). The first author is at the University of Kent and a member of the SANTESIH research group; this paper came out of research conducted while he was with UFR-STAPS at the University of Montpellier 1, France. We would also like to thank the two anonymous referees and the editor of this special issue for their valuable comments.

Notes

[1] Schantz and Gilbert, 'An Ideal Misconstrued'.
[2] Schell and Duncan, 'A Content Analysis of CBS's Coverage'.
[3] Schantz and Gilbert, 'An Ideal Misconstrued'; Thomas and Smith, 'Preoccupied with Able-bodiedness?'.
[4] M. Rose, *The Staff of Oedipus*; Barnes, Mercer, and Shakespeare, *Exploring Disability*, 14.
[5] Barnes, Mercer, and Shakespeare, *Exploring Disability*, 14.
[6] Elliot, 'Moral Responsibilities and the Power of Pictures', 12.
[7] Buysse and Embser-Herbert, 'Constructions of Gender in Sport'.
[8] See, for example, Duncan and Brummet, 'The Mediation of Spectator Sport'; Crolley and Teso, 'Gender Narratives in Spain'; Kane and Parks, 'The Social Construction of Gender Difference'; Klein, 'Women in the Discourse of Sports Reports'; Lee,'Media Portrayals of Male and Female Olympic Athletes'; Salwen and Woods, 'Depictions of Female Athletes on *Sports Illustrated* Covers, 1957–89'; Shugart, 'She Shoots, She Scores'; Marcellini *et al.*, 'D'une Minorité à l'autre?'
[9] Duncan and Messner, 'The Media Image of Sport and Gender'.
[10] Buysse and Embser-Herbert, 'Constructions of Gender in Sport'.
[11] Crossman, Vincent, and Speed, 'The Times They are a-changin'. 29.
[12] Duncan, 'Sports Photographs and Sexual Differences'.
[13] Hardin, Lynn, and Walsdorf 'Challenge and Conformity on "Contested Terrain"'.
[14] Kane, 'Media Coverage of the Female Athlete'.
[15] Hardin, Lynn, and Walsdorf, 'Challenge and Conformity on "Contested Terrain"'.
[16] Messner, Duncan, and Cooky, 'Silence, Sports Bras, and Wrestling Porn'.
[17] Hardin, Lynn, and Walsdorf 'Challenge and Conformity on "Contested Terrain"', 105.
[18] Hooper, 'Fading Starlet. Lack of Success Tarnishes Kournikova's Marketability'. http://sportsillustrated.cnn.com/tennis/2002/us_open/news/2002/08/27/kournikova_tennis/
[19] Vincent *et al.*, 'Analysing the Print Media Coverage of Professional Tennis Players'.
[20] Duncan, 'Sports Photographs and Sexual Differences'.
[21] Fullerton, 'Not Playing Fair'; R. Jones, Murrell, and Jackson, 'Pretty versus Powerful'.
[22] Messner, Duncan, and Jensen, 'Separating the Men from the Girls'; Fullerton, 'Not Playing Fair'.
[23] Pappous *et al.*, 'La Visibilidad de la Deportista Paralímpica en la Prensa Española'.
[24] Thomas and Smith 'Preoccupied with Able-bodiedness?'.
[25] Pekin 2008, http://paralimpicos.sportec.es
[26] See for example, Smith and Thomas, 'The "Inclusion" of Elite Athletes with Disabilities'; D. Jones, 'The Representation of Female Athletes'; Hardin *et al.*, 'Olympic Photo Coverage Fair

to Female Athletes'; Shifflett and Revelle, 'Gender Equity in Sports Media Coverage'; Malec, 'Gender (In)equity in the NCAA News?'.

27 D. Jones, 'The Representation of Female Athletes'.

28 Ibid., 416.

29 G. Rose, *Visual Methodologies*, 66.

30 Schell and Rodriguez, 'Subverting Bodies/Ambivalent Representations', 128.

31 Scherrill, *Adapted Physical Activity*, 51.

32 Hargreaves, *Heroines of sport*.

33 Schell and Rodriguez 'Subverting Bodies/Ambivalent Representations'.

34 Ferri and Gregg, 'Woman with Disabilities', 433.

35 Schell and Rodriguez, 'Subverting Bodies/Ambivalent Representations', 132–133.

36 Ferri and Gregg, 'Woman with Disabilities', 433.

37 Meekosha and Dowse, 'Distorting Images'.

38 Schell and Duncan, 'A Content Analysis of CBS's Coverage'.

39 Crolley and Teso, 'Gender Narratives in Spain'; Higgs, Weiller, and Martin, 'Gender Bias in the 1996 Olympic Games'.

40 Schell and Duncan, 'A Content Analysis of CBS's Coverage', 45.

41 de Léséleuc, Pappous, and Marcellini, 'La Cobertura Mediática de las Mujeres con Discapacidad'.

42 Ibid.

43 Duncan and Messner, 'The Media Image of Sport and Gender', 176: '... the body parts that signaled female sexual difference: – thighs, breasts, buttocks, and crotches – were sometimes highlighted in photos of sportswomen, diverting attention from women as strong and competent athletes ...'.

44 de Léséleuc, Pappous and Marcellini, 'La Cobertura Mediática de las Mujeres con Discapacidad'.

45 Morris, *Pride Against Prejudice*, 93.

46 Barnes, Mercer, and Shakespeare, *Exploring Disability*,196.

47 In de Léséleuc *et al.* 'La Cobertura Mediática de las Mujeres con Discapacidad', it was observed that some newspapers reported stories on male and female disabled athletes focusing on non-sport-related aspects (stories about their professional occupation and their family situation, obstacles that they face in their everyday life) instead of giving sport related information. During the newspaper coverage of Sydney Paralympic Games, a British journalist of *The Independent* (October 28, 2000) referred to a Paralympic champion as '*this young boy of 28 years old*'. By mentioning the age of the athlete, the reader discovers that the article is not talking about a young boy, but about an adult. This lexical contradiction in the same sentence gives the impression that these athletes are not really perceived as adults, although they have more than passed the age of adolescence.

References

Barnes, Colin, Geof Mercer, and Tom Shakespeare. *Exploring Disability*. Cambridge: Polity Press, 1999.

Baroffio-Bota, Daniela, and Sarah Banet-Weiser. 'Women, Team Sports, and the WNBA: Playing Like a Girl'. In *Handbook of Sports and Media*, edited by Arthur Raney and Jennings Bryant, 485–500. Englewood Cliffs, NJ: Erlbaum, 2006.

Buysse, Jo A., and Melissa S. Embser-Herbert. 'Constructions of Gender in Sport: An Analysis of Intercollegiate Media Guide Cover Photographs'. *Gender and Society* 1 (2004): 66–81.

Crolley, Liz, and Elena Teso. 'Gender Narratives in Spain. The Representation of Female Athletes in *Marca* and *El Pais*'. *International Review for the Sociology of Sport* 42 (2007): 149–66.

Crossman, Jane, John Vincent, and Harriet Speed. '"The Times They Are A-Changin": Gender Comparisons in Three National Newspapers of the 2004 Wimbledon Championships'. *International Review for the Sociology of Sport* 42 (2007): 27–41.

Duncan, Margaret C. 'Sports Photographs and Sexual Differences: Images of Women and Men in the 1984 and 1988 Olympic Games'. *Sociology of Sport Journal* 7 (1990): 22–42.

Duncan, Margaret C., and Barry Brummet. 'The Mediation of Spectator Sport'. *Research Quarterly for Exercise and Sport* 58 (1987): 168–77.

Duncan, Margaret C., and Michael A. Messner. 'The Media Image of Sport and Gender'. In *Media Sport*, edited by Lawrence A. Wenner, 170–95. New York: Routledge, 1998.

Elliott, Deni. 'Moral Responsibilities and the Power of Pictures'. In *Images that Injure*, edited by Paul M. Lester and Susan D. Ross, 7–21. London: Praeger, 2003.

Ferri, Beth, and Noel Gregg. 'Woman with Disabilities: Missing Voices'. *Women's Studies International Forum* 21 (1998): 429–39.

Fullerton, Romayne S. 'Not Playing Fair: Coverage of Women & Minorities in the Sports Pages'. *SIMILE: Studies in Media & Information Literacy Education* 6 (2007): 1–13.

Hardin, Marie, Jean Chance, Julie E. Dodd, and Brent Hardin. 'Olympic Photo Coverage Fair to Female Athletes'. *Newspaper Research Journal* 23 (2002): 64–78.

Hardin, Marie, Susan Lynn, and Kristie Walsdorf. 'Challenge and Conformity on "Contested Terrain": Images of Women in Four Women's Sport/Fitness Magazines'. *Sex Roles* 53 (2005): 105–17.

Hargreaves, Jennifer. *Heroines of Sport: The Politics of Difference and Identity*. London: Routledge, 2000.

Higgs, Catriona T., Karen H. Weiller, and Scott B. Martin. 'Gender Bias in the 1996 Olympic Games: A Comparative Analysis'. *Journal of Sport and Social Issues* 27 (2003): 52–64.

Jones, Diane. 'The Representation of Female Athletes in Online Images of Successive Olympic Games'. *Pacific Journalism Review* 12 (2006): 108–29.

Jones, Ray, Audrey J. Murrell, and Jennifer Jackson. 'Pretty versus Powerful in the Sports Pages: Print Coverage of U.S. Women's Olympic Gold Medal Winning Teams'. *Journal of Sport and Social Issues* 23 (1999): 183–92.

Kane, Mary J. 'Media Coverage of the Female Athlete Before, During, and After Title IX: *Sports Illustrated* Revisited'. *Journal of Sport Management* 2 (1989): 87–99.

Kane, Mary J., and Janet B. Parks. 'The Social Construction of Gender Difference and Hierarchy in Sport Journalism: Few New Twists on Very Old Themes'. *Women in Sport and Physical Activity Journal* 1 (1992): 49–83.

Klein, Marie-Luise. 'Women in the Discourse of Sports Reports'. *International Review for the Sociology of Sport* 123 (1988): 139–51.

Lee, Judy. 'Media Portrayals of Male and Female Olympic Athletes: Analyses of Newspaper Accounts of the 1984 and the 1988 Summer Games'. *International Review for the Sociology of Sport* 27 (1992): 197–219.

Léséleuc de, Eric, Athanasios Pappous, and Anne Marcellini. 'La Cobertura Mediática de las Mujeres con Discapacidad. Analisis de la Prensa Cotidiana de 4 Paises Europeos Durante los Juegos Paralimpicos de Sydney 2000'. *Apunts. Educacion Fisica y Deporte* 97 (2009): 80–8.

Malec, M.A. 'Gender (In)equity in the NCAA News?'. *Journal of Sport and Social Issues* 18 (1994): 376–78.

Marcellini, Anne, Nathalie Lefevre, Eric de Léséleuc, and Gilles Bui-Xuan. 'D'une Minorité à l'autre? Pratique Sportive, Visibilité et Intégration Sociale de Groupes Stigmatisés'. *Loisir & Société (Society and Leisure)* 23 (2000): 251–72.

Meekosha, Helen, and Leanne Dowse. 'Distorting Images, Invisible Images: Gender, Disability and the Media'. *Media International Australia* 84 (1997): 91–101.

Messner, Michael A., Margaret C. Duncan, and Kerry Jensen. 'Separating the Men from the Girls: The Gendered Language of Televised Sports'. *Gender and Society* 7 (1993): 121–37.

Messner, Michael A., Margaret C. Duncan, and Cheryl Cooky. 'Silence, Sports Bras, and Wrestling Porn: Women in Televised Sports News and Highlights Shows'. *Journal of Sport and Social Issues* 27 (2003): 38–51.

Morris, Jenny. *Pride Against Prejudice*. London: The Women's Press, 1991.

Oliver, Michael. *The Politics of Disablement*. Basingstoke, UK: MacMillan, 1990.

Pappous, Athanasios, Francisco Cruz, Eric de Léséleuc, Maria Paz García, Antonio Muñoz, Jacqueline Schmidt, and Anne Marcellini. 'La Visibilidad de la Deportista Paralímpica en la Prensa Española'. *Revista de Ciencias del Ejercicio Físico FOB* 3 (2007): 12–32.

Rose, Gillian. *Visual Methodologies*. London: Sage, 2001.

Rose, Martha L. *The Staff of Oedipus: Transforming Disability in Ancient Greece*. Ann Arbor: University of Michigan Press, 2006.

Salwen, Michael B., and Natalie Woods. 'Depictions of Female Athletes on Sports Illustrated Covers, 1957–89'. *Journal of Sport Behaviour* 17 (1994): 98–107.

Schantz, Otto, and Keith Gilbert. 'An Ideal Misconstrued: Newspaper Coverage of the Atlanta Paralympic Games in France and Germany'. *Sociology of Sport Journal* 18 (2001): 69–94.

Schell, Lea Ann, and Margeret C. Duncan. 'A Content Analysis of CBS's Coverage of the 1996 Paralympic Games'. *Adapted Physical Activity Quarterly* 16 (1999): 27–47.

Schell, Lea Ann, and Stephanie Rodriguez. 'Subverting Bodies/Ambivalent Representations: Media Analysis of Paralympian, Hope Lewellen'. *Sociology of Sport Journal* 18 (2001): 127–35.

Scherrill, Claudine. *Adapted Physical Activity, Recreation and Sport: Cross-disciplinary and Lifespan.* Boston: McGraw-Hill, 1993.

Shifflett Bethany, and Rhonda Revelle. 'Gender Equity in Sports Media Coverage: A Review of the NCAA News'. *Journal of Sport and Social Issues* 18 (1994): 144–50.

Shildrick, Margrit. *Embodying the Monster. Encounters with the Vulnerable Self.* London: Sage, 2002.

Shugart, Helene A. 'She Shoots, She Scores: Mediated Constructions of Contemporary Female Athletes in Coverage of the 1999 U.S. Women's Soccer Team'. *Western Journal of Communication* 67 (2003): 1–31.

Smith, Andrew, and Nigel Thomas. 'The "Inclusion" of Elite Athletes with Disabilities in the 2002 Manchester Commonwealth Games: An Exploratory Analysis of British Newspaper Coverage'. *Sport, Education and Society* 10 (2005): 49–67.

Thomas Nigel, and Adrew Smith. 'Preoccupied with Able-bodiedness? An Analysis of the British Media Coverage of the 2000 Paralympic Games'. *Adapted Physical Activity Quarterly* 20 (2003): 166–81.

Vincent, John, Paul M. Pedersen, Warren A. Whisenant, and Dwayne Massey. 'Analysing the Print Media Coverage of Professional Tennis Players: British Newspaper Narratives about Female Competitors in the Wimbledon Championships'. *International Journal of Sport Management and Marketing Issue* 2 (2007): 281–300.

China and the development of sport for persons with a disability, 1978–2008: a review

SUN Shuhan, YAN Rui, MAO Ailin, CHAO Liu and JING Tang

China Disability Institute, Renmin University of China, Beijing, China

The 2008 Beijing Paralympic Games have had a very positive impact on many aspects of Chinese society beyond sport. This article focuses on the wide-ranging changes that have taken place since 1978 for the 83 million persons with disabilities in China. Organizations such as the Chinese Disabled Sports Association (1983) and the Disabled Persons Federation (1988) have been established and the 1995 People's Republic of China Sport Law 'supporting sport for the elderly and disabled' was initiated. New government policies also support fitness programmes, special education policies, National Games, new sports facilities, local recreational activities and the participation of high-performance athletes in the international Far East and South Pacific Games for the Disabled (FESPIC) and Paralympic Games. However, there are many ongoing challenges to increasing opportunities for and the participation of those with disabilities in all areas of sport and fitness. Fortunately, with the rapid development of China's economy, more support for disability sport has been possible.

Disability in China

In 2009, China's 1.2 billion people made up 20% of the world's population. Eighty-three million people in China had disabilities, a number comparable with the population of Germany, making the task of developing disability sport challenging. Ironically, even though China is such a large country and has a considerable impact on world affairs, most people in other countries know little about disability and disability sport in China. This article provides a review of the profound changes that have taken place in relation to disability since 1949 and the Foundation of the New China. Ideology and policies have changed with the development of civil society and the Chinese economy; and we argue that both of these have influenced and shaped the development of disability sport.

As recently as 20 years ago, having a disability meant being defined as ill and marginalized. This began to change after 1990 with the decree by the President of the People's Republic of China to implement the first Law on the Protection of Disabled Persons. Gradually people began to think of disability in a new way as an impairment in physical or mental health. By extension, this meant that those with disabilities were able to take part in all aspects of society. In addition to this, the wide-ranging impact of the 2008 Paralympic Games made it clear to the whole nation that these athletes were no longer to be considered as people with disabilities, but rather people with quite impressive and previously unimagined *abilities*.

The 2006 *Second China National Sample Survey on Disability* sampled 771,797 households (2,526,145 individuals) in 5964 rural and urban communities throughout

China. From this, data on different types of disability and their relative proportions within the total population of those with disabilities were presented.[1] There are 24.12 million people with physical disabilities in China, representing 29.07% of the disabled population and the largest group; 20.04 million people have a hearing disability, 13.52 million have multiple disabilities, 12.33 million have visual disabilities, 6.14 million have a mental health disability, 6.80 million have an intellectual disability and 1.27 million have a speech disability. Table 1 shows the type and severity of disability in people aged over 18 needing care.[2]

The Chinese government has begun to provide some benefits and support to people with different disabilities, including medical services, assistive devices, rehabilitation training, educational subsidies, vocational rehabilitation, employment support, poor relief, accessible facilities and information, and living support, as well as recreational services.[3] Importantly, the overall availability of services and support to disabled persons in China is inadequate. Given that most disabled people in China are poor and in need of basic living arrangements, the government has provided more medical care and poor relief than any other benefits and services. Table 2 presents statistics representing a sampling of China's disabled population (771,797 households; 2,526,145 individuals from rural and urban areas) and highlights the nature of the support received by those with disabilities.[4]

Ideology and policies for people with a disability

As a country with more than 5000 years of recorded history, China has experienced various social systems, including feudalism, semi-feudalism, semi-colonialism and socialism. Ideologies and polices regarding disabled people in China have changed in conjunction with the evolution of Chinese social systems. This section describes the sometimes profound changes that occurred in the twentieth and twenty-first centuries. This era of change is explored in five periods: Old China (up to 1948), New China (1949–1966), the Great Cultural Revolution or the Great Proletarian Revolution (1967–1977),

Table 1. Severity of disability in people aged 18 years and older.

| Diability type | None[a] | Severity of disability | | | |
		Mild	Moderate	Severe	Extreme[b]
Total	48.11	28.89	13.01	6.58	3.41
Percentage of people with a visual disability	53.12	26.85	11.21	6.09	2.73
Percentage of people with a hearing disability	80.15	14.94	3.77	0.90	0.25
Percentage of people with a speech disability	74.02	15.51	5.55	3.23	1.70
Percentage of people with a physical disability	28.41	39.08	18.82	9.25	4.45
Percentage of people with an intellectual disability	44.03	33.28	13.44	6.85	2.40
Percentage of people with a mental disability	35.24	39.87	16.73	6.34	1.81
Percentage of people with multiple disabilities	34.12	28.42	17.39	11.55	8.52

Note:
[a] These people can live independently and do not need assistance;
[b] These people cannot live independently.[3]

Table 2.   Persons with a disability who receive services.

Disability type	Medical service	Assistive devices	Rehabilitation training and services	Educational expenses, subsidy assistance or deduction	Vocational education and training	Employment arrangement or assistance	Poor disabled person support	Legal aid and services	Accessible facilities	Accessible information	Living services	Cultural and recreational services	Other	Not received any service or assistance
Visual disability	9320	1900	1117	99	41	150	2804	108	544	283	1594	549	506	12271
Hearing disability	9803	2938	1152	62	55	125	2134	94	287	302	1747	748	878	25570
Speech disability	711	69	266	42	12	30	289	16	14	20	129	62	62	1474
Physical disability	23441	5726	7651	334	105	426	6513	264	627	289	2591	856	833	19566
Intellectual disability	2547	125	921	221	72	209	2240	103	42	46	858	269	321	6287
Mental disability	5771	106	948	63	27	127	2224	134	48	86	950	218	349	4881
Multiple disabilities	9604	1926	2428	213	122	244	4307	141	257	143	1631	372	562	12887

Number of persons receiving service

Opening-Up and Reform Policies (1978–2001), and the Olympic and Paralympic Games (2002–2008).

China has experienced great poverty and misery, especially during times of environmental disasters such as earthquakes, floods and drought. The foundation of the People's Republic of China (PRC) on October 1, 1949, changed the country profoundly. Key elements in these enormous changes in policy and programmes by the Chinese government are outlined in Table 3.[5] Above all, security and welfare measures and policies established by the Chinese government at the time of the PRC's foundation provided crucial security for disabled persons and were a good start for undertaking new disablity initiatives.

In the past, it was believed that people with a disability had no work skills because of their impairments. This perspective, which treated disability as invalidism, damaged and distorted images of the disabled. Although traditional Chinese culture was oriented towards harmony, which encouraged rulers to take measures in accordance with the ideology of humanism, it was difficult to change the fundamental belief that the disabled were useless, and some Chinese still discriminated against the disabled, who were seen to be a burden to their family and society.[6] Thus, restricted by economic and social conditions, change was slow.

After 1978, China began to implement its Opening Up and Reform Policies.[7] The 1980s was the most important decade for the disabled. China took an active part in the 'United Nations Decade of the Disabled' (1983–1992) which was a milestone for the international disability movement. During this decade, the advanced ideology and successful experiences of the disability rights movements all over the world were combined with the situation in China, which used its own expertise, ways and methods to promote disability services. 'Future Plans for Disabled Persons and their Work in China' (in 1984 and 1987) explained the basic rights of the disabled, such as equal rights as citizens, social inclusion and new ideas about disability. In addition, many organizations by and for the disabled were founded, including: The China Disabled Persons Federation, The Blind Association of China, The Deaf Association of China, The Physically Disabled Association of China, The Intellectual Disabled Association of China, The Mentally Disabled Association of China, and The Associations for Relatives and Friends of Persons with a Disability.

These measures had a great impact on policies for disabled people. However, there remained many informal constraints, such as social prejudice and conservative attitudes towards the disabled which meant exclusion from socially dominant groups and from mainstream society. Moreover, people believed that disabled relatives were a liability, because families were expected to take full responsibility for them. However, in the mid-1980s, China began to gradually change its national social security system, although this initially formed part of the reform of state-owned enterprises.

Although there was no longer overt discrimination towards disabled people, Chinese society and government still utilized the traditional political approach embodied in 'Care and Protection', and these policies inevitably meant that disabled people had no option but to be nursed by their families.[8] After 1990, disability initiatives made greater progress and the legislative system required compliance with 50 codes related to the disabled and their rights. However, in order to ensure that disability initiatives kept pace with social and economic development, China established the 'Future Plans of the Work for Persons with Disabilities During the 8th Five-Year Development Program Period' (1991–1995) and continued through the 9th (1996–2000), 10th (2001–2005) and 11th (2006–2010) with reports at the end of each period to evaluate implementation.

Table 3. China's five historical periods and key factors affecting views on disability.

Period	Key elements
Pre-1948 Old China	Disability as destiny, often seen as a curse resulting from the 'sins' or wrongdoings of the ancestors The disabled were discriminated against in many ways and disabled babies were sometimes killed at birth Typically, the disabled were viewed as useless and a burden on their families Sometimes the disabled were imprisoned in their homes with no rights or freedoms Many disabled people forced to beg and often had little food or clothing
1949–1965 New China. People's Republic of China, October 1, 1949	Disabled people in China asserted their rights and become masters of their own fate[9] From total discrimination to partial inclusion, but people felt sorry for families with disabled children because families were responsible for the disabled person's care Improvement in economic conditions; subsidized 'welfare' factories and special education schools for the deaf and mute were established Charity organizations run by foreigners were replaced by social relief policies in the cities and rural areas for paupers, the unemployed and disabled 1950 – 'Temporary Regulations to Honour the Injured Veterans of the Revolution' (support for veterans of the revolutionary struggles) 1951 – The 'Labour Insurance Regulations of the People's Republic of China' (stipulated methods for helping injured workers) 1956 – 'Demonstrating Rules on Advanced Agriculture Cooperation', which stipulated that agricultural cooperatives had to take care of people with a disability who could not work 1956 – The Constitution of the People's Republic of China, which stipulated that Chinese people had the right to enjoy social security, however, disabled people were excluded and were covered by social relief policies; the few disabled persons who were employed were covered by social insurance, as were employees without disabilities 1960 – Association of the Blind and the Deaf–Mute formed
1966–1976 The Great Cultural Revolution/Great Proletarian Revolution[6]	Similar to Soviet purges China was in a state of chaos, and schools and factories for the disabled were closed No new disability policies initiated during this period
1978–2001 Opening-Up and Reform Policies	1984 and 1987 – 'The Future Plans for Disabled Persons and Their Work in China' (guidelines for the development of disabled services) 1985 – Special Olympics established 1986 – Compulsory Education Law of the People's Republic of China Article IX (special education schools) 1988 – The China Disabled Persons' Federation founded as a nationwide umbrella organization to promote inclusion (other organizations also founded) 1988 to present – 'Working Outline of the Five-year Disability Initiatives in China'

Table 3 – *continued*

Period	Key elements
	Establishment of social service network for the disabled in villages, towns and neighbourhoods to provide rehabilitation, employment, education, entertainment and financial subsides for daily living
	Collaboration with international organizations and a leading role in two 'Decades of Asia-Pacific Disability'
	1990 – The Law of the People's Republic of China on the Protection of Disabled Persons
	1990 – Regulations on the Work of College Sports
	1993 – The Standard Rules on the Equalization of Opportunities for Persons with Disabilities
	1994 – The Ordinance of the Republic of China on Disability Education
	1995 – Nationwide Fitness Plan of China
	1995 – The Outline of National Fitness Plan'
2002–2008 The Impact of the Paralympic Games	The Games had a national impact on many aspects of the country – see main text

Disability policies from 2002 to the 2008 Olympic and Paralympic Games

In this period, China undertook a number of initiatives, both internally and internationally, to support the rights of persons with disabilities. In 2006, China signed the UN Convention of the Rights of Persons with Disabilities. In addition, China cooperated successfully with the disability associations of 30 countries and with related international organizations. Through a combination of learning from the valuable experiences from other countries and its own effective practices in disability affairs, China successfully changed its medical and economic model of disability to a social model, recognizing the importance of social conditions in the creation and labelling of the disabled person.

The Chinese government carried out its second 'China National Sampling Survey of Disability' in 2006 and obtained data about disability which was used to develop policies and initiatives in regard to the disabled. In 2008, the 'Central Committee of the Communist Party of China and the State Council's Guidelines on Accelerating Disability Initiatives' outlined the strategies, tasks and measures for these new initiatives. In future years it is expected that China will greatly improve its social security and welfare programmes for people with a disability such that they will enjoy equality in health rehabilitation, education, employment, housing, communication and recreation in their social and political lives.

The Ordinance of the Republic of China on the Disability Employment was passed in 2007 and the Law of the People's Republic of China on the Protection of Disabled Persons (of 1990) was amended in 2008; the latter is the most important law protecting the equal rights of persons with a disability. These are the two most important administrative laws ensuring education and employment rights for the disabled in China and have had far-reaching impacts.

Initiated by the national government, China explored new ways to expand, support (socialize is the term used in Chinese) and change its welfare system for the disabled by learning from successful programmes in other countries. As the host city of the Paralympic Games 2008, those with disabilities were pushed to the social and political forefront and, as a result, Beijing vigorously expanded its social welfare for the disabled. The social welfare system was improved by combining programmes within the government, promoting social participation and integrating families, communities and welfare institutions. These changes were based on the Constitution of the People's Republic of China, including the Law of People's Republic of China on the Protection of Disabled Persons and dozens of other laws and policies concerning disabled persons. The impact on organizations and support systems for disabled people was extensive, from the State Council of China to local communities. In addition, this also had an impact upon operational work for the disabled in many fields including rehabilitation, employment, education, poverty alleviation, rights protection, culture, sport and so on. More and more people paid attention to the disabled and their lives and initiatives. However, these changes took time to implement. Welfare policies concerning the disabled were improved gradually and accessible environments were constructed step by step. Because of the 2008 Beijing Paralympic Games, the programmes and policies for China's disabled garnered greater attention, as did sports for the disabled.

The Beijing Paralympic Games in 2008 provided a great opportunity for all of Chinese society to abandon conservative attitudes towards the disabled. Through vigorous information campaigns about initiatives and programmes for disability sports, the Games raised awareness around the disabled. People learned more about sports for the disabled and further accepted the disabled under the policy of 'Equality, participation, sharing' programmes.

The development of disability sport in China

After the foundation of the New Republic of China, sporting activities for those with a disability were carried out on a small-scale, mainly through social welfare enterprises and schools for the deaf and mute in economically developed cities. Subsidized factories held broadcast gymnastics (group gymnastics known as broadcast exercises in China because of the use of a loudspeaker) and other sporting activities. Meanwhile, special schools began to have physical education lessons and special schools for the deaf–mute also held sport competitions.[10] All of these provided the foundation for disability sport. The Chinese government also provided a special budget to develop competitive sport for the disabled. The Civil Affairs Bureau organized small-scale sport competitions in some economically advanced provinces, but there were no comprehensive national competitions in China. For example, the first track and field, table tennis and swimming competitions for the deaf were held in Beijing in 1957. In 1959, the first national basketball games for the deaf were held.

The legal system of disability sport in China

Although the Constitution of the People's Republic of China did not directly outline the rules for disability sport, it established the rights of disabled persons. Participating in sporting activities is one of the most important rights of the disabled. It is a central component of rehabilitation, key to equal participation in society and a route to self-fulfilment. Therefore, the Constitution has been the basis for disability sport laws. In 1990, the Law of the People's Republic of China on the Protection of Persons with a Disability came into force (revised in 2008). It provided basic laws for the disabled (and the foundation for disability sport), arguing that:

> The state should protect the education rights, organize and support persons with disabilities in public cultural, sports and recreational activities, stage special art performances, hold sports games, and support participation in major international contests and events.

The law now explicitly protected disabled people's rights in sport and stated that it was the duty of governments and related departments at all levels to ensure that disabled persons participate in sports activities as much as possible, and at their convenience. Meanwhile, the law helped to facilitate these changes by pointing out ways to develop disability sport and to encourage both mass participation and competitive disability sport.

Another important law guiding disability sport is the People's Republic of China Sports Law which came into force in 1995. It is a special law for sporting activities and aims to develop initiatives to improve health and sporting opportunities at all skill levels. The law points out that work in sport should be based on national fitness activities and encourage all types of sporting activities to grow. The law also includes the establishment of public sports facilities that include activities for students, the elderly and the disabled. Article 16 provides that 'the whole of society should show concern and support for the elderly, and the disabled, to participate in sports activities. The People's government at all levels should take measures for the elderly, and disabled to participate in sports without barriers'. Article 46 stipulates:

> Public sports facilities should be open to the community to facilitate the public and the majority of society to carry out sports activities, and provide preferential treatment to students, the elderly and persons with a disability to increase their utilization of sports facilities.

Education and disability sport

Educational institutions have played a central role in the development of disability sport. In part, this is due to legislation such as the Compulsory Education Law of the People's Republic of China (April 1986), in which Article 9 provides that 'local people's governments at all levels should organize special education schools for the blind, deaf, dumb, intellectually disabled children and teenagers'. Another legislative push came from Regulations on the Work of College Sports which came into law in 1990. This addressed the regulations for physical education and health programmes at colleges and universities. It provides that colleges should make available appropriate sports health, therapeutic exercise and rehabilitative medical and sports activities for students who have physiological challenges or certain medical conditions (such as traumatic brain injury and dwarfism), so that they can improve their physical condition and health.

Policies related to disability sport

In recent years, government at all levels has paid more attention to disability sport and, one by one, more policies oriented or related to disability sports have been established. In 2002, the Communist Party of China (CPC) Central Committee and State Council established the 'Guidelines on Further Strengthening and Improving the Work of Sports in the New Era'. This was introduced to help frame the development of sport as part of hosting the Beijing 2008 Olympic Games and Beijing 2008 Paralympic Games. Article 13 states 'pay more attention to and support the selection, training, team organization, and competition of the athletes with a disability'. The push came both internally and externally, because the International Olympic Committee (IOC) required that everything must be done to ensure the success of the 2008 Paralympic Games. This requirement improved competitive sport for the disabled and furthered the ability of China to hold large disability sport events. It also helped lead to the successes of high-performance disabled athletes and the successful hosting of the 2008 Paralympic Games.

Established on May 6, 2007, the 'Guidelines of the General Office of the State Council on Further Strengthening the Disabled Sport Work' systematically addresses disability sport. It points out that, although China had made great progress in disability sport since 1978, it was still undeveloped. This was especially the case for mass participation sport.

It also indicated that the Shanghai 2007 Special Olympics (Olympics for the intellectually disabled) and the Beijing 2008 Paralympic Games would provide great opportunities for the disabled. The State Council believed that disability sport should be improved from the grass roots.

The State Council also recognized the important social, cultural and personal benefits that participation in sport offers those with disabilities. First, it calls for compliance with 'the National Fitness Project' in which fitness programmes will be widely available to people with disabilities to improve their physical health and given them equal opportunity to participate in social activities. Second, it requires strengthening sport teams to develop athletes and sport management teams, and the construction of sport training centres. Third, it requires the construction of a supportive social environment for disability sport through education campaigns about disability sport, volunteer service, accessible stadiums and facilities, and sponsorship. Last, it requires strengthening leadership in disability sport. Government at all levels has to include disability sport in social and economic projects, and all government departments and the disability federations have to actively establish disability sport development projects. Following these guidelines, it can be said that disability sport will make great progress in the next few years.

Another important policy is the CPC Central Committee and State Council's Guidelines on Accelerating Disability Initiatives which was established on March 28, 2008. This requires that 'every place should pay close attention to sports activities for the disabled, develop athletes with a disability and support them by specific state policies'. This further reinforces the message of the 'Guidelines of the General Office of the State Council on Further Strengthening the Disabled Sport Work':

> Make disability culture and sport prosper. Organize the disabled to take part in mass culture, arts and entertainments, enrich their spiritual and cultural life, and encourage them to actively participate in the advanced cultural construction of socialism. Fulfil the National Fitness Project and initiate mass sport and fitness activities for the disabled. Do scientific research and physical education on disability sport. The public facilities for culture and sport have to be open to the disabled at preferential prices. Organize Paralympic competitions, the Special Olympics and the Deaflympics. Hold and participate in major competitive games at home and abroad. Try to have the best events and to successfully host the Beijing 2008 Paralympic Games and the Guangzhou 2010 Asian Disabled Games.

Both sets of guidelines have had, and should continue to have, a great impact on the lives of the disabled, and on disability sport.

Before 2001, there were no statistics concerning disabled persons participating in sport. But anecdotally it has been reported that few people were able to leave their homes to take part in sport or exercise, with the exception of some disabled students who had physical education lessons in their schools. Fortunately, the Chinese government established its 'Nationwide Fitness Plan of China' in 1995 and required improvements in sporting activities for the disabled. Therefore, 'Rules on the Sports Careers of the Disabled during the 10th Five-Year Plan Period' set a participation rate of 10% of the total disabled population as its main goal. According to 'The Statistics Report of Implementing "The 10th Five-Year Outline Plan of Disabled Persons' Initiatives"', these targets have been achieved. Through these programmes, disability sport has made progress.

Article 14 stipulates:

> Widely initiate fitness programmes for the persons with disabilities to improve their physical condition, equal opportunities to participate in social activities. More diverse methods for the disabled should be established to develop key sportsmen and sportswomen to raise the participation rates of the disabled in sports.

Table 4.   Growth of Special Olympics in China.

Year	Number of participants
1998	~ 28,000
2002	179,510
2004	407,026
2006	600,000 +

In 2001, implementing 'Rules on the Sport Careers of the Disabled' the 10th Five-Year Plan was put forward. From 2001 to 2005, China aimed to make the number who regularly attended mainstream sporting activities 10% of the total number of people with a disability in China, and among them, the number of intellectually disabled who would participate in the Special Olympics should increase from 50,000 to 500,000. As surprising or unrealistic as the numbers might seem in comparison with those in other countries, the projected growth figures for persons with intellectual disabilities served by Special Olympics was exceeded (Table 4).[11]

Leadership in disability sport

Several organizations for the disabled share the responsibility of running disability sport. The China Disabled Persons' Federation, sport, education and civil affairs departments all have their own responsibilities and functions depending on the different nature of these organizations. These federations have to select athletes, build sport teams, and organize training and competitions. They also create and develop organizations for disability sport such as disability sports associations and Paralymic committees. Disability sport is also an important part of sport departments.[12] Sport departments have to assist the Disabled Persons Federation to select athletes, build sport teams, and arrange training plans and spaces. They also use their technical expertise to guide and support disability sport and the Paralympic Games.

Education departments at all levels are expected to organize and support sporting activities in high, middle and primary schools, and provide volunteers. Civil affairs departments are expected to actively initiate and organize people with a disability in welfare organizations to participate in sporting activities and create better environments for them. Community, residential and village committees are expected to actively encourage the disabled to take part in fitness projects, and to identify athletes with potential. Meanwhile, all levels of government have to invest more in disability sport. According to the rules of the Ministry of Central Finance, government departments have to provide special funds from the sports lottery and the welfare lottery fund to support disability sport.

Associations for disability sport

There are three major disability sports organizations whose names within China differ from their international names, which can be confusing to the uninitiated, as can be seen in Table 5.

The three associations have a significant presence across China, having set up branches in all provinces, autonomous regions and municipalities, and also in some cities, districts and counties. There are initiatives for local collaboration in disability sport. The 'Guidelines on Further Strengthening Disability Mass Sport and Fitness in Beijing' were issued by the Beijing Disabled Person's Federation, the Beijing Sport Bureau, the Beijing Education Committee, the Beijing Civil Affairs Bureau and the Beijing Municipal Commission of the China Communist Youth League to ensure continued growth in efforts towards

Table 5. Major associations for disability sport in China.

Name used in China	International Name
China Association for the Disabled[a]	China Paralympic Committee
China Sport Association for the Deaf	China Paralympic Committee for the Deaf
China Sport Association for the Mentally Disabled	Special Olympics China

Note. [a] In July, 1991, the China Association for the Injured and Disabled was renamed the China Association for the Disabled and its membership includes the physically disabled, the intellectually disabled, the spinal cord injured and the blind.

development. However, it has sometimes proved difficult for the different organizations to reach agreement. Organizations for disability sport are often too dispersed to work together successfully, and their leadership is often criticized for its ineffectiveness.

In 1983, the first nationwide games for persons with a disability were held and nearly 200 disabled athletes from 13 provinces competed in track and field, swimming and table tennis. After this event, the China Sport Association for the Injured and Disabled was established on October 21, 1983, issuing 'The Policy with Regard to Positively Planning and Implementing Sports Movements for Persons with a Disability',[13] which required the whole of Chinese society to pay more attention to the participation of persons with a disability in sports activities and to establish local disabled people sports associations.

The non-profit sector plays a central role at both the local and national level. The most significant of these organizations are the China Association for Disabled, the China Association for the Deaf, and the China Sport Association for the Intellectually Disabled (Special Olympics) which operate under the guidance and supervision of the China Disabled Persons' Federation, State Sport General Administration of China, and the Ministry of Civil Affairs of China. They consist of sport associations from all provinces, autonomous regions, municipalities and cities in China. Each of the organizations for disabled athletes provides the following services and support for their individual members:

- initiate, organize and guide sporting activities;
- assist related departments to develop campus sports in special education schools and fitness activities in government-supported factories and institutions;
- organize, administrate and train athletes and provide staff for Paralympic Games; build training centres for the Paralympic, Deaflympic or Special Olympic Games; hold nationally comprehensive and single-event sport events;
- organize the participation of athletes with a disability in the international Paralympic, Deaflympic or Special Olympic Games and make international exchanges;
- assist related departments to do research in Paralympic, Deaflympic or Special Olympic science, provide and make special equipment and assistance devices for the Games;
- advise membership units on funding, training, athlete selection and other matters; and
- share and exchange information about disability sport and reward high-performance athletes with a disability.

Sport facilities and stadiums for the disabled

Over the past 20 years there has been a boom in the facilities available for disabled athletes. China has set up more than 3000 sport centres for the disabled, of which more than 1324 are in medium-sized or larger cities; alongside this, China has created public places to provide accessible services to those with disabilities. There are also 10,469 rehabilitation centres ensuring that more people with disabilities can carry out sporting activities suitable to their physical condition and abilities. In communities, subsidized enterprises and special education schools, sitting volleyball, table tennis, goal ball, badminton, wheelchair tai chi, wheelchair aerobics, wheelchair basketball and blind chess are common. To date, there are more than two million disabled amateur athletes across China.[14] In recent years, China has focused effort on balancing mass participation and competitive sport for the disabled. However, despite these advances, there remains a gap between mass participation and competitive disability sport. The difference can be seen by examining disability sport facilities and stadiums. Most disability sport facilities are established within disability training stadiums and these are mostly used as training centres for elite athletes rather than for the general population. To be fair, since the successful bid for the 2008 Olympic Games and Paralympic Games in 2001, there has been great progress in the growth in disability sport facilities and some of these are being opened up to a broader section of the community.

The government has recognized that improvements need to be made in this area. According to China's 2007 11th Five-Year Programme Supporting the Implementation of the Work of Disabled Sports, by the end of 2006, all provinces, autonomous regions and municipalities were expected to have at least one stadium as the main sports resource centre for persons with disabilities, to support self-improvement fitness activities and sports training; public sports facilities must meet the needs of persons with a disability to participate in sports activities, and have to give people with a disability financial support.

To date, 17 training centres have been established (see Figure 1), including: The Comprehensive Training Centre for Disabled Sport of China, Beijing; Shanghai Sport Training Centre for the Disabled, Shanghai Fuzhou Sport Centre, Fujian province; Haigeng Sport

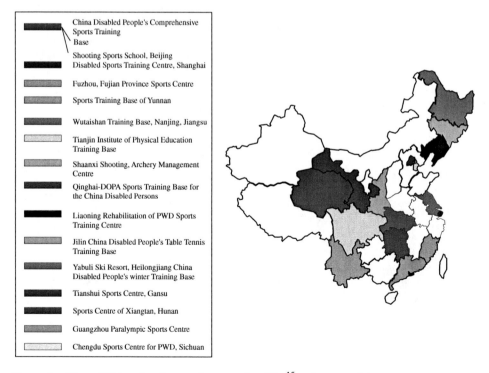

Figure 1.   Map of China showing provinces, major cities[15] and sport training centres.

Training Centre, Yunan province; Sport Training and Rehabilitation Centre, Liaoning province; Nanjing Wutai Mountain Training Centre, Jiangsu Province; Tianjin Physical Education College Training Centre, Tianjin; Huangshi Sport Centre, Hubei province; Shooting and Archery Management Centre, Shanxi province; Duoba Handicapped Disabled Sport Training Centre of China, Qinghai province; Table Tennis Training Centre for the Disabled of China, Jilin province; China Disabled Persons' Winter Games Training Center, Heilongjiang province; Beijing Shooting Sports Technique School; Tianshui Sport Centre, Gansu province; Xiangtan Sport Centre Hunan province; Guangzhou Disabled Olympic Sport Management Centre, Guangdong province; and Chengdu Disabled Sport Centre, Sichuan province.

Supported by the Chinese government and approved by the State Council, the China Disabled Persons' Federation has built a national-level sports training centre in Shunyi district, Beijing, covering an area of 360 mu (360 Chinese acres) and having facilities for 12 of the 20 events in the Paralympic Games. This should ensure that China will continue to support and develop elite athletes long after the 2008 Games.

There has also been a push to improve access to sport spectatorship for the disabled. In Chengdu, Sichuan province, commercial sport stadiums have half-price entry for the disabled and other stadiums provide free access. Stadiums that are not accessible are encouraged to become so. Newly built stadiums have to be accessible to all. In Beijing, the city government not only planned to set up sport facilities for the disabled as part of the national fitness project, but also encouraged public and community sport stadiums to open up to the disabled.

Disability games

Since the First National Games for Persons with a Disability in 1983, China has held seven National Games every four years, and they have been officially included in the State Council-approved budget for large-scale games. The number of competition events has grown from only three in the First National Games to twenty in 2008. In addition, national individual championships are also held every year, and various sports events are held by all levels of government. China Disabled People's sporting events have become the national games for persons with a disability, and the development model is a combination of disabled national individual championships and local events for people to participate in all kinds of sports competitions, promoting the development of mass participation sports.[16]

There are over 20 national and 10 provincial disability sports events every year, and more than 10% of the disabled population regularly participate in these. In recent years, China has, albeit gradually, greatly developed wheelchair darts, rock climbing, tug of war (one of the early Olympic sports) wheelchair tai chi and other group programmes. Rowing, sailing, equestrian and other events have also grown significantly.

Since 1984, China has participated in seven Summer Paralympic Games, two Winter Paralympic Games, seven Far East and South Pacific Games for the Disabled (FESPIC) Games and a number of other international events, and has obtained excellent results. While medal tables can only tell us so much, examining the medal results from the Paralympic Games it is clear that China's disabled sport has made tremendous progress in a period of less than 25 years (Table 6).[17]

Improved opportunities because of the 2008 Beijing Paralympic Games

It is clear that there are many problems and ongoing challenges to improve disability sport in China, but the 2008 Beijing Paralympic Games was a turning point for disability sport.

Table 6. Medals won by China in the Paralympic Games (1984–2008).

Date	Number of disabled athletes taking part	Number of gold medals won	Number of silver medals won	Number of bronze medals won
June 1984 (7th Paralympic Games)	24	2	13	9
October 1988 (8th Paralympic Games)	43	17	17	10
September 1992 (9th Paralympic Games)	34	11	7	7
August 1996 (10th Paralympic Games)	37	16	14	10
October 2000 (11th Paralympic Games)	122	34	22	16
September 2004 (12th Paralympic Games)	200	63	46	32
September 2008 (13th Paralympic Games)	332	87	70	52

From 2001 when the bid for the 2008 Beijing Olympic Games and Paralympic Games was successful, many of China's political, economic and social activities were oriented towards the Games. In 2002, the CPC Central Committee and State Council established 'Guidelines on Further Strengthening and Improving the Work of Sports in the New Era' to guide the development of sport around the 2008 Olympic Games and the Paralympic Games.

Another development due to the games was that cities, in particular Beijing, began to construct accessible environments. Many public places such as the popular Summer Palace in Beijing added ramps and lifts, and installed accessible toilets and transportation. Sport facilities tried to make themselves as accessible as possible. In order to raise awareness around disability sport, China conducted information campaigns. Beijing made outdoor broadcasts about the Paralympic Games. These took place in Beijing Chang'an Street for the first time in 2006 and there were 100 broadcasts along streets and in buildings in Beijing. At the same time, information was provided to TV channels and was broadcast through loudspeakers at schools, on the Internet and in newspapers.

The Bejing Olympic Games Organizing Committee (BOGOC) selected 100,000 volunteers, 30,000 of whom were assigned to be Paralympic volunteers, and trained them in disability awareness and the Games. This training helped young people better understand and care for the disabled. In preparation for the 2008 Paralympic Games, it became apparent that there were many problems, difficulties and deficiencies in China's disability sport which pushed and encouraged China to improve conditions. For example, China is now more aware of the importance of conducting scientific research on facilities, sport equipment items and sport science.

Disabled population and sports participation in schools

Since the establishment of the Chinese Disabled Sports Association in 1983, all provinces, autonomous regions and municipalities, the Federation of Persons with Physical Disability and the Disabled Sports Association have actively held sports events and have successfully organized more than 800 disability sports training and business courses. The number of amateur athletes participating in sports held nationally, in municipalities and in counties increased, and has risen to more than 200,000; the number of people who participate in regular physical activity has reached more than 10 million. Sport schools at all levels have been training disabled athletes who increasingly become members of amateur sports teams. Some university Physical Education departments have also set up disability sports elective courses for programmes in sport, health, rehabilitation and professional sport.[18]

The uneven development of disability sport

As is frequently the case, economics plays a large role in access to sport and facilities. The relative wealth of a region affects the types of opportunities available. Progress occurs at a faster rate in economically advanced regions. Because of their flourishing economy, Beijing, Shanghai, Guangdong Zhejiang and Jiangsu provinces have more sport facilitates and stadiums for the disabled, and more persons with a disability take part in sporting activities than in the poorer central and western provinces in China. At the same time, disabled people in rural areas have fewer opportunities to enjoy sporting activities than those in cities.

Overall, but especially in poorer areas, there remains a considerable gap between opportunities for participation in recreational sport and in competitive sport. For economic and political reasons (as in other countries), more attention has been paid to competitive and elite sport. Disability sport funds, facilities, stadiums and resources are all oriented towards competitive games. At present, recreational disability sport needs more attention, practical measures for implementation and larger investment.

Lack of secure funds

One of the most crucial obstacles to disability sport is a lack of secure funds. There are three major ways to raise money for sport. The first is from the budgets of government financial departments. Although required to provide appropriate funds for disability sport at all levels, the provision of money is not secure, and is on a small scale. The second is money from the sport lottery fund and welfare lottery fund. According to the rules of the Ministry of Central Finance of China, finance departments have to arrange special funds from the sports lottery and welfare lottery to support disability sport. However, the proportions are not laid out clearly and the funds are inadequate. The third way is sponsorship. In the past, this has come from individuals, companies, government bodies and agencies, social associations and so on, however, in the current economic climate this has been greatly reduced. The problem has been compounded by the fact that there is no tradition of charitable donations in this area. As a result, money from charity and sponsorship is very limited. Therefore, China has to make great efforts to solve the problem of a lack of funding.[19]

Inadequate sport equipment and inaccessible stadiums and facilities

To guarantee a disabled person's right to participate in sport, the government needs to provide suitable equipment, accessible facilities and appropriate programming.[20] Stadiums and facilities for disability sport are mainly designed for competitive sport. For disabled people, an accessible environment is a basic precondition to participation in society. Only megalopolises, developed cities and cites with a large number of disabled persons, such as Beijing, Shanghai, Shenzhen, Guangzhou and Tangshan, have begun to construct completely accessible environments. As for other medium-sized and small cities, they have few accessible roads or buildings.

In addition, most equipment is imported and is too expensive for individuals to purchase. Because of their physical impairments, many persons with a disability cannot participate in existing non-adapted sports, but a more urgent problem in China is the lack of physical education facilities and professionally trained educators and coaches.

Poor economic conditions of people with a disability

Sport advancement is restricted by the economic development level of the country, and also by the resources available to the individual. Most disabled people have a low income,

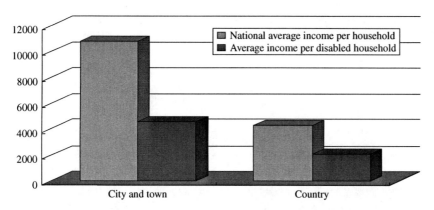

Figure 2. Comparison between national average income and average imcome for families with disabilities.

which prevents them from participating in sport or purchasing sports equipment. One of the major factors in developing disability sport is the need to improve the economic status of the disabled.

Data from the Second China National Sample Survey on Disability reveals that the economic condition of people with a disability is far worse than that of people without disabilities (Figure 2).

Non-supportive social environments for disability sport

The social environment for the disabled is composed of not only societal attitudes and interpersonal interactions, but also the physical environment, which has to be visitable and accessible, including 'visitable housing', accessible transportation and accessible communication. Sadly, China has lagged behind other contries in providing this kind of support. Difficult terrain often means that it is impossible for people to leave their homes. As a result, physical access to sports facilities, let alone the sporting activities themselves, are unattainable for many with impaired mobility. At the same time, societal pressures to not invest in these improvements also act as a roadblock; many people simply cannot understand the desire of disabled people to participate in sport. Larger and longer lasting education campaigns are needed to educate people about this issue of access to sport participation and sporting activities.

Economic growth and support for disability sport

A key element in the discussion of disability sport is the economic foundation of its support. The Chinese economy has experienced 30 years of economic growth at an average rate of 9.8% per year. In 1978, the GDP was US$243,000,000,000 (345,500,000,000 RMB) and in 2007 GDP reached $US3.371,600,000,000 (249,500,000,000,000 RMB), while the average annual growth in the state budget was 14.1%.[21] Therefore, disability sport has a more solid foundation and the government can no longer use its poor economic status as a reason to refuse to invest in disability sport. The government has begun to provide greater support to scientific research on disability sport, facilities and training, while supporting international exchanges to share innovative ideas related to sport. In high school education, more emphasis has been placed on disability sport and adapted physical education. At the same time, companies and factories have begun to develop more products, recognizing that there is a large market for them. With prosperity, the government has paid more attention to the idea of harmony and sharing to build a cooperative society so that the disabled can enjoy their rights and services equally.[22]

Conclusion

Since 1978 when China began implementing its Opening-up and Reform policies there has been great progress for disabled people in China. Founded in 1988, the China Disabled Persons' Federation aimed to promote policies and programmes for the disabled, supporting their equal participation in society. These measures have had a great impact on policies and programmes for the disabled in China. However, there remain many informal constraints, such as social prejudice and conservative attitudes. These constraints have led to disabled persons being excluded from mainstream society.

It is clear that sport in China has also made great progress since 1978. People now believe that participating in sporting activities is a disabled person's right and has to be guaranteed by the government and society. A relatively complete legal system has been formed to protect and guide disability sport. Legal and administrative systems have been formed to support members of the disability community and promote inclusion. The leadership mechanism consisting of several administrative departments is constantly improving. Disability and disability sport associations have been set up and have played an important role in disability sport, including international exchanges. Sporting events have been held across China, and Chinese teams have actively joined in international sport and performed well. In addition, more and more disabled people take part in sporting activities at the grass roots level.

The Beijing 2008 Paralympic Games provided an excellent opportunity for development. People now know more about disability sports and increasingly accept the disabled under the ideal of 'equality, participation, sharing'. However, despite these achievements, disability sport has many ongoing challenges and problems for further development. We need to be aware of the deficiencies in sport programmes for those with a disability and try our best to improve them. Also, we should balance the development between competitive, high-performance sport, mass participation sport and school sport. In other words, we want to build a harmonious society for both disabled and non-disabled people.

Acknowledgements

The authors would like to acknowledge the invaluable support and assistance in translation from Li Jing at the School of International Studies at Renmin University of China, Beijing.

Notes

[1] In addition to the question of a huge population, there is the challenge of a diversity in language use in China that includes Standard Chinese (Mandarin), Putonghua (based on the Beijing dialect), Yue (Cantonese), Wu (Shanghainese), Minbei (Fuzhou), Minnan (Hokkien-Taiwanese), Xiang, Gan, Hakka dialects and other minority languages.

[2] China Disabled Persons' Federation, *The Second China National Sample on Disability* 2, 66–69.'According to the survey data, it is estimated that the total number of persons with disabilities nationwide for all disability types is 82,960,000. In accordance with the survey of the National Bureau of Statistics, the total population of China was estimated to be 1,309,480,000 and with a total disabled population of 6.34%.

3   China Disabled Persons' Federation, *The Second China National Sample on Disability*.
4   Ibid.
5   Zhang and Zhong, 'Historical Retrospect of Disabled Sports', 17–22.
6   Dong Xue, 'The New Concept about Persons with Disabilities', 7.
7   Cong Xiaofeng and Tang Binyao, 'A Study on the Practical Models of Disability', 1–4.
8   Wang Qiyan and Tan Zhilin, 'Social Security of the Handicapped', 20–24.
9   China Disabled Persons' Federation, *The Second National Sample on Disability*.
10 After World War II, there were two major social systems. One is called capitalism and the other is called socialism. China is part of a socialist system (most westerners would use the term communist). In the 1960s, capitalist countries were hostile to socialist countries and at that time China also had a poor relationship with Soviet Russia, which was the largest communist country. The Chinese government was so angry that it refused to connect with other countries. During the period from 1949 to 1978, China was based on a planned economy and focused on various political initiatives. This resulted in a slow improvement in China's economy and a reduction in poverty as a whole. In 1978, the Chinese government decided to open up and connect with other countries all over the world. Since then, the Chinese government has been reforming its planned economic system step-by-step and has set up a market economy within socialism. It has paid more and more attention to its economy and societal progress. Therefore, the reforms beginning in 1978 have been very important for China and its people.'
11 Special Olympics, personal correspondence, July 15, 2009.
12 *Yearbook of Affairs for Persons with Disabilities China* (1983–1994).
13 Chairman Tom Koizumi Qiyue, 'Countdown to the First Anniversary of the Paralympic Games'. News Conference, China Disabled Persons Federation, http://www.beijing2008.cn/.
14 Wikipedia, *Province (China)*, http://en.wikipedia.org/wiki/Provinces_of_China.
15 Tom Koizumi Qiyue, 'Countdown to the First Anniversary of the Paralympic Games'. News Conference, China Disabled Persons Federation, http://www.beijing2008.cn/
16 China Disabled Persons' Federation, http://www.cdpf.org.cn.
17 Zhang and Zhong, 'Historical Retrospect of Disabled Sports', 17–21; China Disabled Persons' Federation, *Statistical Communiqué on the Development of Work*. National compulsory special education schools have increased in number from 423 in 1986 to 1667 in 2007, and special classes attached to ordinary schools have gone up to 678. The number of students with disabilities in schools has grown almost 10 times from 47,200 in 1986 to 413,000 in 2007. Blind, deaf and intellectually disabled children's enrolment rate has reached 80.7%. In senior and secondary schools, the number of students with disabilities has reached 14,000. Ninety-five per cent of students with disabilities who meet university and college admission standards are admitted. Plus, there are 720,000 persons with disabilities studying in all types of vocational training institutions. The persons with disabilities mentioned above have access to sport training courses. Gansheng, 'Report on the Donation Income and Expenses in 1994 and Express Budget in 1995 of China Foundation of Disabled Persons', http://www.cwfh.org.cn/wxzl/cwbg-94.html.
18 'Zhou Fang, 'Present Situation and Influential Factors', 1.
19 Luo Yong,''Research into the Status Quo and Development Measure of Sports for the Disabled in China', 37–39.
20 China Disabled Persons' Federation, *The Second China National Sample*.
21 The Statistics Bureau of China, 'Series of Reports on the Social and Economic Achievements', 2008. In 1978, US$1 was ∼ 1.5 RMB; in 2007, US$1 was ∼ 7.4 RMB; in 2008, US$1 was ∼ 6.9 RMB.
22 Qian, 'Discussion on the Definition and Construction of the Socialism Harmonious Society', 5–8.

References

China Disabled Persons' Federation. *The Second China National Sample on Disability*. Beijing: National Bureau of the People's Republic of China, 2006.
China Disabled Persons' Federation. *Statistical Communiqué on Development of the Work for Persons with Disabilities in 2007*. Beijing: China Disabled Persons' Federation, 2007.
Cong, Xiaofeng, and Tang Binyao. 'A Study on Practical Models of Disability'. *Journal of the Beijing Scientific Universities*, no. 3 (2003): 1–4.
Dong Xue. 'The New Concept about Persons with Disabilities and its Revelations for the Work'. *Chinese Journal of Special Education* 7, no. 61 (2005): 7.

Gao, Xiao-ai. 'The Restrictive Factors of Sports for the Disabled in Gansu, and Countermeasures'. *Journal of Physical Education* 1, no. 1 (January 2005): 13–15.

General Office of the State Council. 'Regulations on the Education of Persons with Disabilities'. Decree by the President of the People's Republic of China, Decree No. 161 (23 August): 1994.

National People's Congress of the People's Republic of China. 'Law on the Protection of Persons with Disabilities'. Decree by the President of the People's Republic of China, Decree No. 3 (10 April), 2008.

Premier Wen Jiabao. 'The Outline of the Work 2006–2010'. State Council 21, 2006.

Tan, Liqing. 'Thoughts on the Development of Physical Education of People with a Disability in China'. *Chinese Journal of Special Education* 66, no. 12 (2005): 21–4.

Wang Qiyan, and Tan Zhilin. 'Social Security of the Handicapped'. *China Civil Affairs, Beijing* 7 (2006): 20–4.

Wu, Yan-dan, and Han-sheng Huang. 'Influences of Beijing Paralympics on Chinese'Sports for the Disabled'. *Journal of Wuhan Institute of Physical Education* 41, no. 7 (2007): 20–2.

Yearbook of Affairs for Persons with Disabilities China (1983–1994). Beijing: The Yearbook Press of China, 2004.

Zhang, Jun-xian, and Quing Tan. 'A Survey on Research of Disabled Sports in the Last 20 Years'in China'. *Journal of Chengdu Sport University* 2 (2007): 104–6.

Zhang Jun-xian, and Yu Zhong. 'Historical Retrospect of Disabled Sports and Attitudes towards Disabled People'. *Sports Science* (2007): 37–22.

Zhang, Jun-xian, and Zhong-gan Yu. 'Historical Retrospect of Disabled Sports and Attitude towards Disabled People'. *China Sport Science* 27, no. 3 (2007): 17–22.

Zhou Fang. 'Present Situation and Influential Factors on Sports for People with Disabilities'. *Zhejiang Sport Science*, no. 1 (2005): 1.

Zhou, Kun, and Tian-zhen Li. 'Investigation on the Physical Exercise Conditioning of Disabled Persons'. *China Sport Science and Technology* 42, no. 3 (2006): 15–16.

Living disability and restructuring International Paralympic Committee sport in Oceania: the challenge of perceptions, spatial dispersal and limited resources

Jagdish C. Maharaj

Faculty of Medicine, The University of Sydney, Sydney, Australia; Executive Management, Lourdes Hospital and Community Service, Dubbo, Australia and Oceania Paralympic Committee

The Oceania region is one of the largest and most diverse. The Sydney 2000 Paralympic Games played a pivotal role for athletes with a disability from this region. A meeting of Oceania representatives led to the establishment of the Oceania Paralympic Committee. This descriptive research reviews definitions and perceptions of living disability, the development of advocacy and sports, and analyses the Paralympic Movement and related challenges with reference to sport administrative structural changes in Oceania. The results indicate that the perception of disability is culturally oriented and tied to superstitious beliefs. Only 29% of eligible nations in Oceania have been able to join the Paralympic Movement. Since 1963, 21 multisports, multinational games have been held in the region without the inclusion of athletes with a disability until 2011 Pacific Games. Attempts at inclusive sports have been unsuccessful so far and efforts at mainstreaming are proving difficult due to attitude, remoteness, the vast dispersal of the countries and resource constraints.

Sport, recreation and leisure activities play a very important role in the lives of many people, including those with a disability; however, opportunities have evolved with varying degrees of success in different communities around the world despite the fact that such activities have been shown to be very beneficial. In a series of in-depth literature reviews, Hashemi and Parnes categorized the benefits of sport for people with a disability as having improvements in physical health and well-being; improvements in mental health and psychological well-being; and increased integration and inclusion into society.[1] The impact of sport as an integral component of medical rehabilitation, socialization and participation,[2] and the birth and development of the Paralympic Games[3] are discussed in other sections of this publication.

Globally, sports for people with a disability grew rapidly from the base of the Stoke Mandeville Games, a competition for disabled ex-servicemen that began in 1948, to other regional Far East and South Pacific (FESPIC) Games for the Disabled in 1975, and evolved into the modern the Paralympic Games and other international and world championships, as well as having an impact on competition events in the Commonwealth Games. Today, the modern Paralympic Games, with its motto 'Spirit in Motion', is no longer rehabilitation focused and social based; instead, it focuses on high-performance elite competition. It is probably far from the ideal of Guttmann, the doctor who founded the

Stoke Mandeville Games, and what used to be the FESPIC Games philosophy. The FESPIC Games entry manual used to stipulate the inclusion of 33% novice athletes on international teams to encourage participation and the development of athletes with a disability. However, the modern Paralympic Games is now the platform for elite high-performance excellence in sport for athletes with a disability. Whereas the philosophy of the FESPIC Games was an excellent way to bring new talents into the international arena, the modern Paralympic Games contributes enormously to the self-esteem, personal self-satisfaction and advancement of a selected few, and supports developments in sport as well as disability-related science, technology and knowledge.

This article outlines some of the recent developments, achievements and shortcomings of participatory, as well as competitive elite sports for people with a disability in the Oceania region, with particular reference to perceptions of disability, recent sport administrative structural changes, and the opportunity for participation and achievements in the area of sport for people with a disability in the Fiji Islands. The case of the Fiji Islands is discussed to illuminate the issues in this article because of its stage of development and the newer initiatives in the arena of sports for athletes with a disability, its dispersed island geography, similar to other island countries, and most of all, the author's personal involvement and experience as an administrator, rehabilitation physician and classifier in sport for athletes with a disability in the Fiji Islands and the region. The journey of an athlete with a disability is also presented to illustrate some of the difficulties encountered by people living on remote, isolated islands who aspire to participate and excel in sports. A number of challenges and possible future directions are discussed. Some country-specific and regional data is also presented to explain the challenges in this region.

Oceania: geography, people, economy and disability

The Oceania region in the western Pacific (Figure 1) is one of the largest and most diverse regions in the world. The 31 million people of the Oceania region are scattered across one-third of the earth's surface, with 96% of the area being water in the form of the Pacific Ocean. Although there are some similarities, cultural and economic variation across the Oceania region is as diverse as the nations are dispersed. Some of the country-specific sociodemographic characteristics are provided below. Oceania encompasses Australasia (Australia and New Zealand) and the Pacific Islands (Melanesia, Micronesia and Polynesia). The boundaries of Oceania are essentially political. In the Pacific Ocean, it excludes Taiwan, Japan, the Philippines, islands associated with the mainland countries of Asia and the Americas, the western half of the island of New Guinea (claimed successively by Portugal, the Netherlands and Indonesia) and the whole of Indonesia; but does include the French possessions, New Caledonia, French Polynesia (aka Tahiti), Wallis and Fortuna Islands.[4]

There is very wide variation in the gross domestic product (GDP) per capita across the region, ranging from only US$600 for Solomon Islands to US$37,500 for Australia.[6] Similarly, national dry land mass in square kilometres, populations and population densities all have very broad ranges, as shown in Table 1.[7] The continent of Australia alone constitutes nine-tenths of Oceania's landmass and has the largest population size, but the lowest population density, whereas Nauru with the smallest landmass has the highest population density.

Disability

What is 'disability' and who are people with a disability? Disability is somewhat difficult to define, regardless of cultural context, but usually presents in a continuum of functional

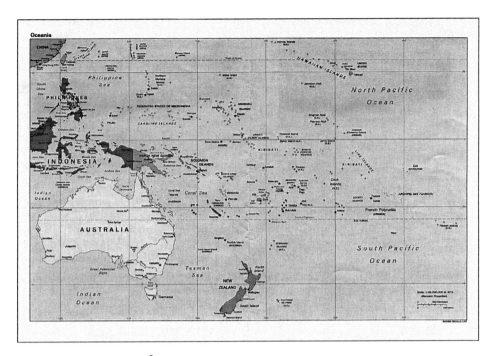

Figure 1.   Map of Oceania.[5]

abilities. The definition has typically been regarded as based on one of two contrasting interpretations, the medical model and the social model. The medical model views certain physical, intellectual and mental impairments as pathological conditions of an individual, causing a person's loss of or reduction in function, participation restriction and various disadvantages in their society. Management of such problems in the medical model revolves around a medical cure and management at tissue, organ and personal levels, adjustments to disability, substitutions and individual and family behavioural changes. The social model views disability as a consequence of social, political, economic and cultural exclusion of those with disabilities. Therefore, in the social model, the management of

Table 1.   National statistics: gross domestic product (GDP), land area, population and population density.

Country	GDP/Capita (US$)	Land area (km^2)	Population	Population density (persons/km^2)
Australia	37,500	7,692,024	19,358,000	2.5
New Zealand	27,300	270,606	3,864,000	14
Palau	7,600	487	19,100	39
Fiji	5,500	18,277	844,000	46
Nauru	5,000	21.2	12,100	571
Marshall Islands	2,900	181	70,800	391
Papua New Guinea	2,900	462,963	5,049,000	11
Vanuatu	2,900	12,195	193,000	16
Micronesia	2,300	702	134,600	192
Tonga	2,200	751	104,000	138
Samoa	2,100	2,831	179,000	63
Tuvalu	1,600	24.3	11,000	453

problems revolves around changing social situations and including and accepting the disabled population as a normal part of society, with the need for society and the environment to change. However, neither of these models, on its own, satisfactorily explains the attributes and management of disability.

More specifically, in 1980, the World Health Organization (WHO) introduced the International Classification of Impairment, Disability and Handicap (ICIDH) which provided a definition by three incremental terms: impairment (reduced function of tissue, an organ or body part); disability (reduced function and activity limitation of a person); and handicap (social, economic and cultural circumstances and restrictions that place persons with impairment or a disability at a role disadvantage relative to their peers or stage in life). This definition embraced social aspects and provided for further different dimensions of disability, but has been criticized by the proponents of 'social-only' model as being too close to the medical model and not including other environmental factors (such as a lack of physical or informational accessibility) as possible contributing causes (contextual factors) of disability. Further evolution of the definition took place in 2001 when the WHO adopted the International Classification of Functioning, Disability and Health (ICF) which draws attention to wider social aspects and views disability as a phenomenon arising from complex interactions of bodily functions and structures, activities and participation, and environmental and personal factors.[8] This definition embraces broader human functioning, takes account of social dimensions, includes contextual factors, uses neutral terminology, provides operational definitions for all categories and gives greater prominence to structural and functional impairments.

There are other internationally recognized definitions of disability that are accepted and in use. The International Labour Organization Vocational Rehabilitation and Employment (Disabled Persons) Convention from 1983 defined disability as: 'Persons with disabilities include those who have long-term physical, mental, intellectual or sensory impairments which in interaction with various barriers may hinder their full and effective participation in society on an equal basis with others'. The chair of the Ad Hoc Committee on the United Nations International Convention suggested the following definition at its 7th session:

> Disability results from the interaction between persons with impairments, conditions or illnesses and the environmental and attitudinal barriers they face. Such impairments, conditions or illnesses may be permanent, temporary, intermittent or imputed and include those that are physical, sensory, psychosocial, neurological, medical or intellectual.[9]

It seems that the definition of disability can vary depending on the contextual application. However, my own understanding (informed by my experience as a rehabilitation medical doctor and as a classifier in the Paralympic sport) is that the drive towards a 'social-only' model of disability, and as such, opposition to WHO model, stems from the fact that majority of people with a disability remain socially disadvantaged. This disparity is believed to stem from and is compounded by barriers such as non-acceptance into society and lack of opportunities available and provided to people with a disability.

It is reported that people with a disability are among the poorest and most vulnerable, with the majority living in low-income (developing) countries. The United Nations estimates that approximately 10% of the world's population, around 650 million people, are living with a disability.[10] There are approximately 400 million people with a disability in the Asia and Pacific region alone, with 80% of them living in developing countries and about a similar percentage (i.e. 80%) dwelling in rural areas.[11] The reported proportion of disabled population in 24 countries of the Asia Pacific region varies greatly from 0.7% to a high of 20%.[12] This data supports the fact that disability prevalence rates differ tremendously across borders not because the populations are so different, but because of the application of different definitions, study methodologies and research capacities for data collection at the local and national level. Once fully implemented, the new ICF is expected and likely to address this anomaly. An estimated 832,900 Pacific Islanders are living with a disability. They rarely enjoy human rights comparable with others and remain invisible to most of the community where discrimination is exacerbated by the negative attitudes, prejudice, ignorance and apathy of policy-makers and the community.[13]

There are various international agencies that are trying to address issues of socio-economic disparity between people with a disability and the non-disabled. One such regional framework is the 'Biwako Millennium Framework for Action towards an Inclusive, Barrier-free and Rights-based Society for Persons with Disabilities in Asia and the Pacific' (BMF). This was the outcome of the high-level intergovernmental meeting to conclude the Asian and Pacific Decade of Disabled Persons, 1993–2002.

Perceptions of disability

Knowledge of how a culture views disability is very important not only for understanding disability from the point of view of the person, family and society, but also in promoting any development of services and programmes for people with a disability. In my opinion, there is growing recognition and acceptance of viewing and understanding disability from a cultural perspective. There is general agreement among anthropologists that judgements of being ill or well are culturally defined and closely related to the views each culture takes of life, values and concepts of personhood. Although there is a scarcity of research data on how disability is exactly viewed by numerous different cultural groups in the societies making up Oceania (including Australia, New Zealand and the Pacific Island countries), the available information points to the fact that illness or disability is viewed not purely as a biological phenomenon, but as being caused by something less tangible, by some misdeed or by somebody. This belief can lead to the rejection and isolation of person with a disability from that society.

Rengiil and Jarrow's study of Palauan terminology for disability suggests that the vocabulary used to describe disability implies that 'the concept conveyed is that the person with a disability is not a true person but rather a less-than-fully-human entity.[14] Other perspectives include those from the Caroline Islands where the general theory of disease is linked to spirits,[15] whereas to be disabled on the Subsistence Atoll is to be of questionable productive power.[16] In the Fiji Island group, it is reported that the Rotuman explanation for ill-fortune often presupposes it to be a punishment for moral transgressions, however, the willingness of households to accommodate members with disabilities as individuals can be attributed, in part, to the importance of generosity in Rotuman culture.[17] Although Western medicine and culture have a prominent presence and are well accepted in Oceania countries, resorting to traditional cures is a common practice in Fiji.[18] In the western Pacific, and specifically in Guam, shame (*mamah'lao*) is a collective concept in the Chamorro language that can assign blame to an entire kinship group for the situation of a single individual.[19] People with a disability are sometimes hidden and disregarded. Thus, cultural beliefs and background appear to have a very strong and important influence on how different societies view people with a disability and consequently may impact upon individual participation and all levels of programme development.

Although awareness and acceptance of people with a disability have improved in the region's culture, perception and attitudes that associate 'a disabling condition with ancestral curse, parental misdeeds, witchcraft, shame and fear' linger.[20] Even with varying degrees of understanding of disability and sociocultural perceptions, and negative beliefs and attitudes towards people with a disability in different societies, many people with disabilities are determined to do their utmost best within their potential and capabilities. An athlete's journey is presented below to illustrate such determination.

Local Fijian challenges en route to the Paralympic Games

RK (a pseudonym) grew up and completed primary education at a small village on one of the remote islands of the Fiji Island group. Although intellectually normal in school performance, RK had underdeveloped and weaker left limbs. Some peers allowed RK to join in their many improvised sporting activities on the island. At the age of 15, when in secondary education and showing promising athletic abilities in running, the parents decided that RK should move to the capital city of Suva on the main island of Viti Levu to continue education and at the same time have the opportunity to further sporting abilities.

The journey to Suva was not without difficulties. The once-a-week flight by air to Suva was prohibitively expensive so the family decided that the fortnightly boat trip was the best option. The boat is usually a cargo/passenger carrier which stops at various islands during the 36-hour trip and if the weather conditions are unfavourable it can take longer and the ride is more treacherous. People from the outer smaller islands prefer to take this painstaking journey by boat rather than by air because of the cost involved. It is cheaper to travel by boat than by air and as most islanders are subsistence farmers or fisherman, this is the most common mode of travel.

To put some resources together to get RK to Suva, the family organized a 'Soli', which is the Fijian traditional way of raising funds through community support. Many members of the clan will throw in few dollars to support a common course. RK's family arranged accommodation with some relatives in Nausori, which is a small satellite town about 15 km from Suva, and RK was to attend a school half way between Suva and Nausori. RK depended on the public transport service to get to school and further transport to get to Suva for training, which was unaffordable. Many times training sessions were missed due to an inability to get to the training and coaching due to a lack of bus fare, difficulty with the accessibility of public transport and time constraints. Thus training was compromised. RK got occasional assistance from sporting organizations, but usually this was unavailable and not sufficient. Because of the potential, the sporting organization arranged a foster family in Suva to house RK during this period. RK found it difficult to adjust to these new arrangements and was set back in both training and schooling programmes. But strong determination and perseverance saw RK through the difficult times. RK got into the national training squad and onto the road to a possible international sporting career.

The following sections discuss the opportunities available to athletes with a disability and the changing dynamics of national, regional and international sport structures that are meant to create and provide the opportunities for athletes like RK and all people with a disability wishing to participate in sport of their choice.

Sports for people with a disability in the Oceania region: FESPIC and International Paralympic Committee restructuring

In terms of sporting regions, until recently, Oceania along with Asia formed the FESPIC Games Federation region. In 2006, the FESPIC Federation had 60 member countries and territories stretching from the Middle East to the mid-Pacific.[21] The first FESPIC Games was organized by Dr Nakamura in Oita, Japan in 1975. As shown in Table 2, the FESPIC Games were held approximately every 4 years in different countries, the final one being the 9th FESPIC Games in Kuala Lumpur, Malaysia in 2006. These Games have provided the main international opportunity for participation and competition for many South Pacific countries. The FESPIC Games had a policy of inviting 33% novice athletes to the Games. This philosophy provided developmental opportunities for novice athletes and sustained an interest in sports, particularly for athletes in developing countries. Illustrating that international participatory sports for people with a disability can lead to organizational developments, it has been reported that a major benefit of the FESPIC Games was that it led to a wide range of rehabilitation and advocacy services and remarkable progress in the countries in the FESPIC Games region.[22] Unfortunately, this spirit of participation opportunity no longer exists at major international competitions.

The author's personal observation is that the smaller nations in the region have had fairly ad hoc sporting activities for people with a disability. In Oceania, apart from Australia and New Zealand, few have any regular sustained sporting programmes. Recently, even fewer athletes participate regularly or have excelled at international level. This is largely due to a lack of any sustained high-performance training programme and opportunities for competition. However, athletes who have, against many odds, managed to take up the challenge report marked self-satisfaction and enrichment. This is later demonstrated by the Fiji's 'Ambassador' programme.

As the International Paralympic Committee (IPC) world regions evolved analogous to the International Olympic Committee (IOC) regions (Figure 2),[24] the FESPIC Games Federation, which originally covered two of the IOC regions, was split into Asia and Oceania. Dissolution of FESPIC Games Federation and the FESPIC Games followed. A FESPIC Games Federation endorsed taskforce specifically looked at post-FESPIC restructuring of the Asian region. There was no such activity undertaken for the Oceania region, leaving the majority of the ex-FESPIC member Pacific Island nations not being able to form National Paralympic Committees (NPCs) or organize regular sport for their athletes with a disability. Not surprisingly, the recommendation of the taskforce was the 'merger' of the FESPIC Games Federation and the existing Asian Paralympic Council, however, 18 Oceania countries that were part of the 60-member FESPIC Games Federation were not part of the Asian Paralympic Council or the Asian region, and as such were left out of the transition arrangements. Fiji had been an active member of FESPIC Games Federation and participated at all nine FESPIC Games, but found itself, along with other South Pacific nations, no longer a part of what had been the previously growing and expanding FESPIC Games family and system.

Table 2. Far East South Pacific Games Federation for the Disabled[23].

Games	Year	Dates	City/Country	Number of nations taking part	Number of athletes taking part
1st	1975	1–3 June	Oita & Beppu, Japan	18	973
2nd	1977	20–26 November	Parramatta, Australia	16	430
3rd	1982	31 October – 7 November	Sha Tin, Hong Kong	23	744
4th	1986	31 August – 7 September	Surakarta, Indonesia	19	834
5th	1989	15–20 September	Kobe, Japan	41	1,646
6th	1994	4–10 September	Beijing, China	42	2,081
7th	1999	10–6 January	Bangkok, Thailand	34	2,258
8th	2002	26 October – 1 November	Busan, Korea	40	2,199
9th	2006	25 November – 1 December	Kuala Lumpur, Malaysia	46	3,641

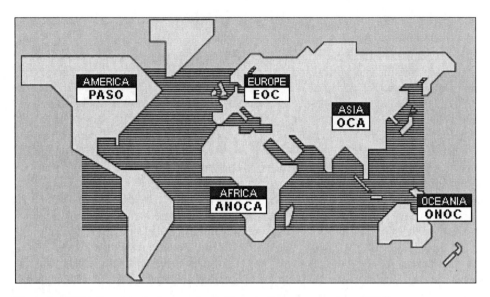

Figure 2.   Map of current the International Olympic Committee regions (2008).

Partnerships: Oceania Paralympic Committee, Arafura Games and Oceania Paralympic Championships

The Sydney 2000 Paralympic Games played a pivotal role in the further development of sports for persons with disabilities in the region. During the Sydney 2000 Paralympic Games, a small delegation of Oceania countries, led by the president of the Australian Paralympic Committee, met with the then Australian minister for sports to discuss the formation of a body to advance sports for people with a disability in the region. After much deliberation and support from the Australian government and the Australian Paralympic Committee, the South Pacific Paralympic Committee (SPPC) was established in 2001. This was later renamed the Oceania Paralympic Committee (OPC), representing one of the five newly formed IPC world regions. Since its inception, the Australian government has continued to fund the activities of the OPC via the Australia Sports Commission and Australian Paralympic Committee that continues to be the custodian of the funds.

The formation of this Oceania body was opportune, as without this development and after the new IPC regionalization, coupled with the FESPIC Games Federation's dissolution, the smaller nations of the Pacific would have been completely isolated and extremely disadvantaged with no regional representation. The primary mission of the OPC is to develop 'Paralympic athletes through regional leadership and cooperation plus increase participation in international sporting competitions'.[25] The expansion of Paralympic Movement in the region has been very slow. So far, since 2001, only 29% of the eligible countries of the region have been able to gain IPC and OPC membership. These include Australia, Fiji, New Zealand, Papua New Guinea, Tonga, Samoa and Vanuatu. The OPC has successfully assisted some island member countries through its development funding grants programme for local talent development, administration capacity building, as well as participation at international competitions. One of the most recent initiatives of the OPC is to provide classification education and training in all member countries. Importantly, the OPC has managed to bring IPC-sanctioned Paralympic Games qualifying championships closer to home. In a historic three-way agreement in 2007 by the Australian

Northern Territory Government, the Australian Paralympic Committee and the OPC, the Arafura Games 2007 incorporated the Oceania Paralympic Championships.

The Arafura Games, named after the Arafura Sea, is now a leading international sporting competition for emerging athletes of the Asia Pacific region and beyond. The Arafura Sea lies west of the Pacific Ocean between Australia and New Guinea. Its boundaries are the Torres Strait through to the Coral Sea to the east, the Gulf of Carpentaria to the south, the Timor Sea to the west and the Banda and Ceram seas to the northwest. Since 1991, the Arafura Games have been held biennially in Darwin, the capital of Australia's Northern Territory. The Games are billed as a meeting of 'sporting neighbours' and attract athletes from all parts of Australia, nations throughout the Asia Pacific and beyond. It began as the Arafura Sports Festival with 1500 participants from seven countries competing in 13 sports. By the time the eighth Games were held in 2005, participation had soared to more than 3000 athletes representing 32 nations, with competition in 30 sports.[26]

The 2007 Oceania Paralympic Championships (incorporated with the 2007 Arafura Games) offered seven sports (athletics, cycling, powerlifting, table tennis, wheelchair basketball, wheelchair tennis) for athletes with a disability. The second Oceania Paralympic Championships in 2009 offered eight sports with inclusion of two new sports (seven-a-side football for Cerebral Palsy athletes and shooting), while wheelchair basketball was dropped.[27] The 3rd Oceania Paralympic Championships with the Arafura Games was held in 2011. It is envisaged that future Oceania Paralympic Championships was incorporated with all the future biennial Arafura Games and grow to offer many more sport events and attract more athletes with a disability from all Oceania countries.

Even with these few successes, there is still a long way to go to include many other Oceania nations into the Paralympic family, the OPC and the Championships. There are probably many reasons for smaller South Pacific nations not being able to join the Paralympic Movement. Most importantly, for any nation to be accepted as an IPC and OPC member the nation must establish its own NPC that is recognized by its government. None of the other eligible Oceania nations have been able to form such a NPC. To provide opportunities to athlete with a disability and develop Paralympic Movement in the region it is imperative to find out why? Amongst other things, some of the reasons for this difficulty seem to be the lack of knowledge of how to go about this task, difficulty with internal structures, poor communication and lack of support and acceptance and isolation within the country and in the region of people with disabilities. This is an essential area that needs further research.

Fiji Islands: sport for people with a disability

The Fiji Islands is a multiethnic, multicultural nation with a population of just over 800,000. It consists of an archipelago of 330 islands of different sizes in the south western Pacific Ocean situated 3000 km northeast of Sydney and 2000 km north of Auckland, straddling the international dateline. The islands are mountainous and covered with tropical forests. It is one of the more developed of the Pacific Island economies, although still with a large subsistence sector. Sugar exports and a rapidly growing tourism industry are the major sources of foreign exchange. The shift from an agricultural-based subsistence economy to a cash economy has influenced the lifestyles of many and has resulted in a rapid increase in the size of urban communities and led to independent nuclear families.

The history of sports for people with a disability in Fiji began in the 1960s when a few selected individuals participated in invited international events. In Fiji, although previous national games for athletes with a disability had been held, regular annual national games for people with a disability started in 1984 and have been held every year since, typically with over 500 athletes participating. Although the initial work commenced in 1984, the umbrella body, the Fiji Sports Association for the Disabled (FSAD), which is the representative NPC, was constitutionally established in 1990. In 2008, to comply with the IPC's requirement that all NPC must include 'Paralympic' in their names, the organization was renamed as the Fiji Paralympic Committee. In this article it is referred to as the 'Fiji National Paralympic Committee'. This organization provides people with a disability in Fiji opportunities for regular local participation and competition, and a vehicle for expansion and preparation for international events. Fiji has participated at all the nine FESPIC Games and in the last four summer Paralympic Games.

Soon after its establishment, Fiji's National Paralympic Committee gained National Olympic Committee (NOC) and government recognition, IPC membership and formed links with various National Sports Federation including athletics, archery, judo, swimming, table tennis and powerlifting, and recently with lawn tennis, to forge inclusive sports. Fiji's National Olympic Committee, the Fiji Association of Sports and National Olympic Committee (FASANOC) has for many years supported sports for people with a disability and treated Olympic and Paralympic athletes on an equal basis in terms of training and tour preparations. Athletes with a disability have been included in all FASANOC award programmes. However, in the past, inclusive sport has been successful to only a limited degree, and in a few sports. This is largely due to athletes with a disability being unable to regularly attend the programmes due to lack of resources to get there. The venues and training facilities originally built for non-disabled athletes are often inaccessible. In some sports, there is a lack of expertise in providing for the athlete with a disability. As a developing country, the biggest constraint is a lack of available funds for the administration, development and elite athlete preparation and competition opportunities. Recently in Fiji, the drive for inclusive sport has increased pace. However, unlike the successes of the Fiji National Paralympic Committee, many smaller nations of the region have not made any advances in the area of sports for athletes with a disability.

Along with the major regional restructuring and changes in opportunities at the international level, Fiji has restructured programmes at the national level. The Abilities Development Program through the Australian Sports Commission has enhanced the programmes by providing funding for 'grass roots', 'sport for all' and 'inclusive sport' development opportunities. The purpose of the programme is to 'increase the number of quality sport programmes that people with a disability can participate in at a level and in a role that they choose'. The activities of the NPC are primarily focused at the sports development level for novice or grass-roots athlete level, advocacy, regional and national games. In 2009 there has been a surge in activities of the NPC, with the acquisition of an office space and the employment of a sports development officer and office staff. In the last few years the Fiji NPC has begun activities at the community and institutional levels; encouragement level; provincial, regional and national level; and international sports development levels. The projects and programmes involve over 1000 children with disabilities from 17 special education schools from around the country. Participation is targeted at regular sporting activities and other new sports for Fiji such as boccia, goal ball and sitting volleyball through corporate sponsorship. Fiji's NPC also organized a very successful subregional sports classification course in 2008 funded and conducted by expertise from the OPC.

One of the most exciting projects has been the Sports Ambassadors Program. This has driven advocacy supporting the benefits of participation in sports. The Fiji NPC embarked on this innovative method of supporting grass-root level sports development where fifteen past elite international athletes formed this group visiting schools and different communities on a weekly basis to advocate, educate and create awareness about the positive impact of sport. The sports development officer regularly monitors all sporting activities in all the special education schools keeping comprehensive records.

In addition to the National Games for the Disabled held annually since 1984, three Regional Games – Central/Eastern, Western and Northern Games are also conducted annually and hosted by local organizing committees. Twenty-three affiliates of the NPC gather with over 500–600 participants in archery, athletics, powerlifting, table tennis, lawn bowls, lawn tennis, swimming and sitting volleyball.

Although the Fiji NPC has been very successful in terms of running annual national games, participating at international competitions, sustaining interest and developing sports for athletes with a disability, huge challenges remain for the regional nations and the individual athletes.

Challenges

Attempts to have a regular regional South Pacific Games for athletes with a disability for the last 20 years have not succeeded. In 1990, on the invitation of the then president of the Fiji NPC, five other regional countries participated in the national games in Fiji. During these Games the idea of starting a South Pacific Games for athletes with a disability was floated. Following this, in 1991, the first and only South Pacific Games for the Disabled was organized in Noumea, New Caledonia through French government support and funding. Owing to a lack of structure, communication and funding, further South Pacific Games for the Disabled have never been organized.

The disabled community of the South Pacific also desired to have inclusive games with the existing non-disabled regional games. Many attempts in the last seven years by the disabled community to be included in the non-disabled South Pacific Games (now known as the Pacific Games) held every four years since 1963 under the patronage of the South Pacific Games Council (now Pacific Games Council) has also not occurred. Requests to have inclusive events in the last two consecutive games in Fiji in 2003 and in Samoa in 2007 were not successful. In both cases, the respective local NPCs supported by the OPC requested the local Games Organizing Committees to include events for athletes with a disability. However, as inclusion or exclusion of any events at such major games has to be approved by the Games Council, although some nations supported the concept, the requests were voted out.

As such, the disabled communities of the South Pacific feel that they are very much discriminated against. In a personal communication, the president of Fiji NPC and a member of Pacific Disability Forum, Mr Vilsoni expressed the following opinion:

> This is clear discrimination for people with disabilities in the name of sports in the Pacific to be excluded by our people and countries … this issue was always raised because hurt and pain to be left out by our own people and countries in sports.[28]

One of the difficulties may be due to the lack of ability of the nations in the region that have established their own NPCs to lobby and demonstrate to general sporting organizations, their NOCs and the community at large the rights to participation and to inclusiveness. Further attempts and lobbying by the OPC and the disabled community of the Pacific to have inclusive events at the Pacific Games to be held in New Caledonia in 2011 were actively underway in 2009–2010 and looked promising. The 2011 Pacific Games held in New Caledonia included 4 'Para Sports' events.

Over the past 20 years, in terms of the general disability movement, there has been sustained progress in the Oceania region. Some countries have managed to establish their non-governmental national advocacy body under the banner of Disabled Peoples International (DPI) and a few have legislative national councils for disabled persons as a governmental statutory body. The advocacy movement in the region has developed into a very active regional umbrella organization know as the Pacific Disability Forum, which organizes regular national and regional development meetings, workshops and forums to advocate on the legislative and human rights platform. It can be noted that the general advocacy movement in the region has been much more successful in terms of development at national and regional levels than the sporting Paralympic Movement has. However, according to the Pacific Disability Forum, the process of general disability movement development has been slow and difficult as the 'awareness of disability movement and self-help organizations of people with a disability remains minimal in the Pacific'.[29]

Almost all smaller nations of Oceania region suffer from lack of funding and corporate and governmental long-term sustained support and sponsorship in the area of sports for people with a disability. Lack of funding compounded by low administrative support, inconsistent communication, shortage of appropriately trained personnel, geographical isolation and poor accessibility seem to be some of the major hindrances in the development and sustenance of Paralympic sports for people with a disability in the Oceania region. There is a large disparity between disabled and non-disabled sports national membership of regional bodies (Table 3).[30] Whereas, 22 Oceania countries are members of the Pacific Games Council, 18 had held FESPIC Games Federation membership in November 2006 and 24 have current Oceania National Olympic Committees (ONOC) memberships (February 2009); they are therefore eligible for International Paralympic Committee/Oceania Paralympic Committee memberships. Only seven, that is only 29% (May 2009), have so far managed to gain IPC status.

The ONOC, under the current leadership, seems to have been extremely successful in promoting Olympism and membership in the Oceania region. The 17 (71%) eligible regional nations that are yet to join the Paralympic Movement should consider soliciting assistance from their NOCs and other appropriate agencies to establish their NPCs and attain IPC status and OPC membership.

Apart from their inability to establish their NPCs, many South Pacific island nations have been left behind by rapidly changing and unaffordable technologies like racing wheelchairs and limb prosthetics. It is now rare to see a South Pacific island athlete competing in a modern racing wheelchair or running with modern leg prosthesis. The needy often are not even able to afford ordinary everyday use wheelchairs or limb prostheses, let alone the modern racing wheelchair or flex foot for elite competition.

Conclusion

Sport for people with a disability has come a long way from the humble beginnings of the Stoke Mandeville Games and the Paralympic Games and Movement; however, it has developed very unevenly in the Oceania region. The recent IPC and Asia–Oceania regional restructuring and dissolution of the FESPIC Games Federation, although it restructured the organization of Paralympic sport in accordance with the International Olympic and Paralympic Movements, seems to have taken away some sporting opportunities for athletes with a disability, particularly those from smaller Oceania nations, without replacing the lost opportunity. The majority of countries in the region have not been able to establish their own NPC and do not seem to be able to muster necessary NOC

Table 3.   Membership of the Oceania Paralympic Committee (OPC), Far East and South Pacific (FESPIC) Games Federation, Oceania National Olympic Committees (ONOC) and Pacific Games (PG).

Countries	Disabled sports		Non-disabled sports	
	OPC (7)	FESPIC (18)	ONOC (24)	PG (22)
American Samoa	0	0	✔	✔
Australia	✔	✔	✔	N/A
Cook Islands	0	0	✔	✔
Fed. Stat. Of Micronesia	0	✔	✔	✔
Fiji	✔	✔	✔	✔
Guam	0	✔	✔	✔
Kiribati	0	✔	✔	✔
Marshall Islands	0	✔	✔	✔
Nauru	0	✔	✔	✔
New Caledonia	0	✔	✔	✔
New Zealand	✔	✔	✔	N/A
Niue	0	0	✔	✔
Norfolk Island	0	0	✔	✔
Northern Mariana Island	0	✔	✔	✔
Palau	0	✔	✔	✔
Papua New Guinea	✔	✔	✔	✔
Samoa	✔	✔	✔	✔
Solomon Islands	0	✔	✔	✔
Tahiti	0	0	✔	✔
Tokelau	0	0	✔	✔
Tonga	✔	✔	✔	✔
Tuvalu	0	✔	✔	✔
Vanuatu	✔	✔	✔	✔
Wallis and Futuna	0	✔	✔	✔

Note: ✔, Current members; 0, not a member; N/A, not applicable as not eligible for membership.

and other sporting federations support for regular and inclusive sporting activity for people with a disability.

Promotion of broad-based participatory and inclusive programmes seems to be lacking. The low-income and dispersed nations in the Oceania region have largely been left behind in the development of sports for people with a disability and the Paralympic Movement. There seems to be no one-size-fits-all solution. There are specific cultural, perceptual, attitudinal, economic and political issues to be taken into account. Foster's[31] wonderful retrospective account of Trobriand cricket, a game made famous in the 1975 documentary film on the Trobriand island of British New Guinea, captures what may have been the dynamics of politicizing sports and an ingenious response to colonialism, but points to a place of sport beyond just cultural assimilation. A clearer understanding of these dynamics is needed if athletes from the Oceania Region are to be able to fully participate in the Paralympic Movement.

The very important question remains as to what model of intervention/development will be most suitable, acceptable and sustainable for this region? Obviously, it has to cater for a wide range of cultures, economies and geography. Apart from the need to work with the local systems, there seems to be an opportunity for research to decipher how to utilize the existing cultural and perceptual values to enhance development for people with a disability, in this region at least.

Whose responsibility is it to ensure that people with a disability in the region wishing to participate in sports are accorded equal rights and opportunities? Is it the people with a disability themselves, their governments, the IPC, the OPC, the NOCs or the NPCs (which do not exist in most countries in the region). The situation should not be seen to be one that perpetuates the culture of ignorance and neglect of people with a disability.

When I stated earlier that the modern Paralympic Movement today is only for elite sport, which is very different from the original goals of Sir Guttmann and the FESPIC Games philosophy, I did not imply that it should not be so. The Paralympic Games should be regarded as only one (elite) end of the continuum, but if not more, equal focus and emphasis needs to be given to the whole continuum – from recreation, participation to excellence. The IPC, the OPC and countries need to actively pursue the establishment and effective functioning of NPCs in all countries within their jurisdiction.

The future of sport for people with a disability and the Paralympic Movement in the Oceania region must extend opportunities to all ages and levels of athletes from all countries to participate in local, national, regional and international multisports as well as sports specific tournaments. It will be a great day when all 24 nations of the Oceania region eligible to be IPC and OPC members join the Paralympic Movement and provide their people with disabilities equal opportunities to participate in sport of their choice.

Notes

[1] Hashemi and Parnes, 'Sport as a Means to Foster Inclusion'.
[2] Steadward and Peterson, 'Sir Ludwig Guttmann', 21–28.
[3] London 2012, 'London 2012 Summer Roadshow'.
[4] Caldwell, Missingham, and March, *The Population of Oceania*.
[5] Oceania Map, http://www.ogram.org/sperry/graphics/images/oceania_pol97.jpg. The map provides the boundaries of Oceania beyond the South Pacific Ocean.
[6] Central Intelligence Agency, https://www.cia.gov/library/publications/the-world-factbook/index.html. *World Fact Book* provides demographic details of countries in Oceania.
[7] 'Oceania – Order of Area, Population and Density'. Globalgeografia. http://www.globalgeografia.com/oceania/oceania.htm. This provides data on area, population and population density for selected countries.
[8] WHO, *Classification*. http://www.who.int/classifications/icf/en/; UNESCAP, *Disability at a Glance*, http://www.unescap.org/esid/psis/disability/publications/glance/disability%20at%20a%20glance.pdf. Disability is defined in the framework of ICF.
[9] United Nations Enable, *Ad Hoc Committee on a Comprehensive and Integral International Convention*.
[10] United Nations Economic and Social Council, *Mainstreaming Disability*. Disability issues and demography are of particular concern in the developing world as this is where the majority of the 650 million people living with a disability are in the world.
[11] International Labour Organization, *Disability in the Pacific*. The majority of people with a disability live in developing countries, a similar percentage dwell in rural areas.
[12] UNESCAP, *Focus Areas of the Pacific Operations Centre*. There is wide variation in the reported numbers of people with a disability in different countries, with the problem of little if any census data in some cases. There is also wide variation in the legally entrenched rights of persons with disability.
[13] Ibid.
[14] Rengiil and Jarrow, 'Culture and Disability in Palau', 6. This, and the following three citations present perceptions of disability in Oceania from anthropological and cultural perspectives.
[15] Alkire, Perceptions of Physical, Mental and Sensory Disabilities', 7.
[16] O'Brien, 'Connection of Ability and Disability', 9.
[17] Rensel and Howard, 'The Place of Disabled Persons', 8.

[18] Cornelius *et al.*, *Fiji Non-communicable Disease (NCD) STEPS Survey 2002*. The use of traditional and cultural 'cures' has been reported to be a common practice in Fiji.

[19] Stephenson, 'Disability in the Western Pacific', 10. Presents the perception of disability in Oceania from an anthropological and cultural perspective.

[20] Tongsiri and Taweesangsuksakul, 'Sports for the Person with a Disability'; UNESCAP, *Developing Role Models and Resources*. Both sources present cultural, perceptual and attitudinal barriers hindering developments for people with a disability.

[21] FESPIC Games Federation, 'FESPIC Games Federation Closure of FESPIC Federation Homepage'. Gives a historical account of the period following the dissolution of the Federation.

[22] Nakamura, A Meaning of FESPIC Games. An account of how FESPIC Games Federation member nations had benefited from the philosophy FESPIC Games.

[23] The FESPIC Games. http://www.kl06fespicgames.com.my/aboutFespic/default.asp?p=about& p1 = about2&what = history

[24] International Olympic Committee, *National Olympic Committees*. The map shows the five IOC regions of the world. Similar regions have been adopted by the IPC.

[25] Oceania National Paralympic Committee, *2007/2008 Annual Report*.

[26] Northern Territory Government, *Arafura Games History*. The Arafura Games started as a 'sports festival' in 1991, and have grown to become a large international event for both disabled and non-disabled emerging athletes. Now hosts the biennial Oceania Paralympic Championships.

[27] Oceania National Paralympic Committees, *2007/2008 Annual Report*.

[28] Vilsoni, personal communication, 2008. Vilsoni made this comment as the President of Fiji National Paralympic Committee and a member of the Pacific Disability Forum. He is a former elite athlete with a disability.

[29] UNESCAP, *Developing Role Models* Presents cultural, perceptual and attitudinal barriers hindering developments for people with a disability.

[30] Oceania National Paralympic Committees. *2007/2008 Annual Report*; FESPIC Games Federation, 'FESPIC Games Federation Closure of FESPIC Federation Homepage'; Oceania National Olympic Committees, 'Pacific Games Council'; 'Our Countries'.

[31] Foster, 'From Trobriand Cricket to Rugby Nation', 739–758.

References

Alkire, William. 'Perceptions of Physical, Mental, and Sensory Disabilities on Woleai and Lamotrek, Caroline Islands'. *International Exchange of Experts and Information in Rehabilitation INTERCHANGE* Special Issue (1993): 7.

Caldwell, John, Bruce Missingham, and Jeff March. *The Population of Oceania in the Second Millennium*. Canberra: Australian National University. 2001 http://htc.anu.edu.au/pdfs/Oceania% 20manuscript.pdf

Cornelius, M., M. Decourten, J. Pryor, S. Saketa, T. Waqanivalu, A. Laqeretabua, E. Chung, *Fiji Non-communicable Disease (NCD) STEPS Survey 2002*. Ministry of Health, Suva 2008.

FESPIC Games Federation. 'FESPIC Games Federation Closure of FESPIC Federation Homepage'. FESPIC Games Federation, 2006. http://www.gzapg2010.cn/09/0606/13/5B4LT5FE0089016C. html

Foster, Robert. 'From Trobriand Cricket to Rugby Nation: The Mission of Sport in Papua New Guinea'. *The International Journal of History of Sport* 23, no. 5 (2006): 739–58.

Hashemi, Goli, and Penny Parnes. 'Sport as a Means to Foster Inclusion, Health and Well-being of People with Disabilities'. Sport for Development and Peace International Working Group, 2007. http://iwg.sportanddev.org

International Labour Organization. *Disability in the Pacific: Fact Sheet*. http://www.ilo.org/public/ english/region/asro/bangkok/download/yr2007/iddp_fact.pdf

International Olympic Committee. *National Olympic Committees*. http://www.olympic.org/en/ content/The-IOC/Governance/National-Olympic-Committees/

London 2012. 'London 2012 Summer Roadshow launches on 15 June'. May, 2007. http://www. london2012.com/press/media-releases/2007/05/london-2012-summer-roadshow-launches-on-15-june.php.

Nakamura, T. (1999). *A Meaning of FESPIC Games*. http://209.85.173.104/search?q=cache: knEChIbO2IYJ:members.tripod.com/campaign99/C99/21/21a.doc+FESPIC+Games+history& hl=en&ct=clnk&cd=5&gl=au

Northern Territory Government. *Arafura Games History*. Darwin, Australia: Northern Territory Government. http://www.arafuragames.nt.gov.au/

O'Brien, Patrick. 'The Connection of Ability and Disability on a Subsistence Atoll'. *International Exchange if Experts and Information in Rehabilitation INTERCHANGE* Special Issue (1993): 9.

Oceania National Olympic Committees. 'Oceania National Olympic Committees: Our Countries'. *Oceaniasport*, 2008. http://www.oceaniasport.com/index.php?id=19

Oceania National Olympic Committees. 'Oceania National Olympic Committees: Pacific Games Council'. *Oceaniasport*, 2008. http://www.oceaniasport.com/index.php?id=19

Oceania National Paralympic Committees. *2007/2008 Annual Report*. Sydney: Oceania National Paralympic Committees, 2008.

Rengiil, Yoichi K., and Jane E. Jarrow. 'Culture and Disability in Palau'. *International Exchange of Experts and Information in Rehabilitation INTERCHANGE* Special Issue (1993): 6.

Rensel, Jan, and Alan Howard. 'The Place of Disabled Persons in Rotuman Society'. *International Exchange if Experts and Information in Rehabilitation INTERCHANGE* Special Issue (1993): 8.

Steadward, Robert, and Cynthia Peterson. 'Sir Ludwig Guttmann – Father of the Paralympics'. *Paralympics: Where Heroes Come*, Chapter 2. Edmonton, AB: One Shot Holdings 1997.

Stephenson, Rebecca. 'Disability in the Western Pacific: Perspective from Guam'. *International Exchange if Experts and Information in Rehabilitation INTERCHANGE* Special Issue (1993).

Tongsiri, Sirinart, and Ratana Taweesangsuksakul. 'Sports for the Person with a Disability: The 7th FESPIC Games in Bangkok, Thailand'. *Asia and Pacific Journal on Disability* 2 (1999): 101–4.

United Nations Economic and Social Commission for the Asia Pacific. *Developing Role Models and Resources: Self-determination in the Pacific*. Bangkok: The Secretariat of the United Nations Economic and Social Commission for the Asia Pacific, 2008. http://www.unescap.org/esid/psis/publications/spps/13/chap2.htm

United Nations Economic and Social Commission for the Asia Pacific (UNESCAP). *Disability at a Glance: A Profile of 28 Countries and Areas in Asia and the Pacific*. Bangkok: Secretariat of UNESCAP, 2008.

United Nations Economic and Social Commission for the Asia Pacific (UNESCAP). *Focus Areas of the Pacific Operations Centre: Disability in the Pacific*. Bangkok: Secretariat of UNESCAP, 2008. http://www.unescap.org/epoc/r4_disability_in_the_asiapacific.asp

United Nations Economic and Social Council. *Mainstreaming Disability in the Development Agenda*. Report of the Secretary General, 48th session, 2008. http://www.un.org/disabilities/documents/reports/e-cn5-2008-6.doc

United Nations Enable. *Ad Hoc Committee on a Comprehensive and Integral International Convention on the Protection and Promotion of the Rights and Dignity of Persons with Disabilities*, 7th session, 2006. http://www.un.org/esa/socdev/enable/rights/ahc7pddisability.htm

World Health Organization. *Classification: International Classification of Functioning, Disability and Health (ICF)*. Geneva: World Health Organization, 2009.

Physical activity and sport as a tool to include disabled children in Kenyan schools

José Frantz, Julie S. Phillips, Joseph M. Matheri and Joanne J. Kibet

University of the Western Cape, South Africa

This article presents a brief history of the disability movement in East Africa and is the first study of its kind in Kenya. The study aimed to determine the physical activity levels of disabled and non-disabled children at schools in selected provinces in Kenya. A cross-sectional study was conducted with children in three high schools offering inclusive education and in three government boarding high schools. Thirty-six per cent of the disabled children were physically active compared with 64% of the non-disabled children. However, there are barriers to participation and there is a need to increase physical activity participation and to create awareness of the health benefits of physical activity among the disabled population.

Disability movement in Africa

The disability movement in Africa is generally young and has its roots in Zimbabwe. This movement is a product of the post-independence era, and started in the 1970s when a group of physically disabled people began to organize themselves in the long-term healthcare institution in Zimbabwe in which they lived and worked. The development of the disability movement has been charted through a series of interviews with key individuals, one of whom, Joshua Malinga, became the main link with Disabled People International (DPI) from its inception in 1981; he was later elected chairperson of DPI. According to Disability Rights Promotion International (DRPI), the first institution for the disabled was established in 1953 and was called the Association for the Physically Disabled of Kenya. Later, the Kenya Society for the Blind and the Kenya Society for Deaf Children were also created through legislation. Non-governmental organizations offered rehabilitation, and included the Christian Blind Mission (CBM), Sense International, the Leonard Cheshire Foundation and Handicap International.[1]

In 1989, after various initiatives on the part of advocacy groups, national organizations, as well as 130 community-based organizations and Disabled Peoples Organisations (DPOs), came together under one vocal umbrella organization to form the United Disabled Persons of Kenya (UDPK). The UDPK then worked hard to influence the Attorney General's 1993 Task Force to review disability laws and the Persons with Disabilities Act was passed in 2003. A provision of this Act included the establishment of a National Council for Persons with Disabilities, with which the responsibility to implement the rights of people with disabilities fell.[2] The United Nations Convention on the Rights of People with Disabilities adopted in December 2007 clearly highlighted the rights of people with disability as it relates to health (Article 24), education (Article 24), work and employment (Article 27), as well as improved accessibility (Article 9),[3] and the disability movement in southern Africa was strongly influenced from its early stages by international disability politics.

Disability in sport

When linking the disability movement in Kenya to sport, it is important to note that this movement is in its early stages. According to the *State of Disabled People's Rights in Kenya*, the disability movement is still in an 'early transition from medical rehabilitation to the human rights model'.[4] This is also evident in the findings of a study by the African Union of the Blind, who reported that people with a disability in Kenya are reporting 'experiences of oppression, discrimination and violation of their basic human rights'. The study also highlighted that there is a need 'to promote equal enjoyment of human rights for disabled persons and to respond to their economic, socio-cultural and political needs through various mechanisms'. Thus the authors concluded that sport can be used as a tool to overcome these negative experiences and to promote the human rights of people living with disabilities.

Kenya is active in a number of sports, including cricket and soccer, road rallying,[5] rugby union and boxing, but it is known globally for its dominance of middle- and long-distance running. Kenya won 14 medals at the Beijing Olympic Games and making it the African country with the most medals. There have been few successful Kenyan Paralympic athletes, but Teresia Nganga is quite well-known because she competed in the 800 metres at the 2002 Commonwealth Games in Manchester.[6] Efforts have been made, however, to develop Paralympic sport and the National Women in Paralympic Sport Leadership Summit was held in 2006 in Nairobi with the aim of supporting women and Paralympic sport.[7]

Sport or participation in physical activity can be a powerful tool to address various inequalities and barriers identified by disabled people. Sport can be used to empower, and to offer inclusion, socialization and independence. As it relates to socialization, sport and involvement in physical activity create peer interaction, cooperative relationships and teamwork.[8] Participation in sport also allows for independent growth, both physically and mentally, thus facilitating empowerment which leads to increased self-confidence.[9] Furthermore, participation in physical activity and sport with non-disabled peers allows for a better understanding and sensitivity about one another and can thus assist in preventing social exclusion. Sport and participation in any form of physical activity have an important role in the lives and communities of many individuals. They allow for young people to develop both socially and physically. Sport and physical activity can be seen as a means of social inclusion because of the visibility of the positive aspects that sport brings in relation to people with and without a disability, making those with a disability the subject of the action and empowering them with the capacity and potential to be active members of society. 'While sport has value in everyone's life, it is even more important in the life of a person with a disability. This is because of sport's rehabilitative influence and the fact that it is a means to integrate the person into society'.[10] The benefits of participation in sport for people with disabilities have been widely cited in terms of an improved quality of life, self-esteem and social acceptance.[11]

It is a fact that around '10% of the world's population, or 650 million people, live with a disability and 80% of these people live in developing countries'.[12] These numbers continue to increase as a result of political conflict, accidents and a high incidence of untreated disease. Interestingly, although the number of people with disabilities in Kenya is not well known, it has been reported to be less than 1% although this might be due to differing definitions of disability and poor monitoring systems. The actual figure is estimated to be approximately 3,000,000, reflecting the world's average of 10%.[13] This lack of information could be due to poor monitoring systems in the country. Given such numbers, people with a disability are a target population within the global agenda of sport for development. Sport has an important role in the lives and communities of many individuals, but for individuals with disabilities it has benefits beyond those applicable to all. Historically, disability sport has been viewed as a form of rehabilitation rather than a form of recreation and competition. However, if we are to move towards the inclusion of people with disabilities in all aspects, then disability sport should focus on recreation and competition rather than rehabilitation.

Education, disability and sport in Kenya

After independence in 1963, the three-tiered education system defined by race (European, African and Asian) changed and developed into government, private and/or missionary schools, as well as *harambee* (a grass-roots movement of self-help schools). Government schools, formerly reserved for whites, and private schools were the best equipped.[14] Currently, Kenya's education system consists of early childhood education, primary, secondary and college education, and the current educational curricula, (introduced in 1985 and commonly referred to as the 8-4-4 system), is comprised of eight years of primary education, four years of secondary education and four years of university education.[15]

Kenya is actually ahead of many sub-Saharan African countries in terms of providing education for all. In 2003, primary education became free and enormous efforts have been made to improve primary school education with additional support from overseas. Initiatives to service children with disabilities began in 1975 as indicated in the *State of Disabled Peopled Rights in Kenya Report*. This included the incorporation of coordinated efforts for children with special needs and training by specialized staff for every disability category.[16] Three special areas of disability were catered for, namely visual disability, hearing disability and intellectual disability. Education for people with physical disabilities was introduced later.[17] Since 2003, the Kenyan government has offered educational support for children with special needs who are attending special schools.

These days, access to special schools is limited and fewer than 30% of disabled children are enrolled in them. Kenya is, however, committed to Education for All, which involves including children with disabilities into 'normal' schools, as well as ensuring gender equity.[18] Currently, there are 57 primary schools for children with disabilities. In addition, there are 103 integrated units in regular primary schools and three high schools for persons with physical disabilities.[19]

Hemmingson and Borrell describe physical activity behaviour or participation in sporting activities as 'the interaction between the person, the task and the environment'.[20] Therefore, participation in physical activity is a function of the individual's experience of their local environment. Arising out of the adolescent−task−environment interdependence, none of these three elements can be held as an independent entity in behaviour change models and interventions. Mihaylov *et al.* stated that ideal environment should include:

- the way the individual perceives the environment as influencing participation in physical and social activities with minimal or no assistance;
- the attitudes of persons without disabilities towards those with disabilities; and
- the way in which local authorities where disabled individuals live recognize their right to (implement national disability policy guidelines) barrier-free physical and

social environments (including transport, health, employment) that promote participation.[21]

Young people with physical disabilities often find themselves excluded from the physical activities that their peers participate in. The most common activities that Kenyan young people participate in include rugby, soccer, cricket, athletics and running. The vulnerability of young people with physical disabilities is reflected in research evidence of their participation in physical activity. In one such study, Law et al. found that the participation of children with physical disabilities in structured school activities was lower than that of their peers without disabilities and was less vigorous.[22] According to MacPhail, Kirk, and Eley, adolescents with physical disabilities do not participate in physical activities because they do not enjoy sport, parents control their decisions, they lack time or friends to play with, they have limited access to opportunities for physical activity, they do not have a preferred choice, andf they need more encouragement.[23]

Adolescents with disabilities might also have fewer opportunities to show their abilities and may experience social isolation because of limited mobility.[24] These factors often lead to the loss of opportunity to interact with peers, preventing them from developing an age-appropriate identity and engaging in habitual physical activity behaviour.[25]

In general, the move towards inclusive education was intended to create an environment that allowed adolescents with disabilities to participate in sport and physical activities with their able-bodied peers, thus promoting understanding and social inclusion. According to the *Integrated National Disability Strategy for South Africa*,[26] one of the main policy objectives for the disabled relating to sport is 'to develop and extend sporting activities for people with disabilities in both mainstream and special facilities so that they can participate in sport for both recreational and competitive purposes'. Coinciding with barriers highlighted by people with disabilities in Kenya, such as discriminatory attitudes, negative perceptions and limited access, the strategy document highlights an inadequacy of sport and recreational facilities, as well as sport federations, to address needs of people with disabilities, and also points to inaccessible public transport as one of the major barriers to full participation in sport. Inclusive education might, therefore, be seen as a mechanism to overcome these barriers.

Inclusion of the disabled into society, education, and sport and recreation is a top priority for many governments, however, it continues to be very challenging. According to various researchers, people with a disability are more likely to be sedentary relative to the general population;[27] this was indeed the case in Kenya. In the *Global School-based Student Health Survey* (GSSHS) in Kenya, among all students aged 13–15 years, 12% were found to be physically active for a total of 60 minutes per day on all seven days preceding the survey.[28] In the same survey, it was found that overall 37.8% of the students spent three or more hours per day sitting and watching television, playing computer games, talking to friends or doing other sitting activities.[29]

Comparing physical activity rates in Kenyan schools

The aim of this study was to compare the exposure of disabled and non-disabled young people to sport or physical activity at schools. A cross-sectional study was conducted in selected high schools in Kenya that offer inclusive education to adolescents with disability and in schools offering education for able-bodied learners. The question raised was: 'Are learners with physical disabilities afforded the same health and socialization opportunities as their peers without a disability'?

Methods

This study is cross-sectional and used a quantitative design. The adolescents were drawn from six high schools in Kenya, three of which were offering inclusive education and three of which were not. Currently, there are three high schools in Kenya for adolescents with physical disabilities that have moved towards inclusive education (Rift Valley, Mombasa and Thika) and there are six boarding high schools in Nairobi. A stratified random sampling technique was used to select the participants from the three government schools and purposive sampling was used to select adolescents from the schools offering inclusive education to ensure that adolescents with disabilities were adequately represented. The schools for adolescents with disabilities were located in different provinces; a secondary school in Thika, Central Province, a secondary school in Kisumu, Nyanza Province and a high school in Mombasa, Coast Province. The three schools are national high schools and are jointly sponsored by the government of Kenya and the Salvation Army church. All three schools offered high school education only to learners with physical disabilities until 2005/2006, but now offer inclusive education curricula, specifically to adolescent learners with and without physical disabilities. The children without disabilities were drawn from three government boarding high schools in Nairobi Province, Kenya.

The study sample consisted of 365 able-bodied adolescents and 234 adolescents with a disability. Only adolescents with physical disabilities were included in the study. Data was collected using self-administered questionnaires that were designed based on the literature.[30] The questionnaire was divided into two sections, namely demographic data and physical activity data. The physical activity level questionnaire for the disabled was based on the Physical Activity Scale for Individuals with Physical Disabilities (PASIPD) which is a valid and reliable scale and the physical activity questionnaire for the able-bodied learners was the Sub-Saharan African Questionnaire (SSAQ). When analysing the data, the physical activities were divided into vigorous, moderate and light activities, according to the World Health Organization (WHO) classification. In addition, the daily amount of activities of the PASIPD was converted to monthly time spent in order to compare it more accurately with the SSAQ.

The WHO recommended that the average adolescent engage in at least 30 minutes of physical activity of moderate intensity every day, or most days of the week, should be sufficient to gain health benefits. This is considered a standard guideline and is also applicable for Kenyan youth. In addition, these 30 minutes can be accumulated throughout the day in small bouts of activity.[31] A pilot study was conducted to pre-test the research questionnaire in Kenya among young people ($n = 15$) with physical disabilities, who were not included in the main study. The test yielded a Cronbach's alpha value of 0.807 [ICC = 0.807]. Descriptive statistics was used to describe the sociodemographic information and inferential statistics were reported as chi square and p-values.

Results

A total of 720 questionnaires were distributed, of which 420 were sent to the enrolled able-bodied adolescents and 300 to the enrolled adolescents with disabilities. The response rate to the questionnaire was 83.2% ($N = 599$). The demographic data of participants are presented in Table 1. Of the total number of participants ($N = 599$), 39% had a disability ($n = 234$). Of the total number of males ($n = 319$), 40% had a disability and 38% of the total number of females ($n = 280$) had a disability. Figure 1 highlights the types of disabilities among the participants.

According to the WHO classification, 52% of the total sample was physically active and 48% were physically inactive. Within the physically active group, 27% of the children

Table 1.   Demographic data of the participants ($N = 599$).

	Adolescents with a disability ($n = 234$)	Adolescents without a disability ($n = 365$)	Total $N = 599$ (100%)
Gender			
Male	129 (55%)	190 (52%)	319 (53%)
Female	105 (45%)	175 (48%)	280 (47%)
Age (years)			
14	20 (8.5%)	8 (2.2%)	28 (4.7%)
15	35 (15.0%)	94 (25.8%)	129 (21.5%)
16	30 (12.8%)	108 (29.6%)	138 (23.1%)
17	55 (23.5%)	132 (36.2%)	187 (31.2%)
18	59 (25.2%)	22 (6.0%)	81 (13.5%)
19	20 (8.5%)	1 (0.2%)	21 (3.5%)
Older than 19	15 (6.5%)	0 (0.0%)	15 (2.5%)
School Form			
2	89 (38.1%)	121 (33.2%)	210 (35.1%)
3	85 (36.3%)	122 (33.4%)	207 (34.6%)
4	60 (25.6%)	122 (33.4%)	182 (30.3%)
Level of activity			
Active	85 (36.3%)	228 (62.5%)	313 (52.3%)
Inactive	149 (63.7%)	137 (38.5%)	286 (47.7%)

Note: School form is equivalent to the year at high school, e.g. Form 3 is the third year at high school.

had a disability, thus 72% of the active participants were able-bodied. The relationship between physical activity levels and presence of a disability was statistically significant ($x^2 = 39.05$; $p < 0.00$). Among those who were physically active, males (52.3%) were found to be more active than females (47.3%). The mean age for Form 2 was 15 (± 0.56) years, for Form 3 was 16 (± 0.55) years and for Form 4 was 17 (± 0.45) years.

Levels of activity were significantly influenced by age, gender and school form within the groups, i.e. disabled and non-disabled groups ($p < 0.00$). There was a significant decrease in the prevalence of participants who were physically active from Form 2 (64.2%) to Form 4 (42.4%) ($x^2 = 18.67$; $p < 0.00$). There was also a significant difference in the prevalence of adolescents who were classified as physically active by age ($x^2 = 16.13$, $p < 0.00$). Older participants were significantly more likely to be classified as more sedentary than the younger participants and this was evident in both groups (Figure 2). There was a significant relationship between gender and physical activity participation ($x^2 = 23.09$, $p < 0.00$).

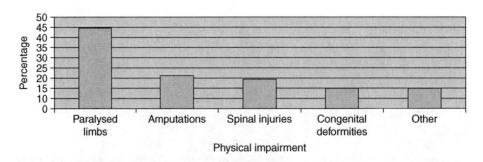

Figure 1.   Types of disabilities present among children.

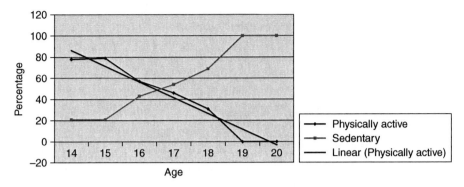

Figure 2. Physical activity levels according to age.

Table 2. Factors influencing participation in physical activity.

Factors identified by disabled adolescents	Factors identified by able-bodied adolescents
Lack of transport has been a problem for me (43%)	Neighbourhood safety (26%)
Uneven playgrounds and compounds makes it difficult to do exercise (41%)	After-school activities (32%)
I have an injury or disability that stops me (35%).	Active role models (27%)
I haven't got the right clothes or equipment (35%)	Illness (22%)
There are no suitable facilities or sports at the school (34%)	Physical education at school (15%)
I haven't got time (36%)	Finances (10%)
People at home do not assist me to become active (22%).	Encouragement from friends and family (73%)
Making new friends (85%)	Social support (82%)
Positive attitude towards me from schoolmates and teachers (75%)	
Positive attitude towards me from other people (71%)	

Factors identified by the adolescents as influencing participation in physical activity varied between the two groups and are presented in Table 2. It is evident that both environmental and personal factors influenced participation in physical activity.

Discussion

Although this study is small it is the first to examine the physical activity levels in children in inclusive education schools in Kenya compared with levels in children in public schools. The study clearly shows that non-disabled children were more active than disabled learners. Although the disabled learners were interacting with non-disabled children at school, they still tended to be less active. When comparing factors such as age, gender and grade, there were statistically significant differences within the groups, but no difference between disabled and able-bodied groups. In order to bridge this gap, schools need to modify activities according to the abilities of the children to promote participation.[32] In addition, schools could also take responsibility for providing children with the correct clothes and equipment, as 35% indicated that this was lacking.

Social support for physical activity and sport participation from friends and family members are strong predictors of physical activity levels. It is a common assumption that most healthy or unhealthy habits originate, at least in part, in family socialization. The findings of our study are similar to others[33] and showed that social inclusion and acceptance were also influences for participation in physical activity. Peer motivation, in particular by family members and friends, is one of the main factors influencing participation in physical activity among populations, primarily in adolescence and young adults.[34] Thus, it is evident that if sport and participation are seen to encourage social inclusion and socialization then more emphasis should be given to this in schools.

In developing countries, great attempts have been made to include people with disabilities in sport. However, Onyewadume's recent research has identified that in Africa people with disabilities have not been afforded their rightful place in sports and physical activity participation.[35] Research has indicated that in schools adolescents with disabilities may need more exposure to physical activity than children without disabilities.[36] French and Hainsworth highlighted that the integration of people with disabilities should change to inclusion of people with disabilities as this describes the way disabled people become full members of society with the similar values and rights as everyone else.[37]

Conclusion

Participation of all children, including those with disabilities, in sports and physical activity promotes physical, emotional and social well-being. Inclusive education should assist the participation of children with disabilities in all areas of life, which should include sport. However, we need to be careful that we are not only promoting integration, but also placing more emphasis on true inclusion. True inclusion should make the child feel that they belong and accommodations should be made to include the child with disabilities in sport. We thus need to be more definite about how we achieve an inclusive environment that promotes sports and physical activity as part of everyday life for all young people. Training of teachers and coaches should perhaps be considered as an intervention to promote physical activity among the disabled.

Notes

[1] Disabled Rights Promotion International, *State of Disabled People's Rights in Kenya*.
[2] Ibid.
[3] United Nations, *Convention on Rights of People with Disabilities*.
[4] Ibid.
[5] The KCB Safari Rally began as the East African Coronation Safari in 1953.
[6] Davies, 'Disabled Sport'.
[7] Women, gender, equality and sport. http://www.un.org/womenwatch/daw/public/Women%20and%20Sport.pdf
[8] Dykens, Rosner, and Butterbaugh, 'Exercise and Sports in Children'.
[9] International Disability in Sport Working Group, *Sport in the United Nations Convention*, 6.
[10] Disabled Rights Promotion International, *State of Disabled People's Rights in Kenya*.
[11] Disabled in sport. http://www.hksi.org.hk/hksdb/html/pdf/research/Report12.pdf
[12] United Nations. http://www.un.org/disabilities/default.asp
[13] Disabled Rights Promotion International, *State of Disabled People's Rights in Kenya*.
[14] Kenya Educational System Overview, http://education.stateuniversity.com/pages/772/Kenya-EDUCATIONAL-SYSTEM-OVERVIEW.htmlixzz0KOn26zSF&D.
[15] Ibid. The education structure in Kenya comprises of two years of early childhood education for children aged 4–5 years, primary education of eight years for children aged 6–13 years and secondary education of four years for those aged 14–17years.
[16] Disabled Rights Promotion International, *State of Disabled People's Rights in Kenya*.
[17] Ibid. The Kenya Institute of Special Education provides specialized training at diploma level to teachers already trained to teach in ordinary schools but with interest in special education. It also

introduced short-term certificate courses for teachers in special schools, units and integrated programmes. It has recently introduced distance-learning programmes with a current enrolment of more than 7000. Special education is also now offered in two public universities: Kenyatta University and Moi University.

[18] International Labour Organization, *Employment of People with Disabilities*.

[19] Ibid.

[20] Hemmingson and Borell, 'Environmental Barriers in Mainstream Schools', 163.

[21] Mihaylov *et al.*, 'Identification and Description of Environmental Factors'.

[22] Law *et al.*, *Patterns and Predictors of Recreational and Leisure Participation*.

[23] MacPhail, Kirk, and Eley, 'Listening to Young People's Voices'.

[24] Blomquist *et al.*, 'Transitioning to Independence'.

[25] Heath and Fentem, 'Physical Activity Among Persons with Disabilities'; Rimmer, Rubin, and Braddock, 'Barriers to Exercise in African American Women with Physical Disabilities'.

[26] South African Government Information, Office of the Deputy President, *Integrated National Disability Strategy White Paper*.

[27] Heath and Fentem, 'Physical Activity Among Persons with Disabilities'; Rimmer, Rubin, and Braddock, 'Barriers to Exercise in African American Women with Physical Disabilities'.

[28] World Health Organization, *Global School-based Student Health Survey*.

[29] Ibid.

[30] Washburn *et al.*, 'The Physical Activity Scale'; Sobngwi *et al.*, 'Development and Validation and Questionnaire for Assessment of Physical Activity'.

[31] World Health Organization, 'Children and Young People'.

[32] Ainsworth *et al.*, 'Personal, Social and Physical Environmental Correlates'; Wharf Higgins *et al.*, 'Factors Influencing Physical Activity Levels'.

[33] Tergerson and King, 'Do Perceived Cues and Benefits and Barriers to Physical Activity Differ Between Male and Female Adolescents?'; Sallis and Owen, 'Physical Activity and Behavioural Medicine'.

[34] Onyewdume, 'Adapted Physical Activity in Africa'.

[35] Ibid.

[36] Sit *et al.*, 'Physical Activity Levels of Children in Special Schools'.

[37] French and Hainsworth, 'There Aren't Any Buses and the Swimming Pool is Always Cold!'

References

African Union of the Blind in collaboration with Kenya Union of the Blind and Centre for Disability Rights, Education and Advocacy. *State of Disabled Peoples Rights in Kenya*, African Union of the Blind, Kenya 2007.

Ainsworth, Barbara, Sara Wilcox, Winifred Thompson, Donna Ritcher, and Karla Henderson. 'Personal, Social and Physical Environmental Correlates of Physical Activity in African American Women in South Carolina'. *America Journal of Preventive Medicine* 23 (2003): 23–9.

Blomquist, Kathleen, Gayle Brown, Anja Peersen, and Elizabeth Presler. 'Transitioning to Independence: Challenges for Young People with Disabilities and their Caregivers'. *Orthopeadic Nursing* 17 (1998): 27–35.

Davies, Gareth. 'Disabled Sport: Kenyan Loses Race But Wins Hearts'. *The Telegraph* (July) 2002. http://www.telegraph.co.uk/sport/3031880/Disabled-Sport-Kenyan-loses-race-but-wins-hearts.html

Disability Rights Promotion International (DRPI). *State of Disabled Peoples Rights in Kenya, 2007*. Disability Rights Promotion International, 2009. http://yorku.ca/drpi/Kenya07Ch3.html African Union of the Blind, Kenya

Dykens, Elisabeth, Beth Rosner, and Grant Butterbaugh. 'Exercise and Sports in Children and Adolescents with Developmental Disabilities: Positive Physical and Psychosocial Effects'. *Child Adolescent Psychiatric Clinics in North America* 7, no. 4 (1998): 757–71.

French, David, and Jenny Hainsworth. '"There Aren't Any Buses and the Swimming Pool is Always Cold!": Obstacles and Opportunities in the Provision of Sport for Disabled People'. *Managing Leisure* 6 (2001): 35–49.

Heath, Gregory, and Peter Fentem. 'Physical Activity Among Persons with Disabilities: A Public Health Perspective'. *Exercise Sport Science Reviews* 25 (1997): 195–234.

Hemmingson, Helena, and Lena Borell. 'Environmental Barriers in Mainstream Schools'. *Child: Care, Health and Development* 28, no. 1 (2002): 57–63.

International Disability in Sport Working Group. *Sport in the United Nations Convention on the Rights of Persons with Disabilities*. Centre for the Study of Sport in Society. Boston, MA: Northeastern University, 2007.

International Labour Organization. *Employment of People with Disabilities: The Impact of Legislation (East Africa): Kenya Country Profile*. Geneva, Switzerland: International Labour Organization, 2004. http://www.ilo.org/skills/what/pubs/lang–en/docName–WCMS_107837/index.htm

Law, Mary, Gillian King, Susanne King, Marilyn Kertoy, Patricia Hurley, Peter Rosenbaum, Nancy Young, Steven Hanna, and Theresa Petrenchik. *Patterns and Predictors of Recreational and Leisure Participation for Children with Physical Disabilities*. Hamilton, ON: CanChild Centre for Childhood Disability Research. 2006 www.canchild.ca/

MacPhail, Ann, David Kirk, and Diann Eley. 'Listening to Young People's Voices: Youth Sports Leaders' Advice on Facilitating Participation in Sport'. *European Physical Education Review* 9, no. 1 (2003): 57–73.

Mihaylov, Svetozar, Stephen Jarvis, Allan Colver, and Bryony Beresford. 'Identification and Description of Environmental Factors that Influence Participation of Children with Cerebral Palsy'. *Developmental Medicine and Child Neurology* 46, no. 4 (2004): 299–304.

Onyewadume, Ignatius. 'Adapted Physical Activity in Africa: Problems and the Way Forward'. *Sobama Journal* 12, no. 1 (2007): 58–63.

Rimmer, James, Stephen Rubin, and Demetrios. Braddock. 'Barriers to Exercise in African American Women with Physical Disabilities'. *Archives of Physical Medicine Rehabilitation* 81 (2000): 182–8.

Sallis, James, and Neville Owen. *Physical Activity and Behavioural Medicine*, Vol. 3. Thousand Oaks, CA: Sage, 1999.

Sit, Cindy, Allison McManus, Thomas McKenzie, and John Lian. 'Physical Activity Levels of Children in Special Schools'. *Preventive Medicine* 45 (2007): 424–31.

Sobnqwi, Eugene, Jean-Claude Mbanya, Nigel Unwin, Terence Aspray, and George Alberti. 'Development and Validation and Questionnaire for Assessment of Physical Activity in Epidemiological Studies in Sub Saharan Africa'. *International Epidemiological Association* 30 (2001): 1361–68.

South African Government Information, Office of the Deputy President. *Integrated National Disability Strategy White Paper*. Republic of South Africa Pretoria: Government Communications Information System, 1997.

Tergerson, Jennifer, and Keith King. 'Do Perceived Cues and Benefits and Barriers to Physical Activity Differ Between Male and Female Adolescents?'. *Journal of School Health* 72 (2002): 374–77.

United Nations. *Convention on the Rights of Persons with Disabilities*. New York: United Nations, 2006. http://www.un.org/disabilities/documents/convention/convoptprot-e.pdf

United Nations. *Women 2000 and Beyond: Women, Gender Equality and Sport*. New York: United Nations, Division for the Advancement of Women, 2007.

Washburn, Richard, Weimo Zhu, Edward McAuley, Michael Frogley, and Stephen Figoni. 'The Physical Activity Scale for Individuals with Physical Disabilities: Development and Evaluation'. *Archives of Physical Medicine Rehabilitation* 83 (2002): 193–200.

Wharf Higgins, J., Catherine Gaul, Sandra Gibbons, and Geraldine Van Gyn. 'Factors Influencing Physical Activity Levels Among Canadian Youth'. *Journal of Public Health* 94 (2003): 45–51.

World Health Organization. 'Children and Young People: Physical Activity for Various Populations Groups'. Non-Communicable Disease Prevention and Health Promotion. World Health Organization Geneva. 2003. http://www.who.int/hpr/phsactiv/economic.benefits.shtml

World Health Organization. *Global School-based Student Health Survey, National Dataset*. Nairobi, Kenya: Ministry of Health Geneva, 2003. http://www.who.int/chp/gshs/kenyadataset/en/index.html

Contested perspectives of 'marvel' and 'mockery' in disability and sport: Accra, Ghana

Anne-Marie Bourgeois

Graduate Department of Development Studies, York University, Toronto, Canada

In the past, persons with disabilities and the relationship between disability and sports were excluded from discussions of development. Within the past 15 years, however, there has been a proliferation of 'development through sport' initiatives and a widespread promotion of the intended and unintended outcomes of participation in sport for persons living in low- and middle-income countries. From the vantage point of development studies, and drawing on qualitative research methods, this article examines sport as a vehicle for the human development of persons with disabilities in a Ghanaian community. It presents the athletes as active agents, and highlights their engagement in daily struggles and strategies to be respected and recognized in both sport and society, as well as links their efforts to questions of marvel and mockery. The setting is the city of Accra, Ghana, and the athletes are female and male athletes of the Ghana Society of the Physically Disabled.

Until recently, persons with disabilities (PWD), and the relationship between disability and sport, had generally been excluded from development discussions. Within the past 15 years, however, there has been a proliferation of 'development through sport' initiatives and a widespread promotion of the intended and unintended outcomes of participation in sport for persons living in low- and middle-income countries.[1] Participation in sport has been touted to involve more than mere improvements in sport skills.[2] Indeed, sport and physical activity have gained rapid recognition as both an end and a pragmatically simple, low-cost and effective means to further aspects of international development, such as the Millennium Development Goals.[3] Most pertinently, sport has become increasingly lauded as a means with which to foster inclusion, integration and empowerment of marginalized groups, namely PWD and women and girls. Various critiques have surfaced, however, in response to such claims and promotions; of particular relevance is the argument that sport is a social construct and thus should not be represented uncritically in an essentialist or positivist light.[4] Furthermore, there remains a dearth of empirical evaluative evidence on the relationship between disability sports and development.

Drawing upon four months of fieldwork (June to September 2008), this article seeks to fill some of these lacunae. A series of vignettes selected from qualitative data collected from focus groups, semi-structured interviews and observations serve to present the voices of disabled athletes and to guide an interpretative narrative. In so doing, hegemonic, able-bodied standards are questioned, whilst the notion that sport serves as a vehicle for the human development of PWD is concomitantly reviewed. Human development is viewed in accordance with Amartya Sen and seen primarily as the ability to expand choices[5] as well as the ability to foster well-being, health, inclusion and integration.[6] The setting is the city of Accra, Ghana, West Africa, and the athletes are both female and male athletes of the Ghana Society for the Physically Disabled (GSPD), Greater Accra Sports Wing. From the vantage point of development studies, the primary purpose of this article is therefore, to provide a local illustration not of what sport is *meant* to do, but rather what sport actually *does* do for a particular group of urban Ghanaian women and men with disabilities.

Through the Ghanaian example, this article will first, provide information regarding the country, Ghana, the organization, GSPD and the female and male athletes themselves. Second, I briefly touch on the relationship between disability and gender. Third, the prevalence of the beggar as the dominant image of 'disableds' in Accra is outlined, as are the ways in which athletes' through sport, seek to be seen as separate, or rather identified as different from beggars. Fourth, the perspectives of the athletes will be foregrounded, namely in relation to how they link acquired respect and recognition from some family and community members to regular participation in sport, and how such notions of respect and recognition play out in terms of cultural, and to an extent, gendered, contexts. Finally, I show that although many athletes do speak of increased respect and recognition, their visible participation in sport also brings out the uneasy underlying question as to whether spectators, rather than respecting or recognizing them as athletes, may actually be marvelling at them as 'supercrips'[7] or mocking them as deviants. The article concludes with a summary of the key findings, their wider implications, and recommendations for further exploration.

Ghana: the (dis)abled state?

A West African coastal country of 23.9 million,[8] and former British colony, Ghana became, in 1957, the first black sub-Saharan African nation to achieve independence from a colonial power. With no history of civil war, Ghana is home to various ethnic groups, primarily Akan, Ga, Ewe and Dagomba, as well as various religious affiliations, primarily Christian, Islam and indigenous beliefs.[9] Sprawling along the southern coast of Ghana and with a population of 1,658,937, Accra is the national hub for the administrative, communication and economic sectors,[10] as well as the centre of the rights-based disability movement. Of note is that US President, Barack Obama, chose Ghana as the site for his July 2009 inaugural presidential visit to sub-Saharan Africa, praising the country for its 'good governance' and promoting it as a model for African development.[11]

Ghana is a particularly suitable site for disability sport and development research given its reputation as a leader in development through sport[12] and its active disabled community. Former President John Kufuor (2001–2009) had stressed the commitment of the government of Ghana to use sport as a strategy for poverty reduction and national development. Additionally, the Deputy Minister for Education, Science and Sports, has emphasized sport's inclusion in the Poverty Eradication Programme (Ghana was one of the first countries to do so) given its supposed contribution to sociocultural development; he has also called for plans to create opportunities for Ghana's youth (to the exclusion of youth with disabilities) to realize their dreams to become sports heroes.[13]

Within the broader national landscape, the late 1980s saw the emergence of a disability movement within Ghana, likely in large part to resist the retrenchment of the Ghanaian state during the 1980s–1990s and the corresponding cuts to social welfare characteristic of the Structural Adjustment Programmes implemented during that time.[14] Funded by the Danish International Development Agency, GSPD is a registered non-governmental organization that since 1987 has been representing the physically disabled community to the wider disability movement. GSPD continues to promote the welfare of their members by creating awareness of the capacities and capabilities of persons with physical disabilities; as well as advocating and lobbying for their rights.[15] With the establishment of Sports Wings in Ghana's 10 regions, GSPD is the primary organization for physical disability sports in Ghana; they envision harnessing sport as a tool for advocacy and empowerment through the provision of sport and recreation opportunities.[16]

Athletes of Accra

Owing to the incomplete societal and sport structures provided, these athletes have found themselves near the bottom of the given economic and sport hierarchical standings and face diminished moral standing. Ranging in age from 20 to 35 years (9 women; 13 men),[17] their group, similar to other marginalized or even non-marginalized collectives, was neither homogeneous nor entirely cohesive; education and employment levels varied, as did social hierarchies and socio-economic statuses. The majority of the athletes had, however, been able to obtain some sort of vocational training, primarily in tailoring, shoemaking, hairdressing or chalk-making, and worked with varying degrees of regularity, for varying, yet always small incomes. Ethnic backgrounds differed to include Akan, Ga, Ewe, Fante; religious affiliations to various Christian (predominantly) and Islamic denominations were present.

All nine women and eleven of the men were lower limb impaired; the remaining two men had upper arm(s) impairments. Various types of wheelchairs and crutches were the primary mobility methods; the majority had had polio and the entire group had been living with their impairment since infancy or early childhood. Although the athletes had access, all be it limited, to a variety of sports, including basketball, football, table tennis, and track and field events, it was basketball that involved the most members as well as was the most regularly occurring, and is thus the sport in which most stories are rooted. The majority of the athletes first became involved in sports by becoming members of GSPD and learning of disability sports at the monthly general meetings.

Unique to the group is that although they are funded externally, there was a lack of structured external support and thus their activities were largely self-led. This situation thus differs greatly from many 'development through sport' initiatives such as those of international development through sport non-governmental organization, *Right to Play* for example. Also unique to the group was that at the basketball court, the context was co-ed, such that women and men trained together weekly, running basketball drills and playing practice matches in a mixed-gender setting. However, upon the rare occasions when these athletes travel or host interregional competitions, they would play women versus women and men versus men.

Disability: a gendered development issue

It seems necessary at this juncture to address the language and literature surrounding disability, in general and in this article. The use of PWD is in light of the 'person-first approach' as is predominantly used in North America. However, in the UK, 'disabled persons' is most often used, given the predominant 'society is disabling approach'. In this latter way, 'disabled' may be seen as a statement that their social and economic status as 'rejected bodies' in a world that privileges an idealized, perfect or perfectable body is restrictive of life chances.[18] Given that in Ghana the athletes' self- and collectively identified as 'disableds', the inconsistency in language throughout this article is deliberate.

When dealing with the literature I use 'PWD' at times, and use 'disabled persons' at others, whereas while voicing and discussing the perspectives of these Ghanaian athletes, I switch to 'disableds'.

When considering gender, although men share with women many of the effects of impairment and disability, as circumscribed by 'the prevailing normativities of the body,' they unsurprisingly are likely to experience them and be affected by them in very different ways.[19] Women with disabilities have been deemed doubly disadvantaged, as per their gender and their disability, and as per most frequently used economic, employment and education indicators.[20] In addition, women with disabilities are often seen as unable to procreate, rear children or be in a relationship.[21] In similar language, yet different manifestations, men with (physical) disabilities have been deemed 'doubly bound,' because they are often judged according to standards of hegemonic masculinity that are difficult to achieve due to the limitations of their bodies.[22]

Of course, existing social understandings of masculinity and femininity, or socially accepted ways of expressing what it means to be a woman or a man in a particular social context play a role in determining access, levels of participation and benefits from sport.[23] As elsewhere, in Accra what it means to be a human being is, first and foremost, defined by socially accepted ways of expressing 'normalcy';[24] because of the way sport itself is socially constructed, its norms have historically and systematically excluded PWDs.[25] By conducting qualitative research with female and male athletes with disabilities, this paper offers a preliminary exploration of how such 'doubly disadvantaged' or 'doubly bound' gendered notions of disability play out in this urban Ghanaian context.

'Ballers' and beggars

In discussing the individual and collective motivations for, and benefits of, participation in sport, most significant to the majority of the athletes or 'ballers' [basketball players] was the respect that they felt they had acquired from some family and/or community members. Of the material, economic and cultural contextual influences of urban Accra, the prevalence of the disabled beggar as the negative counter-image of disability featured most prominently, and has as result shaped and reshaped the actions and experiences of these athletes or 'ballers'. Given that the athletes spoke in terms of 'separating themselves' or 'being seen as separate' from those begging, their corresponding actions have been interpreted as 'separation strategies'. To increase their chances of acquiring such respect, and to ultimately increase their chances of being seen as separate to or different from those begging, the athletes, as will be explored in greater detail, utilized the three key separation strategies of movements, 'having something doing' and appearance.

Further, the visibility of these culturally creative separation strategies may be considered in terms of the relationship between the moral order and the figure of the beggar. By rhetorically distancing themselves from those at the roadside, the athletes are distancing themselves from a significant proportion of the disability community so as to assert their claims to the respect that is due full moral persons.[26] It is important to note that Ghanaian researcher Kwesi Kassah found through interviews with numerous beggars in Accra, that not all beggars interpreted their begging in the city streets as extremely stigmatizing or something to be pitied, rather, they felt it to be 'both personally liberating and a valid form of community participation'.[27] Thus, as Nepveux has noted, Kassah's work suggests 'social recognition' and 'independence' are indeed in the eye of the beholder;[28] and are not strictly economic in nature. While athletes had varying (re)actions towards those begging, and felt varying yet limited degrees of socio-economic stability, they did not want to be on the road begging, primarily because there is [little to] no dignity or respect in doing so. However, beggars did not want to be on the court playing as there is little to no benefit or material reward in doing so, as recounted to me by several of the athletes who have tried to encourage some of the beggars to join.

Spurred by their involvement in sport, the rhetorical distancing of the athletes from 'those at the roadside' may provide for greater inclusion and integration within the dominant order, however, this may be to the further exclusion of 'their kind'. Deal puts forth the notion that there is potential for those perceived as less accepted by society to be further isolated as a further level of social oppression from within one's community (if, that is, one agrees with the notion of disability as a defining feature of self-identification).[29] This resonates, as does the possibility that this may contribute to reinforcing and/or recreating negative perceptions of disability, or rather *some* 'disableds', and their continued use within society.[30]

In pointing out the exclusionary aspects of the athletes' varying degrees of increased inclusion, the intent is not to criticize them as individuals or as a collective, or to outshine in any way, the profoundly positive effects of their participation in sport and their efforts to treat each other respectfully and inclusively. Rather, the aim is to attract attention to the dominant narrative surrounding the shame of disability and poverty, as well as show that sport plays a role in this dominant narrative. Athletes tended at times, as did members of the wider disability community, and members of society in general, to reinforce this dominant disability narrative by their resisting what they perceived to be the dominant image of 'disableds', the beggar. Further, if the fostering of inclusion and integration is seen as a key positive outcome of development through sport initiatives for PWD, this article must also then acknowledge, and recommend future acknowledgement, that with inclusion, there is the very real potential for new forms of exclusion to surface on and off the court, despite inclusive intentions or expectations. The complex and socially constructed nature of the notion and the practice of development through sport are therefore illuminated.

Respect

But what did the athletes say? How *did* participating in sport affect their everyday lives? The following section explores the idea of respect, given that the respect athletes' felt they had acquired from some family and community members due to their involvement in sport was felt by the majority to be the most significant motivation for, and benefit of, their participation in sport. This idea of respect was expressed most evidently and consistently vis-à-vis the separation strategies of movement, 'having something doing' and appearance. Both the *fact* that they were seen moving as well as the *way* in which they were seen moving, served to demonstrate their difference. In light of the predominance of perceptions of incapacity, 'disableds' were frequently seen as incapable of 'having something doing,' rather they were expected to be 'always in the house' or 'at the roadside' [begging] having 'nothing doing'; not, for example, regularly working, schooling or training [playing basketball]. Thus, 'having something doing' is not seen purely in terms of economic activity. Finally, their appearance whilst moving and 'having something doing' seemed to help athletes gain respect.

Movement

A female athlete explained, 'You know these people [beggars] are always there, dull … they don't do anything, even they themselves see that you are more active than they are'.

Of additional importance is that a lack of movement may exacerbate or act to affirm perceptions of incapability, given that 'When you are sitting in one place going nowhere ... it makes people look down on you. But when people see you "going" and "coming" it really gives respect'. A male athlete added:

> OK ... the time that I will spend by the roadside will make them [others] know whether I'm a beggar or not, because most beggars spend most of their time at the roadside or they will stop by cars and will be taking money from them. But they [others] see me going where I am going – I will not spend most of my time at the roadside.

Although the fact that the athletes were moving was of utmost importance, almost all felt that the *way* they moved contributed more to rhetorically distance themselves from those begging and aligned them more with society's conceptions of normalcy. According to a male athlete:

> Yes, I would say that before I joined the sports, I wasn't active, I wasn't active in my movements, also [I didn't know] how to wheel the wheels fast to get to a particular object.... And [now] even the way I feel when somebody calls me and the way I will cruise to the person and then apply my brake!

A second male athlete commented that before he became involved in sports, he had felt dull and slow. However, he now performs his daily tasks as well as his training with vim and vigour or as others framed it, 'with purpose'. While in agreement, a female athlete acknowledged that the notion of visible and purposeful movements is not necessarily a sport-specific phenomenon as she has also felt respected when she was attending the apprenticeship component of her vocational training in tailoring, as she was seen to have had a purpose, that she needed to be somewhere in a timely fashion. It seemed then that the point was not to simply appear as *able* as possible but to defy perceptions of incapability by offering a positive counter-image of disability, one that involved strong, confident movements, more regular 'going' and 'coming', or put differently, 'having something doing'.

'Something doing'

The phrase 'having something doing' was repeated by the majority of the athletes, often in relation to 'being not always in the house,' the enactment or demonstration of which indeed served as an important separation strategy. Regularly attending weekly sport trainings better aligned the athletes with the regular 'goings and comings' of the majority of the rest of society, and as will be further detailed in the next section, led to their increased social recognition. Visibly having 'something doing', in the case of sport, defied perceptions of incapability and corresponding expectations of 'being always in the house', as well as allowed the athletes, in tandem with their movements as described above, and their appearance as explored below, to separate themselves from their dominant negative counter-image, that of the beggar who is perceived to be 'just there at the roadside with nothing doing'. Moreover, it is tied tightly to respect and by extension to status, as in Ghana 'having something doing' or exercising purpose and/or independence is seen as 'moving forward' with merit; again these ideas are not necessarily economic in nature. By contrast, 'having nothing doing' for anyone, disabled or temporarily non-disabled, was frowned upon. 'Having nothing doing' or 'being always in the house' perpetuates negative notions of disability.

Appearance

Not merely moving, or coming and going, but one's appearance whilst doing so was the third separation strategy utilized by athletes, and referred both to their actual dress as well as to an outward show of being busy with 'something doing'. Virtually all athletes deemed attention to appearance an important means by which to better differentiate themselves from beggars and to subsequently increase their chances of being treated with respect. According to a female athlete, 'going to the sports and wheeling the wheelchair and playing the basketball, helps you to look smart', in contrast to 'those "disableds" who are always begging outside, they're almost always dirty' as claimed by a second female athlete. Further testament to the significance of appearance, a male athlete admitted:

> If it [appearance] is neat, like say wearing nice shoes you may say 'Hi', but you do it very fast, and you keep going. But say if the person is dirty, you don't even want to associate yourself with the person, you don't want to look at him.

When questioned as to why he behaved this way, he exclaimed 'Because if you don't take care, people will say "that's how they all are!" This is how it is in Ghana!'

Indeed, many of the athletes felt that PWD encountered extra pressure to 'look smart'. Such extra pressure seemed compounded by their perceived incapability, and they felt that looking smart may serve to portray a positive, attractive and capable counter-image. Sarah Andrews, Ghanaian Research Assistant, and GSPD member, shared a story about how her brother followed her to a general GSPD monthly meeting to see 'what is going on', as her family had been 'worrying her' about the time it usually took her to dress. She returned home, marvelling to the family that everyone [at the meeting] was 'looking smart' and that *'Even the women in the wheelchairs were wearing high heels* [emphasis hers]!' Additionally, it seems that this extra pressure to look smart may also manifest itself materially due to the many difficulties PWD face in terms of obtaining regular and adequate income. Interestingly, it was observed that the women usually looked neater than the men, a phenomenon that many of the women had turned into a unique defence strategy. For example, quite often during a conflict or disagreement within the group – on or off the basketball court – the women use their neater appearance 'to look down on the men' or to insult them with taunts of 'you guys are always dirty, so how can we have a relationship with you guys?!'

Recognition

How did the athletes know they were being respected? While acknowledging the difficulties of measuring outcomes of sport, in asking how they knew that they were being respected more, athletes' responses pointed to their increased social recognition. Such recognition manifested itself through a variety of means, including: (1) for *not* being always in the house; (2) *for* being in the house; (3) increased popularity; and (4) media attention, both in terms of media coverage and peoples' reactions to such coverage.

Oh! Are you now coming from training?'

Many athletes felt that having their movements and activities, namely sport training, noticed signified respect.

As a female athlete related:

> I feel big, like proud. Every Saturday when I am not in the house and somebody comes up to the house and they are looking for me, and people are saying 'Oh she is gone to training!' And when I come back they will tell me 'Oh when you went to training this person came to look for you!' or [others may say] 'Are you now coming from training?'

'Hey! Why didn't you go to training?'

Although having their sport-related and routine movements recognized was important and in the minds of many of the athletes indicated they were being respected, having their absence of movements recognized was equally deemed a sign of respect. For example, a female athlete commented that 'I feel good that people know what I am doing and that I am training [such that] if some Saturday I didn't go to training, maybe I am sick or something and if they [others on the compound where I live] come out and see me they will say "Ah, you're here; you didn't go to training. Today you are not going, why?"'

'You become popular'

One male athlete felt that sport enabled him to meet and be greeted and/or acknowledged by people he had not previously encountered, because they had seen him going to training or playing sport, 'People know you – you become popular!' A second male athlete felt that being seen as a 'disabled' who plays on a sports team garners him respect 'Because *now people really see me* [emphasis his], everybody is saying "Hey Shera!" that's my guy name [nickname] "Shera how?!" [Shera what's up!?], so it really gives a respect.' This notion of 'now people really see me' points to the fact that his presence has not always been acknowledged and to his desire to be seen, of course as capable, but ultimately as a human being.

The media – 'And then you, you who nobody regards'

Many athletes attributed the media as having a positive role in the increased recognition they felt from both community and family members, in fact media attention seemed to be a key point of reference for almost all of the athletes, due in large part to the fact that:

> Maybe most of your family has never been featured in the media before and then *you, who nobody regards* [emphasis hers] are on TV and here they think that being on TV you are somebody big [important]. Not only that but you are doing something, doing the disability sports and showing that you are capable.

A male athlete spoke about his family and how it was not just his athletic ability but also his ability to express himself in interviews during media coverage about disability sports that had helped him become more included in family decision-making discussions. He smiled and recounted that some people will say: '"Hey last time I saw you on TV! And ah the way you were speaking!" and I will say "Yeah." *And the way they look down on you is different'*.

Marvel or mockery?

It is indeed significant that these athletes have described gaining respect as defined by their receiving increased recognition from family and/or community members. Their visible participation in sport, however, has brought out uneasy underlying questions as to whether spectators may, rather than respect them as athletes, marvel them as 'supercrips' or mock them as deviants.

Marvel

Several of the female athletes commented about how others have marvelled at their involvement in sport.

According to one female athlete:

Sports has changed how others see me ... one time I travelled to Kumasi [a city in southern central Ghana] and people saw me on television playing basketball. People marvelled – they were surprised as they were not expecting it at all [to see me on television, playing sports].

Gerschick found during his work with men with physical disabilities in the USA, that many males with disabilities who were involved with sport felt frustrated that they were often not taken seriously; they were often patted on the head or seen as brave or courageous, or that their athletic performances were less socially recognized or validated than they were trivialized and devalued.[31] Similarly, in my Ghanaian study, one male athlete expressed his frustration, 'Disability sports? No one even minds you [cares about you]; they may just think you are having fun!'

Since athletic performance embodies gender performance not being taken seriously as an athlete may, for example, symbolize not being taken seriously as a man or woman. For example, and in correspondence with Gershick's findings,[32] it is interesting that it was primarily GSPD's male athletes who were less comfortable with feeling that they were being either marvelled at or perceived as courageous for playing sports. For example, one male said 'This can get annoying' and that 'People can't believe it'. A second male athlete saw his involvement in sport as a challenge, not as courageous, or by extension anything to marvel about. Other female and male athletes spoke of the constant convincing required by members of their families and communities that they played basketball, for example, as one female athlete recited, 'Yes, from our wheelchairs and yes, on a court of the same dimensions as those able-bodied, and yes, using nets of the same height'.

Depicting disabled persons as heroic in light of their (cap)ability to perform acts normally deemed not possible for PWD or their (cap)ability to live a 'regular' life in spite of disability, is representative of the 'supercrip' model, and has been said to promote ableism. Although the above conversations did not directly address 'supercrip', they were reminiscent of its tenets. Interestingly, a key finding from Hardin and Hardin's US-based work, again with male, physically disabled athletes and disability sports media coverage, was the preference of the athletes to be framed by the media such that their athleticism may be seen as a legitimate activity and not as a human-interest story, or by extension, as a marvel or marvellous feat. Accordingly, numerous male, physically disabled athletes spoke to Hardin and Hardin about their wish to have their athletics foregrounded as opposed to their disability.[33] In correspondence and across genders, all the female and male athletes of this Ghanaian study saw themselves as athletes and preferred their dominant identity to be that of athlete, not of disabled.

In a unique and rather poignant twist to this notion of foregrounding the athlete and/or the activity instead of the disability, one athlete referred, as did most, to the failure of any of those invited (mainly dignitaries, as is custom) to attend a Disability Sports Workshop, organized by GSPD's Greater Accra Sports Wing for their Eastern Region colleagues. She suggested that perhaps focusing on their sporting identity rather than their disabled identity might have served to their advantage, not just to their dignity; it may have brought out the 'big men'. A male athlete agreed and in an accurate and humorous reference to the air-conditioned comforts of the 'big men' in their 'storey buildings,' felt that 'Maybe they would have come out instead of sitting in their office with their coats and other things!' Thus, though the athletes may be marvelled by some, they remain 'shunned' by those with access to the resources to help change their situation.

Or mockery?

This particular vignette pertains to one male athlete who plays primarily football and table tennis and had until very recently always, despite his upper limb impairments, played with non-disabled athletes on non-disabled teams, described the discomfort he felt whilst playing in a particular football match. The match was held between a lower-limb amputee team and a recently put together team of, as he described, 'those ["disableds"] who didn't need crutches or any of those things to move around'. He recounted that the spectators present were mocking the match and the movements of the players, that they had seen it [the match] as funny. According to him 'It made people laugh "because of the way the disability is and the way they played the ball", not because they were enjoying the game'. This realization maddened and saddened him so much that he felt like coming out of the game, 'Though I'd never seen such a game before, I tried my best to show what disableds can do'. When asked if anyone else there expressed similar feelings, he said they had not. It is difficult to speak to why no other athlete shared similar sentiments, perhaps they had never experienced this before, perhaps they had, but chose to withhold such information, or perhaps they chose to remain oblivious, or maybe some were so accustomed to being mistreated and misperceived that they had developed 'thick skin'. Still others may have subscribed by lack of choice to the notion that 'any recognition is good recognition' and they could not afford to be too selective of the limited attention they received. Warranting further inquiry is the nature of spectator expectations of different games and their possible place within Ghanaian nationalisms, especially given that the flagship sport is men's football. Finally, the gender implications of this scenario should be explored, especially because all the football players were male, as were the majority of the spectators.

Though feeling mocked was explicitly mentioned by just one male athlete, the idea of marvel and/or mockery as prompted by visible disability-focused development through sport initiatives should be subsequently seen as a crucial area for more in-depth exploration, not to prove one or the other, or to view marvel and mockery as dichotomous nor fixed. Instead, valuable insights into the various ways in which spectators, and by extension society, take up or react to their witnessing of disabled athletes playing sports may be provided. For, 'To a stranger, unfamiliar with the peculiar ways of paraplegics, the sight of ten wheeled chairs in hurtling pursuit of a ball must seem odd, if not a little frightening'.[34] This would allow for a deeper understanding of some of the hidden or unforeseen complexities brought about by 'development through sport' initiatives that target the greater inclusion of PWDs. Additionally, it becomes necessary to recognize that spectators and/or members of society may feel unnerved or threatened by such visible disruptions of their dominant perceptions, perceptions which include the disabled as incapable or as beggar.

Conclusion

The main purpose of this article was, through a case illustration, to explore the notion that sport serves as a tool for the human development of PWD. The main question was how participation in sport affects the everyday lives of female and male athletes of GSPD in Accra, Ghana. Through a discussion of the perspectives and experiences of this group, there emerged expected and unexpected benefits and applications regarding how the athletes see themselves socially. Sport was seen to provide a space for the (re)creation of self, serving as both a site, and a springboard, for resistance to the marginalization or disability oppression(s) faced by the athletes. It can be contended then that sport acts as a catalyst for the human development of these athletes primarily by helping them combat the prevailing perceptions of their incapability as held by others in their family and in their communities, as measured by their increased respect and recognition. However, the paper also illuminates the potential exclusionary aspects of inclusive initiatives as well as highlights the importance of interrogating underlying questions of marvel and mockery. Given that the shifting languages of disability and development continue to coincide with the languages of respect and recognition and to collide with the questions of marvel and mockery, what lingers then, is the larger question of whether the language, practice, and institutions of development are appropriate to disability, specifically, sport and disability.

The voices of both female and male athletes with disabilities were sought so as to form the foundation of a gender analysis. However, due to the time and resource constraints of this study, as well as the spatial constraints of this article, some of the more salient 'on-/off-court' negotiations carried out by women and men with disabilities are highlighted as they relate to, and resist, notions of hegemonic masculinity. Despite the fact that all athletes emphatically asserted that disabled women and men face many challenges, most felt that women with disabilities have somewhat different, and markedly more, worries than men with disabilities, as manifested 'off-court,' primarily in terms of relationships, marriage, education and employment. 'On-court' ability- and gender-based battles played out for women (and for some men) in terms of access, playing time and nature of play. Both women and men seemed to enact their agency and assert their presence by way of creative resistance strategies to counter on- and off-court power imbalances amidst navigations of 'male and able' hegemonic masculinity. The general consensus of the athletes coincided with observations that men with disabilities were not without 'worries' or negotiations. However, women with disabilities, although not without agency or resistance or action, were decidedly disadvantaged in relation to the aforementioned aspects of everyday life.

In light of its interdisciplinary nature, this article poses a plethora of points for more in-depth future research within sport, development, disability and gender studies, respectively, but even more so, calls for further engagements and conversations with their convergences. Additionally, individual factors such as, but not limited to, gender, nature of disability, age at onset of disability, class, ethnicity, age, cultural context, sexuality, religious affiliations and urban and urban versus rural dynamics, should be taken up in greater detail. To conclude, the aim of this article was to, together with the athletes, emphasize the importance of disability as a development issue in and of itself, given the overall and continued marginalization of Ghanaian women and men with disabilities both in sport and in society. With this emancipatory aim of working together towards improving the 'disability situation' for Ghanaian and global citizens, in society and in sport, it becomes imperative that the perspectives of those involved are not just voiced, but heard. This is in order to better understand and better take into account the contextual and cultural meanings and practices that comprise their everyday existence.

Acknowledgements

The author would like to acknowledge the support of the Social Science and Humanities Research Council of Canada (SSHRC) through their graduate student fellowship. She also wants to express her deep appreciation of the assistance provided by Ghanaian research assistant Sarah Andrews, without whose help this research would not have completed.

Notes

[1] 'Low- and middle-income countries' is used instead of 'developing country' or Global South, given that such classification by income does not necessarily reflect development status. See Sport for Development and Peace International Working Group Secretariat, 'Sport as a Means to Foster Inclusion', 128.

[2] United Nations, *Sport for Development and Peace*.

[3] Van Eekeren, 'Sport and Development', 19.

[4] See Kidd, 'New Social Movement'; Donnelly, 'Sport and Human Rights'; Giulianotti, 'Human Rights'.

[5] United Nations Development Programme, *Human Development Report*; Sen, *Development as Freedom*.

[6] Sport for Development and Peace International Working Group Secretariat, 'Sport as a Means to Foster Inclusion', 124.

[7] 'Supercrip' is a term which depicts disabled persons as heroic in light of their (cap)ability to perform acts normally deemed not possible for PWD or their (cap)ability to live a 'regular' life in spite of disability, as such it has been said to promote 'ableism'. Hardin and Hardin, 'The "Supercrip" in Sport Media'.

[8] Brittain, 'Perceptions of Disability', 443.

[9] Amnesty International, *Amnesty International Report 2009*. http://www.unhcr.org/refworld/docid/4a1fade9c.html.

[10] British Broadcasting Corporation, *Country Profile*.

[11] City Population, *Regions, Maps, Urban Localities*; British Broadcasting Corporation, *Country Profile*.

[12] Reuters Africa, 'Obama's Speech on Africa in Ghana's Capital'.

[13] Right To Play, *Ghana Newsletter* 2.

[14] *The Statesman* [Accra], July 30, 2007.

[15] Konadu-Agyemang, 'The Best of Times, 474.

[16] Ghana Society of the Physically Disabled, *About Us*.

[17] Ghana Society for the Physically Disabled Sports Wing, www.gspdsportswing.com. The Association of Sports for the Disabled national office is located on the third floor of Accra's recently renovated national football stadium. There are no ramps. There are no elevators.

[18] Nepveux, 'In the Same Soup'.

[19] Hargreaves, *Heroines of Sport*, 185.

[20] Emmett and Alant, 'Women and Disability', 445; Edmonds, *Disabled People and Development*; Department for International Development, 'Disability'; Sport for Development and Peace International Working Group Secretariat, 'Sport and Persons With Disabilities', 178.

[21] Groce, 'Women with Disabilities in the Developing World'; Traustadottir, 'Part II; Obstacles to Equality'. The majority of the women shared their encounters and experiences with such stereotypes during the female focus group discussion.

[22] McKay, Messner, and Sabo, *Masculinities*, 9.

[23] Sport for Development and Peace International Working Group Secretariat, 'Sport as a Means to Foster Inclusion', 131. Of course, gender is only one such category, class, race and ethnicity also deserve mention, however, their in-depth consideration proved beyond the scope of this article.

[24] Davis directs the bulk of his attention to the construction of normalcy, he claims that the 'problem' is not with persons with disabilities. At issue, rather, is the way that the construction of normalcy creates the 'problem' of the disabled person (Davis, *The Diability Reader*).

[25] Nixon, 'Constructing Diverse Sports Opportunities', 111.

[26] Jarvie, *Sport, Culture, and Society*, 291. Unfortunately, typical of the role disability ought to play, Jarvie's *Sport, Culture, and Society* is thoroughly bereft of any discussion of disability.

[27] Nepveux, 'In the Same Soup', 511.

[28] Kassah, *Begging as a Way of Life*.

[29] Nepveux, 'In the Same Soup', 55.

[30] Deal, 'Disabled People's Attitudes', 907.

[31] Jarvie, *Sport, Culture, and Society*, 287–288.

[32] Gerschick, 'Sisyphus in a Wheelchair'.

[33] Hardin and Hardin, 'The "Supercrip" in Sport Media'.

[34] *The Chord* 1950, 19 cited in Hargreaves, *Heroines of Sport*, 181.

References

Amnesty International. *Amnesty International Report 2009 – Ghana*. London: Amnesty International, 2009.

British Broadcasting Corporation. *Country Profile: Ghana*. http://news.bbc.co.uk/2/hi/africa/country_profiles/1023355.stm

Brittain, Ian. 'Perceptions of Disability and Their Impact on Involvement in Sport for People with Disabilities at all Levels'. *Journal of Sport and Social Issues* 28, no. 4 (2004): 429–52.

City Population. *Regions, Maps, Urban Localities*. Thomas Brinkhoff. http://www.citypopulation.de/Ghana.html

Davis, Lennard, J. *The Disability Reader*. New York: Routledge, 1997.

Deal, Mark. 'Disabled People's Attitudes Toward Other Impairment Groups: A Hierarchy of Impairments'. *Disability and Society* 18, no. 7 (2003): 897–910.

Department for International Development. *Disability, Poverty and Development*. London: Department for International Development, 2000. http://www.dfid.gov.uk/Documents/publications/disabilitypovertydevelopment.pdf

DonnellyPeter. 'Sport and Human Rights'. *Sport in Society* 11, no. 4 (2008): 381–94.

Edmonds, Lorna J. *Disabled People and Development*. Philippines: Asian Development Bank, 2005.

Emmett, Tony, and Erna Alant. 'Women and Disability: Exploring the Interface of Multiple Disadvantage'. *Development Southern Africa* 23, no. 4 (2006): 445–60.

Gerschick, Thomas J. 'Sisyphus in a Wheelchair: Men with Physical Disabilities Confront Gender Domination'. In *Everyday Inequalities: Critical Inquiries*, edited by Jodi O'Brien and Judith Howard, 189–211. Malden, MA: Blackwell, 1998.

Ghana Society of the Physically Disabled. *About Us*. Accra, Ghana: Ghana Society for the Physically Disabled, 2008. www.gspd.webs.com

Ghana Society for the Physically Disabled Sports Wing. *About Us*. Accra, Ghana: Ghana Society for the Physically Disabled, 2009.

Giulianotti, Richard. 'Human Rights, Globalization, and Sentimental Education: The Case of Sport'. *Sport in Society* 7, no. 3 (2004): 355–69.

Groce, Nora. 'Women with Disabilities in the Developing World: Arenas for Policy Revision and Programmatic Change'. *Journal of Disability Policy Studies* 8 (1997): 177–93.

Hardin, Myers, and Brent Hardin. 'The "Supercrip" in Sport Media: Wheelchair Athletes Discuss Hegemony's Disabled Hero'. *Sociology of Sport Online* 7, no. 1 (2004).

Hargreaves, Jennifer. *Heroines of Sport: The Politics of Difference and Identity*. London: Routledge, 2000.

Jarvie, Grant. *Sport, Culture, and Society: An Introduction*. London: Routledge, 2006.

Kassah, Kwesi A. *Begging as a Way of Life*. Baltimore, MD: Publish America, 2005.

Kidd, Bruce. 'A New Social Movement: Sport for Development and Peace'. *Sport in Society* 11, no. 4 (2008): 370–80.

Konadu-Agyemang, Kwadwo. 'The Best of Times and the Worst of Times: Structural Adjustment Programs and Uneven Development in Africa: The Case of Ghana'. *The Professional Geographer* 52, no. 3 (2000): 469–83.

McKay, Jim, Messner, Michael, and Sabo, Donald, eds. *Masculinities, Gender Relations and Sport*. Thousand Oaks, CA: Sage, 2000.

Nepveux, Denise. 'In the Same Soup'. PhD diss., University of Illinois at Chicago, 2008.

Nixon, Howard, II. 'Constructing Diverse Sports Opportunities for People With Disabilities'. *Journal of Sport and Social Issues* 3, no. 4 (2007): 417–31.

Reuters Africa. 'Obama's Speech on Africa in Ghana's Capital'. *Reuters Africa*, July 11, 2009. http://af.reuters.com/article/ghanaNews/idAFLB24117320090711?sp=true

Right to Play, *Ghana Newsletter* 2, no. 1 (2008).

Sen, Amartya. *Development as Freedom*. Oxford: Oxford University Press, 1999.

Sport for Development and Peace International Working Group Secretariat. *Literature Reviews on Sport for Development and Peace*. Toronto, ON: University of Toronto, Faculty of Physical Education and Health, 2007.

Traustadottir, Rannevig. 'Part II: Obstacles to Equality: The Double Discrimination of Women with Disabilities'. *Journal of Leisurability* 19 (1992): 2–15.

United Nations. *Sport for Development and Peace: Towards Achieving the Millennium Development Goals*. UN Inter-Agency Task Force on Sport for Development and Peace, 2003. http://www.un.org/themes/sport/reportE.pdf

United Nations Development Programme. *Human Development Report 1990*. New York: Oxford University Press, 1990.

United Nations Development Programme. *Ghana Human Development Report: Towards a More Inclusive Society*. Ghana: United Nations Development Programme, 2007.

United Nations Enable. *Convention on the Rights of Persons with Disabilities*. New York: United Nations Enable, 2006.

Van Eekeren, Frank. 'Sport and Development: Challenges in a New Arena'. In *Sport and Development*, edited by Y. Auweele, C. Malcom, and B. Meulders, 19. Leuven, Belgium: Lannoo Campus, 2006.

The use of sport by a Health Promoting School to address community conflict

Patricia Struthers

School of Public Health, University of the Western Cape, Bellville (Cape Town), South Africa

Sport has been utilized as a tool to address situations of conflict globally. This article describes one South African primary school that has identified itself as a Health Promoting School and its use of sport to strengthen the role of the school as a safe place in the community and thus facilitate the learning taking place in the school. The school is situated in a socio-economically deprived community, with a culture of gangsterism and drug abuse, in a densely populated area in Cape Town. Within the school there are very few students with physical disabilities, however, intellectual disability is common and emotional instability, closely associated with violence in the community, is a major disabling factor. The concept of who is considered 'other' in this community is explored. A netball tournament organized by the school enabled all students, boys and girls, regardless of ability or gang alliance, to participate, and brought different factions of the community together.

Sport has been utilized as a tool to address situations of conflict globally. This article describes one South African primary school that has identified itself as a Health Promoting School and its use of sport to strengthen the role of the school as a safe place in the community and thus facilitate the learning taking place in the school. The school is situated in a socio-economically deprived community, with a culture of gangsterism and drug abuse, in a densely populated area in Cape Town.

The Western Cape Province, one of nine provinces in the Republic of South Africa, had a population 5.3 million in 2007, 10.9% of the total population of South Africa (48.5 million).[1] It occupies 10.6% of the land surface area. In some respects, the Western Cape Province is different from the other provinces. Although black Africans form the majority of the population (73.8–97.2%) in most provinces,[2] the Western Cape is one of two provinces where, for historical reasons which did not allow for urban migration of black Africans, the majority of the population (50.2%) identify themselves as coloured[3] although this group only comprises 9% of the national population. Despite having 11 official languages in South Africa, the three languages most commonly spoken in the Western Cape are Afrikaans, a language derived from Dutch (55.3%), isiXhosa (23.7%) and English (19.3%). Amongst the coloured population 79.5% speak Afrikaans.

The educational colour level in the Western Cape is higher than the national average, with 5.7% of adults aged over 20 years having no education compared with 17.9% nationally. The Western Cape has the lowest unemployment figure of all the provinces (18% of persons aged 15–65, compared with 29% nationally). Although considered a lesser problem in the Western Cape than in other provinces, poverty has a major impact on education. Poorer communities have a shortage of housing, with amenities such as toilets and water taps shared among families. Child hunger, substance abuse including alcohol and other drug abuse, and HIV are major problems affecting the health of students. School drop-out is very high and youth unemployment as high as 50%. In 2004, the under-five mortality rate was 58.09 per 1000 in the Western Cape – a long way off the Millennium Development Goal target of reducing child mortality to 20 deaths per 1000 live births by 2015.

Definitions of disability

In any community, the World Health Organization (WHO) has estimated that approximately 10% of the population has a disability. The 2001 South African Census estimated that 5% of the population has a disability with the Western Cape having a disability prevalence of 4.1%.[4] The percentage of disabled people with a sight disability was the highest (32%) followed by physical disability (30%), hearing disability (20%), emotional disability (16%), intellectual disability (12%) and communication disability (7%).[5] Gathering this information in developing countries is difficult, not least because there first needs to be recognition that there is impairment, followed by a professional diagnosis. This understanding of disability stems from a medical or individual model where disability is understood as being the consequence of the impairment. The World Health Organization definition does not necessarily correlate with local understandings as to what constitutes disability at either the personal or medical level. Disability activists internationally, and in South Africa, criticize this model and argue that disability needs to be viewed within a social model that reflects the social and political aspects of disability.[6] Within this model there is an interaction between personal factors, including the impairment, and the context in which the person lives, including the external environment and the attitudinal or social factors. This interaction will lead to either disability or functioning, depending on whether the other factors act as barriers or facilitators. Thus changing the environment, and providing appropriate support, can act as the facilitation needed to change the impact of the personal health condition and enable functioning.[7]

The school environment

With the international trend towards inclusive education,[8] students with disabilities are encouraged by governments to attend mainstream schools or ordinary schools.[9] In South Africa, education policy changes have been based on a human rights perspective, in line with the South African Constitution. The rights of persons with disabilities have been affirmed by South Africa signing and ratifying the 2006 UN Convention on the Rights of Persons with Disabilities.[10] The key policy document on the establishment of an inclusive education system, *Education White Paper 6* (EWP6),[11] links this development to the establishment of a caring and humane society. Historically, a separate inequitable system of schooling was developed for children with disabilities, with schools being disability specific and racially segregated. Most special schools for children with disabilities only provided education for white children with only a small proportion of coloured and African children having the opportunity to attend a special school. Coloured and African children with less severe or less obvious disabilities attended their local school with no additional support to the student or the school. This led to a gap between the education support provided to students with diagnosed disabilities who attended special schools and those with undiagnosed disabilities attending ordinary schools, with the result being large numbers of students having difficulties with learning not getting appropriate support.

Furthermore, in 1997 it was estimated that 70% of children with disabilities of school-going age were out of school[12] and in 2001 the South African EWP6[13] estimated that between 260,000 and 280,000 children with disabilities had no proper care or educational provision.

School and community violence

A serious challenge to schools in South Africa and internationally is conflict and violence within the school and within the community. In a study in the Western Cape Province, South Africa, 100% of schools reported weapons on school premises, 90% reported vandalism, 90% reported drug abuse, 60% reported incidents of assault and 25% reported incidents of rape.[14]

The violence in South African society is deep rooted, affecting the political, social and community life of all.[15] With the extreme poverty and economic inequity in the country, the political differences that were encouraged under apartheid led to conflict within communities and, in combination with unemployment, developed into criminal activity.[16] Additionally, violent behaviour in the home is common. The reported incidence rate of sexual assault on children aged 0–13 years is 1.7 per 1000 children.[17] This daily experience of aggression has resulted in a generation of young people who find violence acceptable and human life cheap.[18] Intentional injuries, including stabbing and shooting, are one of the highest causes of mortality,[19] with young males at particular risk.

One form of community conflict, in many communities internationally, has been the development of gangs whose activities are frequently linked to violence and drug trafficking. Rocha-Silva and Ryan argue that there is a complex relationship between drugs and violence.[20] In their view, this link can be best understood by using the tripartite conceptual framework of Goldstein that describes the systemic connection between drugs and violence.[21] This is typical of the violence that results from within the underground economy of the drug-distribution system in areas in Cape Town, the largest city in the Western Cape, and some neighbouring small towns.[22] Without any legal means of settling disputes and disagreements related to drug distribution this is done through intimidation, extortion, bribing and violence. Shoot-outs are used with killing continuing until an equal number of members of different gangs or their family members have been killed. Taylor and Chermack also emphasize the importance of the environment in violence.[23]

While the violence has an effect on the social capital of community, the effect of violence on the individual is also profound. Physical disability, resulting from gunshot wounds or stabbing is more common among adults, in particular young men, than among children. However, the emotional trauma that the children experience growing up in a violent home and community has a lasting impact on their emotional stability. Additionally, the heavy drug and alcohol use associated with the violence has led to a high proportion of children in the community having learning or intellectual disabilities.

Social and economic inequities in many communities are the root cause of this conflict. The gang violence in the community inevitably spills over into the local schools and the presence of members of gangs in schools affects the learning process of gang members and other students as well as the day-by-day life of the school.

Health Promoting School

Health for all

A framework that is identified as appropriate for a successful inclusion of students with disabilities or different learning needs is the Health Promoting School.[24] This framework, developed by the WHO and the outcome of the First International Health Promotion Conference in Ottawa, Canada, in 1986, is the Ottawa Charter.[25] The framework is based on five principles: to develop healthy school policies; to develop a healthy school environment including both the physical environment and the psychosocial environment; to develop a healthy network between the school and the community to help empower the community; to develop healthy personal skills of all in the school community, including students, teachers, parents and other community members; and to develop support services that give appropriate support to the school.

The importance of the school as a setting for the promotion of health was also identified by the WHO in the Jakarta Declaration in 1997.[26] Health Promoting Schools have been developed internationally to promote the health of all in the school community, including students, teachers, parents and others in the community. There is evidence from Denman *et al.* that this development has an impact on the health of students, teachers and parents.[27]

In South Africa there are Health Promoting Schools in all nine provinces,[28] often in poorer communities, where the particular schools are striving for change and improvement. These schools have been identified as a tool for whole school development, in the support for activities that encompass both the formal and informal curriculum.[29] While the formal curriculum includes the syllabus, the informal curriculum relates to the aims and purpose of the entire school programme and how these are carried out.[30]

From biomedical to social definitions of health

Within the Health Promoting School context, the concept of health is understood broadly and holistically. The concept goes beyond the traditional biomedical view of health to incorporate the WHO's definition of health as being: 'A state of complete physical, mental and social well-being, not merely the absence of disease or infirmity'.[31] The South Africa Department of Health further states that all aspects of life impact on one's health and well-being, including physical, mental, social, environmental, economic and spiritual aspects.[32] Consequently, the Health Promoting School takes all these aspects into consideration in the development of the school and the support that it gives to a diverse population of students.

> The Health Promoting School aims at achieving healthy lifestyles for the total school population by developing supportive environments conducive to the promotion of health. It offers opportunities for, and requires commitments to, the provision of a safe and health-enhancing social and physical environment.[33]

It is within this context that there are opportunities for students with different needs, including students with disabilities, to feel at home and supported. Students who come from unhealthy home situations, with families affiliated to gangs, and those who do belong to gangs, are able to learn and play sport together. Team sport can be seen as an alternative to the gang activities as it can provide a sense of belonging and sense of achievement. However, gangs do play sport, mostly soccer, against each other. Additionally, gangs have grown out of the sports clubs – either when members engage in delinquent activities and turn to violence or, as an indirect result of the closure of soccer clubs in the Western Cape.

Sport and cohesion in school and in the community

Harms describes how, first, sport can be a tool for social integration to overcome cultural barriers and 'otherness';[34] second, sport programmes can be occasions of collective experience and involve direct physical contact, which have an intense effect on both parties with the potential to build cohesion; third, sport can be a medium that transcends class divisions; and fourth, sport can be used as a cultural instrument with the norms and rules of the sport that transcend the divisions between groups. This theoretical framework is valuable in planning and reflecting on any sports intervention.

Sport has been identified as a tool for addressing conflict and has been utilized in peace-building interventions internationally.[35] It has been used to convey a message of non-violence, mobilize and develop communities. Anecdotally, sport is considered to make a significant difference in children's lives by boosting self-confidence, increasing understanding of difference, leading to tolerance and mutual acceptance. It has been described as a tool for the development of the social capital of the community.[36]

Unfortunately, it is frequently found that students with disabilities attending ordinary schools in South Africa, unlike the USA or UK, are excluded from the sporting activities.[37] Adapted physical education is not offered in ordinary schools so students with disabilities can only take part in the regular sports offered by the school for students without disabilities.[38] Only a very few better resourced schools offer students with disabilities opportunities to participate in sport. Consequently, students with disabilities will sit on the sidelines during this time. By cintrast, most special schools for students with disabilities do offer adapted sports and sporting events are organized between special schools.

This article reports on an ordinary primary school in the Western Cape Province that has identified itself as a Health Promoting School. The research question is: In a community with a high level of social conflict, as a major disabling factor, how effective is school sport as an implementation of the Health Promoting Schools framework?

The research setting

Primary school A is situated in a township on the Cape Flats, a socio-economically deprived community in a densely populated area of the city of Cape Town. In the 1960s, under the apartheid era, the community was formed when people classified as 'coloured' by the government were forcibly removed from residential areas that had been declared for 'whites' only. During this time, by law, people were classified by the government into different racial groups which determined the area where people were allowed to live. There were separate (and unequal) facilities such as hospitals, post offices, beaches and schools for people of different racial groups. The implementation of this policy involved the social restructuring of areas people lived in to ensure that people of different racial groups lived in their own area. During this restructuring, a class separation was implemented by the state with 'coloured' people identified as 'poorer' placed in communities, including this township, where smaller houses or apartments were built and rented to the residents by the city council. Piped water, inside flush toilets and electricity were provided. Forty years later in this high-density area there are rows of apartments, two or three stories high separated by washing lines, groups of unemployed youth on street corners, and very few trees, parks or recreational facilities in the area. Where there is small piece of land attached to the home/apartment a small wood and iron structure is frequently built and rented to a family needing accommodation (the backyard dwellings). There are a few small shops for bread, milk and cigarettes, but no street markets and people do the bulk of their shopping outside the area. Many households are made up of extended families, with several generations living together in two or three small rooms. The average household size in the coloured community is 4.3 persons compared with 3.8 persons nationally. Single-parent families are common. Socializing happens at home with a lot of time spent watching TV and parents hesitant to allow young children outside to play. Five kilometres away from this slice of the third world are the leafy suburbs of Cape Town where wealthier people have large homes, private swimming pools and easy access to a first world lifestyle. The large numbers of unemployed people living in this community have produced a culture of gangsterism, with extensive involvement in drugs and violence.

Since the 1990s there has been a proliferation of gang-related violence in the Western Cape.[39] Kinnes argues that many young people, who have been rejected by their families or the community, have joined gangs to gain a sense of identity and of belonging. Others join gangs to gain materially. It is estimated that approximately 60% of the population of this township, including women and children, are aligned to one gang or another. Jensen describes the township as the 'zone' from which gangsters living in that area go to steal and commit acts of violence in other equally disadvantaged surrounding areas 'zones of poverty and social disintegration'.[40] It is considered by the council officials as a particularly violent space within a broader geographical area and is described as 'a special case where the prevalence of gangs, poverty, crime and overcrowding went hand in hand with a civil society in sharp opposition to state agencies'.[41]

Methodology

Primary school A has been actively developing as a Health Promoting School for a number of years. While this development was initiated by the school nurse who visits the school from the Department of Health, it is fully supported by the principal and school personnel who work closely with the school nurse to develop healthy school policy, a healthy school environment, make links with the community, develop the skills of the teachers, students and parents, and to make links with support services.

In-depth interviews were conducted at the school. The school was visited several times over a period of 18 months. With the use of an interview guide, open-ended questions were asked. Ethical considerations included getting consent from participants and the understanding that there would be anonymity for participants and the school.

Results and discussion

School: a neutral zone

Primary school A, a small school with 450 students, is one of 11 primary schools in this township. Despite being situated in a very poor community, the leadership of the school has been determined to turn a very ordinary, struggling primary school into a centre of excellence and a creative centre of learning for all in the community.[42] Despite this, only 27% of students in the school have reached the expected literacy level, according to national literacy standards. In a partnership between the principal, teachers and the school nurse, this school has actively worked to implement the principles of the Ottawa Charter towards developing the school into a Health Promoting School, including prioritizing the development of the relationship between the school and the community.[43] The school has been striving for the identity of being a 'neutral zone' within this strife-torn community, with the top priority being to provide world-class education that parents in the community would be proud to send their children to. Parents are encouraged to visit the school and have learnt to respect the fact that parents from rival gangs may be at the school.

Despite attempts for a 'neutral zone', many activities in the school must be duplicated to allow students and families of different gangs to attend. As an example, the development of a counselling centre at the school included training for some mothers as lay counsellors. Training for mothers aligned to different gangs was necessary as women would not go for counselling with a woman linked to another gang.

The 'Other' populations: who is 'different', and what is 'deviant' behaviour?

In schools across the world there are groups of students that can be described who are considered different from the 'ordinary' students. In primary school A two groups considered 'others' by the teachers are the students with disabilities and the students who are gang members. What is unusual is that the 'other' may even be the majority in a particular school class, challenging the teachers who have on average 40–45 students in a class. Additionally, many students who experience difficulties with learning come from homes where adults have a low level of literacy so are not viewed as 'other' within the family. Likewise, the students who are members of gangs often have older siblings or even parents who are gang members. Consequently, within this township, these students do not have the identity of being 'other'.

Students with an intellectual disability

In the past, there have been a small number of students at the school with moderate intellectual disability.[44] However, teachers at primary school A are not keen to have students with moderate intellectual disabilities in their classes as they feel they do not have the skills to assist these students to learn. They complain that there is no extra support provided by the Department of Education for the students or teachers when students experience barriers to learning. Some students have been referred from this school to special schools, but the principal reports how the students struggle in the different cultural environment of the special school, where there is no understanding of the students' daily experience of poverty, and the low levels of literacy in their homes. Additionally, students feel stigmatized by having a 'special bus' collect them from home instead of being able to walk to the local school, and most students soon stop attending any school.

A common cause of intellectual disability in South Africa is foetal alcohol syndrome. This township has been identified as a community with a very high prevalence of alcohol use and abuse, and, as a consequence, there is a high prevalence of students with foetal alcohol syndrome or mild intellectual disabilities; many of whom would not have had any formal diagnosis of this problem. Advocacy programmes in the community, such as the 'Sensible Drinking Campaign' have been discontinued due to a lack of funding. A second common cause of intellectual disability is the use of methamphetamine (locally known as Tik), the most frequently used illegal drug in the community, with reports of children as young as seven years using Tik.

Students with emotional instability

There are a very large number of students at primary school A with emotional difficulties. According to the school principal, recent psychological tests on all students throughout the primary school found 90% of students to be emotionally unstable; 70% of students having a feeling of complete helplessness; 10% being extremely aggressive; and 5% with attention deficit disorder and not on any medication or treatment. The latter two groups (15% of students) are described as 'taking over the school' (according to the principal) and disrupting learning. This apparent 'norm' of emotional instability has established an alternate reality for these children who have no experience of life in a different community.[45]

The principal explains that this emotional instability is partly the result of the conflict in the community, with normal developmental activities unable to take place for months at a time while there is active violence. Parents do not allow their children outside and they may be absent from school for long periods as the same gangs that are present in the community have a presence in the school. Even when the students are allowed out of the home, there are unwritten rules about where people may go in the community, for example, 'the library is in the "Clever Kids" area so the "Hard Livings" people [two opposing gangs] don't cross the boundaries to go to the library'. There is a similar difficulty with the use of 'sports fields' in the area unless they are in your own territory. There is only one real sports field in the township, the Greens. This was developed subsequent to the netball tournament described below, and in part as an outcome of this tournament. Other than this, there are a few small playgrounds for young children in the community with asphalt areas that people use to play sport on or they use the roads in the community as their 'sports fields'. This lack of opportunity in the environment to interact normally with others affects children's emotional and cognitive development.

Many students in the school come from single-parent families where the mothers have very poor parenting skills. Teenage pregnancies are common in this community with students as early as Grades 7 and 8 (14–15 years old) becoming pregnant. Consequently, when their children start school in Grade R and Grade 1 (at 6–7 years) the mothers are still trying to complete secondary school. This has an impact on the learning of both the mother and the child. The mother is unable to take appropriate responsibility for her child, in turn affecting the broader community.

Students who are members of gangs

Primary chool A stands geographically between the territories of two rival powerful gangs with a number of other gangs in the area. Social interaction in the community occurs within, and not between, rival gangs. While the men and boys in families tend to become more directly involved in violent activities, such as shooting, the women and girls provide support by carrying weapons or drugs as they are considered less likely to be searched by the police. Nevertheless, many of the children from different gangs attend primary school A. According to their principal:

> There is an alley directly opposite the school. One side of the alley is the territory of the one gang and the other side of the alley is the territory of the other gang. When the gang war was active male gang members would line up behind the fences along each side of the alley. Then the women and girls from each gang would come with the guns, and walk down the alley to hand out the guns. Then the shooting would start and would continue until an equal number of gang members on both sides had been killed. Afterwards the women and girls would walk down the alley and collect the guns, so that when the police arrived the men would not have the guns and the women and girls could disappear with the guns hidden in their clothes.

The school considers itself fortunate as it has a solid fence and gates that lock to stop the gangsters running through the school. However, this does not ensure complete protection. 'One day two students at the school got into a fight. One girl left the school, went home and came back to school with her father's gun to settle the fight'. On this occasion, the principal successfully intervened to control the situation. The principal, teachers and the school nurse are not members of this particular community making it easier for them to stay out of gang-related alliances.

Need for healing

The high proportion of students who experience emotional instability is reflected in the wider community, which can thus be described as an emotionally unstable society, where much of the social structure has disintegrated. It is a community with intense power struggles, both between rival gangs and between politicians (unrelated to the gangs) in the area, leading to many factions in the community.

In the school, emphasis is placed on understanding the needs of the students and the community with all programmes being directed to addressing the need for healing. The notion of South Africa as a wounded society has been offered by Pinnock and Van Wyk and Theron in describing the disintegration of society following the Group Areas Act when family and community networks were destroyed.[46] The greatest need of the individual students and the community, emphasized by the principal, is the need for healing the emotional instability and hurt: healing of individual students; healing of the students' families; and healing of the community.

Sport and healing

Sport has been identified by the school as one tool for addressing this need for healing. The township has a number of sports clubs with a variety of sports offered including soccer, cricket, swimming, karate, table tennis and weight lifting. A popular sport offered by clubs that is played by children, including boys and girls, and adults is netball. This sport, similar, in some respects, to basketball, is often played in schools in South Africa by girls and increasingly some boys. Netball teams are developed for the range of age groups – under 13, under 15, a B team and an A team, often for adults. With the community divided into different 'areas' associated with specific gangs, sports clubs are associated with one specific area. Although these clubs do not strictly belonging to a specific gang, people will not walk into another gang's territory. For example, in the Hard Livings' (gang) area, the people who participate in that particular club will all live in the area.

The outcome of this is that each club has its own netball teams with little interaction between the different clubs. The teams usually practise on the asphalt in the courtyards of their apartments and when they want to play a game they ask the schools if they can borrow the netball posts for the weekend. For the game, they will find a larger piece of asphalt to play on or use the road. Occasionally, they may get the opportunity to use the one proper sports field in the area 'The Green' but it is largely used for soccer, the most popular of all sports in the area.

In 2006, on June 16, National Youth Day, and the following day a two-day netball tournament for the whole community was organized at primary school A bringing girls and boys from 20 community netball teams together from all the clubs in the community. The tournament had taken months of organizing with regular meetings between a school committee, from primary school A, and the chairladies of the sports clubs. This organizing group decided on how the day would be structured and the rules that the teams would have to follow. The clubs indicated that it was easier to make these decisions with the school committee seen as a neutral body to negotiate with, that was not affiliated to any particular team and that respected the clubs knowledge of the rules.

The supporters of the clubs, the families of the players, including the parents, brothers, sisters and other relatives, came as spectators to watch the tournament and enjoy a fun-filled family day. Many of the spectators had disabilities as a number of young adults in the community have physical disabilities, such as paraplegia, resulting from the violence in the community. All were there to support their teams. They came from different factions in the community, 'to support the youth within an atmosphere of peace and calm', while the school saw its role as being 'to force integration in a very diplomatic way' (according to their principal). Small stalls were set up at the school and food and drinks were sold by teachers and families. Live entertainment was organized between the netball matches. There was a special speaker as it was National Youth Day and an exhibition for all to learn more about, or remember the political background to the day. At the end of the two days trophies, donated by sponsoring companies, were given out to the winning teams.

The question must inevitably arise about violence at the tournament. Holding the tournament and ensuring there would be no violence was partly dependent on what was happening in the community. The school nurse explained: 'The community is like a volcano that sleeps and then erupts'. The tournament needed to be held during the time the volcano was asleep and there are periods when things are quieter in the community and this was one of those times. The school went ahead with organizing the tournament and the people from the community who attended respected the school's position of being a neutral zone and 'so there was no fighting'.

Students with mild intellectual or learning disability were included in the teams as many of them excelled in playing sport. In addition, it was an opportunity for not only the 90% of students from primary school A with emotional difficulties to participate, but also for many other emotionally scarred students and adults in other teams in the community to experience the tournament and the days when integration was possible in the community.

The event was repeated the following year. On this occasion, there were spectators from outside the community including the Western Province Netball Association who subsequently worked with the teams to develop a Netball Union. For two years the event was very successful. The principal then describes how the local politicians became involved, insisting that the event be held away from the school, in the community, in commemoration of June 16, 1976 when youth were shot by the police in Soweto, Johannesburg. Public holidays in South Africa are used by politicians as an opportunity to hold political rallies which the local community is expected to attend. This kind of rally cannot be held at a school. By insisting on the move away from the relative safety of the school, the 'neutral zone', the members of the community were no longer willing to attend the sports event. By 2008, this netball tournament had stopped.

Conclusion

The years of building primary school A as a Health Promoting School, as a safe place for all students and their families, has had an important impact on the relationship between the school and the community. Additionally, there has been improved trust of the school by the community through using sport as a tool to bring the community together at a neutral venue. Members of opposing gangs could jointly participate in this community sporting event. This sports development suggests that the use of the Health Promoting Schools framework, as a tool to improve the relationship between the school and the community, can have a positive impact on the social and emotional health of the whole school community including students, teachers and the families.

The outcome demonstrates that sports can be used as a specific tool to strengthen the community. The development of a Netball Union is a positive development for the community which will assist in the sustainability of netball in the community. Unfortunately, the annual netball tournament has stopped. It appears an element of conflict between the school and political organizations led to reduced support from the school for an event outside the school. In hindsight, the prominent role of the principal and the time and work put into the making the event a success needs to be acknowledged and continued to ensure future joint community netball events either at the school or in the community. Perhaps the most strategic way forward would be for the school to work with other schools in the community, rather than directly with political organizations, and reinstitute the netball tournament on a day that does not have strong political associations.

However, the principal is sceptical of whether it would be possible to get the commitment of other schools in the area to the work that is needed for a successful tournament to take place.

There is evidence that the sports intervention has had an impact on the development of social capital in the community with the transformation in the use of the local disused park from an illicit meeting place to a fenced sports field, this is known as the Greens and is well maintained, with markings on the ground for soccer and soccer goal posts. It is used by all the community. This suggests that the development of the netball tournament has strengthened the ties in the community by enabling sports teams associated with the different gangs to meet on neutral community territory where there is seldom violence.

The study does not provide information on the direct impact of sports on the gangs in the area. However, there was an important outcome for the school in strengthening its goal from being a 'neutral zone' to a zone where all can meet; a zone where all can learn; a zone where the steps towards healing a community are being undertaken. Although prior to the tournament students from rival gangs were already integrated in the classroom, the principal indicates that sport has helped to ease the tensions. It has forced further integration and normalization of the broken community. Through a change to the environment the school has had an impact on the students who have disabilities, including those with intellectual disabilities or learning difficulties, and those who have experienced emotional trauma, facilitating their full participation in this community event. Through the lens of the social model of disability, the effect of facilitating changes in the physical and the psychosocial environment surrounding the netball tournament could reduce the experience of disability. What is also of significance is the involvement of the families of the students, extending the impact beyond the school to the broader community.

On its own, sport cannot solve the enormous social problems in Cape Town or more widely in developed and developing countries, where there is extreme poverty, endemic violence, unemployment and rampant HIV/AIDS. With multiple social factors involved it is not easy to find hard evidence of the impact of a sports intervention on a community. However, the evidence does suggest that using sport as a tool for social change may offer some impetus for change. The sustainability of this change will depend, in part, on whether the intervention is viewed as a sports 'plus' or 'plus' sports intervention.[47] In the first instance, sports 'plus', the sports intervention is considered more important than addressing the wider social issue of violence. In the second instance, 'plus' sports, sport is only used as a tool to achieve the objective of addressing violence. Changes in conflict are generally considered more important than the sustainability of the sports; however, perhaps it is possible for both sports development and changes to happen in a community simultaneously.

It is recommended that more extensive evaluation is done on the impact of Health Promoting Schools on reducing violence in the community. Evidence is needed to back the experience of the principal on the value of addressing the needs of the students and the school holistically through the use of the Health Promoting School framework: 'If I don't do that (develop a Health Promoting School) I cannot take anybody forward.'

Acknowledgements

I would like to acknowledge the principal of primary school A whose commitment to the community is an inspiration and Dr Brian van Wyk, UWC, for gang-related information.

Notes

1. Groenewald, 'Western Cape', 11.
2. Statistics South Africa, *Census in Brief.*
3. The last census in South Africa was in 2001. People are still classified by racial group in South Africa in order to monitor the progress in moving away from the apartheid-based discrimination of the past. Statistics South Africa uses the following options for self-classification: Black African, Coloured, Indian or Asian, White and Other. 'Coloured' includes a varied group of persons, for example, a person of mixed race or with ancestry from countries such as Malaysia might consider themselves as Coloured. (http://www.statssa.gov.za/keyindicators/keyindicators.asp)
4. Statistics South Africa, *Census 2001.*
5. Ibid.
6. Howell, Chalklen, and Alberts, 'Disability Rights Movement'. The Disability Rights Movement in South Africa has a history of opposing oppression and has been active in the promotion of inclusive policy.
7. World Health Organization (WHO), *International Classification of Functioning.*
8. United Nations Educational, Scientific, and Cultural Organization (UNESCO), *The Salamanca Statement.* This document supporting inclusion of children with disabilities in all schools was the outcome of a conference with representatives of 92 governments and 25 international organizations, hosted by UNESCO, in Salamanca, Spain in 1994.
9. Mainstream schools are referred to as 'ordinary schools' by the South African Department of Education. These are public schools that any child or adolescent from the community can attend.
10. South Africa signed the UN Convention on the Rights of Persons with Disabilities on March 30, 2007 and it was ratified on November 30, 2007.
11. Department of Education, South Africa, *Education White Paper 6.* This paper outlines an inclusive education system for South Africa; Department of Education. 'Report of national commission' is an important document for background to inclusive education in South Africa.
12. Office of the Deputy President of South Africa, *White Paper Disability Strategy.*
13. Department of Education, South Africa, *Education White Paper 6.*
14. Frank, *Missed Opportunities.*
15. Schärf, 'Resurgence of Urban Street Gangs', cited in van Wyk and Theron, 'Fighting Gangsterism in South Africa', 54.
16. Pinnock, 'Rituals, Rites and Punishment', cited in van Wyk and Theron 'Fighting Gangsterism in South Africa', 54.
17. Dawes and Ward, 'Levels, Trends and Determinants of Child Maltreatment', 111.
18. Lombard and van der Merwe, 'Preventive Programmes for Schools', 371.
19. Bradshaw *et al.*, *Initial Burden of Disease.* Mortality causes in South Africa: HIV/AIDS (29%), cardiovascular disease (16.6%), infectious and parasitic diseases (10.3%), malignant neoplasms (7.9%), intentional injuries (7.0%), unintentional injuries (5.4%).
20. Rocha-Silva and Ryan, 'Drugs and Violence'.
21. Ibid.
22. Van Wyk and Theron, 'Fighting Gangsterism in South Africa'.
23. Ibid.
24. Department of Education, South Africa, *Report OF THE National Commission on Special Needs.*
25. WHO, *Ottawa Charter.*
26. WHO, *Jakarta Declaration.*
27. Denman *et al.*, *Health Promoting School.*
28. Department of Health, South Africa, *School Health Policy.*
29. Department of Health, South Africa, 'Draft Guidelines for the Development of Health Promoting Schools'.
30. Donald, Lazarus and Lolwana, Educational Psychology in Social Context. 2.1.
31. WHO, *Constitution.*
32. Department of Health, South Africa, 'Draft Guidelines for the Development of Health Promoting Schools'. These guidelines have remained in this draft format.
33. WHO, 'The overall progress of the European Network of Health Promoting Schools', cited in Tones and Tilford, *Health Promotion: Effectiveness, Efficiency and Equity*, 223.
34. Harms, cited in Keim, 'Sport as Opportunity for Community Development'.
35. Keim, 'Sport as Opportunity for Community Development'.

[36] The development of social capital through sport is discussed by a number of authors: Bailey, 'Evaluating the Relationship'; Misener and Mason, 'Creating Community Networks'; Lindström, Hansen, and Östergren, 'Socioeconomic Differences'; Stone, *Research Paper 24*.

[37] Reiman, 'Sports for Learners'; Block, *Teacher's Guide to Including Students*.

[38] Reiman, 'Sports for Learners'.

[39] Kinnes, 'Struggle for the Cape Flats'.

[40] Jensen, *Gangs, Politics and Dignity in Cape Town*.

[41] Ibid., 116.

[42] The school has attempted to address widespread illiteracy in the community. First, within the school, a small library has been started and computer laboratories have been provided by the Department of Education and Microsoft. Second, for adolescents who have left secondary school without qualifications, a night school has been organized with more than 100 registered students, to enable them to complete their matriculation examinations. Third, for adults who are illiterate, the night school provides adult literacy classes. The school hosts a food kitchen which cooks meals at a very low cost for students or for community members to buy. This facility, housed in a small container, remains open throughout the year for the community.

[43] Activities have included addressing substance abuse, as there is widespread use of 'Tik' (methamphetamine), 'dagga' (marijuana) and heroin from as young as 8 or 9 years. This has included the use of role plays, students demonstrating against the use of drugs, and holding posters in a human chain on the side of the busy road. The school has a policy related to drug use. A school drug-action committee, comprising staff and parents, supports students using drugs to go for counselling.

[44] Despite the South African policy of inclusive education, there are few, if any, students attending School A with moderate or severe physical disabilities, visual disabilities, hearing disabilities or severe intellectual disabilities as these students are expected to attend the special schools in neighbouring areas. This may change in the future as the policy of an inclusive education system is implemented, but implementation is still in its infancy with minimal additional support available for ordinary schools.

[45] Lindegaard. 'Navigating Terrains of Violence'. Lindegaard discusses the challenges experienced by young people who attempt to break away from these violent communities.

[46] Van Wyk and Theron 'Fighting Gangsterism in South Africa', 54.

[47] Keim, 'Sport for Community Development'.

References

Bailey, Robert. 'Evaluating the Relationship Between Physical Education, Sport and Social Inclusion'. *Educational Review* 57, no. 1 (2005): 71–90.

Block, Martin E. *A Teacher's Guide to Including Students with Disabilities in General Physical Education*. 3rd edn. Baltimore: Brookes, 2007.

Bradshaw, Debbie, Pam Groenewald, Ria Laubscher, Nadine Nannan, Beatrice Nojilana, Desiree Pieterse, and Michelle Schneider. *Initial Burden of Disease Estimates for South Africa, 2000*. Cape Town: Medical Research Council, 2003.

Andy, Dawes, and Catherine Ward. 'Levels, Trends and Determinants of Child Maltreatment in the Western Cape Province'. In *The State of the Population in the Western Cape Province*, edited by Ravayi Marindo, Cornie Groenewald, and Sam Gaisie, 97–125. Cape Town: HSRC, 2008.

Denman, Susan, Alysoun Moon, Carl Parsons, and David Stears. *The Health Promoting School: Policy, Research and Practice*. London: Routledge, 2002.

Department of Education, South Africa. *Report of the National Commission on Special Needs in Education and Training and National Committee on Education Support Services. Quality Education For All: Overcoming Barriers to Learning and Development*. Pretoria: Department of Education, 1997.

Department of Education, South Africa. *Education White Paper 6, Special Needs Education: Building an Inclusive Education and Training System*. Pretoria: Department of Education, 2001.

Department of Health, South Africa. *Draft National Guidelines for the Development of Health Promoting Schools/Sites in South Africa*. Pretoria: Department of Health, 2000.

Department of Health, South Africa. *School Health Policy and Implementation Guidelines*. Pretoria: Department of Health, 2003.

Donald, David, Sandy Lazarus, and Peliwe Lolwana. *Educational Psychology in Social Context*. 2nd edn. Cape Town, South Africa: Oxford University Press, 2001.

Frank, Cheryl. *Missed Opportunities: The Role of Education, Health and Social Development in Preventing Crime*. Pretoria: Institute for Security Studies, 2006.

Groenewald, Cornie. 'Western Cape: An Overview'. In *The State of the Population in the Western Cape Province*, edited by Ravayi Marindo, Cornie Groenewald, and Sam Gaisie, 7–24. Cape Town: HSRC, 2008.

Howell, Colleen, Shuaib Chalklen, and Thomas Alberts. 'A History of the Disability Rights Movement in South Africa'. In *Disability and Social Change: A South African Agenda*, edited by Brian Watermeyer, Leslie Swartz, Theresa Lorenzo, Marguerite Schneider, and Mark Priestley. Cape Town: HSRC, 2006.

Jensen, Steffen. *Gangs, Politics and Dignity in Cape Town*. Johannesburg: Wits University Press, 2008.

Keim, Marion. 'Sport as Opportunity for Community Development and Peace Building in South Africa'. In *Sport and Development*, edited by Yves Van den Auweele, Charles Malcolm, and Bert Meulders. Leuven, Belgium: LannooCampus, 2006.

Kinnes, Irvin. 'The Struggle for the Cape Flats'. In *Now that We are Free: Coloured Communities in a Democratic South Africa*, edited by Wilmot James, Daria Caliguire, and Kerry Cullinan. Cape Town: IDASA, 1996.

Lindegaard, Marie Rosenkrantz. 'Navigating Terrains of Violence: How South African Male Youngsters Negotiate Social Change'. *Social Dynamics* 35, no. 1 (2009): 19–35.

Lindström, Martin, Bertil S. Hanson, and Per-Olof Östergren. 'Socioeconomic Differences in Leisure-Time Physical Activity: The Role of Social Participation and Social Capital in Shaping Health Related Behaviour'. *Social Science & Medicine* 52, no. 3 (2000): 441–51.

Lombard, Susan, and Andri van der Merwe. 'Preventive Programmes for Schools and Other Institutions'. In *Violence in South Africa: A Variety of Perspectives*, edited by Elirea Bornman, René van Eeden, and Marie Wentzel, 373–98. Pretoria: HSRC, 1998.

Misener, Laura, and Daniel Mason. 'Creating Community Networks: Can Sporting Events Offer Meaningful Sources of Social Capital?'. *Managing Leisure* 11 (2006): 39–56.

Office of the Deputy President of South Africa (ODP). *White Paper on an Integrated Disability Strategy*. Pretoria: ODP.

Pinnock, D., *Rituals, Rites and Punishment: Rethinking Youth Programs in South Africa*, 1990 Institute of Criminology, University of Cape Town, South Africa.

Reiman, L. 'Sports for Learners with Physical Disabilities in Ordinary Schools in the Western Cape'. Masters thesis, University of the Western Cape, 2008.

Rocha-Silva, Lee, and Timothy Ryan. 'Drugs and Violence Nexus'. In *Violence in South Africa: A Variety of Perspectives*, edited by Elirea Bornman, René van Eeden, and Marie Wentzel, 323–46. Pretoria: HSRC, 1998.

Schärf, W. 'Resurgence of Urban Street Gangs: Community Responses'. In *Towards Justice: Crime and State Control in South Africa*, edited by D. Hansson and D. Van Zyl Smit, 232–63. Cape Town: Oxford University Press, 1990.

Statistics South Africa. *Census in Brief*. Pretoria: Stats SA, 2003.

Statistics South Africa. *Census 2001: Prevalence of Disability in South Africa*. Pretoria: Stats SA, 2005.

Stone, Wendy. *Research Paper No 24. Measuring Social Capital: Towards a Theoretically Informed Measurement Framework for Researching Social Capital in Family and Community Life*. Melbourne: Australian Institute of Family Studies, 2001.

Tones, Keith and Sylvia Tilford. *Health Promotion: Effectiveness, Efficiency and Equity*. 3rd edn. Cheltenham: Nelson Thornes, 2001.

United Nations Educational, Scientific, and Cultural Organization (UNESCO). *Salamanca Statement and Framework for Action on Special Needs Education*. Paris: UNESCO, 1994.

Van Wyk, Brian E., and Wilhelmina H. Theron. 'Fighting Gangsterism in South Africa: A Contextual Review of Gang and Anti-Gang Movements in the Western Cape'. *Acta Criminologica* 18, no. 3 (2005): 51–60.

World Health Organization (WHO). *Constitution*. Geneva: WHO, 1946.

World Health Organization (WHO). *Ottawa Charter. First International Conference on Health Promotion*. Geneva: WHO, 1986.

World Health Organization (WHO). *The Jakarta Declaration on Leading Health Promotion into the 21st Century*. Geneva: WHO, 1997.

World Health Organization (WHO). *International Classification of Functioning, Disability and Health*. Geneva: WHO, 2001.

'Bladerunner or boundary runner'?: Oscar Pistorius, cyborg transgressions and strategies of containment

Moss E. Norman[a] and Fiona Moola[b]

[a]Department of Sociology, Memorial University of Newfoundland, St. John's, Canada; [b]Graduate Department of Exercise Sciences, The University of Toronto, Toronto, Canada

This article uses disability studies and cyborg theory as lenses to explore the disabled body in contemporary sporting contexts and situates the reader by critically reviewing social theory. Using the case of Oscar Pistorius, a South African Paralympian, we explore how the intense scrutiny on his prostheses forecloses examining how scientific discourses are called upon as arbiters to discern the 'truth' of his body. Moreover, while Pistorius invariably transgresses the boundaries of the modern sporting project and liberal humanist subject, he is subjected to powerful strategies of containment and domination. Threatening to undo secure notions of humanness, we illustrate how Pistorius is both fascinating and anxiety-provoking, and renders moral angst in the public consciousness. In order to rethink the stranglehold of ability and disability in the collective psyche and 'do' disability sport differently, this article calls for a radical cyborg politics.

Ablest Western culture has always had a troubled relationship with disability. Where 'normalcy' is at the very heart of the Othering process, ability constructs itself as normal by excluding 'deviant' disabled bodies.[1] The relationship with disabled bodies is complex and is indicative of a cultural obsession with high-functioning, flawless and perfect bodies. The fear, trepidation and anxiety[2] associated with the pathological body is psychic and runs deep. Disability is 'lived closely'; the 'risk' of becoming disabled is ever-present, and, for this reason,[3] we fear and reject it. Indeed, disability continues to be landscaped by powerful language structures which invariably connote deficiency, inadequacy, negativity, diminishment and tragedy[4] and raise tensions and questions about the essence of personhood.

Sport is a cultural space in which the relationship between ability and disability, the skilled and the unskilled, is magnified. Modern sport idealizes the 'universality of non-disabled social order'[5] and is a site in which competitive physicality is revered, flawless bodies are idealized, and desirable cultural values are inculcated. Indeed, the disabled body stands in greatest contrast to the very ideals upon which the modern sporting project was founded[6] and provides an appropriate forum in which to interrogate the relationships between ability and disability.

In order to address the disabled body in sporting cultures, we set out to accomplish three objectives in this article. First, we aim to situate the reader within the context of contemporary issues in disability as well as disability in sporting cultures, through a critical review of the existing literature. Second, we draw upon disability studies and cyborg theory to encourage a critical discussion of disabled 'cyborg' bodies in sporting cultures. Finally, using the case of Oscar Pistorius, a Paralympian known as 'blade runner' who runs on two prosthetic legs, we explore the interface between humans and technology in sporting cultures.

Disability debates: moral, medical, and social interpretations

Different theoretical insights have been proposed in order to articulate ability's complex relationship to disabled bodies. Prior to the ascendancy of medicine, discourses of religion were the dominant paradigm through which disability was read. While meanings were not always negative – sometimes, persons with certain disabilities were thought to possess unique skills – disability was associated with the divine. In most cases, disability was regarded as a moral sin or punishment for a certain wrong-doing or transgression.[7]

In the West, the medical model of disability was associated with the rise of medicine in the late nineteenth century and the institution of medicine was heralded as the only legitimate way of knowing disability.[8] Rather than disability resulting from vexed and tortured spirits, discourses of medicalization, reductionism, individualism and biological determinism sought to reduce disability to a problem associated with individual bodies. As such, disability was located in the body and named as a bodily problem to be eradicated by expert medical interventions. In addition to devising elaborate taxonomic systems to differentiate disabilities, the medical system is curative; it is oriented towards diagnosis, classification, treatment and cure. Moreover, with the assistance of medical intervention, the individual is configured as personally responsible for recovery[9] and powerful moral connotations are invoked. Medical practitioners replaced the clergy as the gatekeepers of health, policing the boundaries between wellness and illness, ability and disability, and normal or not. Today, the medical model remains entrenched and is the dominant framework through which disability is interpreted. Waging an attack on the medical model, the social model of disability has sought to undo the linguistic stranglehold which defines the disabled body

Language

The social model of disability reflects the efforts of disabled grass-roots activists to secure what is thought to be a more liberating and humane way of knowing the disabled body. They contest the notion that disability is located within individual pathological bodies, and rather, impairment and disability are differentiated; while impairment has a biological or structural origin in the body, disability is proposed to reside within disabling and oppressive social environments.[10] While it is important to not lose sight of the lived experience of impairment, or to obscure its fleshy physical embodiment, disability is located in the environment. Proposing that the environment itself is in need of 'rehabilitation', these authors discuss the complex network of physical, social, cultural, institutional and ideological barriers which magnify the burden of disability.[11] These include: the inherently negative way in which dominant speech acts construct disability in our everyday lives; the inaccessibility of the built environment; the ablest nature of the institutional work day; and the stereotypes that are reified when people with disabilities are showcased in the media.

Disability studies and the critical turn

Social model theorists have advanced a critical research agenda. This includes discussing the way in which disability elicits a politics of the visual which 'troubles space'. We come to know disability as spectacle and establish limited meanings, such as the wondrous, the monstrous or the sentimental, based on disability's visual representation.[12] Conjuring up notions of awe, marvel, monstrosity and pity, these visually mediated meanings compel a middle class 'call to rescue' and are always partial.

Informed by Marxism, social model theorists understand disability to be embedded within the context of the rise of modern capitalist industrial states. Disability arises as a concern in industrial cultures, as a 'problem of work'. Disability represents the unproductive body and therefore is read as an economically untenable embodiment.[13] More radical theorists suggest that entire human service industries of rehabilitation professionals are sustained by disabled bodies as the subjects of rehabilitation.

While meanings are not always negative, other social model insights suggest that disability is 'narrative prosthesis'; while it is used as a crutch to propel and launch fictional stories in film and literature and further the plot, it is rarely interrogated as a social construct or described as a desirable embodiment.[14] Examples of narrative prosthesis include 'Dying Beth' in *Little Women*, the 'Lame Boy' from *The Pied Piper of Hamlin*, 'The Hunch Back of Notre Dame', *Jane Eyre*'s crazy 'Bertha Mason', or more contemporaneous examples such as 'Maggie Fitzgerald' in *Million Dollar Baby*. Illustrating the complex ways in which literature and film both centre and erase disability from critical social thought at one and the same time, social theorists ask what cultural truth, ill, or evil is evaded when disability is called upon to play a central role in the plot?

Finally, these theorists illustrate how the notion of disability is related to the interests of dominant groups. Abelism is perpetuated as natural, inevitable and taken for granted, such that the binaries between ability and disability are presumed to exist.[15] Although the boundary between ability and disability is always ideological and entrenched within the cultural psyche, there are very real material consequences for how the able body and its disabled other experience their embodiment. The ascendancy and hegemony of ableism represents a material and ideological straightjacket that forecloses the critical interrogation of disability, not as a real embodiment, but produced as a complex social and cultural phenomenon.

Transgressive theories of the body in contemporary research offer up critical and radical means for thinking about disabled bodies. By proposing a series of troubling questions, efforts are made to undo the presumed binary between ability and disability and include: when we look to disability as a problem, what in culture do we look away from? What must culture be, such that this representation of disability is possible?[16] What is society's investment in policing disability at its borders? These theorists remind us that the boundary between ability and disability is fragile, tenuous and ultimately porous, and labours to highlight the leakiness, instability and incompleteness of all human embodiment. The divine, medical, social and transgressive models of disability are theoretical propositions which illustrate how disability is understood within contemporary Western culture and the invariably shifting nature of these interpretations. The following section on sport, disability and culture will situate the reader within the broader context of the literature and provide an overview and critique of current socio cultural issues.

Situating sport, disability, and culture: 'I love to dance, but I can't … everything that I can't do physically, I do in my mind'[17]

Critical sport sociologists have provoked novel insights with respect to the disabled body in sporting cultures. These include recognizing sport as a universal human right for persons with disabilities and working towards more diverse and inclusive sporting models.[18] Critical literature has also addressed dominant cultural representations and stereotypes and how these are taken up by disabled athletes in the constitution of the self.[19] These authors have noted the contextual and multiple nature of identity construction in athletes with disabilities and the central role of physical activity in allowing children with disabilities to legitimate their status as children.[20] Moreover, the complex social relations which occur in disability-sport settings illuminate the shifting nature of hierarchies and oppressions.[21] The novel concept of disability-through-sport illuminates the inherent contradictions of elite athleticism and the sport-through-disability narratives which are rendered sayable.[22] Finally, while inclusion for people with disabilities in sport offers up more humane choices, it is not immune from normalizing forces.[23]

While efforts have been made to offer athletes with disabilities more liberating sport opportunities, this work is couched in rights-based and inclusion discourses. Rather than overturning and transgressing the ablest modern sport project, this work negotiates the terms under which some disabled athletes may enter. Thus, disability, and the conditions for participation, are still heavily policed, surveilled and guarded; ability functions as the gatekeeper and final arbiter into a world of legitimate and privileged sport participation. Moreover, while critical theorists have identified some of the normalizing forces which underpin disability sport, the categories of ability and disability remain firmly entrenched and little headway is made in terms of interrogating these binaries. Finally, the social model of disability and its application to sport has exposed how environmental barriers are implicated in the oppression of people with disabilities. However, the notion of disability as a real and material embodiment that is presumed to exist outside language, cultural forces and discourse is assumed and entrenched in and through this literature.

Thus, while sociocultural considerations have seemingly advanced a more critical research agenda, the disabled sporting body is still landscaped by rights-based and inclusion discourses. In doing so, what it would mean to transgress the modern sporting project and undo the presumably natural categories of ability and disability remain unconsidered. The following section extends the current discussion of sport, disability and culture by deploying a cyborg analysis of the disabled sporting body.

Border crossings: cyborg theory as a challenge to the humanist subject

The cyborg is a term deployed to characterize the human–machine coupling. Cyborgs can be envisaged as human–machine hybrids ranging from the seemingly trivial, such as corrective eye wear or orthodontics, to more anxiety-inducing forms, such as restorative prosthetics, eye surgery and gene manipulation. The metaphor of the cyborg problematizes the supposedly clear boundary between human and machine, revealing that what is commonly assumed to be the 'natural' body is indeed a complex amalgamation of science, technology and flesh.[24] Since it forces a reconsideration of what counts as the natural body,[25] the cyborg provokes anxiety in a Western ontology founded upon the assumption of a pure, uncontaminated organic body standing outside, and in opposition to, the machine.[26] Thus, the metaphor of the cyborg connotes a leaky body, one that pollutes the tidy binary categories that structure the modern humanist subject (i.e. human/machine, able-bodied/disabled-bodied). Rather than existing safely on one side of the binary division or the other, the cyborg forces the radical revelation that all human embodiment exists in the interstitial space between sameness and difference.

Theories of the post human or cyborg are not homogeneous. Some theorists are uncritically celebratory of the technological problematization of the human subject. In this article, however, we are particularly interested in the cyborgian theories and politics inspired by Donna Haraway. Haraway negates a reductionist account of technology, refusing to envision it as either negative or positive.[27] Haraway's cyborg is less about concrete or virtual humanness and 'more a matter of stories, political mythologies and a form of writing' that is concerned with 'seizing the tools to mark the world' and 'recoding communication and intelligence to subvert command and control'.[28] Haraway's cyborgian feminist politics are twofold. The cyborg provides a forum for conceptualizing how information and technology have intensified the categories that are constitutive of the human subject (that is able-bodied/disabled, human/machine). At the same time, the cyborg exposes these categories as ontologically unstable or 'dirty ontologies' that are vulnerable to redeployment and reinvention through mutant feminist refigurations.

Brian Pronger refers to Haraway's politics as a politics of transgression. Here, politics is about seeing how the boundaries that are constitutive of the humanist subject, such as the boundary between able-bodied and disabled, are conditions of domination and control. Through transgression, these conditions can be reworked such that individuals take more control over the projects that dominate their identities. Thus, transgressive cyborgs might reimagine their identities outside an 'informatics of domination'[29] that fixes them into a series of hierarchical and binarized subject positions. Rather, they may actively work to foster mutant, less dominating cyborgian connectivity's through a politics of transgression.

A responsible and ethical cyborg politics must recognize that the cyborg body does not guarantee a transgressive politics of reinvention. Technological advancements are indeed ideology-in-progress that reproduce dominant cultural embodiments.[30] Moreover, while it is crucial to recognize that information and technology serves dominant cultural constructions, it is also important to be aware that access to emerging technologies and their cybernetic possibilities – dominant and otherwise – are disproportionately available. To this end, it is important to consider how the cyborg's boundary blurring, while allowing for metaphoric potentials, cannot be separated from its historical links to capital and to social and economic control.[31] Therefore, questions of context, access and consequences of one's cyborgian projects are elemental to a feminist cyborg politics. Informed by Haraway, we deploy the metaphor of the cyborg as a means of both revealing ablest conditions of domination, as well as a strategy for reimagining other ways of conceiving disabled embodiment and collapsing and polluting the very constitutive categories of ability and disability themselves. In the following section, we explore existing literature on the cyborg body in sporting cultures.

Athletes as 'always already cyborgified': sport and the cyborg body

Sport is a central discursive site for producing and reproducing the modern body.[32] Pronger conceptualizes modern sport as a 'project of differentiation and socio-cultural boundary maintenance', where the boundaries of the humanist subject are constructed, disciplined and regulated.[33] Sport is not a neutral physical engagement governed by a disinterested arrangement of rules, values and beliefs, but a discursive set of practices that are productive of certain bodies through the normalization, regulation and disciplining of the boundaries of the humanist subject. Cole (1998) draws upon drug testing to illustrate how sport is a boundary project that faces a 'crisis of the natural'.[34] Informed by Derrida and Sedgewick, she argues that drug-testing is a strategy deployed to prop up the myth of the natural, uncontaminated athletic body. When considering the role that playing surfaces, sporting equipment, nutritional supplements, rehabilitative technologies and various prostheses play in the production of both sport and sporting bodies, other scholars argue that there is no such thing as an athlete untainted by technologies. To this end, Butryn argues that elite athletes should not be seen as 'technological tabulae rasae', but as 'cyborgs who are inextricably tied to a range of sport technologies', a recognition that he claims serves to 'alleviate the tension between 'natural' and 'artificial' athletes and performances.[35]

Despite the recognition of the impossibility, absurdity even, of the preservation of the natural athletic body, it remains an ideological mainstay of modern sport.[36] This is evident in Butryn and Masucci's analysis of Lance Armstrong's cyborgified dominance as Tour de France champion. They argue that the transgressive potential of Armstrong is ambivalent. While he undeniably occupies a cyborg identity as a thoroughly biomedicalized cancer survivor and savvy agent of the most up-to-date cycling technology and scientific knowledge, he preserves his body as natural by refuting claims of doping. He invokes, somewhat ironically, the technology of drug-testing and his negative tests to argue for his natural athletic body, thereby legitimating his athletic performances. The transgressive potential of Armstrong is contained by the aggressive policing of governing sporting bodies that enable and legitimize some forms of cyborgification, while limiting others.

In his exploration of elite track athletes' negotiation of technology, Butryn found that all of the athletes felt compelled to 'tread the line between a natural athletic status, while at the same time, borrowing and maximizing performance enhancing technologies'.[37] He argues that a constitutive component of their relationship with technology is discursively constructing a natural athletic identity through denying the cybernetic or unnatural properties of the self. This is because technologically enhanced bodies challenge the constitutive notion of humanness and the principle of pure and natural athletic accomplishment. However, Butryn's analysis demonstrates that the boundary projects of sport are not reflective of real categories (i.e. natural/cultural, man/woman, etc.). Rather, we would argue that these boundaries are productive of the very objects which they purportedly divide, and thus the boundary must be continuously enacted to bestow the fiction of reality through rules, laws and even the actions and narratives of the athletes themselves. By denigrating banned performance-enhancing technologies and their associated performances while simultaneously erasing those cyborgifying properties of so-called legitimate technologies, the 'proper' athlete comes into being through producing, policing and shoring up the boundary between self and other, pure and impure, human and cyborg, and so on.

Despite the fact that all athletes are 'always-already-cyborgified',[38] disabled athletes bear a disproportionate burden of cyborg embodiment because of the hypervisibility and spectacle of their cybernetic sporting selves (i.e. prostheses, wheelchairs, etc.). Moreover, the visibility of sports is also variable. For example, certain athletic events, such as track and field, function as the pinnacle of human excellence and are likely to garner greater public surveillance. In the following section, we examine how the cyborg is a site for thinking about and reimagining both disability and normative embodiment in sporting cultures through an analysis of the career of Oscar Pistorius.

The multiple transgressions and containments of Oscar Pistorius

The career of Oscar Pistorius, a double-amputee South African runner, is one instance of disability as transgression. Oscar Pistorius was born with a congenital condition which required amputation in early life. Arguably, the experiences of those with acquired versus congenital disabilities are different. Whereas a congenital condition is a state of embodiment which one has always 'known', acquiring a disability may shatter and disrupt ones' sense of self and embodiment. Pistorius, champion runner and world record holder in the Paralympic Games (100 m, 200 m and 400 m, T44 category), recently applied to run in the non-disabled Olympics. Because Pistorius uses high-tech prostheses called Cheetahs, he has sparked waves of controversy. Pistorius's explicitly technologized body blurs the foundational categories of modern Olympic sport, including those separating human and machine, ability and disability, independence and dependence.[39] Rationalizations for excluding Pistorius from the non-disabled Olympic Games typically centre around the argument that his prostheses represent an unfair advantage.[40] Constituting a performance-enhancing technology, some detractors even argue that Pistorius is 'not even running',[41] a contention which arguably suggests that he is less-than-human. By contrast to these positions, we follow in the steps of other critical sport theorists in arguing that the search for the truth about Pistorius's prostheses is ultimately misplaced and serves only to bolster the presumption of a real human body that is reducible to biologically neutral categories. In place of the tyranny of the natural, we argue for a critical analysis of the category of human itself. Using the representational struggle over Oscar Pistorius's body as an embedded case study, we take up this task in the following section.

It's all about the legs!

Shortly after Pistorius took part in his first non-disabled international competition in 2007, the International Association of Athletics Federations (IAAF) asked German professor Gert-Peter Bruggemann to test the performance-enhancing potential of his prosthetic legs. Bruggemann concluded that Pistorius enjoyed 'considerable advantages over athletes without prosthetic limbs'.[42] On the basis of these findings, the IAAF ruled in January 14, 2008 that the Cheetah prostheses were ineligible for use in non-disabled competitions, thus blocking Pistorius from competing for a position on the South African Olympic team. Our objective is not to weigh into the already well-trodden terrain that examines the merit of arguments over whether Pistorius's prosthesis represents an 'unfair advantage'. Rather, we examine how debates are almost exclusively focused on his prosthetic legs, which serves to foreclose a series of more culturally pressing moral and ethical questions about the limits of human ontology and the humanist subject upon which it is founded. We ask: by turning to the scientific truth of Pistorius's technologized body,[43] and focusing primarily on the 'empirical' question of what is considered an athletic advantage,[44] what other aspects of his cyborgified embodiment are left uninterrogated? Although notions of a level playing field are ostensibly questions for a supposedly objective science to answer, we intend to show how they are more properly understood as philosophical and ethical questions about what it is to be human and are founded upon the presumption of a natural body.

The discourse of science figures prominently in determining the eligibility of Pistorius to compete in non-disabled competitions and structures the form and content of the debate. The governing bodies of sport, as well as Pistorius and his advocates, turned to science to decipher the truth of his cyborg body. Central to this debate is the assumption that there is in fact a stable, natural body that can be apprehended through science. Moreover, the debate presumes that notions such as fair play and a level playing field are real possibilities and ideals worthy of struggling towards. In contrast to these assumptions, we argue that the institution of modernist sport is a manifestation of liberal humanism that assumes an organic body and a self-contained human subject. These are concepts that we intend to destabilize with our cyborg analysis of Oscar Pistorius.

Elite modern sport continues to operate through a 'naturalistic metaphysics',[45] in which the category of the natural remains the central mode of classifying sporting bodies.

Thus, the notion of fairness or a level playing field is rooted in the presumption of a natural, self-contained human body, an ideal which is thought to be polluted or corrupted by technological enhancement. Therefore, the idea of technological enhancement presumes that 'something clear can be said about humanness that is lessened or removed by the use of some technology'.[46] Equally relevant is the presumption that science is the privileged medium for discerning the 'truth' of both what it is to be human and the essence of the natural body. Indeed, under the auspices of nature, the natural sciences obscure the cultural and political work that goes into the production of the natural body, presenting the body as an inert mass waiting to be uncovered through the medium of science.[47] Informed by feminist post-structuralism,[48] we understand that what has come to be accepted as the natural body in sport, should be rethought of as a natural*ized* body, inscribed into a culturally meaningful form through a series of normalizing technologies, including science and information. For us, the notion of the natural body is not an ontological reality, but the outcome of sociocultural technologies of corporeal inscription, including the disciplines that are productive of the sporting body – both able-bodied and otherwise – such as sports nutrition, sports psychology, biomechanics and other techno-scientific innovations.[49]

The sporting body is constituted alongside and in tandem with science and technology. Given that the elite athlete is inevitably and always-already-cyborgified what comes to mark the IAAF's boundary between fair and unfair advantage is not governed by objective scientific fact, as we so often assume, but is rather a fluid, shifting and somewhat arbitrary boundary that is determined by contemporaneous cultural and moral values and beliefs.[50] Nonetheless, the governing bodies of sport, such as the IAAF and the CAS, ostensibly turn to scientific expertise as a means of shoring up and policing the boundary between fair and unfair, technologically enhanced and pure, human and non-human.

Although science is seemingly deployed as the final arbiter of what constitutes a pure and authentic athletic performance, it is possible to see how moral anxieties are powerful mediators of how technological innovations are received. This is apparent in the words of Elio Locatelli, director of development for the IAAF, when he comments with respect to Pistorius that 'we cannot accept something that provides advantages … it affects the purity of the sport. Next will be another device where people can fly with something on their back'. Here, Locatelli relies on hyperbole and 'cyborg anxiety',[51] not rational and objective scientific reasoning (assuming such a science exists), to discount Pistorius as an eligible – and thus normative – non-disabled competitor.

There are other examples which illustrate how scientific facts about Pistorius make little difference to the value laden moral conclusions that people draw, such as commentary by Robin Brown, a journalist for the Canadian Broadcast Corporation's *The Inside Track*. Brown concluded that it is likely impossible for science to quantify the difference between human flesh and Pistorius's prostheses. Regardless, she states as fact that Pistorius's 'scientifically designed carbon-fibre limbs' are 'different from someone who races on flesh and bone'.[52] These illustrative examples demonstrate that science is always embedded in a social and cultural context, and, in drawing attention to them, we are not arguing for a so-called better or more accurate science to evaluate Pistorius's body. By contrast, we show that although science is called upon as adjudicator, the questions that science asks and the structure of the debate are always cultural. Moreover, moral, philosophical and ethical sentiments are brought to supposedly scientific facts and influence the nature of the conclusions that people come to about Pistorius.

Focusing upon Pistorius's prostheses acts as a discursive constraint, fixing our gaze on the issue of an 'unfair advantage' and conceptually effacing the argument. In looking to

Pistorius's prostheses, we invariably turn away from how scientific discourses are called upon to discern how governing bodies render who can participate and who cannot, who can attain the status of normative embodiment and who cannot. Therefore, questions of level playing fields and technological advantage, we contend, are more properly thought of as techniques for shoring up the boundaries of the humanist subject and the natural body upon which it is founded. Moreover, this section illustrated how values and morals are inevitably brought to the interpretation of 'scientific facts'. Next, we turn to an analysis of the more transgressive aspects that Pistorius's cyborg embodiment represents to the institution of modern sport, and the humanist subject more generally.

The transgressive potential of Oscar Pistorius

Swartz and Watemeyer have provocatively asked 'what does the case of Pistorius threaten to de-stabilize?'[53] We argue that Pistorius disrupts the boundaries of modern sport. Perhaps more importantly, he threatens the accepted and foundational binary categories of the humanist subject, and the intense public scrutiny he has garnered attests to this. His bid to compete for a place on the South African Olympic track and field team received international media attention and was the topic of numerous, intense and highly divisive public discussion forums, including media phone-ins and on-line discussions. Indeed, Pistorius does fascinate and provoke anxiety at one and the same time – but why?

Jere Longman has attempted to explain Pistorius's grasp on the public imagination. In his *New York Times* column, he writes that Pistorius represents a 'searing athletic talent who has begun erasing the lines between abled and disabled.'[54] Indeed, the boundary between ability and disability is a central division that organizes modern sport. While this might explain why sport governing bodies and athletes express anxiety over Pistorius's transgressions, it offers scant insight into why the public imagination is so heavily invested in this case. It is Pistorius's broader disruption which extends beyond the confines of sport and its athletes, that is of particular interest to us.

To address the question, we turn to critical theorists who situate sport as a central site for the production and naturalization of difference among bodies. They argue that the construction of the 'natural' body (i.e. able-/normal/human, etc.) is largely produced through excluding its other (i.e. disability/abnormal/machine, etc.). This cultural process must be reiteratively enacted through multiple cultural institutions, including the rules, laws and discursive mediations which govern modern sport. The category 'normal' 'secures its self-identity and shores up its ontological boundaries by protecting itself from what it sees as the continual predatory encroachment of its contaminated other',[55] the abnormal. The sporting body is thus produced through marking itself as different and superior from its excluded other; in the case of Oscar Pistorius, the disabled-bodied athlete.

However, the boundary between the included (i.e. ability, natural and the normal) and the excluded (i.e. disability, the cyborg and the abnormal) is tenuous and unstable, as Oscar Pistorius's bid to gain eligibility to the Olympics demonstrates, and thus must be produced and policed with vigilance. Nonetheless, disability is always already inside ability as the constitutive conditions of its emergence. As Judith Butler writes, the 'exclusionary matrix by which [able-bodied] subjects are formed ... requires the production of ... those who are not yet "subjects" [the disabled-bodied], but who form the constitutive outside to the domain of the subject'.[56] Ability is constituted and knows itself through the repudiation of its other, disability. The integrity of ability is shored up and maintained through keeping disability in its place. Thus, when Oscar Pistorius transgresses the boundary between ability/disability, nature/machine and so on, he reveals the margins of ability as porous, leaky, and unstable, thereby threatening to collapse the very ontological and corporeal security of the humanist subject.

The symbolic and material implications of sport's boundary projects, however, extend far beyond the reach of sport and the bodies that participate in it. Certainly, the modern Olympic Games serve as a primary forum for meaning-making in contemporary societies. Haraway explains that any form of 'boundary sorting ... is always a specific mode of worlding'.[57] Thus, we come to understand the world, our identities and subjectivities, and our place in it through the various boundary projects that render it meaningful, including the spectacle of sport. Thus, it is hardly surprising that the world follows with scepticism, fascination, anxiety, desire and fear as Oscar Pistorius challenges the boundaries that organize modern sport. Indeed, his disabled cyborg body threatens to collapse the very categories upon which our comprehension of what it is to be 'human' is premised.

Swartz and Watemeyer argue that Oscar's disabled, cybernetic body disrupts the public's imagination of the embodiment of the Olympic ideal – namely, a body that is the paragon of aesthetic and athletic perfection. Here, the authors claim that the elite modern athlete is supposed to embody the ideal human form, including aesthetic beauty and bodily integrity, ideals that the inclusion of Pistorius's 'pathological', disabled cyborg body in the Olympic Games potentially places under suspicion. In this regard, the case of Pistorius has maintained its stranglehold on the public's imagination largely because he disrupts the 'apparently stable binaries ... that constitute the very ground of our embodied selves.'[58] He is disruptive to normative Olympic sporting ideals and problematises the very categories of ability/disability, nature/machine – some of the founding binary coordinates of the humanist subject.

While the material and metaphorical impact of the cyborg body centres on its potential to reveal the conditions of domination that structure contemporary embodiment and aspire to do embodiment differently, there is nothing inherently destabilizing about cybernetic embodiment. It is imperative that a feminist cyborg analysis consider the broader context in which the cyborg operates, asking about the conditions of its transgressions, the ends to which it aspires, and the power relations that are served. Here, we interrogate the ways in which Pistorius is contained.

Strategies of containment

Science is deployed as the final arbiter of the truth of Pistorius's body and thus serves as a means of policing both the natural and sporting body. However, we also argue that the destabilizing transgressions of Pistorius's cyborg body are undermined through two interconnected strategies of containment.

The first strategy of containment is to be found in the ruling of the Court of Arbitration of Sport (CAS). Although the CAS overturned the earlier ban issued by the IAAF, thereby allowing Pistorius to compete in the Olympic trials, the details of their ruling contained several important caveats that made the positive ruling a tenuous victory at best. The CAS ruling is limited to the specific case of Oscar Pistorius and the prosthetics he uses. Moreover, the CAS made it clear that future scientific evidence that conclusively demonstrates that the Cheetah prostheses provide an 'unfair advantage' would be grounds for repeal of their present ruling. Thus, Oscar Pistorius is situated as an anomaly, as a specific and isolated case that is clearly not to be confused with a radical rethinking of the criteria and categories of normal embodiment. Instead, we should envision the CAS ruling as a gate separating ability/disability, normal/abnormal, human/less-than-human, opening just long enough for Pistorius to squeeze through to the other side, before quickly slamming shut. Even at that, his position is tenuous. Under the auspices of fair play, we can imagine that scientific experts may be diligently working to prove the unfair advantage of Oscar Pistorius's prostheses, thereby shoring up the boundaries of the humanist subject. Thus, Pistorius is discursively constructed as an anomaly, a one-off case, as opposed to an emergent form of embodiment that demands opening up new ways of imagining human physicality.

The second way in which the disruptive potential of Pistorius is contained is through the discourse of individualism, which he actively positions himself within. As discussed earlier, modern sport is premised on the construct of the liberal humanist subject; an autonomous, rational, self-contained human agent at the centre of discourse, is assumed. In order for Pistorius to qualify as a 'natural athlete', one whose success is founded in his extensive and disciplined training and *not* his technological enhancement, he must reiteratively disavow his dependence on any connectedness to an external environment, or that which is beyond the margins of his own body. One way in which he accomplishes this is by reiteratively enacting the discourse of individualism. For example, Pistorius states that 'if they [IAAF] ever found evidence that I was gaining an advantage, I would stop running because I would not want to compete at a top level if I knew I had an unfair advantage.' Here, Pistorius shores up the boundaries of his bodily integrity by renouncing any advantage that may be gained from his dependence on technologies outside his own disciplined training and mental toughness. Those around him, such as coach, Ampie Louw, likewise deploy the discourse of individualism to preserve his bodily integrity. Louw comments that Pistorius 'is a born champion ... He doesn't settle for second best'.[59] In referring to Pistorius as 'a born champion', as opposed to one who is made through the hybridization of flesh, technology, and hard work, Louw labours to individualize and naturalize Pistorius.

Indeed, the discourse of individualism also mitigates against an exploration of how Pistorius is located at the cross roads of privilege and oppression. As a disabled body that must fight for legitimacy in able-bodied sports, he invariably encounters a range of oppressive anti-disability sentiments. While being heralded as an 'incredible supercrip' who cannot be ordinary, his legitimacy as an athlete is called into question due to his technologically enhanced self. Moreover, when concerns about legitimacy are only raised in relation to participating in non-disabled activities, this reveals telling information with respect to the perceived seriousness of disability sport.

However, while Pistorius is entrapped by oppressive discourses that thwart his legitimacy as a sporting body, his sport career has also arguably been enabled by his social position and matrices of privilege. Pistorius hails from Sandton which is one of the wealthiest neighbourhoods in South Africa and is commonly known as the 'Manhattan' of Johannesburg. Where South Africa brings to bear stark material and symbolic disparities between rich and poor, this illustrious and economically productive business town is located just next door to Alexandra, what was once one of the poorest black South African townships. Pistorius is also situated at the cross roads of a cultural and historical boundary project, straddling the interface between the apartheid and post-apartheid era. This raises telling questions about the other boundaries that structure Pistorius's life, including his privileged gender, social class, education and racial background. His privileged background may have facilitated access to exclusive health, sport and restorative technologies; we can only speculate on how Pistorius's lived reality may have been radically different if he were on the other side of the boundaries of race, class and gender, and were a poor, black, disabled South African from a township. In this regard, situating Pistorius entails unpacking how his social position affords him with relative privilege and disadvantage at one and the same time. It also entails thinking about how discourses of individualism may render these complex intersections invisible.

Finally, the discourse of individualism also acts as a strategy of containment in the way that Pistorius comes to articulate himself as an athlete. Although Pistorius is an articulate and outspoken advocate, his voice is invariably constrained. Disabled athletes come to constitute themselves through dominant cultural representations and Pistorius draws upon discourses of individualism and individual reparation in order to articulate his sporting self. Pistorius states that 'I don't see myself as disabled … there is nothing I can't do that able bodied athletes can do'.[60] He thus not only leaves the categories of ability and disability intact and entrenched, but articulates himself as a liberal humanistic subject who is neither enabled nor constrained by sociocultural forces. As a rugged individualist, there is nothing that can stand in his way or prevent his progress. Another unintended consequence of Pistorius's disavowal and erasure of disability, is foreclosing the diversity of disabilities, the way in which disabilities are differently embodied, and the pain, anguish and burden of exclusion that some disabled bodies do encounter. In this way, discourses of individualism are taken up in how Pistorius comes to know himself as a sporting subject.

In focusing on Oscar Pistorius as an individual agent and labouring humanist subject, discourses of individualism are drawn upon as strategies for disavowing the other social, cultural and technological forces that go into the construction of the human body. The disruptive potential of Pistorius is usurped. In this section, we argued that by locating the governing officials of sport as the gatekeepers of normative human embodiment, the transgressive potential of Oscar Pistorius is contained. Additionally, we argued that the discourse of individualism serves to situate Pistorius as an isolated and contained individual, thereby obscuring the complex social, cultural and technological influences that construct his always-already-cyborgified identity.

Conclusion, inclusion, or cyborg openings?

This article illuminated the troubling relationship that ablelist Western culture has always had to disability and the various cultural interpretations through which it has been landscaped. Cyborg theory was considered as a lens for thinking about 'doing' disabled embodiment differently. Oscar Pistorius, a disabled cyborg athlete who both fascinates and troubles the public's imagination was deployed as an embedded case study. In doing so, it is evident that the notion that 'it is all about the legs forecloses the investment of science in uncovering 'the truth' of Pistorius's body. In addition, Pistorius both transgresses the boundaries of the modern sporting project and liberal humanist subject, while simultaneously being dominated and constrained by strategies of containment. In undertaking this critical analysis of disabled sporting cultures and the case of Pistorius, we call for a radical cyborg politics; in doing so, athletes like 'Bladerunner' will not be cast as anomalies, but, rather, a testament of how to rethink and disrupt the normative boundaries of ability, disability and modern sport.

Notes

[1] Huang and Brittain, 'Negotiating Identities through Disability Sport'.
[2] Shakespeare, *The Disability Studies Reader*.
[3] Hoyle and White, 'Physical Activity in the Lives of Women'.
[4] Ibid., 256.
[5] Huang and Brittain, 'Negotiating Identities through Disability Sport', Swartz and Watemeyer, 'Cyborg Anxiety'.
[6] Garland-Thomson, 'The Politics of Staring'.

[7] Barnes, 'The Social Model of Disability'; Barton, 'Sociology, Disability Studies and Education'.
[8] Wheatley, 'Disciplining Bodies at Risk'.
[9] Shogan, 'The Social Construction of Disability'; Zola, *Missing pieces.*
[10] Barton, 'Sociology, Disability Studies and Education'; Zola, *Missing pieces.*
[11] Garland-Thomson, 'The Politics of Staring'.
[12] Barnes, 'The Social Model of Disability'; Davis, *Enforcing Normalcy*; Abberly, 'The Spectre at the Feast'.
[13] Mitchell, 'Narrative Prosthesis and the Materiality'.
[14] Barnes, 'The Social Model of Disability'.
[15] Titchkosky, *Reading and Writing Disability Differently.*
[16] Hoyle and White, 'Physical Activity in the Lives of Women'.
[17] Nixon, 'Constructing Diverse Sports Opportunities'.
[18] Brittain, 'Perceptions of Disability'; Goodwin, Thurmeier, and Gustafson, 'Reactions to the Metaphors of Disability'.
[19] Taub and Greer, 'Physical Activity as a Normalizing Experience'.
[20] Hoyle and White, 'Physical Activity in the Lives of Women'; Lindemann and Cherney, 'Communicating in and Through Murderball'.
[21] Smith and Sparkes, 'Changing Bodies, Changing Narratives'.
[22] Shogan, 'The Social Construction of Disability'.
[23] A poststructural cyborg analysis would mitigate against trying to draw a line between 'more or less' technologically produced cyborg bodies. It recognises that some forms of technological advancement are more visible than others and insists that all bodies are always already cyborgified.
[24] Balsamo, *Technologies of the Gendered Body.*
[25] Lupton, 'Monsters in Metal Cocoons'.
[26] Gane and Haraway, 'When We Have Never Been Human'.
[27] Shields, 'Flanerie for Cyborgs', 211.
[28] Shields, 'Flanerie for Cyborgs', 211; Haraway, 'A Cyborg Manifesto', 175.
[29] Balsamo, *Technologies of the Gendered Body.*
[30] Hitchcock cited in Parker-Starbuck, 'Shifting Strengths', 96.
[31] Cole, 'Oscar Pistorius's Aftermath'; Pronger, 'Post-sport'; Shogan, *The Making of High-Performance Athletes.*
[32] Pronger, 'Post Sport', 281.
[33] Cole, 'Addiction, Exercise, and Cyborgs'.
[34] Burtryn, 'Posthuman Podiums', 18.
[35] Miah, 'Re-thinking Enhancement in Sport'.
[36] Burtryn, 'Posthuman Podiums', 19.
[37] Ibid.
[38] Our intent in naming Oscar Pistorius a cyborg is not to discount his agency and transformative accomplishments for disability sport. Rather, we are interested in how representations of him both construct and constrain his agency as an athlete and disabled body.
[39] Edwards, 'Should Oscar Pistorius be Excluded'.
[40] The discourse of 'unfair advantage' was dominant at the time the paper was written. Since that time, the discourse of athlete health and safety has gained prominence. Interestingly, both discourses rely on a seemingly neutral and objective scientific foundation in building an argument for the exclusion of Pistorius from able-bodied competition.
[41] 'Oscar Pistorius'. Wikipedia, July 8, 2009 from http://en.wikipedia.org/wiki/Oscar_Pisotirus
[42] Here, we deliberately use the more neutral term 'technologized body' as opposed to the more morally laden term 'technologically enhanced' as a means of remaining outside the 'unfair advantage' debate that surrounds Oscar Pistorius's Cheetah prostheses, a debate, we argue, forecloses the consideration of more interesting and relevant questions about the limits of human ontology.
[43] Van Hilvoorde and Landeweerde, 'Disability or Extraordinary Talent', p. 106.
[44] Cole, 'Addiction, Exercise, and Cyborgs'.
[45] Miah, 'Rethinking Enhancement in Sport', 308.
[46] Pronger, 'Post Sport'.
[47] Butler, *Bodies that Matter*; Cole, 'Resisting the Canon'; Grosz, *Volatile Bodies.*
[48] Cole, 'Resisting the Canon'; Pronger, 'Post Sport'; Shogan, *The Making of High-Performance Athletes.*

[49] Miah, 'Rethinking Enhancement in Sport'.
[50] Cited in Jere Longman, J. (May 15, 2007) 'An Amputee Sprinter: Is He Disabled or Too-abled?'. *The NewYork Times*, http://www.nytimes.com/2007/05/15/sports/othersports/15runner.html; Swartz and Watemeyer, 'Cyborg Anxiety'.
[51] Robin Brown (January 18, 2008) 'How Can we Quantify Disability in Sport?' *From the Inside Out*, http://www.cbc.ca/sports/brown/2008/01/how_can_we_quantify_disability.html
[52] Swartz and Watemeyer, 'Cyborg Anxiety', 308.
[53] Jere Longman, J. (May 15, 2007) 'An Amputee Sprinter: Is He Disabled or Too-abled?', *The NewYork Times* [online], http://www.nytimes.com/2007/05/15/sports/othersports/15runner.html
[54] Judith Butler cited in Shildrick and Price, 'Breaking the Boundaries of the Broken Body', 443.
[55] Butler, *Bodies that Matter*, 3.
[56] Gane and Haraway, 'When We Have Never Been', 148.
[57] Shildrick and Price, 'Breaking the Boundaries of the Broken Body', 433.
[58] Jere Longman, J. (May 15, 2007) 'An Amputee Sprinter: Is He Disabled or Too-Abled?, '*The NewYork Times* [online], http://www.nytimes.com/2007/05/15/sports/othersports/15runner.html
[59] Ibid.
[60] Ibid.

References

Abberley, Paul. 'The Spectre at the Feast: Disabled People and Social Theory'. In *The Disability Reader: A Social Science Perspective*, edited by T. Shakespeare, 79–94. London: Cassell, 1998.
Balsamo, Anne. 'Forms of Technological Embodiment: Reading the Body in Contemporary Culture'. In *Feminist Theory and the Body: A Reader*, edited by Janet Price and Margrit Shildrick, 278–89. New York: Routledge, 1999.
Barnes, Colin. 'The Social Model of Disability: A Sociological Phenomena Ignored by Sociologists'. In *The Disability Reader: A Social Science Perspective*, edited by T. Shakespeare, 64–78. London: Cassell, 1998.
Barton, Len. 'Sociology, Disability Studies and Education: Some Observations'. In *The Disability Reader: A Social Science Perspective*, edited by T. Shakespeare, 53–64. London: Cassell, 1998.
Birrell, Susan, and Cheryl Cole. 'Renee Richards and the Construction and Naturalization of Difference'. In *Reading Sport: Critical Essays on Power and Representation*, edited by Susan Birrell and Mary McDonald, 279–310. Boston: Northeastern University Press, 2000.
Brittain, Ian. 'Perceptions of Disability and Their Impact Upon Involvement in Sport for People with Disabilities at all Levels'. *Journal of Sport and Social Issues* 28, no. 4 (2004): 428–52.
Butler, Judith. *Bodies That Matter: On the Discursive Limits of Sex*. New York: Routledge, 1993.
Butryn, Ted. 'Cyborg Horizons: Sport and the Ethics of Self Technologization'. In *Sport Technologies: History, Philosophy, and Policy*, edited by Andy Miah and Simon Eassom, 111–34. Oxford: Elsevier Science, 2002.
Butryn, Ted. 'Posthuman Podiums: Cyborg Narratives of Elite Track and Field Athletes'. *Sociology of Sport Journal* 20 (2003): 17–39.
Butryn, Ted, and Matthew Masucci. 'It's Not About the Book: A Cyborg Counternarrative of Lance Armstrong'. *Journal of Sport and Social Issues* 27, no. 2 (2003): 124–44.
Cole, Cheryl. 'Resisting the Canon: Feminist Cultural Studies, Sport and Technologies of the Body'. In *Women, Sport, and Culture*, edited by Susan Birrell and Cheryl Cole. Champaign, IL: Human Kinetics, 1994.
Cole, Cheryl. 'Addiction, Exercise, and Cyborg. Technologies of Deviant Bodies'. In *Sport in Postmodern Times*, edited by G. Rail, 239–61. Albany: State of University of New York Press, 1998.
Cole, Cheryl. 'Oscar Pistorius's Aftermath'. *Journal of Sport and Social Issues* 33, no. 1 (2009): 3–4.
Davis, Lennard. *Enforcing Normalcy*. London: Verso, 1995.
Edwards, S. 'Should Oscar Pistorius Be Excluded from the 2008 Olympic Games?'. *Sport, Ethics, and Philosophy* 22, no. 2 (2008): 112–25.
Gane, Nicholas, and Donna Haraway. 'When We Have Never Been Human, What Is to Be Done? An Interview with Donna Haraway'. *Theory, Culture, & Society* 23, no. 7 (2006): 135–58.
Garland-Thomson, Rosemarie. 'The Politics of Staring: Visible Rhetoric's of Disability in Popular Photography'. In *Disability Studies: Enabling the Humanities*, edited by Brenda Brueggemann,

Sharon Snyder, and Rosemarie Garland-Thomson, 56–76. New York: Modern Language Associations of America, 2002.

Goodwin, Donna, Robin Thurmeier, and Paul Gustafston. 'Reactions to the Metaphors of Disability: The Mediating Effects of Physical Activity'. *Adapted Physical Activity Quarterly* 21 (2004): 379–98.

Grosz, Elizabeth. *Volatile Bodies: Towards a Corporeal Feminism*. New York: Routledge, 1994.

Haraway, Donna. 'A Cyborg Manifesto: Science, Technology, and Socialist Feminist'. In *Simians, Cyborgs, and Woman: The Reinvention of Nature*, edited by Donna Haraway, 149–82. London: Free Association Press, 1991.

Hoyle, Jennifer, and Philip White. 'Physical Activity in the Lives of Women with Disabilities'. In *Sport and Gender in Canada*, edited by Philip White and Kevin Young, 182–96. Toronto: Oxford University Press, 1999.

Huang, C., and Ian Brittain. 'Negotiating Identities through Disability Sport'. *Sociology of Sport Journal* 23 (2006): 352–75.

Lindemann, Kurt, and James L. Cherney. 'Communicating In and Through Murderball: Masculinity and Disability in Wheelchair Rugby'. *Western Journal of Communication* 72, no. 2 (2008): 107–25.

Lupton, Deborah. 'Monsters in Metal Cacoons'. *Body & Society* 5, no. 1 (1999): 57–72.

Miah, Andy. 'Re- Thinking Enhancement in Sport'. In *Progress in Convergence: Technologies for Human Wellbeing. Annals of the New York Academy of Sciences*, edited by William Bainbridge and Mihail Roco, 301–20, 2006.

Mitchell, David. 'Narrative Prosthesis and the Materiality of Metaphor'. In *Disability Studies: Enabling the Humanities*, edited by Brenda Brueggemann, Sharon Snyder, and Rosemarie Garland-Thomson, 15–30. New York: Modern Languages Association of America, 2002.

Nixon, Howard. 'Constructive Diverse Sports Opportunities for People with Disabilities'. *Journal of Sport and Social Issues* 31, no. 4 (2007): 417–33.

Parker-Starbuck, Jennifer. 'Shifting Strengths: The Cyborg Theatre of Cathy Weiss'. In *Bodies in Commotion: Disability and Performance*, edited by Carrie Sandahl and Philip Auslander, 95–108. Ann Arbor: The University of Michigan Press, 2008.

Pronger, Brian. 'Post Sport: Transgressing Boundaries in Physical Culture'. In *Sport in Postmodern Times*, edited by Geneviève Rail, 277–98. Albany: State University of New York Press, 1998.

Schwartz, Leslie, and Brian Watermeyer. 'Cyborg Anxiety: Oscar Pistorius and the Boundaries of What It Means to Be Human'. *Disability and Society* 23, no. 2 (2008): 187–90.

Shakespeare, Tom, ed. *The Disability Reader: A Social Science Perspective*. London: Cassell, 1998.

Shields, R. 'Flanerie for Cyborgs'. *Theory, Culture, & Society* 23, no. 7–8 (2006): 209–20.

Shildrick, Margrit, and Janet Price. 'Breaking the Boundaries of the Broken Body'. In *Feminist Theory and the Body: A Reader*, edited by Janet Price and Margrit Shildrick, 432–44. New York: Routledge, 1999.

Shogan, Debra. *The Making of High- Performance Athletes: Discipline, Diversity, and Ethics*. Toronto: University of Toronto Press, 1999.

Shogan, Debra. 'The Social Construction of Disability in a Society of Normalization'. In *Adapted Physical Activity*, edited by G. Wheeler, R. Steadward, and J. Watkinson, 65–74. Edmonton: The University of Alberta Press, 2003.

Smith, Brett, and Andrew Sparkes. 'Changing Bodies, Changing Narratives, and the Consequences of Tellability: A Case Study of Becoming Disabled through Sport'. *Sociology of Health and Illness* 30, no. 2 (2008): 217–36.

Taub, Diane, and Kimberly Greer. 'Physical Activity as a Normalizing Experience for School- Aged Children with Physical Disabilities'. *Journal of Sport and Social Issues* 24, no. 4 (2000): 395–414.

Titchkosky, Tanya. *Reading and Writing Disability Differently: The Textured Life of Embodiment*. Toronto: University of Toronto Press, 2007.

van Hilvoorde, Ivo, and Laurens Landeweerd. 'Disability or Extraordinary Talent- Franscesco Lentini (Three Legs) Versus Oscar Pistorius (No Legs)'. *Sport, Ethics, and Philosophy* 2, no. 2 (2008): 97–111.

Wheatley, Elizabeth. 'Disciplining Bodies at Risk: Cardiac Rehab and the Medicalization of Fitness'. *Journal of Sport and Social Issues* 29, no. 2 (2005): 199–221.

Zola, Irving. *Missing Pieces: A Chronicle of Living with a Disability*. Philadelphia: Temple University Press, 1982.

Participation rates of developing countries in international disability sport: a summary and the importance of statistics for understanding and planning

Jackie Lauff

CEO, SportMatters, Sydney, New South Wales, Australia

This study analyzes the historic participation of developing countries in international disability sport competition to determine how the increases in international participation around the world have presented in developing countries. The data analysis evaluates participating and non-participating developing countries along with the ratio of male to female participation. This analysis provides new insights into the international participation of developing countries and creates a platform for further qualitative investigation to guide development assistance and work towards greater participation from developing countries.

Statistical information is of vital importance to organizations and governments in order to allow them to understand what is really taking place and to plan effectively. Frequently, records vary, or are sometimes inflated.[1] International disability sport is relatively new in many contexts and often there is limited published data available. Participation data in the form of total number of countries and athletes is often used to indicate the size of international games. Interestingly, international governing bodies including the International Olympic Committee (IOC), struggle to maintain accurate data of athletes that participate in each games.

This article summarizes an analysis conducted in 2007 of the participation of developing countries in the Deaflympics, Paralympics and Special Olympics World Games between 1991 and 2006, encompassing four winter and four summer Games. This study provides new insights into the international participation of developing countries in the context of sport, disability and international development. It is intended to provide a platform for further research to guide development assistance and improve international participation in disability sport in developing countries.[2]

Definitions of what is meant by developing country vary considerably, but for the purposes of this analysis, the level of 'Developing Degree' is in accordance with the list of Official Recipients of Aid determined by the Development Assistance Committee (DAC) of the Organization for Economic Co-operation and Development (OECD). Countries are classified as least developed, other low income, lower middle income and upper middle income based on per capita gross national income (GNI). The DAC list revised on December 7, 2005 was used to determine the countries included in the analysis as it was current for reporting on aid flows for 2005, 2006 and 2007. If a country does not appear on the DAC list it is listed as a developed country, with the exception of former states and regional teams.[3]

Table 1. Developing country participation by region, 1991–2006

Results by region	Africa		America		Asia		Europe		Oceania	
	Summer	Winter	Summer	Winter	Summer	Winter	Summer	Winter	Summer	Winter
Number of countries participating	42	7	29	21	30	14	12	9	5	0
Number of countries not participating	13	48	7	15	4	20	0	3	11	16
% Participation	76	13	81	58	88	41	100	75	31	0
% Non-participation	24	87	19	42	12	59	0	25	69	100
Total number of developing countries	55		36		34		12		16	

There are three key areas of analysis addressed in the research:

1. Which developing countries participated in Deaflympic, Paralympic or Special Olympics World Games from 1991 to 2006?
2. Which developing countries did not participate in Deaflympic, Paralympic or Special Olympics World Games from 1991 to 2006?
3. What was the ratio of male to female participation in developing countries in Deaflympic, Paralympic and Special Olympics World Games from 1991 to 2006?

Participation data was collected from the headquarters of each international governing body; International Committee of Sports for the Deaf (ICSD), International Paralympic Committee (IPC) and Special Olympics International (SOI). Within a sport history framework, the electronic databases maintained at each international governing body provided the most accurate primary sources of participation data. The names of countries are as they appear on the DAC list and a country was classified as participating if they participated in at least one Games during the period of analysis (Table 1). The IOC regions of Africa, America, Asia, Europe and Oceania (Figure 1) have been used in the analysis as they allow the best comparison of the disability sport data presented.[4]

Overall, developing country participation increased over time from 1991 to 2006. However, 23% of developing countries had not participated in any games during the period of analysis. Female participation is still less than half the total male participation. Oceania was identified as the region with the least participation historically, followed by Africa and Asia. Special Olympics World Games have comparatively higher participation in Summer and Winter Games in America.[5] The Paralympics saw the greatest increases overall, particularly in Asia. Winter Games participation from developing countries is very low, whilst the participation of women in winter sport is even lower and declining with time.

The following factors may have influenced the participation of developing countries in international disability sport competition:

- political change and the creation of 31 new countries since 1990;
- location of the host city and associated travel costs;
- historic origins and regional growth of international governing bodies and their membership;
- prevalence of disability – intellectual disability, physical and sensory disability, and deafness;
- specific initiatives from international governing bodies including increases in sports, events and classifications offered at international games;

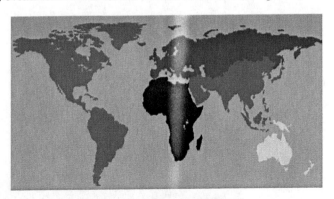

Figure 1.   The five International Olympic Committee regions.

Table 2. Non-participating countries by region.

Region	Number of non-participating countries	
Africa	13	Burundi, Comoros, Democratic Republic of the Congo, Djibouti, Equatorial Guinea, Eritrea, Guinea-Bissau, Liberia, Mayotte, Mozambique, Sao Tome & Principe, Somalia, St. Helena
America:	7	Anguilla, Belize, Dominica, Grenada, Haiti, Montserrat, Turks & Caicos Islands
Asia	4	Bhutan, Democratic People's Republic of Korea, Maldives, Timor-Leste
Europe:	0	
Oceania	11	Cook Islands, Kiribati, Marshall Islands, Federated States of Micronesia, Nauru, Niue, Palau, Solomon Islands, Tokelau, Tuvalu, Wallis & Futuna
Total	35	

- climate and geographic barriers particularly for winter games; and
- economic development, given that one third of the countries listed in Table 2 that did not participate in any Games are Heavily Indebted Poor Countries.

Participation data does not, on its own, explain cause and effect relationships for specific countries. For example, in 2001 Uganda sent 96 athletes to the Summer Deaflympics in Rome and four years later had no athletes at the next Deaflympics in Melbourne. The decrease could have been influenced by any number of factors and the participation data alone cannot tell the story.

This research is a starting point to stimulate evidence-based qualitative and quantitative analysis to guide international development in disability sport. Further research into sporting and organizational structures, case studies and best practice models for development are sorely needed to improve the participation of developing countries.

For the first time, participation data for developing countries has been presented in such a way that researchers can use this data to compare regional and country-specific participation rates, between disability sport movements, male and female participation and analyze trends over time.

Researchers can refer to the thesis at the Norwegian School of Sport Science.[6] A CD-ROM is also available with the full participation data of developed and developing countries from 1991 to 2007 by contacting the author by email or visiting www.sportmatters.org.au. SportMatters is an Australian based NGO launched in 2011 with the aim of making a difference to the people's lives through sport in the Pacific, Asia and Africa.

Notes

[1] Lauff, 'Developing Country Participation', 2007, 12–14.
[2] Lauff, 'Developing Country Participation', 2.
[3] Lauff, 'Notes on Countries and Regions'; Lauff, 'Developing Country Participation', 14–16; Organization for Economic Cooperation and Development, 'History of DAC Lists.
[4] The IPC uses the IOC regions, ICSD have four regions combining Asia and Oceania into Asia–Pacific and SOI have seven regions in their structure.
[5] Data was not available for Special Olympics World Games in 1991, 1993 and 1995 which limits analysis over time.
[6] Lauff, 'Developing Country Participation'. http://assets.sportanddev.org/downloads/70__developing_country_participation_in_international_disability_sport_competition.pdf

References

Lauff, Jackie. 'International Disability Sport Competition: Participation data 1991 to 2007 [CD-ROM], Berlin, Germany: Freie Universität Berlin.

Lauff, Jackie. 'Developing Country Participation in International Disability Sport Competition'. Master's thesis, Norwegian School of Sport Science, Oslo, Norway 2007.

Organization for Economic Cooperation and Development. 'History of DAC Lists of Aid Recipient Countries'. http://www.oecd.org/document/55/0,2340,en_2649_34447_35832055_1_1_1_1,00.html

New direction: disability sport in Malaysia

Selina Khoo

Sport Centre, University of Malaya, Kuala Lumpur, Malaysia

Disability sport in Malaysia has a short history, not much of it has been documented and there remains little published research. This article touches in brief upon the development of disability sport in Malaysia within the context of the broader disability movement. Positive trends and persistent challenges for persons with disabilities within both sport and society are highlighted, as are new directions for future research. These are drawn from interviews of key Malaysian disability sport figures, as well as from recent qualitative data regarding the challenges and barriers faced by high performance athletes in Malaysia.

Disability sport in Malaysia has a short history, not much of which has been documented, and there remains little published research. To address these absences, this article touches briefly upon some historical developments of disability sport in Malaysia within the broader context of disability. Given Malaysia's leading role in the region, and drawing on qualitative data from interviews with key Malaysian disability sport figures, and high-performance athletes, positive trends are highlighted, as are, however, the persistent and corresponding challenges for persons with disabilities within sport and society. Further, new directions for future research are recommended.

Challenges faced

Malaysia is a middle-income country in South East Asia with a per capita gross national income (GNI) in 2010 of RM 26,841 (approximately US$6,764). In 2011, the population was estimated at 26 million, with a diverse population of different cultural values; 54.5% of the population is Malay, 24.9% Chinese, 7.4% Indian, 11.8% other indigenous ethnic groups (aborigines in Peninsula Malaysia and indigenous groups in East Malaysia who are not Muslim) and 1.4% others (including Eurasians, as well as Malaysians of European and Middle eastern descent).[1]

Unfortunately, there are no exact figures for the number of persons with disabilities in the country. This problem is also faced by many other countries in East Asia and the Pacific.[2] A lack of accurate statistics has made it difficult to formulate policies and plan programmes, intervention and training for the disabled in Malaysia. Moreover, given that government registration of persons with disabilities is currently voluntary, the numbers are often underreported. A total of 220,250 persons with disabilities were registered with the Department of Social Welfare in 2007; this represents less than 1% of Malaysia's total population of 25.5 million.[3] It remains unclear whether this is due to choice or to a lack of information about the registration process. According to Shamsiah Abdul Rahman, former Advisor to the Minister of Women, Family and Community Development, many persons with disabilities only register when they need benefits[4] (such as educational allowance, income tax relief, medical care in government hospitals and concessions on travel).

Government policy towards persons with disabilities: support for, and challenges of, inclusion

The definition of persons with disabilities has shifted from the medical model to incorporate the social model (Persons with Disabilities Act 2008), 'those who have long term physical, mental, intellectual or sensory impairments which in interaction with various barriers may hinder their full and effective participation in society'.[5] Further, Ng Yen Yen, former Minister of Women, Family and Community Development, claims that Malaysia has moved from a charity-based programme to a rights-based approach so as to address the issues affecting persons with disabilities.[6] Finally, the language that is used around disability in Malaysia has changed, as can be seen in both the official Malay language and English. In the past, the Malay word used for persons with disabilities was 'cacat' meaning handicapped. This word is no longer used, but rather 'orang kurang upaya' (the equivalent of persons with disabilities) is used and accepted by both the government and the general public. Given Linton's claim that language about disability is a powerful tool in defining disability culture (cited in Gilson and Depoy 1998),[7] this may indeed be seen as positive.

Since the launch of the World Programme of Action Concerning Disabled Persons in 1982, the government of Malaysia has introduced various policies and programmes, including Job Coach, to improve the quality of life of persons with disabilities.[8] According to the then Director of Rehabilitation of the Department of Social Welfare, Md Rashid Ismail, policies and programmes for persons with disabilities in the country are guided by the strategic goals of the National Social Welfare Policy (introduced in 1990 to create an independent, equitable, caring society)[9] which emphasizes the attainment of self-reliance, equalization of opportunities for the less fortunate and fostering the spirit of mutual help and support towards enhancing a caring culture.[10] The Biwako Millenium Framework was adopted in 2002. Additionally, but not before many years of lobbying by disability organizations, the Persons with Disabilities Act of 2008 marked a major legislative milestone.

The Act provides 'for the registration, protection, rehabilitation, development and wellbeing of persons with disabilities, the establishment of the National Council for Persons with Disabilities, and for matters connected therewith'.[11] The functions of the National Council for Persons with Disabilities include overseeing, coordinating, monitoring and evaluating the implementation of national policies and plans pertaining to persons with disabilities. The Act states that persons with disabilities have the right to public transport, housing, education, employment and health care.

The Act, though a major step forward, does not offer remedies for persons with disabilities who face discrimination in these areas, nor does it impose sanctions for non-compliance.[12] This is a sore point for representatives from various disability organizations who advised on the initial draft of the bill, and who claim that the Act is a watered down version of the original draft. Moreover, persons with disabilities lack the opportunity to fight legally; instead they are limited to fight for their rights via the media and government memorandums.

Government support for disability sport

It is thus within the broader context of disability in Malaysia that the government has begun to support sport for persons with disabilities. For example, despite its limitations, the Persons with Disabilities Act 2008 states explicitly the right of persons with disabilities to participate in recreation, leisure and sports activities.[13] Additionally, the National Sports Policy has (since 1988) been stressing the importance of Sport for All, which includes disability sport.[14] Further, funding for disability sport currently comes from the Ministry of Youth and Sports, who are also responsible for the development of disability sport and a unit under the ministry run programmes like coaching clinics, annual recreation activities for persons with disabilities and sports circuits for various sports. Unfortunately, however, funding for disability sport is considerably less compared with funding for non-disabled sport, and according to Radha Krishnan, General Manager of the Malaysian Paralympic Council, such circuits have not been very successful in identifying new athletes and developing sports in the states[15] due in large part to a lack of publicity or awareness of these circuits.

Under the National Sports Council, the Paralympic division (established 2007) provides training and support for athletes with a disability, including nutrition and sports psychology. The government also promotes equal opportunities for athletes with a disability, namely training in the same venue (National Sports Council facility, Kuala Lumpur) and receiving the same allowance during training. Unfortunately, the rewards for winning at the Olympic and Paralympic Games are not equal, for example, as of 2008 Malaysian Olympic gold medal winners earn more than three times that of Paralympic gold medallists.[16]

Disability sports organizations in Malaysia: the Malaysian Paralympic Council

The disability sport movement in Malaysia runs parallel to the non-disabled sport movement. Given that both have their own structures in place, cooperation between disability and non-disabled sport has proved minimal. There are, however, some national sports associations that are opening their doors to disability sport, such as cycling, sailing and table tennis, and the government provides support to coaching and sport science through the National Sports Council and the Ministry of Youth and Sports.

The national governing body for sports for persons with disabilities is the Malaysian Paralympic Council.[17] The objectives of the Council are to prepare athletes for international events, encourage an active lifestyle for persons with disabilities, introduce new sports and recreation programmes, establish more training facilities for greater participation, and train coaches, classifiers and technical officials.[18] The Malaysian Paralympic Council has organized international accredited technical and classification courses in a variety of sports, such as athletics, archery, wheelchair basketball, powerlifting, swimming and table tennis. Many of these courses were held prior to Malaysia hosting the 2006 Far East and South Pacific (FESPIC) Games (a multidisability and multisport competition for Asia and the South Pacific) for the purposes of creating more accredited technical officials and classifiers in the region. Despite Malaysia gaining numerous internationally accredited classifiers and technical officials in a variety of sports, this has not significantly impacted the development of disability sport in the country, primarily because most of these qualified personnel only provide support during sport events, but do not initiate any new programmes.

Competitions: participating and hosting

The Malaysian Paralympiad, a national multisport and multidisability sport competition, has been organized biennially in Malaysia since 1982, and has grown steadily in terms of the variety of sports and number of participants, with the aim of training coaches and developing technical skills.[19] Despite such growth, the Malaysian Paralympiad has helped to develop sport to only a limited degree given that there is no year-long training, rather most of the training for the athletes is held prior to competition; also there are hardly any regular sports activities and competitions.

Malaysia has been taking part in international multisport and multidisability competition since the 1970s, namely the Paralympic, FEPSIC and Association of Southeast Asian Nations (ASEAN) Para Games (a biennial multisport and multidisability championship for athletes with a disability in South East Asia). The 1992 Paralympic Games was the first time that Malaysian athletes with a disability who won medals at international competitions received cash incentives from the government. Malaysian athletes did not win any medals at subsequent Paralympic Games, until Siow Lee Chan notably became the first female Malaysian medal winner, earning a bronze for powerlifting at the 2008 Beijing Paralympic Games.

Within the Asia–Pacific region, disability sport first began with the FESPIC Federation. The FESPIC Federation was originally established in 1974 to encourage disability sport in the Far East and South Pacific, as well as to promote disability sport in the region given the limited opportunities for persons with disabilities to participate in sports.[20] The first FESPIC Games were held in Oita City in Japan in 1975. Malaysia first participated in 1982 in Hong Kong,[21] with their participation and medal counts improving over the years; their best performance occurred in 2006 at the 9th and final FESPIC Games where Malaysia won 44 gold, 60 silver and 71 bronze medals. There are a number of reasons for this huge increase in medal success including home advantage and a bigger Malaysian contingent. The athletes also trained more aggressively for the competition. Unfortunately, the success of the Malaysian team at the 2006 FESPIC Games did not translated into more funding for disability sport. It did, however, slightly improve media coverage for the Games.

At the 2006 FESPIC Games, disability sport in the region was restructured. The FESPIC Federation was dissolved and the Asian Paralympic Committee was established, this was done so that these international games would coordinate with the International Paralympic Committee's new regional structure in which each region has its own committee. A Malaysian, Zainal Abu Zarin was elected President of the Asian Paralympic Committee. Zainal had also been instrumental in establishing the ASEAN Para Sports Federation in 2001 with the aim to enhance solidarity among South East Asian nations.

In addition to participating in international competitions, Malaysia has also played host to numerous international disability sport competitions. Malaysia's active role in hosting disability sport events is mainly due to the vision of the Malaysian Paralympic Council and its aim to raise the profile of disability sport in Malaysia. Members of the council also hold positions in international disability sports organizations, including the International Paralympic Committee. Despite an increased awareness of disability sport in the country, media coverage of disability sports remains minimal. Moreover, few spectators attend the free competitions; in fact most of them are volunteers and athletes from other teams.

Conclusion

It can be concluded that there is indeed government support for persons with disabilities in Malaysia, both within society and within sport. Yet, there remains a discrepancy between policy and practice, for although *policies* are in place which promotes the right to participate in recreation, leisure and sport, in reality there are few *programmes* in place. Moreover, accessibility to existing programmes, both in terms of facilities and transportation, remains an enormous obstacle. Additionally, acknowledging the Malaysian government's endorsement of participation in, and hosting of, national and international sport competitions, and the marked improvement in media coverage over the years, sponsorship, coaching and athlete incentives, as well media attention and public awareness for athletes with a disability, all remain lower than their non-disabled counterparts.

The disparities between non-disabled and disability sport should be addressed and emphasis given to equality and equity. Athletes with a disability should be provided with training and incentives that equal their non-disabled counterparts, for they too don the national colours and can bring glory to their country. In fact, the positive inroads, and remaining roadblocks, encountered by Malaysian athletes with a disability, prompt questions both of rights and of nationhood, given the national pride tied to sporting performance and the assertion by athletes with a disability of their right, not just to be permitted equal access to sporting opportunities, but to be held in equal regard to able-bodied athletes, or rather their fellow country women and men.

Malaysia, with its great diversity, limited disability statistics, short, poorly documented history of disability sport, as well as its various societal and sporting disability inroads and roadblocks, actually plays a leading role in the Asia–Pacific region. Leading in a multitude of capacities, such as disability language and policies, as well as medal counts and hosting history, Malaysia inspires a variety of new research directions and questions. For example, in terms of gender, why did it take until 2008 for the first female to win a medal? Are issues of access or perceptions different for women and men with disabilities?

There should also be more effort to encourage Malaysians with disabilities to take up sport. This is because sport is a means of social integration and rehabilitation, as well as a way of improving quality of life. More parties should be involved in providing sports for persons with disabilities. Ways to overcome current barriers like inaccessible facilities and transport should be sought. Future research can look at ways to attract more persons with disabilities into sport. This will not only ensure a healthy population, but will also produce a bigger talent pool from which to choose for elite competition. An investment in mass sports would benefit high-performance sport in the future.

Acknowledgements

The author would like to express appreciation for the invaluable information provided in personal interviews by the following: Shamsiah Abdul Rahman, former Advisor to the Minister of Women, Family and Community Development, Radha Krishnan, the General Manager of the Malaysian Paralympic Council, Azahari Abdullah, Committee Member of the Little People Welfare Association of Malaysia, Joseph Lau, Chairman of Special Olympics Malaysia and Naziaty Mohd Yaacob, Senior Lecturer, Department of Architecture, Faculty of Built Environment, at the University of Malaya.

Notes

[1] Department of Statistics, http://www.statistics.gov.my; *Monthly Statistical Bulletin Malaysia*, 9.
[2] Takamine, 'Disability Issues in East Asia', 9. In Malaysia, the number of persons with disabilities per household was not asked in the last population census in 2000. The question was asked in the 2010 census so there would be more accurate statistics on the number of persons with disabilities in Malaysia.
[3] Official website of the Depatrtment of Social Welfare of Malaysia, http://www.jkm.gov.my.
[4] Shamsiah Abdul Rahman, in discussion with author, May 25, 2009.
[5] Government of Malaysia, *Laws of Malaysia Act 865*, 9.
[6] Yee, 'Rights of Disabled People To Be Taken Care Of'.
[7] Gilson and Depoy, 'Multiculturalism and Disability', 212.
[8] Official website of the Depatrtment of Social Welfare of Malaysia, http://www.jkm.gov.my.
[9] Department of Social Welfare, *National Social Welfare Policy*, 3–4.

[10] Ismail, 'Country Paper'. Paper presented at Expert Group Meeting and Seminar on an International Convention to Protect and Promote the Rights and Dignity of Persons with Disabilities.

[11] Government of Malaysia, *Laws of Malaysia Act 865*, 7.

[12] Yue, 'Falling Short'. The Barrier-Free Environment and Accessible Transport Group is a collation of 18 disability groups that has lobbied extensively for accessible transportation and inclusiveness in all aspects of society including sport.

[13] Government of Malaysia, *Laws of Malaysia Act 865*, 26.

[14] Ministry of Youth and Sports, *National Sports Policy 1988*, 5, 10.

[15] Radha Krishnan, in discussion with author, May 25, 2009.

[16] Ibid. Malaysians who win a gold medal at the Olympic Games will receive RM 1 million (approximately US$303,030), whereas gold medallists at the Parlaympic Games receive RM 300,000 (US$90,909). A silver medallist at the Olympics will receive RM 300,000, whereas a silver medallist at the Paralympics will receive RM 200,000 (US$60,606). A bronze medallist at the Olympics will receive RM 200,000, which is double that received by the bronze medallist at the Paralympics. In addition, only Olympic athletes receive a pension.

[17] Khoo, 'Paralympic Organizations', 154. The Malaysian Sports Council for the Disabled, a non-profit organization, was established on May 18, 1989, and renamed the Malaysian Paralympic Council in 1996.

[18] Ibid. Medical classifiers have been trained in wheelchair basketball, badminton, tenpin bowling and powerlifting, and accredited technical officials for athletics, table tennis, wheelchair basketball, goalball, powerlifting, boccia, lawn bowls, archery and volleyball.

[19] Ibid. The competition was originally called the National Sport for the Disabled. The name was changed to the Malaysian Paralympiad in 1998.

[20] FESPIC Federation, *FESPIC Federation*. The FESPIC Games were the largest competition for athletes with a disability in Asia and Oceania and the second largest after the Paralympic Games. The Games followed a four-year cycle and was held in the even years that alternate with the Olympic Games.

[21] Malaysian Paralympic Council, *Participation in International Sports Competitions*, 2.

References

Department of Social Welfare. *National Social Welfare Policy 1990*. Kuala Lumpur, Malaysia: Government of Malaysia, 1990.

Department of Statistics. *Monthly Statistical Bulletin Malaysia April 2011*. Kuala Lumpur, Malaysia: Department of Statistics, 2011.

FESPIC Federation. *FESPIC Federation: Its Games and History: A Comprehensive Guide*. Kuala Lumpur, Malaysia: FESPIC Federation, 2006. http://www.taiyonoie.or.jp/fespic/.

Gilson, Stephen French, and Elizabeth Depoy. 'Multiculturalism and Disability: A Critical Perspective'. *Disability and Society* 15, no. 2 (2000): 207–18.

Government of Malaysia. *Laws of Malaysia Act 865: Persons with Disabilities Act 2008*. Kuala Lumpur, Malaysia: Percetakan Nasional Malaysia Berhad, 2008.

Ismail, Md Rashid. 'Country Paper: Malaysia'. Paper presented at Expert Group Meeting and Seminar on an International Convention to Protect and Promote the Rights and Dignity of Persons with Disabilities, Bangkok, Thailand, June 2–4 2003.

Khoo, Selina. 'Paralympic Organizations and National Competitions'. *Encyclopaedia of Malaysia: Sports and Recreation*. Singapore: Archipelago Press, 2008.

Malaysian Paralympic Council. *Participation in International Sports Competitions*. Kuala Lumpur, Malaysia: 2008.

Ministry of Youth and Sports. *National Sports Policy 1988*. Kuala Lumpur, Malaysia: Government of Malaysia, 1988.

Takamine, Yutaka. 'Disability Issues in East Asia: Review and Ways Forward'. Working Paper No. 2004-1 (May) 2004.

Yee. 'Rights of Disabled People To Be Taken Care Of'. *The Star Online*, August 18, 2008. http://thestar.com.my

Yue. 'Falling Short'. *The Star Online*, January 28, 2009. Lifestyles section. http://thestar.com.my

Risk of catastrophic injury in sports and recreation

Charles H. Tator

Division of Neurosurgery, Toronto Western Hospital, University of Toronto, Toronto, Canada; Founder, ThinkFirst Canada

Many factors have contributed to the increasing risk of sustaining a catastrophic injury in sports and recreation that has occurred in most countries. Greater involvement in high-risk activities, more aggressive play and advanced technology have increased the speed and force of collisions in team sports such as hockey and football, and in individual recreational activities such as snowmobiling or driving an all-terrain vehicle (ATV). There is also more public attention and greater participation in extreme manoeuvres in risky activities such as snowboarding, BMX and mountain bicycling, and paragliding. Thrill seekers are stimulated to attempt stunts and actions for which they are often untrained and unskilled. In some high-risk activities, alcohol, drugs and superficial media portrayal overcome or cloud the normal instinct towards risk aversion and self-protection. Unfortunately, catastrophic injuries are very costly in terms of grief, disappointment and financial burden for the participants, families and societies. The purpose of this article is to describe the problem of increased participation in an increasing array of risky sports and recreation activities and to offer some strategies for reducing the risk of catastrophic injury. Further research is required to identify and mitigate risk. It is also important for individuals and for societies to develop and propagate effective injury prevention strategies.

Trauma in general is a major burden to the individual and to society, and many Western societies consider trauma to be at epidemic proportions. Sports and recreation comprise a significant percentage of trauma in most developed countries, with some estimates as high as 20%.[1] Furthermore, there is evidence that the incidence of these injuries is rising in many countries because there is more risk-taking behaviour.[2] The personal, familial and societal costs of injuries are very high, in particualrt the costs of catastrophic injuries to the central nervous system in children and youth, including such major trauma such as head injuries in bicycling or spinal cord injuries in diving into shallow water. Most injuries in sports and recreation are considered preventable, and studies of their incidence, causes and demographic features can lead to targeted effective prevention strategies.[3] This is especially important because even with the major advances in the field of neuroscience, there is still no proven treatment for regeneration of lost neural tissue in the brain or spinal cord. The focus of this article is the province of Ontario in Canada. Climate, geography and cultural factors tied to tradition, gender and socio-economic factors impact on sport injuries, and unfortunately there is a limited literature from low and middle income countries to make comparisons.

Although there have been several studies addressing risk factors and risk management in sports,[4] there have been very few reports from anywhere in the world with actual data on the population risk of catastrophic injuries in sports and recreation. Also, few studies have documented the relative risk of various sports and recreation injuries, either catastrophic or non-catastrophic. Indeed, of the multitude of studies of injuries in sports and recreation, only a small number have focused on catastrophic injuries.[5] Mueller's catastrophic sports injury registry at the University of North Carolina in the USA has been a rich source of information about catastrophic head and spine injuries, but mainly covers high school and college players with an emphasis on American football.[6] This group analysed the risk factors in American football and found higher risk in games rather than practice, and higher risk in those with a history of prior injury, older players, players with additional years of playing experience, and when there is less coaching experience.[7] Most studies have included all types of injuries, and this has made it difficult to extract data on catastrophic injuries. Examples of such studies are those by Spinks and McClure[8] who surveyed injuries in 14 activities in Australia, and de Loes and Goldie who surveyed 17 activities in Sweden;[9] in both studies, ice hockey had the highest risk. The Spinks and McClure study was a meta-analysis of 48 reports from various countries and showed the relative risk among sports for youths aged 15 and under in a total of 14 sports: as noted above, ice hockey had the highest injury rates and soccer the lowest. Pringle et al., surveyed injuries in New Zealand in only three activities and in the 5–15year-old group.[10] Schmikli et al., conducted a nationwide telephone survey in the Netherlands and derived national data on the overall incidence of injuries in all activities, but only in those aged less than 55 years, and many recreational activities were excluded such as all-terrain vehicles (ATVs).[11] Chang et al., assessed the relative risk of various water-related activities in Hawaii,[12] and there are analyses of specific risk factors such as body checking in ice hockey.[13] The risk of overuse injuries in a specific age group in a specific sport has also been assessed.[14]

A small number of reports have calculated the risk of sports/recreation injuries from the standpoint of injury prevention. For example, an analysis of risk behaviours among youths in grades 6–10 injured in physical activities in schools showed that interventions modifying the environment were more effective for prevention than those targeting the participants.[15] In the same age group, Koven et al., divided the risks of head and neck injuries between psychological and lifestyle risks in sports and other activities, and found that only lifestyle risks were directly related to injury incidence.[16] Pickett et al., found that a supportive home and school environment provided some protection against injury in youths aged 10–16 years.[17]

The risks of specific injuries among several countries have also been compared. For example, Ackery et al., performed an international study of head and spinal injuries in alpine skiing and snowboarding,[18] and showed the rising incidence of catastrophic injuries in these sports in many countries. They attributed the rise to increased speed and risk-taking behaviour, especially aerial manoeuvres.

Recommendations for future studies of catastrophic sports and recreation injuries
Definition of sports and recreation activities
With respect to the type of activities to be included, all individual or team sports and fitness programmes, supervised and unsupervised, amateur and professional, should be included. Similarly, all recreational activities should be included such as motor sports, bicycling, diving, boating and other water sports, supervised or unsupervised. All bicycling injuries in children should be included, but adults injured bicycling to work or bicycling

for transportation rather than for sport or recreation should be excluded. Injuries to either participants or officials in sports shows should be included, but injuries to spectators should be excluded.

Definition of catastrophic injury in sports and recreation

There is no universally accepted definition of catastrophic injury in sports and recreation. In the Ontario study referred to above, catastrophic injury was defined as any injury causing death or permanent or long-term disability as a result of participation in a sport or recreational activity. Injuries such as extradural haematoma in which blood accumulates between the brain and the skull are obvious inclusions, but so are almost all eye injuries because of their *potential* to cause permanent or long-term disability. The following should be included as catastrophic injuries: drowning; head injury of severity greater than concussion; spinal injury with fracture or ligamentous spinal injury leading to instability, or disc herniation; spinal cord injury, even if transient; nerve root injury; eye injury; facial fracture, except nasal fracture; internal injury to the thoracic, abdominal or pelvic organs; arterial injury to the neck or limbs; laryngeal injury; and major nerve or brachial plexus injury (injury to the large nerve trunks supplying the upper limbs). Multiple injuries are frequent in sports and recreation, especially in motor sports, and therefore, the number of catastrophic injuries in most sports or recreational activities usually exceeds the number of participants who sustain the injuries. The following types of injuries should be excluded: simple, uncomplicated concussion; musculoskeletal injury to the limbs including fractures; soft tissue injuries such as contusion, sprain or dislocation, except those with actual or threatened loss of a limb; whiplash injury; neck or back strain; and nasal fracture. Near-drowning should be included because of its potential to cause permanent disability. One might question the exclusion of concussion since it is a brain injury, and repeated concussions can have catastrophic long-term consequences such as dementia.[19]

Methods for calculation of risk rates in sports and recreation

The calculation of personal and population risk rates requires 'denominator data' that quantitates participation in sports and recreational activities. As indicated in the review by Spinks and McClure referred to above there are many ways to calculate participation or exposure, varying from a 'season' to an individual exposure such as a bicycle ride.[20] Participation may also be defined as any taking part in a given activity during a given period, such as in a sports 'season' or calendar year. Participation for a population may be obtained by actual counting of participants at sporting venues or by surveillance techniques such as random telephone surveys that employ questionnaires. However, population participation data based on surveillance has serious limitations for assessing catastrophic injury, especially for less-popular sports. Surveillance alone will miss many catastrophic injuries because of their relative rarity. Also, since catastrophic injuries are much less common than non-catastrophic injuries, they would represent the minority of injuries in surveillance studies.

Tator recently reported a comprehensive study of catastrophic injuries in all sports and recreation activities in Ontario, a province in Canada with apopulation of approximately 10 million. Several population risks were identified including age, gender, activity, season, terrain/location, alcohol consumption, supervision, rules and enforcement and safety equipment.[21] Annually, during each of the years of the study from 1986 to 1995, 539 Ontarians, 158 of whom died, sustained catastrophic injuries in approximately 100 different sports and recreation activities. Head and spine injuries and drowning were the most frequent types of injury. Males comprised 82.7% of the injured participants and 17.3% were female. For both genders, the mean and median ages of survivors were 23.6 and 20.0 years, respectively, and for fatalities the mean and median ages 31.6 and 29.0 years, respectively. Although the ages ranged from 3 to 85 years, it was primarily young participants who were injured. Risk was calculated in two ways: population risk was defined as the number of injuries per 100,000 of the population and reflects the risk to society; and personal risk was defined as the number of injured participants per 100,000 participants which reflects the personal risk undertaken by the participant. The top ten population risk activities in order were snowmobiling, bicycling, hockey, fishing, boating, diving, swimming, baseball, ATV riding and alpine skiing. The top ten personal risk activities in order were diving, snowmobiling, parachuting, tobogganing, hang gliding, water polo, equestrian activities, scuba diving, hunting and fishing.

Demographic risk factors in catastrophic injuries in sports and recreation

Age

Age is a major risk factor in determining injury. In general, catastrophic injuries in sports and recreation affect young people, although the mean age of the population at risk varies greatly among activities. Young age groups sustain catastrophic injuries in bicycling, tobogganing, snowboarding, hockey and on playgrounds. By contrast, in other activities such as fishing or hunting, the mean age is much older.[22] Flying and other air sports also affects older participants.

Gender

Males are much greater risk takers than females, and most studies of catastrophic injuries show much higher incidence rates in males. In Tator's Ontario study, the male/female ratio for catastrophic injuries was 4.8, indicating that injuries to males were 4.8 times more frequent than injuries to females; and in all activities except equestrian sports, injuries to males outnumbered those to females, usually by a large percentage.[23] In that study, the male gender risk factor was one of the strongest risks for catastrophic injury in almost all activities, and this contrasts markedly with non-catastrophic injuries, or injuries in general in sports and recreation, where injury rates in females are generally equal to or higher than injury rates in males.[24]

Alcohol consumption

In the Ontario study, water and motor sports had the highest incidence of alcohol consumption, approaching 50% of fatalities in the water sports group, whereas in other activities such as hockey there were virtually no instances of injured participants having consumed alcohol.[25]

Type of activity

The type of activity is a major factor determining both population risk and personal risk. Water sports as a group were the leading cause of injury in the Ontario study, accounting for 24.4% of all injuries.[26] Motor sports were second at 19.8%, winter sports third at 16.3%, and bicycling fourth at 13.4% of all injuries. With respect to the 631 fatalities in the Ontario study, water sports accounted for 52.9% of all fatalities, while 23.1% were due to motor sports and

10.6% were due to bicycling. There were no fatalities in some activities such as baseball and racquet sports.[27] In the water sports category, the major activities producing injury were fishing, boating, swimming and diving. Fishing caused 18.5% of all fatalities and was the highest cause of all fatalities in the water sports group and the second highest in fatalities overall, second only to snowmobiling which caused 19.0% of all fatalities. Snowmobiling was the highest single activity leading to catastrophic injury and accounted for 13.5% of all fatal and non-fatal catastrophic injuries. ATV crashes were another frequent cause of catastrophic injury. Bicycling caused 13.4% of all injuries and was the second highest cause (second only to snowmobiling) of total injuries including survivors and fatalities, and accounted for 10.6% of fatalities. Hockey caused the highest number of injuries in the winter activities group, and alpine skiing and tobogganing also produced large numbers of injuries in this group. Field sports as a group did not cause many catastrophic injuries, and there were only small numbers of injuries in football and rugby. Although only 25 hunters sustained catastrophic injuries, 15 were fatal (2.4% of the total number of fatalities).

Terrain, venue

The location or terrain of catastrophic injuries varies greatly with the type of activity. In the Ontario study, the most frequent site was lakes and rivers (24%), followed by roads/streets (19%) and open terrain (15%).[28] Arenas (10%), playing fields and playgrounds (9%) and pools (4%) were also frequent sites. It was of major interest that there were more diving injuries in pools than in lakes or rivers. A large number of the catastrophic snowmobiling injuries occurred in lakes and rivers, most of which were drowning, as opposed to injuries on open terrain and on streets and roads. Avalanches are an increasing cause of fatalities in Canada.

Supervision and organizations involved

In the Ontario study, only 22.4% of catastrophic injuries occurred under supervision.[29] The injuries most likely to occur in supervised settings were hockey, baseball, floor sports and field sports, whereas activities with a much greater preponderance of injuries in unsupervised settings were water sports, bicycling hunting, and motor sports. The types of organizations frequently involved were schools, sports leagues and clubs or fitness centres. The majority of hockey injuries occurred in organized community league settings. Baseball injuries also frequently occurred in community leagues. By contrast, almost none of the water-related injuries occurred in organized settings. In badminton, field sports, floor hockey, football, rugby and gymnastics, approximately half the cases with available data occurred in schools. Most injuries in motor sports such as snowmobiling and ATV riding did not occur in organized settings.

Season and months

The seasonal nature of many high risk sports and recreation activities leads to high risk and low risk months for many catastrophic injuries, especially relevant for water sports in the summer months and snow sports in the winter months.

Location and country

The lack of population-based studies for most countries makes it impossible to compare the risk rates among countries for catastrophic injuries in sports and recreation.

Training and knowledge

Lack of training is a major factor for most types of catastrophic injuries in sports and recreation. Similarly, lack of knowledge of safety measures is frequently cited for high speed activities such as motor sports but also for water and snow sports.[30]

Safety equipment

Failure to use safety equipment is a major risk factor in almost every type of sport or recreational activity. Personal flotation devices and life jackets are extremely effective for preventing drowning in all water activities. Helmets are now mandatory in an increasing number of high-risk activities such as alpine racing and ice hockey, and strongly recommended in many additional activities such as tobogganing and sledding. In bicycling, helmets have been shown to provide about 85% protection against head injury.[31]

Rules/enforcement

The introduction of new rules targeting high risk behaviours identified by analyses of injury mechanisms has resulted in a reduction in catastrophic injuries in team sports. For example, cervical spinal cord injuries have been reduced in ice hockey as a result of the introduction of specific rules against pushing/checking from behind which had been identified as a common mechanism of injury.[32] Similarly, in rugby, a rule against collapse of the scrum has also resulted in a reduction in cervical spinal cord injuries.[33] Lack of enforcement of effective rules is also a major risk factor.

Risk compensation

Proponents of the risk compensation theory in sports and recreation would say, for example, that the wearing of safety equipment such as helmets might increase risk taking behaviour among participants or increase the tolerance threshold of their parents or coaches.[34] However, Pless et al. found no evidence for risk compensation in their study of youth with respect to the wearing of protective equipment,[35] and Tator found no evidence that risk compensation had any role to play in the Ontario study.[36]

Conclusions

Many factors affect the population and personal risks of catastrophic injuries in sports and recreation. The population and personal risk rates vary greatly among the various activities and depend on age, gender, training, terrain/location, season, alcohol and drug abuse, protective equipment and other factors that are amenable to injury prevention strategies. Introduction of new rules where appropriate and enforcement of existing rules are effective injury-prevention strategies. It is concluded that the majority of catastrophic injuries in sports and recreation are preventable by a combination of measures. Greater attention to identified risk factors and prevention programmes could save many lives, prevent the disablement of many athletes and participants, and reduce the costs to society. Few studies have documented the relative risk of various sports and recreation injuries, either catastrophic or non-catastrophic. It would be useful if additional studies were conducted to help in the better understanding of the risk factors in diverse cultural settings, particularly as there is little in the literature about injuries in low and middle income countries where there is increasing participation in higher risk sport activities by both tourists and residents.

Notes

1 Spinks and McClure, 'Quantifying the Risk of Sports Injury', 548–557; discussion, 557.
2 Lord, Tator, and Wells, 'Examining Ontario Deaths Due to All-Terrain Vehicles', 343–349; Ackery et al., 'An International Review of Head and Spinal Cord Injuries', 368–375.
3 Tator, *Catastrophic Injuries in Sports and Recreation*.
4 Emery, 'Risk Factors for Injury in Child and Adolescent Sport', 256–268; Fuller, 'Managing the Risk of Injury in Sport', 182–87. Fuller and Drawer, 'The Application of Risk Management in Sport', 349–356; Hopkins et al., 'Risk Factors and Risk Statistics for Sports Injuries', 208–210; Meeuwisse et al., 'A Dynamic Model of Etiology in Sport Injury', 215–219.
5 Mueller, 'Catastrophic Sports Injuries', 57–58.
6 Boden et al., 'Catastrophic Cervical Spine Injuries', 1223–1232; Cantu and Mueller, 'The Prevention of Catastrophic Head and Spine Injuries', 981–986.
7 Knowles et al., 'Risk Factors for Injury Among High School Football Players', 302–310.
8 pinks and McClure, 'Quantifying the Risk of Sports Injury', 548–557; discussion, 557.
9 de Loes and Goldie, 'Incidence Rate of Injuries During Sport Activity', 461–467.
10 Pringle, McNair, and Stanley, 'Incidence of Sporting Injury in New Zealand', 49–52.
11 Schmikli et al., 'National Survey on Sports Injuries', 101–106.
12 Chang et al., 'Risk Factors for Water Sports-related Cervical Spine Injuries', 1041–1046.
13 Emery and Meeuwisse, 'Injury Rates', 1960–1969.
14 Gerrard, 'Overuse Injury and Growing Bones', 14–18.
15 Janssen et al., 'Influence of Multiple Risk Behaviours', 672–680.
16 Koven et al., 'Multiple Risk Behaviour', 240–246.
17 Pickett et al., 'Associations Between Risk Behaviour and Injury', 87–92.
18 Ackery et al., 'An International Review of Head and Spinal Cord Injuries', 368–375.
19 McKee et al., 'Chronic Traumatic Encephalopathy in Athletes', 709–735.
20 Spinks and McClure, 'Quantifying the Risk of Sports Injury', 548–557; discussion, 557.
21 Tator, *Catastrophic Injuries in Sports and Recreation*.
22 Ibid.
23 Ibid.
24 Spinks and McClure, 'Quantifying the Risk of Sports Injury', 548–557; discussion, 557.
25 Tator, *Catastrophic Injuries in Sports and Recreation*.
26 Ibid.
27 Ibid.
28 Ibid.
29 Ibid.
30 Ibid.
31 Macpherson and Spinks, 'Bicycle Helmet Legislation'.
32 Tator, Provvidenza, and Cassidy, 'Spinal Injuries in Canadian Ice Hockey', 451–456.
33 Bohu et al., 'Declining Incidence of Catastrophic Cervical Spine Injuries', 319–323.
34 Morrongiello and Major, 'Influence of Safety Gear on Parental Perceptions of Injury Risk', 27–31; Morrongiello, Walpole, and Lasenby, 'Understanding Children's Injury-Risk Behaviour', 618–623.
35 Pless, Magdalinos, and Hagel, 'Risk-Compensation Behaviour in Children', 610–614.
36 Tator, *Catastrophic Injuries in Sports and Recreation*.

References

Ackery, A., B.E. Hagel, C. Provvidenza, and C.H. Tator. 'An International Review of Head and Spinal Cord Injuries in Alpine Skiing and Snowboarding'. *Injury Prevention* 13 (2007): 368–75.
Boden, B.P., R.L. Tacchetti, R.C. Cantu, S.B. Knowles, and F.O. Mueller. 'Catastrophic Cervical Spine Injuries in High School and College Football Players'. *American Journal of Sports Medicine* 34 (2006): 1223–32.

Bohu, Y., M. Julia, C. Bagate, J.C. Peyrin, J.P. Colonna, P. Thoreux, and H. Pascal-Moussellard. 'Declining Incidence of Catastrophic Cervical Spine Injuries in French Rugby: 1996–2006'. *American Journal of Sports Medicine* 37 (2009): 319–23.

Cantu, R.C., and F.O. Mueller. 'The Prevention of Catastrophic Head and Spine Injuries in High School and College Sports'. *British Journal of Sports Medicine* 43 (2009): 981–86.

Chang, S.K., G.T. Tominaga, J.H. Wong, E.J. Weldon, and K.T. Kaan. 'Risk Factors for Water Sports-related Cervical Spine Injuries'. *Journal of Trauma* 60 (2006): 1041–46.

de Loes, M., and I. Goldie. 'Incidence Rate of Injuries During Sport Activity and Physical Exercise in a Rural Swedish Municipality: Incidence Rates in 17 Sports'. *International Journal of Sports Medicine* 9 (1998): 461–67.

Emery, C.A. 'Risk Factors for Injury in Child and Adolescent Sport: A Systematic Review of the Literature'. *Clinical Journal of Sport Medicine* 13 (2003): 256–68.

Emery, C.A., and W.H. Meeuwisse. 'Injury Rates, Risk Factors, and Mechanisms of Injury in Minor Hockey'. *American Journal of Sports Medicine* 34 (2006): 1960–69.

Fuller, C., and S. Drawer. 'The Application of Risk Management in Sport'. *Sports Medicine* 34 (2004): 349–56.

Fuller, C.W. 'Managing the Risk of Injury in Sport'. *Clinical Journal of Sport Medicine* 17 (2007): 182–87.

Gerrard, D.F. 'Overuse Injury and Growing Bones: The Young Athlete at Risk'. *British Journal of Sports Medicine* 27 (1993): 14–18.

Hopkins, W.G., S.W. Marshall, K.L. Quarrie, and P.A. Hume. 'Risk Factors and Risk Statistics for Sports Injuries'. *Clinical Journal of Sport Medicine* 17 (2007): 208–10.

Janssen, I., S. Dostaler, W.F. Boyce, and W. Pickett. 'Influence of Multiple Risk Behaviours on Physical Activity-related Injuries in Adolescents'. *Pediatrics* 119 (2007): 672–80.

Knowles, S.B., S.W. Marshall, M.J. Bowling, D. Loomis, R. Millikan, J. Yang, and F.O. Mueller. 'Risk Factors for Injury Among High School Football Players'. *Epidemiology* 20 (2009): 302–10.

Koven, R., M.A. McColl, P. Ellis, and W. Pickett. 'Multiple Risk Behaviour and its Association with Head and Neck Injuries: A National Analysis of Young Canadians'. *Preventative Medicine* 41 (2005): 240–6.

Lord, S., C.H. Tator, and S. Wells. 'Examining Ontario Deaths Due to All-Terrain Vehicles, and Targets for Prevention'. *Canadian Journal of Neurological Sciences* 37 (2010): 343–49.

Macpherson, A., and A. Spinks. 'Bicycle Helmet Legislation for the Uptake of Helmet Use and Prevention of Head Injuries'. Cochrane Database Syst Rev:CD005401.2008.

McKee, A.C., R.C. Cantu, C.J. Nowinski, E.T. Hedley-Whyte, B.E. Gavett, A.E. Budson, V.E. Santini, H.S. Lee, C.A. Kubilus, and R.A. Stern. 'Chronic Traumatic Encephalopathy in Athletes: Progressive Tauopathy After Repetitive Head Injury'. *Journal of Neuropathology and Experimental Neurology* 68 (2009): 709–35.

Meeuwisse, W.H., H. Tyreman, B. Hagel, and C. Emery. 'A Dynamic Model of Etiology in Sport Injury: The Recursive Nature of Risk and Causation'. *Clinical of Journal of Sport Medicine* 17 (2007): 215–19.

Morrongiello, B.A., and K. Major. 'Influence of Safety Gear on Parental Perceptions of Injury Risk and Tolerance or Children's Risk Taking'. *Injury Prevention* 8 (2002): 27–31.

Morrongiello, B.A., B. Walpole, and J. Lasenby. 'Understanding Children's Injury-Risk Behaviour: Wearing Safety Gear Can Lead to Increased Risk Taking'. *Accident Analysis and Prevention* 39 (2007): 618–23.

Mueller, F.O. 'Catastrophic Sports Injuries: Who is at Risk?'. *Current Sports Medicine Reports* 2 (2003): 57–8.

Pickett, W., S. Dostaler, W. Craig, I. Janssen, K. Simpson, S.D. Shelley, and W.F. Boyce. 'Associations Between Risk Behaviour and Injury and the Protective Roles of Social Environments: An Analysis of 7235 Canadian School Children'. *Injury Prevention* 12 (2006): 87–92.

Pless, I.B., H. Magdalinos, and B. Hagel. 'Risk-Compensation Behaviour in Children: Myth or Reality?'. *Archives of Paediatrics and Adolescent Medicine* 160 (2006): 610–4.

Pringle, R.G., P. McNair, and S. Stanley. 'Incidence of Sporting Injury in New Zealand Youths Aged 6–15 Years'. *British Journal of Sports Medicine* 32 (1998): 49–52.

Schmikli, S.L., F.J. Backx, H.J. Kemler, and W. van Mechelen. 'National Survey on Sports Injuries in the Netherlands: Target Populations for Sports Injury Prevention Programs'. *Clinical Journal of Sport Medicine* 19 (2009): 101–6.

Spinks, A.B., and R.J. McClure. 'Quantifying the Risk of Sports Injury: A Systematic Review of Activity-Specific Rates for Children Under 16 Years of Age'. *British Journal of Sports Medicine* 41 (2007): 548–557, discussion 557.

Tator, C.H., ed. *Catastrophic Injuries in Sports and Recreation, Causes and Prevention: A Canadian Study*. Toronto: University of Toronto Press, 2008.

Tator, C.H., C. Provvidenza, and J.D. Cassidy. 'Spinal Injuries in Canadian Ice Hockey: An Update to 2005'. *Clinical Journal of Sport Medicine* 19 (2009): 451–6.

Reflections on the participation of Muslim women in disability sport: hijab, Burkini®, modesty and changing strategies

Sima Limoochi[a] with Jill M. Le Clair[b]

[a]Physical Education College, University of Alzahra, Tehran, Iran; National Paralympic Committee of Iran, IPC Women in Sport Committee; [b]Humber College ITAL; Global Disability Research in Sport and Health Network

The inclusion of women and girls in sport has been contested for centuries, tied to differences in the gendered view of what is seen as 'suitable' or appropriately 'modest'. Disabled women in many low- and middle-income countries face triple challenges related to gender, the lack of economic resources and disability. This article reflects upon some of the issues for global disability sport organizations, and for Muslim women, in the context of diverse religious and cultural attitudes towards Islamic Dress (hijab), the presentation of the female self, and interactions with males. Different strategies have been used to increase the participation of women; some international organizations have included training for women in low- and middle-income non-Western countries, and the Islamic Federation of Women's Sport instituted the Islamic Women's Games, held in Iran, offering separate women-only international sport events. Debate is global and heated, as researchers and communities are deeply divided on these issues.. The authors argue for more research, and the collection of data to allow for innovation and for a two-way and more informed discourse.

Emerging field

The participation of women in sport has a long history of exclusion based on gender discrimination tied to traditional, cultural and religious values.[1] Today many now regard sport as a basic right for all human beings and increasingly women with disabilities are exercising their right to participate in sport by invoking various initiatives both global in nature, such as the 2006 UN Convention on the Rights of Persons with Disabilities, and local.[2] The initiatives described here are also in response to data that demonstrates the many health benefits women derive from an active lifestyle.[3] However, in the 1996 Paralympic Games, 47% of the nations participating had no women on their teams.[4] Muslim women, representing one fifth of the world's female population, often have not been included in international sport.[5] Disability in sport research about Muslim women in low- and middle-income countries is an emerging field and we would like to suggest some areas that need further examination, especially given the complexity of these issues, as frequently there are both oversimplifications and a lack of information.[6] This article suggests that there is a need to examine strategies to increase the participation of Islamic women and girls in sport as this issue is much contested within diverse cultural contexts.

Importance of Islamic dress (hijab)

Although rejecting an historically influenced, colonial perspective and essentialist, 'Orientalist' view of veiled women that sees them as fundamentally 'different', and as 'other', the authors recognize that there are special circumstances related to the importance of tradition, and religious and cultural values in the context of Islam that influence specific rules about the presentation of the female self and Islamic dress (hijab).[7] These values impact on the participation of Muslim women in sport, and the different requirements for appropriate 'modest' dress which vary by country and by region, as well as by varying religious and cultural values, and class/socio-economic factors.

Limoochi's experiences as a coach and official in Islamic countries (Bahrain, Egypt, Iran, Malaysia, Qatar, Sudan, the United Arab Emirates and Yemen) have led her to conclude that clothing is one of the key issues in the participation of disabled Muslim women in sport, related to what are framed as religious values, but are also often cultural.[8] Sporting attire can be an issue for Muslim women when dress codes prohibit them from wearing Western-style sport clothes and they want to respect the code itself. This is a concern not only for local community sports, but also for Muslim women participating in international events and the issue often results in emotional responses. For example, Algerian Hassiba Boulmerka, who won the 1500 m in the 1992 Olympic Games wearing shorts, was forced into exile following the Games because of death threats.[9] There are few globally accessible publications written by women living in Muslim countries about sport so we often find misconceptions or stereotypes about Muslim women, and the meaning of the hijab, niqab, abaya, burqa, or chador as symbols of their cultural or religious beliefs. However, it is important to make it clear that there are considerable variations in what is considered hijab or appropriate Islamic dress that is tied to the history and cultural values of the region or country, and impact on sport choices. Table 1 provides some examples of the diversity in choices of appropriate attire.

In some countries such as Iran and Saudi Arabia, clothing 'rules' are enforced by the government. In others, such as Malaysia, there is considerable variation as to what is defined as appropriate within the country itself. In addition, there are often regional and class differences in choice, with changes tied, in part, to fashion preferences and there are different terms used for the varied clothing used by Muslim women. Hijab is used differently too, sometimes to refer to Islamic dress as a whole, at other times to describe only the head covering.[10] Different requirements impact differently depending on the sport. The Islamic dress code consists of covering the hair and wearing modest clothing defined as covering the head, arms and legs and sometimes the feet. For this reason, it is not considered appropriate for women to participate in sport activities such as swimming and gymnastics where men are present as players, officials or spectators. However, women can take part in sports such as archery, volleyball, tennis and table tennis since they can play in their Islamic clothing without having to expose their hair or body.

Uniforms and technology

FIFA (the world soccer organization) barred the Iranian team from participating in the 2010 Youth Olympics because the team insisted on wearing head scarves, arguing it was for safety reasons and to prevent religious and political statements on the field. However, a compromise was achieved between FIFA and the Iran Football Federation and the Iran National Olympic Committee in which all parties agreed that the players could wear a cap that covered their heads but not their necks.[11] Western sport organizations can increase the participation of women by introducing accommodations that allow greater flexibility in team uniform requirements in this manner.

Table 1. Diverse women's clothing in Muslim countries

Head and face coverings	
Hijab	There is some confusion in usage because some use the term to simply to mean a headscarf, whereas in Iran, hijab has a general meaning as Islamic dress and refers to any covering for the body and head including chador, roosari (headdress – scarf), manteau, etc. A head covering or scarf may sit loosely on the head (as was worn by the Prime Minister of Pakistan, Benazir Bhutto) or it may include one tightly fitting piece that covers the hair and a second covering on top of that, somewhat reminiscent of the head covering of Catholic nuns in the past.
Niqab	An Arabic word that means to patch up or sew up, this is a face veil attached to the hijab and can either cover the face entirely or be attached at the side and leave the eyes exposed. Today it is made out of fabric, but in the past it was made out of leather when worn by Bedouin women in the Middle East. Some variants of niqab are used in Saudi Arabia, Qatar and Yemen, and in some southern parts of Iran.
Purdah or pardah	A Persian word meaning curtain, and sometimes in literary or poetic sense means hijab in general. It refers to a face veil or curtain to separate women from men.
Body coverings (to cover the body, arms and legs)	
Abaya	The Arabic word for cloak and is worn over other clothes. It is the required national dress in Saudi Arabia and the United Arab Emirates. It is also worn by women in Qatar, traditional abaya are black.
Burqa or chadri	The burqa has been at the centre of political battles in Afghanistan and northern Pakistan where the Taliban have insisted that women wear this loose fitting garment that covers the entire body as well as the face, which has an open woven net 'grille' or a slit at the eyes to see through. Historically, they were worn by both women and men and gave protection in sand storms. It is sometimes called the 'shuttlecock burqa' in Pakistan because of the design.
Kaftan or caftan	(from Persian) Originally worn by sultans in the Ottoman Empire and the takchita and jellaba are now worn by Arab women in Morocco and consist of a long loose dress and an outer cover.
Chador	The Iranian name for the loose abaya. Chador is a large piece of cloth cut and sewn in the shape of a half-circle that is wrapped around the head and body leaving the face exposed.
Dupatta	Is a long scarf or shawl worn around the head or over the shoulders, usually worn with the shalwar kameez and is less restrictive than wearing a burqa and commonly worn in Pakistan.
Shalwar kameez	It is the national dress for women in Pakistan and is worn with salvars or shalvars (Punjabi word, but from Persian) which are loosely fitting pants.

A most challenging sport is swimming where the body is exposed, whereas in Para Table Tennis, the wearing of a headscarf or long sleeves has not made any difference to sport competition and performance, as Limoochi has witnessed in a variety of Islamic countries where she has umpired or coached. Technology has had an impact in many aspects of sport including in clothing. Two of the most recent innovations have been the Burkini® and Hijood® designed by a Lebanese–Australian woman Ahdea Zanetti. The first covers an athlete's entire body including the head, and provides modesty in the pool and on leaving it; the second covers the arms, legs and head for track and field events. In 2008, in contrast to other runners who have been wearing ever briefer and shorter garments to compete, the Bahrain sprinter Ruqaya Al Ghasara won the 200-m sprint at the 2008 Olympic Games while covered from head to foot.

> It is great to finally have a high performance outfit that allows me to combine my need for modesty with a design made from breathable moisture controlled fabric that allows freedom of movement and flexibility. ... I hope that the Hijood Sports Top will inspire other women

to see that modesty or religious beliefs don't have to be a barrier to participating in competitive sport.[12]

Not surprisingly, this item has been adopted by others who want either more modest sport wear or protection from the sun.

The question of the rights and roles of Muslim women is also linked to global politics and to the cultural tensions between liberal democracies and Muslim countries, and the Muslim populations living in traditionally non-Muslim Western countries.[13] The West assumes that its perspective on women is correct, even though there is much heated debate in the public discourse on the changing roles of women. Some Muslim countries regard aspects of individualized and sexualized 'Western culture' with horror and take pride in the centrality of the family in their own countries, while others are envious of the entrenched rights in western democracies. Sometimes it is difficult for women on both sides of the debate to argue their position because of the complexity of the issues, the politicized confrontational nature of debate and the fact that in some countries questioning official government policy may have serious consequences and can lead to potential imprisonment.

Sport participation: accommodations and strategies for inclusion

As incredible as it seems to athletes today, in the early twentieth century women played tennis in white dresses with long sleeves *and* stockings, and swimmers wore wool costumes that extended to their ankles and wrists in order to comply with social expectations. Battles for the right of females to participate in sport were accompanied with battles to have the right to move freely without restricting clothes, and were particularly heated regarding the sports of bicycling and swimming as there was a gendered and sexualized analysis of these two activities tied to the use of the bicycle and the revealing impact of the water.[14] Modern international sport has its origins in the West, and sport federations enforce participation rules that require compliance in regards to required team uniforms, which vary by sport. These rules have evolved over time, reflecting changing Western attitudes towards women. However, to some in non-Western countries the inflexibility towards the rules represents attitudes that seem ethnocentric, biased and even an infringement of their human rights.

> According to Dr Ghafouri Fard, the head of the Physical Education Organization of Iran, the leaders of world sport have created a cruel imposition whereby Muslim women are 'deprived of taking part in World and Olympic events due to having their Islamic cover'. (*Salam Iran*, November 28, 2001) He goes on to criticize the IOC for the cruel violation of human rights to exclude these women from the world's athletic stage.[15]

The Islamic Federation of Women Sport

It has been argued that regional and international events can be held that are in compliance with the rules and regulations of Paralympic and Olympic sport, but also meet the concerns of athletes as regards hijab, so as to allow increasing numbers of women and girls to participate in sport and physical activity.[16] Although women in the West see segregation as reminders of the past discrimination and reminiscent of the racial policies of 'separate and unequal', many women in Muslim countries want to abide by their religious views on modesty and feel that holding separate sports events is a good solution. As in most religions, there are differences of opinion in interpretation, but the Qur'an states that women are equal to men before God; according to the Qur'an, Islam also promotes good health and fitness for both men and women. There are guidelines within which sports are expected to be practised and this entails women following their faith by not engaging in mixed-gender sports, as well as by observing a dress code. There was a desire to provide opportunities for women to engage in healthy exercise and sport and this served as the basis for the establishment of the Islamic Federation of Women Sport (IFWS) in 1991 and the hosting of the Women's Islamic Games in 1993 which included the disability sport of Para Table Tennis. At present, the organization has many members from Islamic countries, as well as athletes who are Muslims living in non-Islamic countries. The most important aims of the IFWS include building international solidarity and peace through sport, developing women's abilities in technical, executive, managerial and practical fields of sport through training courses in member countries, and through facilitating the exchange of scientific information through congresses, assorted international gatherings and the publishing of books and literature.[17]

An important aspect of this initiative was that the organization operates *within the framework of the Olympic Charter*. It coordinates the 'Women Islamic Games' every four years, as well as individual 'Solidarity Cup Competitions'. Notably, in all four 'Women Islamic Games' held in Tehran, participating athletes came from many countries including Afghanistan, Azerbaijan, Bahrain, Bangladesh, Benin, Brunei, Congo, Gabon, Guinea, India, Indonesia, Iran, Iraq, Kuwait, Kyrgyzstan, Lebanon, Libya, Malaysia, Oman, Qatar, Pakistan, Senegal, Syria, Tajikistan, Uganda, the UK, the USa and Yemen.[18] According to Sarah Hillyer, coach of the American team at the Fourth Games, the games have been successful in providing a venue for Muslim women to celebrate self-expression and develop self-confidence.[19]

Table 2 illustrates that if the conditions are met in compliance with their beliefs, cultural norms, religious values and requirements, the participation of Muslim women will increase.[20]

All the officials including umpires, coaches, referees, managers and others were female. Compliance with Islamic modesty requirements in sport were met as men and the photographing media were only allowed to attend the Opening Ceremonies and some events where women were covered such as chess and shooting. All the rules and regulations of these Games were in compliance with the corresponding international federations and since there were no men around at the competition venues, women were free to act without any clothing-related restrictions; this meant that the Women's Islamic Games garnered considerable support from families and governments. In international and Paralympic Games, however, the conditions are of course very different due to the presence of men.

Western sport organizations

In response to criticisms of the International Olympic Committee (IOC) and its exclusion of Islamic women, the American member Anita DeFrantz argues that it is the international sport federations who determine team uniform requirements,[21] and they can adapt and modify sport rules and regulations. Some sports have done so.

International Paralympic Committee (IPC) initiatives

Even though in 2004, a record 31% of participants in the Summer Paralympic Games in Athens were women, this was still below the 40% participation of women in the 2004 Olympic Games.[22] Because of this lower number of women participating in the

Table 2. Increasing women's participation in sport in the Women's Islamic Games

Round of Games	Date	Place	Countries	Teams	Disciplines	Athletes	Referees	International observers	Registration in Ifs	Workshops
1st Islamic Countries Women Sport Games	February 1993	Tehran, Islamic Republic of Iran	11	46	8	456	190	1	–	–
2nd Islamic Countries Women Sport Games	December 1997	Tehran, Islamic Republic of Iran	25	95	12	748	290	6	–	–
3rd Muslim Women Games	October 2001	Tehran, Islamic Republic of Iran	23	84	15	795	389	8	2	27
4th Women's Islamic Games	September 2005	Tehran, Islamic Republic of Iran	39	203	18	1587	374	16	12	58

Paralympic Games, the IPC felt it was necessary to address this issue by introducing programmes to support the training of women and to appoint a special Women in Sport Committee (WISC) committed to changing this situation, and Limoochi was the first Muslim woman appointed to the committee in 2006. Its purpose was:

> To advocate and advise on the strategies and policies to obtain the full inclusion of women and girls at all levels of Paralympic sport and the Paralympic Movement and identify barriers that restrict participation, recommend policies and initiatives to increase participation. ... The committee also reviews existing IPC initiatives and policies including research and data collection, universality wild card system, publications and solidarity funding allocation.[23]

The IPC has its roots in Europe and although criticized in the past for its Western bias, it has worked hard to increase and sustain the participation of women from around the world and has held numerous regional initiatives and included in these initiatives were the Islamic countries of Egypt, Iraq, Qatar, Iran, Kuwait, Jordon, Niger, Lebanon, Malaysia and Algeria.[24] To support development the WISC held regional and national training sessions on different continents between April 2005 and June 2008.[25] With numerous initiatives to bring about change, WISC reported that 27.3% of the official delegates at the IPC General Assembly in 2007 were women; also 42 National Paralympic Committee presidents and secretary generals were women from 38 NPCs.[26]

Inclusion and International Table Tennis Federation and Para Table Tennis

The International Table Tennis Federation (ITTF) and Para Table Tennis[27] have been at the forefront of initiatives to include women from low- or medium-income countries in all aspects of sport and to encourage participation and leadership, primarily through athlete development (targeting developing countries) and coach development. Additionally, they use and fund world and continental forums to provide training in officiating, administrating and tournament organizing for women. ITTF working jointly with Para Table Tennis has found a significant growth in the participation of women in its sport because, in addition to training and funding initiatives, these organizations have stipulated that athletes and officials can wear Islamic dress of their choice. Thanks to the support provided by the international sport organizations such as the IPC, the IOC, the ITTF and Para Table Tennis, as well as the National Paralympic Committee of Iran and other IPC sport federations like the Shooting Federation, Sitting Volleyball Federation and the Track and Field Federation, Muslim women are able to participate in international sport events up to elite levels as both athletes and officials. Today, Muslim women can access the websites of international sport federations, and are increasingly able to take up the sports which are in compliance with their cultural and religious values and take part in world sport events.

Conclusion

Guthrie and Castelnuovo observe that 'in order to produce the greatest good for the greatest number, more opportunities for women with disabilities in both sport and exercise must be made available, and those that do exist must be made more accessible and accommodating'.

There are different strategies to increase the opportunities for women to participate in sport while meeting the constantly changing cultural and religious values about appropriate behaviour for women. The IPC and its Women in Sport Committee, and other sport federations like the ITTF and Para Table Tennis have made considerable efforts to provide training and financial support to increase the number of women in the different areas of sport within a gender-integrated, but often male-dominated system, and by modifying rules to include women with Islamic dress. Technological innovations in fabrics and design with clothing like the Burkini® and Hijood® can support the participation of women in sport events, while meeting the requirements of Islamic dress.

The Islamic Women's Games have taken a different approach and held separate women-only international competitions. Many women are pleased to see the significant growth in the participation of women from many countries though this initiative. However, some are dismayed at what they see as a traditional or sexist approach to the role of women in sport through the Islamic Women's Games. They feel the differential expectations about women in sport are simply discriminatory, especially when some women have been forced to leave their own countries to be able to continue their sport. The authors argue that if sport federations and the IPC allow accommodation in the area of team uniforms, and support officially recognized regional women-only events there will be an increase in participation within global sport organizations; and until such time as a boycott of countries with men-only teams takes place, women who see themselves as pragmatists are pleased that various Islamic sport organizations and governments support the participation of women and prefer that women have the opportunity to participate in women-only events, than not at all. This is particularly the case for those women who love sport dearly.

Notes

[1] Hargreaves, *Sporting Females*.
[2] La Rivière-Zijdel, 'The Convention as an Instrument'.
[3] Guthrie and Castelnuovo, 'Disability Management Among Women with Physical Impairments'; Oglesby, 'Positive Embodiment'; UN Inter-Agency Task Force on Sport and Development, *Sport as a Tool for Development*; United Nations Division for the Advancement of Women, *Women 2000 and Beyond*.
[4] International Paralympic Committee, *Women and Sport Progress Report*.
[5] Hargreaves, 'Sport, Exercise and the Female Muslim Body'.
[6] Also there are challenges for analysis as most sport organizations such as the IPC do not track the religious affiliations of their athletes.
[7] Scott, *The Politics of the Veil*.
[8] Limoochi has a MSc in physical education, is Muslim, lives in Tehran, Iran and draws on her experience as a former member of the Iranian table tennis team, a current international Paralympic Table Tennis member, International Table Tennis Federation course conductor, umpire, a member of the IPC Women in Sport Committee and a member of the Iran National Paralympic Committee (NPC); she has travelled extensively while a member of these organizations.
[9] Murray, *Unveiling Myths*, http://www.womenssportsfoundation.org/cgi-bin/iowa/issues/part/article.html?record=863.
[10] Scott, *The Politics of the Veil*.
[11] 'FIFA Clears way for Iranian Girls to Play: Islamic Head Scarves to be Swapped for Caps'. *Toronto Star* May 4, 2010, S6.
[12] 'Bikini to Burkini – The Choice is Yours'. South Asian Generation Next: Uniting South Asian Youth with Canada, February 3, 2010, http://www.sagennext.com/2010/02/03/bikini-to-burkini-%E2%80%93-the-choice-is-yours/; 'Muslim Sprinter wins Olympic Sprint Dressed Head to Toe in Hijab'. *Mail Online*, August 19, 2008, http://bing.search.sympatico.ca/?q=Ruqaya%20Al%20Ghasara&mkt = en-ca&setLang = en-CA.
[13] 'Muslim Women in Sport: A Minority within a Minority'. Women's Sports Foundation UK, Fact File, http://www.isrm.co.uk/technical/docs/2008120510265810_-_Muslim_women_in_sport_-_a_minority_within_a_minority.pdf
[14] Hargreaves, *Sporting Females*.

15 Murray, *Unveiling Myths*, http://www.womenssportsfoundation.org/Content/Articles/Issues/Participation/U/Unveiling%20Myths%20Muslim%20Women%20and%20Sport.aspx.
16 Pfister, 'Islam and Women's Sport', 12–15.
17 Islamic Federation of Women Sport, http://www.ifws.org/English/Default.aspx?page=AsasName.
18 Ibid.
19 Cultural Heritage News Agency, 'Objectives of Women Islamic Games Met, American Coach', http://www.chnpress.com/news/?section=1&id=1251.
20 Organization of the Islamic Culture and Guide Ministry, *The Fourth Women Islamic Games Technical Handbook*.
21 Women's Sports Foundation, Muslim Women in Sport, http://www.womenssportsfoundation.org/cgi-bin/iowa/issues/part/article.html?record=863.
22 International Paralympic Committee, *Women and Sport Progress Report*.
23 Ibid.
24 IPC Women in Sport Leadership Summit. Tehran, Iran. Final Report: 1–3 December, 2004, http://www.paralympic.org/export/sites/default/IPC/Organization/Standing_Committees/Women_in_Sport/2005_11_16_Final_Report_Middle_East_IPC_Women_in_Sport_Leadership_Summit.pdf.
25 International Paralympic Committee, *Women in Sport Committee Network Update*, http://www.paralympic.org/release/Main_Sections_Menu/IPC/Organization/Standing_Committees/Commission_Women_Sport/2008_06_26_WIPS_2008_Issue_2.pdf.; Limoochi, 'How to Increase Opportunities'.
26 ITTF Para Table Tennis, 2010, http://206.191.35.210/; Para Table Tennis, the official website of the Paralympic Movement, 2010, http://www.paralympic.org/Sport/IF_Sports/Table_Tennis/index.html.
27 Guthrie and Castelnuovo, 'Disability Management Among Women'.

References

Guthrie, Sharon, and Shirley Castelnuovo. 'Disability Management Among Women with Physical Impairments: The Contribution of Physical Activity'. *Sociology of Sport Journal* 18, no. 1 (2001): 5–20.
Hargreaves, Jennifer. *Sporting Females: Critical Issues in the History and Sociology of Women's Sports*. London: Routledge, 1994.
Hargreaves, Jennifer. 'Sport Exercise and the Female Muslim Body: Negotiating Islam, Politics and Male Power'. In *Physical Culture, Power, and the Body*, edited by Jennifer Hargreaves and Patricia Vertinsky, 74–100. London: Routledge, 2007.
International Paralympic Committee. *Women and Sport Progress Report*. Bonn, Germany: International Paralympic Committee, 2001. http://www.paralympic.org/release/Main_Sections_Menu/News/Current_Affairs/2001_10_31_a.htm
International Paralympic Committee. *Women in Sport Committee WIPS Network Update. July 2008 Report*. Bonn, Germany: International Paralympic Committee, 2008.
La Rivière-Zijdel, Lydia. 'The Convention as an Instrument to Advance Sport Participation of Women and Girls with Disabilities: A Response from the International Working Group on Women and Sport'. In *Sport in the United Nations Convention on the Rights of Persons with Disabilities*, edited by International Disability in Sport Working Group. Boston, MI: Northeastern University, 2007.
Limoochi, Sima. 'How to Increase Opportunities for Para Table Tennis Athletes and Officials within the ITTF'. Paper presented at the Women in the ITTF Meeting, Beijing 2008 Paralympic Games, September 12, 2008.
Murray, Sarah. *Unveiling Myths: Muslim Women and Sport*. New York: Women's Sports Foundation, 2002.
National Paralympic Committee of Islamic Repubic of Iran. *Iranian Paralympic Medalists*. Tehran, Iran: NPC Publications, 2008.
Oglesby, Carole, in collaboration with the International Working Group on Women and Sport, Women Sport International, the International Association of Physical Education for Women and Girls, and the International Council of Sport Science and Physical Education. 'Positive Embodiment: Contributions of Sport, Exercise and Physical Recreation to the Life-long

Development of Girls and Women'. Brief prepared for the United Nations Division for the Advancement of Women, 2006.

Organization of the Islamic Culture and Guide Ministry. *The Fourth Women Islamic Games Technical Handbook*. Tehran, Iran: Project Executive IFWS.

Pfister, Gertrud. 'Islam and Women's Sport: More and More Muslim Women are Taking up Sports, and Tehran is Setting an Example'. *SangSaeng Summer* (2006): 12–15.

Scott, Joan Wallach. *The Politics of the Veil*. Princeton, NJ: Princeton University Press, 2007.

United Nations Division for the Advancement of Women, Department of Economic and Social Affairs. *Women 2000 and Beyond: Women, Gender Equity and Sport*. Geneva: United Nations, 2007.

United Nations Inter-Agency Task Force on Sport for Development and Peace. *Sport as a Tool for Development and Peace: Towards Achieving the United Nations Millennium Development Goals*. Geneva: United Nations, 2003.

Women's Sports Foundation. *Muslim Women in Sport: A Minority within a Minority*. UK: Women's Sports Foundation, 2006.

Index

Page numbers in *Italics* represent tables.
Page numbers in **Bold** represent figures.